WITHDRAWN

A POLITICAL APPROACH TO PACIFISM

Book 1

A POLITICAL APPROACH TO PACIFISM

Book 1

Will Morrisey

Symposium Series
Volume 39a

The Edwin Mellen Press
Lewiston/Queenston/Lampeter

Library of Congress Cataloging-in-Publication Data

Morrisey, Will.
    A political approach to pacifism / Will Morrisey.
        p.   cm. -- (Symposium series ; v. 39a-b)
    Includes bibliographical references and index.
    ISBN 0-7734-8910-X (v. 1). -- ISBN 0-7734-8912-6 (v. 2)
    1. Peace. 2. Pacifism.   I. Title. II. Series
JX1952.M62   1996   95-12482
303.6'6--dc20   CIP

This is volume 39a in the continuing series
Symposium Series
Volume 39a ISBN 0-7734-8910-X
SS Series ISBN 0-88946-989-X

A CIP catalog record for this book is available from the British Library.

All rights reserved. For information contact

The Edwin Mellen Press   The Edwin Mellen Press
Box 450   Box 67
Lewiston, New York   Queenston, Ontario
USA 14092-0450   CANADA L0S 1L0

The Edwin Mellen Press, Ltd.
Lampeter, Dyfed, Wales
UNITED KINGDOM SA48 7DY

Printed in the United States of America

To my Aunt Sophia

Stalin to Churchill: "How many divisions can the Pope supply us?"

Pius XII to Churchill: "Tell my son Joseph that he will meet my divisions in eternity."

TABLE OF CONTENTS

BOOK 1

BOOK 2

END NOTES

ACKNOWLEDGMENTS

A grant from the United States Institute of Peace enabled me to undertake the research for this book. I am grateful to Kenneth M. Jensen, Director, Research and Studies Program, for their encouragement.

The staff at the Swarthmore Peace Collection, the Friends Historical Library, and McCabe Library — all located at Swarthmore College — proved most helpful during the months I spent in Swarthmore, Pennsylvania. I am also grateful to the staffs at the New York Public Library, the Library of Congress, Firestone Library at Princeton University, the Dana Library and the Alexander Library at Rutgers University, the Founders Library at Howard University, the Guggenheim Library at Monmouth College, the Eastern Branch of the Monmouth County Library, the Oceanic Free Library in Rumson, New Jersey, and the Red Bank Public Library in Red Bank, New Jersey.

The Robert H. Horwitz Memorial Foundation generously provided financial assistance in the final stages of the project. I am grateful to the Foundation's Board of Trustees — Mrs. Mavis Horwitz, Philip N. Marcus, Thomas L. Short, Charles T. Rubin, Richard A. Baehr, and Maynard H. Murch, IV.

Indispensable clerical assistance was provided by Mrs. Carol Morrisey and Ms. Nancy G. Smith.

I owe a debt of gratitude of a different kind to Carol Portlock, M. D., Acting Chief of the Lymphoma Service at Memorial Sloan-Kettering Cancer Center in New York, Subhash C. Gulati, M. D., formerly of the Center and now Director, Clinical Research and Stem Cell Transplantation at New York Hospital-Cornell Medical Center, and their colleagues, particularly Patricia O'Keefe, R.N., and Jill Kaplan, M.S.W.

Finally, the editorial and production staff at The Edwin Mellen Press guided the manuscript through the publication process with great professionalism.

INTRODUCTION: PACIFISM AND THE POLITICAL ORDERS

Writings about war and peace proliferate ineffectually. 'Moralists' and 'realists' have at each other, firing cannonades of such adjectives as 'immoral' and 'irresponsible.' Shrewd word-generals talk of 'synthesizing' moralism and realism, but the job never gets done.

The impasse will continue so long as partisans pretend nonpartisanship, continue to speak of war and peace as if the decision to make war or to seek peace could be governed by moral principles alone, physical-historical forces alone, or some combination of the two.

The typical moralist talks as if war and peace are part of his own psychodrama, as if personal morality forms the core of reality. This is as true of the typical contemporary advocate of just-war doctrines as it is of pacifists. The typical realist, impatient with this high-toned narcissism, wants to cut the chatter and get to the supposed realities of brute force. Syntheses of these two dogmatisms merely indulge in double-gaited dogmatism.

What is needed is neither moralism nor realism but political philosophy. Political philosophy requires an understanding of war and peace in terms of the political orders or regimes. The first political philosophers whose written works survive – Plato, Aristotle, and Xenophon – describe a variety of such regimes and present classifications of them. My intention is to understand war and peace as they relate to the political orders. Such understanding will provide a theoretical ground for the politics of peacemaking.

There are several basic political orders and many more subspecies. This accounts for the complexity and length of the argument. Despite that complexity and that length, the reader who keeps my intention in mind will not find these materials diffuse or randomly-selected.

Pacifism and the political orders: although I shall venture far from 'modern' rules or method, I shall begin by undertaking the modern practice of 'defining my terms.' The argument I make will be new to many readers, partly because it is so old, so obscured by certain mental habits. An apparent novelty needs to be introduced through the medium of the familiar. So, to the terms: starting with 'pacifism.'

Historians trace the English words 'pacifism' and 'pacificism' to the French *pacifisme*, coined by Emile Arnaud in *Les États-Unis d'Europe* the newspaper he edited just prior to the Franco-Prussian War. *Le pacifisme* meant internationalist peacemaking, the construction of a world order that would make wars unnecessary. Until that order was achieved, defensive wars might be necessary to resist aggression[1] Initially interchangeable, 'pacifism' and 'pacificism' now have distinct meanings, at least in the United States. 'Pacificism' means what *le pacifisme* meant to Arnaud. More often than not it retains its association with efforts to extend the political regime of commercial republicanism – the regime first seen in the United States of America – to all the nations of the earth. Failing this, pacificists often look to international law and to various international institutions – the League of Nations yesterday, the United Nations today – for the settlement of disputes that threaten or break the peace.[2] 'Pacifism' can mean all of this (or none of it). Primarily, it means a principled refusal to employ military force internationally.

An outstanding historian writes that "Pacificism is relativist; pacifism is integral, absolutist."[3] For this reason pacificism is usually but not always associated with secular thought, pacifism with religion – particularly (in the West) Christianity.[4] There is some question whether pacifism existed at all in the West before Christianity.[5] Much more research will be needed to determine pacifism's status in non-Western civilizations.[6]

War itself may be of limited duration in human history. Anthropologists date the origin of war (as distinguished from personal conflicts) at approximately 4000 B.C.E. – that is, at the time of the development of agriculture. The great empires of Assyria and Persia systematized conquest, making it possible to consolidate victory in war.[7] Changed socioeconomic and political institutions thus made war possible and useful; certain institutions have made some rulers more likely to perceive it as useful than other rulers do.[8] It is therefore not surprising to see one modern pacifist contend, with Aristotle, that "politics is the supreme science and art, embracing all pursuits and callings and professions," productive of an ethos that profoundly affects civil and international peace.[9] The consideration of the character of political regimes is prior to consideration of relations among countries because the relations derive from the regimes, and the character of the countries derives decisively if not exclusively from the regimes. The structure whereby justice is established within each country has more profound consequences internationally than does any international structure designed to establish justice.[10] The priority of political regimes to 'international relations' was so well understood for so long that Gentili could complain of the neglect of international law: "In fact, it does not appear to be the function either of the moral or of the political philosopher to give an account of the laws which we have in common with our enemies and with foreigners," a deficiency his book was to correct.[11]

A political regime is an arrangement of a community with respect to its offices, particularly those offices or institutions that have *de facto* authority over all the others. The regime is the configuration of these offices animated by certain kinds of human beings pursuing certain purposes in association.[12] Writers in the Machiavellian tradition scant the importance of political regimes, particularly insofar as regimes encourage certain human virtues; these writers often speak of 'the state' as if it did not much matter what regime forms 'the state.'[13] Among some pacifists and pacificists (who do not conceive of themselves as Machiavellians but who remain under his influence in some respects) the political cause of war is not a specific political regime or set of regimes but 'the state' in its sovereignty.[14] Civil and international wars result from sovereignty itself or, even more imprecisely, 'the times,' the historical epoch and all the forces at play within it.

Algernon Sidney takes the more rigorous view that Rome's fall did not proceed from the corruption of "the age" but from corruption "proceeding from the government." "[T]ime changes nothing, and the changes produced in this time" − just as in ancient Rome − "proceed only from the change of governments."[15] Changes in governments proceed from the people governed (except in instances of conquest), although seldom from all of the people governed. Uncorrupt peoples

> ... think it a small matter to destroy a tyrant, unless they can also destroy the tyranny. They endeavor to do the work thoroughly, either by changing the government entirely, or reforming it according to the first institution, and making such good laws as may preserve its integrity when reformed.[16]

Because, as Benjamin Constant remarks, "the internal constitution of a state and its external relations are intimately connected," those concerned with promoting peace do well to consider regime questions.[17]

Constant endorses representative government for the purpose of promoting peace. "[I]t is curious and interesting to discover why this form of government, the only one in the shelter of which we could find some freedom and peace today, was totally unknown to the free nations of antiquity," which subjected the private individual to community authority (as for example in its practice of civil religion) even while individuals collectively enjoyed civic freedom, sometimes as democrats voting directly on public policies. The ancient republics were spirited, warlike. The modern republics are commercial, with citizens more jealous of private than of public liberties. Ancient liberty was "an active and constant participation of public power." Modern liberty "must consist of peaceful enjoyment and private independence."[18]

> Individual liberty... is the true modern liberty. Political liberty is its guarantee, consequently political liberty is indispensable. But to ask the peoples of our day to sacrifice, like those of the past, the whole of their individual liberty to political liberty, is the surest means of detaching them from the former and, once this result has been achieved, it would be only too easy to deprive them of the latter.... We still possess today the rights we have always had, these eternal rights to assent to the laws, to deliberate on our interests, to be an integral part of the social body of which we are members. But governments have new duties; the progress of civilization, the changes brought by the centuries require from the authorities greater respect for customs, for affections, for the independence of individuals.[19]

A challenge of citizenship in the commercial republic will be to defend political rights and public life against the blandishments of privacy. The advantage of commercial republicanism will be its achievement of civil and international peace insofar as the principles of representative government are extended. Thomas Paine sees this clearly if over-optimistically:

> If there is a country in the world, where concord, according to common calculation, would be least expected, it is America. Made up, as it is, of people from different nations, accustomed to different forms and habits of government, speaking different languages, and more different in their modes of worship, it would appear that the union of such a people was impracticable; but by the simple operation of constructing government on the principles of society and the rights of man, every difficulty retires, and all the parts are bought into cordial unison.[20]

The American Civil War and persistent interracial tensions may be said to have qualified these claims. But subtract the rhetoric (with Paine, this will not leave much) and a measure of truth remains. As for international peace, Paine crosses the line from optimism to fatuity, imagining that "When another nation shall join France [in her republicanism], despotism and bad government will scarcely dare to appear," and peace will become inevitable in Europe.[21] Moreover, Paine notoriously fails to distinguish between American and Jacobin republicanism, the latter being an incoherent attempt to synthesize 'ancient' and 'modern' principles. Still, Paine does see the possibilities commercial republicanism offers for international peace even as he grossly overestimates their likelihood of easy realization and exhibits extraordinarily poor practical judgment in assessing actual political situations.

One of the best statements of commercial republican pacifism was published not by a European or a North American but by the Argentinian writer Juan Bautista Alberdi. In his 1870 book *The Crime of War* Alberdi writes that "war may be the only means of carrying out justice for want of a judge, but it is a primitive, savage, and anti-civilized medium" whereby the parties to a dispute judge their own case. As such it is, "almost always, a counter-crime." There are three remedies for the causes of this crime: commerce, Christianity, and republican government, all of which are in principle "international and universal" as well as peaceful. In South America republicanism has been vitiated by too-powerful military establishments, remnants of Caesarism — the Roman law as reinvented by Machiavelli. "South American liberals want two inconsistent things at once — *glory* [that is, "the rule of victory"] and *freedom*." The revival of Caesarism in Latin America originated in intellectuals' acceptance of the notions of German historicists who believe "facts" to be "the aspiration of natural reason and a revelation of the laws of Providence." "*Might*, from that time forward, is placed above *right*." Accordingly, "modern Germany has made warfare a policy, an industry, a branch of ethics." The elevation of might over right in practice abrogates the republican principle of popular sovereignty. In Prussia the government is independent, and independent of the country under its rule; "the individual is absorbed and disappears into the pantheism of the *Fatherland*, represented and personified by the monarch," who leads 'his' militarized nation to war against other nations. Alberdi himself avoids nationalism, admiring "the free institutions of the early Germans" and noticing that Bismarckian Germany "plagiarizes the France of Napoleon I," which in turn borrowed Rome's imperial iconography. He would have recognized the same imperial ambitions in such later Machiavellian 'Romans' as Mussolini and Hitler.[22]

Recent empirical studies have confirmed the expectations of political philosophers and statesmen. Commercial republics do not fight one another. Two *commercial* regimes may fight if only one or neither regime is republican. Two *republics* may fight if only one or neither regime regime is commercial. And commercial republics fight other kinds of regimes. But commercial republics seldom if ever fight each other.[23] Limited though it may be, this claim cannot be made on behalf of monarchies, tyrannies, aristocracies, or oligarchies. Attempts to deny this claim invariably misstate it, triumphantly refuting the notions that commerce by itself leads to peace or that republicanism by itself does, or that commercial republics will remain at peace with other regimes.[24]

Commercial republics achieve their relative peaceableness at the cost of what might be described as cultural high drama. Proudhon's complaint may be taken as representative of thousands:

> The modern world has beneath its eyes the spectacle of a
> society which, born of a vigorous blood, a strong and intelligent

race, placed in exceptional conditions, has been developed, for eighty years, only by the works of peace. Certainly, the American is an indefatigable pioneer, an incomparable *producer*. But, apart from the products of his agriculture and his industry, what has this self-described young nation given? Neither poets, nor philosophers, nor artists, nor politicians, nor legislators, nor captains, nor theologians: not one great work, not one of the figures who represent humanity in the pantheon of humanity.[25]

The complaint is overdrawn; even as Proudhon wrote those words the generation of Emily Dickinson, Walt Whitman, Abraham Lincoln, Frederick Douglass, and Robert E. Lee prepared themselves for the work that would commend them to the attention of whatever gatekeeper Proudhon envisioned at the entrance to his pantheon. It is nevertheless true that commercial republics often need the help of cultural archeologists to unearth intelligence from the slag of popular culture. Commercial republicanism frustrates moralists and intellectuals alike; when the observer is both a moralist and an intellectual, the frustration doubles.

Commercial republics also make enemies among stern souls, 'left' and 'right.' Some of these may be suspected of cynicism – as when Stalin surveyed the borders of his empire in the years after the Second World War and declaimed that West Germany and Japan were "now languishing in misery under the jackboot of American imperialism."[26] Some only suffer from a colic of delusion:

Two centuries ago, a former European colony decided to catch up with Europe. It succeeded so well that the United States of America became a monster, in which the taints, the sickness, and the inhumanity of Europe have grown to appalling dimensions.[27]

Still others fear civilization's shipwreck in a wave of vulgarity:

But what terrible difficulties there may be in the future with this self-complacent and self-righteous nation, which is as convinced as the Germans were in 1914 that their *kultur* is the only civilization worth having, and that they cannot do another people a better service than by abolishing its customs and traditions and turning English and French towns into duplicates of *Main Street*.[28]

There is snobbery here. (Americans cannot do much in England or France that the English or the French don't want done; the real worry is that ordinary folks will *like* the American demi-culture.) But there is also a genuine sense of loss, a sense that the glory of Europe *is* gone forever, that indigenous traditions everywhere dissolve, that the price of peace is blandness. While it is hard to sympathize with the German scientists who warned in 1914 that "Without German militarism German civilization would be wiped off the face of the earth,"[29] and while intellectuals' enthusiasms for anti-bourgeois tyrannies will remain among the most deplorable wonders of this century, it is not hard to see the honest concerns beneath the contemptible follies and bizarre excesses. Such concerns often prevent individuals concerned with peacemaking from appreciating the very regimes that most effectively promote it.

Commercial republicanism generates some of its own most virulent critics, who disturb its peace. As these lines are being written, commercial republicanism nonetheless enjoys a worldwide prestige unprecedented since the aftermath of the First World War, perhaps since the nineteenth century. Because I agree with the wise pacifist who said, "Political prophecy is the most gratuitous form of error,"[30] I shall not venture any predictions on how things will go. This book is not an historical study, anyway, and does not address itself to peacemaking as a 'movement.' There are several recent histories of pacifism; adding another would be nearly superfluous at this time.[31]

This book addresses the principles of peacemaking, both pacifist and pacificist. Although some writers have called these principles strictly relative to the times and places in which they were first formulated, I have not found this to be so.[32] While new principles are discovered and new conventions invented, old principles qualified and old conventions discarded or adapted, much of pacifism and pacificism has remained constant for centuries, with certain questions and doctrines reappearing persistently. Still, however persuasive this book may be, contemporary historians will likely come away from it still convinced of the superiority of 'historical thinking' to 'abstract philosophizing.' And however unconvincing this book is, philosophers are unlikely to be shaken form their convictions that history is properly philosophy's handmaiden.

I begin where I am, in the United States. Understood by its founders as the first commercial republic in world history, the American regime provides a fortuitous beginning point for the study of pacifist and pacificist doctrines. The American founders were themselves pacificists, in large measure. They expected their regime to promote civil and international peace. The first chapter explores this regime with a view to this purpose. The second chapter discusses those American pacifists who have attempted to build upon 'American' regime principles. The third chapter discusses American pacifists who rejected the principles of commercial republicanism for those of philosophic historicism.

Many of the American Founders were Christians, and their Declaration of Independence refers to God as Creator – the God of Abraham, Moses, and Jesus of Nazareth. Accordingly, the book's Second Part begins with a chapter on Christian pacifism and on the just war doctrines that have been adopted and adapted by most Christians. This chapter takes the form of a dialogue. I think this form appropriate to the subject, but claim no literary aptitude where none exists. (Roger Kahn once said of his book on the Brooklyn Dodgers that "*King Lear* is on the same subject as *The Boys of Summer* – not so much baseball as "time, and what time does to us all" – "and my work differs from *Lear* in that it isn't as good." I say that my chapter is on not quite the same subject as Plato's *Republic*, but my work also differs from the *Republic* in that it isn't as good.) The Second Part's second chapter returns to essayistic normalcy in its discussion of the influence of Gandhi's principles and practice on Christian pacifism.

A few of the American Founders did not adhere to any Christian orthodoxy. The Declaration of Independence refers to the Laws of Nature and of Nature's God, who in this formula may or may not be taken to be the Biblical God – an ambiguity that Benjamin Franklin and Thomas Jefferson may be said to have understood. The Third Part deals with secular pacificism: Chapter Six does so with respect to war in general, Chapter Seven with respect to war fought with weapons of mass destruction.

Taken together, the book's three sections are intended to clarify the relation of peacemaking to the variety of political orders or regimes, particularly the American regime, and to political order as such. Without any pretensions to philosophy, the book may therefore be useful to philosophers.

FIRST PART

PACIFISM AND THE AMERICAN REGIME

God grant that not only the love of liberty, but a thorough knowledge of the rights of man, may pervade all the nations of the earth, so that a philosopher may set his foot anywhere on its surface and say: This is my country.

Benjamin Franklin

CHAPTER ONE
Peace and the American Founding

The American Founders resolved to establish a regime of peace. They succeeded in one respect: When, where, and insofar as men establish political regimes based upon the principles of the American founding, peace prevails so long as citizens live by those principles, and foreigners respect them. When citizens of the United States or the other commercial republics abandon 'American' principles – American only because implemented first and maintained longest by Americans – they will likely make war, civil or foreign. When foreign countries with rulers animated by other principles refuse to respect 'American' principles, war may ensue. Because many such rulers detest 'America' in principle, 'American' regimes worldwide find themselves embattled, regardless of their inclinations.

Book-battles precede real ones. For this reason it matters practically if contemporary historians deny that the American Founders shared a coherent set of intentions, peaceful or otherwise. If in 1787 the Pennsylvania State House in Philadelphia was a Tower of Babel, then self-destructive civil war, not peace, must be the Founders' real legacy. 'American' principles contradict themselves, these historians claim. The incongruity thesis does not flourish on the extreme ends of the modern political spectrum; rightists and leftists call the regime all too coherent, damning it accordingly.[1] Rather, certain liberals and conservatives who object to one or more of the Founders' principles find it useful to posit a stew, the better savor preferred morsels.[2]

Forrest McDonald, a conservative, finds incoherence in the sources of the Founders' political thought. Of the Virginia gentlemen (a favorite target) he smiles, "Because there was not much else to do, they read a great deal: they read Thucydides, Virgil and Cato in Greek and Latin, and Coke, Blackstone, Montesquieu and Bolingbroke, Locke and Hume in English: and not only could they cite this incongruous conglomerate of authorities to justify any action, they believed them all as well."[3] This argument fails to consider the possibility that ideas from thinkers who contradict each other do not necessarily themselves contradict. Poor Richard advises, "The ancients tell us what is best; but we must learn from the moderns what is fittest."[4] The Founders selected from diverse and self-contradictory thought-systems and experiences; a selection need not share the incompatibility of its sources.

McDonald believes he finds contradictions within the new system because "repeated compromises" occurred at the 1787 Constitutional Convention. "It should be clear from this survey", he concludes, "that it is meaningless to say that the Framers intended this or that the Framers intended that: their positions were diverse and, in many particulars, incompatible." This argument illogically conflates the need for compromise in particulars with the presence of *systemic* contradiction. Once reached, a compromise may or may not cohere logically; it has its own logical status independent of the original intentions of the compromisers. A compromise becomes the new intention.[5]

Gordon S. Wood, a liberal, claims "there was and is no 'real' Constitution against which we can measure the conflicting statements of the Federalists and the Anti-Federalists," only conflicting opinions.[6] The 1787 Constitution conflicts with the principles of the Declaration of Independence because the Articles of Confederation the Constitution superseded *did* adhere to those principles. Wood mistakenly assumes that the Constitution could not consist of a superior (or worse) attempt to give the Declaration's principles better institutional protection; perhaps the conflict between Federalists and Anti-federalists amounted to a dispute over this prudential task, not over the Declaration they all affirmed. The Rev. Stanley Griswold, writing in 1801, was historically and in principle closer to the truth when he affirmed, "The precious maxims of the Declaration of Independence are transplanted into the Constitution. And as under the former the country marched to victory, so under the latter she may advance to prosperity.[7]

In arguing that "a fundamental transformation of political culture" occurred between 1776 and 1787,[8] Wood means two things. First, "the Declaration of Independence did not deny the principles of the English Constitution" — a mixed regime of monarchic, aristocratic, and democratic elements; the United States Constitution did, being an unmixed republic whose every branch derived its authority directly or indirectly from the people, not from hereditary lineages. Second, the 'Spirit of '76' moved in an "atmosphere of suspicion and jealousy" with respect to governmental power; representatives were to obey faithfully the instructions of their constituents, conceived as virtuous, self-sacrificing citizens of small republics. To the delegates who wrote the 1787 Constitution, such faith in popular virtue, issuing in a strongly democratic republicanism institutionally dominated by legislatures, clearly needed qualification; separation of powers, a stronger national government and a stronger executive issued from the rough experience of excessive 'democracy'.[9]

Wood does not sufficiently reflect on the complementary characters of these two tendencies. The move away from a reliance upon the English *institutional* principles of mixed government went in an unmistakably 'democratic' direction: popular sovereignty, the derivation of all branches of government from the people. The move away from believing the people the *embodiment* of virtue, and towards a more 'aristocratic' conception of representation — itself qualified by the separation and balance of powers, that guard against the vices of all representatives, not only legislative ones — counterbalanced the 'un-English' steps toward popular sovereignty, but did so in a then-uniquely American way.[10]

Neither of these tendencies Wood identifies, taken together, contradicts the principles of the Declaration of Independence. Popular sovereignty affirms the Creator-endowed unalienable equal rights to life, liberty and the pursuit of happiness; institutional safeguards preventing direct expression of the fluctuating *will* of the sovereign people, equally affirm those rights, preserving them from impassioned popular misjudgments and injustices.

The failure of these outstanding historians to convict the American Founders of self-contradiction does not by itself prove the coherence of the Founders' enterprise with respect to the question of peace. Here historians help us less than the Founders themselves, seldom reluctant to say what they wanted to do, for what purpose.

Benjamin Franklin anticipated several main principles of the American approach to peace. In the 1740's in Pennsylvania, Quakers controlled the colonial Assembly, blocking any military establishment on the Christian pacifist grounds laid down by William Penn one-half century before.[11] In his *Autobiography*, Franklin recalled with characteristic glint of eye, "I had some cause to believe that the defense of the country was not disagreeable to many of them, provided they were not required to assist in it."[12] To help assuage troubled consciences, Franklin offered a commentary on Jesus' admonition, "All they that take the Sword, shall perish by the Sword" (Matt.26:52). This "cannot be understood in an absolute literal sense, as to Individuals," Franklin assured his readers; "it being evident that all Men who have taken the Sword, have not perished by the Sword." And to "presume," alternatively, that Jesus refers to the perishing of souls not bodies would be "uncharitable." Franklin appeared somewhat puzzled, but helpfully suggested that Jesus may mean the sword should not be used to "propagate the Christian religion," inasmuch as His Kingdom is not of this world.[13] Some thirty years later, in a private letter, Franklin was more brutally succinct: "[T]here is truth in the old saying, that *if you make yourself a Sheep the Wolves will eat you.*"[14] Pennsylvania got its militia.

A moderated Christianity, neither pacifist nor crusading, will permit military self-defense. To this Franklin added the spirit of commerce. "[I]n my opinion, *there never was a good War, or a bad Peace.*" War-monies would better go to "works of public utility."[15] Cost-accounting may cool militarism: [I]f glory cannot be valued, and therefore the wars for it cannot be subject to arithmetical calculation so as to show their advantage or disadvantage, at least wars for trade, which have gain for their object, may be proper subjects for such computation; and a trading nation as well as a single trader ought to calculate the probabilities of profit and loss, before engaging in any considerable adventure." Franklin immediately admitted, "This, nations seldom do..."[16] But they should. He also hoped that modern technology, in the form of the invention of the hot-air balloon, might bring an end to war: "Convincing sovereigns of the folly of wars may perhaps be one effect of it, since it will be impracticable for the most potent of them to guard his dominions."[17] The love of economic gain, the fear of losing property and life — will powerfully supplement a liberalized religious morality.

Will the combination of commerce and religion yield not pacificism but passivity, a spiritless refusal to defend oneself? Franklin anticipated the problem and sought to solve it with the same commercial spirit that inclines men to peace. Commerce feeds the desire for peace, but it also teaches suspicion, and a certain kind of pride which, though not militant, may exercise the sinews of defensive war. It is the suspicion of a cheat, pride in avoiding cheats, fear of being 'taken.' Christianity too teaches suspicion, suspicion of the devil's snares. Franklin brilliantly played on the spirits of commerce and (Protestant) Christianity in his 1761 essay, "The Jesuit Campanella's Means of Disposing the Enemy to Peace," an attempt to warn his fellow-Englishmen of French machinations.[18] Purporting this to be a translation of an extract, "the famous Jesuit *Campanella's* discourses address'd to the King of *Spain*," the essay betrays a master of propaganda who chooses to reveal the arts of propaganda, in order to bring his people to defend themselves better.

"If the *minds* of enemies can be *changed*, they may be brought to grant willingly and for nothing, what much gold would scarcely have otherwise been prevailed to obtain." Teach bribed speakers and writers in the country of your enemy to "magnify the blessings of peace and enlarge mightily thereon, which is not unbecoming grave Divines and other Christian men; let them expatiate on the misery of war..." Have them describe the war as advantageous to some of their countrymen, and these alone, "thereby to excite envy." Have them teach that victory in war merely brings more wars, as the conquered will burn resentment and plot revenge. Have them pretend public spiritedness. "For in this war of words, the avarice and ambition, the hopes and fear, and all the crowd of human passions, will, in the minds of your enemies, be raised, armed, and put in array, to fight for your interests, against the rest and substantial interest of their own countries." Eight classes of citizens will prove vulnerable to this rhetoric: "the simple and undiscerning many," who will be duped by the show of good intentions and plausible arguments; "rich men" and moneylenders; "book-statesmen," who malign the bold conducters of the war, and envy the glory they may have thereby attained; "those timorous by nature, amongst whom be reckoned men of learning that yield sedentary lives, using little exercise of body, and thence obtaining but few and weak spirits"; prominent politicians "whose natural spirits be exhausted by much thinking or depressed by over-much feasting"; "all women, whose power, weak as they are, is not a little among such men:; and "all the worldly-minded clergy." If the Spanish King follows this strategy, Campenella concludes, "no sound but that of *Peace, Peace, Peace,* shall be heard from every quarter"; this echo of Jeremiah 6 reminds Franklin's readers of Jerusalem under God's judgment, where "from the least of them even to the greatest of them, every one was greedy for gain." The civil societies Franklin promoted require the rule of a kind of reason: prudential calculation, never overwhelmed by sheer greed, the lust for power, or even religions ardor.[19]

These themes found a metaphor in Franklin's reconception of the game of chess. With its ecclesio-monarchic trappings, inviting players to put intellect at the service of spiritedness in a kind of mock-war, chess obviously embodies an ethos Franklin intended to undermine and replace. Hence his essay, "The Morals of Chess." Chess "is so interesting in itself, as not to need the view of gain to induce engaging in it; and thence it is seldom played for money" − a fact that Franklin might not have viewed as an unmitigated good. Actions not undertaken for money may incline toward mere entertainment, or toward fanaticism, or toward excessive political power. Sure enough, he quickly called chess "not merely an idle Amusement" but an exercise "useful in the conduct of human life." "Life is a kind of Chess," and Franklin's kind of chess comports with Franklin's kind of life. Chess, he writes, teaches four virtues: foresight, circumspection (viewing "the whole Chessboard, or scene of action," not just a part of it), caution (especially in war), and hope (seeking favorable change, avoiding discouragement when 'checked'). If one considers the classical virtues − courage, moderation, wisdom and justice − and the Christian virtues − faith, hope, and charity − the metamorphosis Franklin effects becomes clear. His are the virtues of commerce and diplomacy. Add to these Franklin's admonitions to observe the rules and to play with "generous civility," and you have a new chess, a chess of commercial republicanism.[20]

Franklin resolved the question of peace on the level of civil society – economic and religious reforms – and military preparedness. It remained for James Madison and George Washington to add the final, architectonic component: the political regime of republicanism.

Washington understood and appreciated Franklin's insights into the peaceful benefits of commerce, religion, and military preparedness. Consonant with his character and position, he emphasized courage more than Franklin did, but the difference remained primarily one of degree. In 1776, as commander of the Continental Army, he urged each "officer and man" to "endeavor so to live, and act, as becomes a Christian Soldier defending the dearest Rights and Liberties of his country."[21] This was no crusading, muscular Christianity; upon becoming President of the United States, Washington wrote to the principal American religious denominations of the time, including Catholic and Jesuit congregations, stressing the virtues of religious toleration, exemplified by his very act of writing.[22] Commerce too will conduce to peace, as "the benefits of a liberal and free commerce will, pretty generally, succeed to the devastations and horrors of war."[23] Washington prudently linked the desire for commerce with the need for military preparedness; "if we desire to secure peace, *one of the most powerful instruments of our rising prosperity*, it must be known that we are at all times ready for war..."[24] He detested imperial ambition, as inconsistent with the unalienable rights of all human beings.[25] But above all, the sight of the great general becoming the first President of the first unmixed republic, his manner of governing and of then leaving office, after a self-limited period of two terms, in accordance with Constitutionally-oriented procedures, demonstrated for Americans and for the world the peaceful character of the new republicanism.

James Madison explicitly addressed the question of peace and American republicanism in two articles published in 1792. In "Universal Peace," he commented on Jean-Jacques Rousseau's *A Project of Perpetual Peace*, forerunner to Immanuel Kant's now better-known *Perpetual Peace*. "Among the various reforms which have been offered to the world, the projects for universal peace have done the greatest honor to the hearts, though they have done very little to the heads of the authors." Rousseau, "the most distinguished of these philanthropists," proposed a confederation of sovereign states. Madison rejected this as impossible, given the "many allurements to war" felt by governments, and undesirable, liable to the "perpetuation of arbitrary power wherever it existed."

"As the first step towards a cure, the government itself must be regenerated." Not a confederation of existing, defective regimes but a new kind of government for each nation will help to make a general peace possible. In the new regimes, first the government's will "must be made subordinate to, or rather the same with, the will of the community," as in the United States and France. Next, the will of each society must itself be subjected to the reason of society "by establishing permanent and constitutional maxims of conduct, which may prevail over occasional impressions, and inconsiderate pursuits." For example, statesmen should legally require each generation to pay for its own wars, and not to carry them "at the expense of other generations"; thus "avarice would be sure to calculate the expenses of ambition; in the equipoise of these passions, reason would be free to decide for the public good." Governments would expend resources only for "wars of necessity and defense"; republican governments would have no reason to fight one another. Once republican governments predominate in the world, fewer wars will occur. If all governments were commercial-republican, none would.[26]

In "Spirit of Governments," Madison cited not Rousseau but Montesquieu, the Francis Bacon of political science: Bacon "lifted the veil from the venerable errors which enslaved opinion, and pointed the way to those luminous truths of which he had but a glimpse himself." With his tripartite political typology — governments of fear (despotisms), governments of honor ("regulated" or constitutional monarchies), and governments of virtue (republics), Montesquieu did just that. Madison's improved typology presents the political truth American thought and experience had made more visible. There are military governments — "the governments under which human nature has groaned through every age" — governments of "corrupt influence" — which substitute "the motive of private influence [i.e. patronage for favorites and bribes to opponents] in place of public duties" – and a third type, republican governments. This third type of government "deriv[es] its energy from the will of the society," but not its policies. Rather, "operating by the reason of its measures, on the understanding and interest of the society," it improves society's will and rechannels society's energy in the direction of justice. "Such is the government for which philosophy has been searching, and humanity has been sighing, from the most remote ages." The philosophic quest for wisdom and the humane search for the protection of the unalienable rights to life, liberty, and the pursuit of happiness, come together in "the republican governments which it is the glory of America to have invented, and her unrivalled happiness to possess."[27] Twenty-three years later, after the War of 1812 had brought President Madison and his republic to its most severe test since the Revolutionary War itself, he proudly told Congress, "[W]e can rejoice in the proofs given that our political institutions, founded in human rights and framed for their preservation, are equal to the severest trials of war, as well as adapted to the ordinary periods of repose."[28]

Madison's 'corrections' of Montesquieu served the purposes of a statesman's pedagogy. Madison replaced "despotism" with "military government," thus dispensing with the numerical criteria of the ancients (Aristotle's governments of the one, the few, and the many) and of the moderns (Machiavelli's principality and republic). 'Government militant' is despotic, whether one, few, or many control it.[29] Madison refused publicly to credit honor to constitutional monarchy (and, perhaps, constitutionalism to monarchy); like militarism, corruption can afflict governments of one, few, or many. Opposing the vices of physical oppression political militarism brings, and the vices of desire corruption encourages, republicanism inculcates public virtue. It does not do so as directly as Montesquieu's republics do; America is no Sparta, no early Rome – no pagan republic. The American republic derives spiritedness from the society, but also allows society to moderate its sternest spirit, its ambitions, militant tendencies (often expressed in violent religious conflicts and factious political strife), with the more peaceful passion for economic gain. In this, republicanism resembles "corrupt government" insofar as it too gives range to private passion. But, crucially, it does not permit private passion to *govern*. Private passion remains on the level of civil *society*. The moderation of national spiritedness by the private desire for gain gives government not so much the traditional political virtue, courage, but rather the opportunity to employ its reason, to refine and elevate the public views. Whereas Montesquieu classified governments by the ruling element's number and by the *sentiments* rulers inculcate in the citizens, Madison classified governments by their methods and rather more by their effects on the *minds* of citizens, that is, on moral sentiments and intellects.[30]

Of the major American founders, only one seemed to deny the peaceful character of commercial republicanism. This was Alexander Hamilton. But close examination of his arguments in *The Federalist* reveals certain inconspicuous logical flaws in service of a very conspicuous political purpose, namely, the ratification of the United States Constitution. "To judge from the history of mankind, we shall be compelled to conclude that the fiery and destructive passions of war reign in the human breast with much more powerful sway than the mild and beneficent sentiments of peace; and that to model our political systems upon speculations of lasting tranquillity would be to calculate on the weaker springs of the human character."[31] Hamilton made this argument concerning the likelihood of foreign wars with nations of differing regimes – an argument all of the founders made – apply equally to relations among commercial republics. "Visionary or designing men" may claim that commercial republics "will never be disposed to waste themselves in ruinous contentions with each other." Such men forget three things. First, "momentary passions and immediate interests" influence governments and nations more "than general or remote considerations of policy, utility, or justice." To those (like Madison, only four years later) who might suggest that the American regime is new, and that this true observation respecting other regimes will not hold among the new republics, Hamilton replied that human nature will not change, that popular assemblies are as impassioned as monarchies. "There have been...almost as many popular as royal wars." As for commerce, "Has commerce done anything more than change the objects of war?" Athens and Carthage were commercial republics, and they "as often engaged in wars, offensive and defensive, as the neighboring monarchies." So were, and so did, Venice and Holland. "Is it not time to awake from the deceitful dream of a golden age and to adopt as a practical maxim for the direction of our political conduct that we, as well as the other inhabitants of the globe, are yet remote from the happy empire of perfect wisdom and perfect virtue?" With these cautions in mind, Americans should ratify the United States Constitution in order to establish a Federal government strong enough to prevent war among the states over territorial disputes, the "competitions of commerce," disputes over the public debt incurred by the Union under the then-existing Articles of Confederation, disputes over one state's laws injuring the legitimate interests of private individuals outside the state, and "incompatible alliances" with foreign powers.[32]

Contrasting Hamilton's observations with those of Madison, the rhetoric becomes clear. Madison, Washington, Jefferson, and Franklin never proclaimed a new golden age of *perfect* wisdom and *perfect* virtue, only a new republic of improved wisdom and virtues made possible by the counteraction of passion by ambition, ambition by passion, thereby enabling (imperfect) wisdom to govern. Athens, Carthage, Venice, and Holland were indeed commercial, but they were not republics in the American sense, that is, they were not unmixed republics. Human nature has not changed, so the nature of popular assemblies, or of republicanism by itself, has not changed; commerce, by itself, has indeed done nothing more than to change war's objects. But Madison and Washington proposed neither commerce nor republicanism *by itself*; they proposed to combine them in a new regime, a regime that would limit if not change the objects of war. Hamilton first subjected commercial republicanism to an analysis, true in itself but not necessarily true in synthesis; he then claimed as examples of the synthesis *mixed* regimes, regimes only partially republican.

Perhaps Hamilton honestly disagreed with his colleagues, and even dreamed of a republican imperialism; perhaps he agreed, but preferred to magnify the dangers of weak federalism in order to lend urgency to the task of ratification. Without a strong federal union, Hamilton predicted, powerful forces would cause legal, political, and economic strife. Internecine war might not occur, but weakness would, sufficient weakness to make America vulnerable to foreign conquest.[33] Whatever his intentions in making it, Hamilton's argument requires Americans to remain guarded in their optimism, never to divorce commerce from republicanism, and never to mistake false or partial republics for true.

The Founders' general intention to seek peace and secure it found expression in the public statements and private correspondence of individuals. It also found expression in their most notable compacts, the Declaration of Independence and the United States Constitution. The Declaration set down the Founders' principles; the Constitution established the governmental structures designed to secure these principles. Although both of these compacts seem over-familiar, neither American nor foreign commentators as a rule consider them as instruments of peace. The Founders themselves thought differently.

The Declaration of Independence: A War for Peace Against a Peace of War

"Nothing short of Independence, it appears to me, can possibly do," George Washington wrote in April 1778. "A Peace, on other terms, would, if I may be allowed the expression, a Peace of War."[34] Animosity between America and Britain would linger, yet foreign help for the colonies would disappear. Some four years earlier, Washington had opposed the Peace of War on the fundamental level of unalienable right. Several months after the Boston Tea Party, he asked a correspondent, "For, Sir, what is it we are contending against? Is it against paying the duty of three pence per pound on tea because burthensome? No, it is the right only, we have all along disputed," the right of government by consent and therefore no taxation without representation.[35] "[W]e must assert our rights, or submit to every imposition, that can be heaped upon us, till custom and use shall make us tame and abject slaves, as the blacks we rule over with such arbitrary sway."[36] A year later, Washington saw "no alternative but Civil war or base submission."[37] Nor had he ignored nonviolent possibilities. In 1769 he had told George Mason, "that no man should scruple, or hesitate a moment to use arms in defense of so valuable a blessing" — liberty — "on which all the good and evil of life depends; is clearly my opinion; yet Arms I would beg leave to add, should be the last resource." He discussed the possibility of a boycott of British goods, but judged its effectiveness improbable.[38]

The Declaration provided a clear and profound defense of the War for Peace against the Peace of War, in principle and in practice. The Declaration might have been titled, "The Defense of Independence"; as its first sentence implies, the actual dissolution of "the political bands" between American and Englishmen constituted a separate act.[39] Just as the Apology or Defense of Socrates remains the greatest well-known vindication of philosophic life, the Declaration or 'Defense' of Independence remains the greatest well-known defense of political life. Both philosophy or love of wisdom and politics or the life of ruling and being ruled in the city proceed principally by deliberation and speech, which require peace much if not all of the time. Both the defense of philosophy and the defense of politics require serious thought about peace — what it is, how to secure it.

The Declaration begins with what we now call "history" — time and occurrences "When in the course of human events..."). The human things, not the divine things, or nature as a whole, come first, in a reversal of the order of history according to both Genesis and natural theology. The next phrase narrows the focus still further: "it becomes necessary for one people to dissolve the political bands which have connected them with another..." A "people" cannot mean an ethnic group, as Americans were mostly of English stock, and at the same time by no means exclusively of English stock. Nor can it mean a shared political authority, as Americans were Americans before the "bands" dissolved. Commercial relations continued after 1776, so "people" is no economic category. Geographical contiguity alone could not constitute a people; at one time Americans surely regarded themselves primarily as Englishmen, while living far closer to American Indian tribes than to Londoners. Nathan Tarcov makes a more plausible suggestion: "The acts of naturally free individuals, in particular the expenditure of life, liberty, and property that by nature belong to each of them" in the acquisition of land, following their emigration to that land, "are what constitutes a people."[40] A people, then, is a group of individuals who have established what John Locke calls a civil society. Necessity causes individuals, living in the scarcity of the state of nature, implicitly and prudently to agree to a "social contract" guaranteeing each others' lives, for which the guarantee of individual civil liberty is an indispensable necessary support. In declaring the *necessity* of *dissolving* some but not all of the political bands of their society, the Signers immediately implied that those bands now threaten their civil society, the lives of its individual constituents. They would soon explicitly affirm this implication.[41]

The Declaration's focus immediately widens. By dissolving its political bands to another, a people takes its place "among the powers of the earth"; no longer simply a people, they are now a sovereign or self-governing people. This place is not exclusively a fact of *Realpolitik*: the people "assume[s]...the separate and equal station which the Laws of Nature and of Nature's God entitle them..." This phrase situates a people not merely in history, in the course of human events, but in a lawful natural order and a lawful divine order. Entitlement is not mere existence; the Declaration distinguishes 'what happens' from 'what should be'. A people may or may not successfully assume what they are entitled to, namely, separation from and equality with other sovereign peoples. The people's separation and equality guard the individuals' necessity for preservation. *Both* as individuals and as a people, "necessity" has a moral dimension; it is a naturally and divinely ordained entitlement. This combination of individuality with sociality distinguished the Signers from such modern political philosophers as Thomas Hobbes and John Locke, who believe society an entirely artificial construction; the Signers affirmed the natural sociality of human being.[42]

The Declaration affirms this sociality by deriving from it "a decent respect for the opinions of mankind," which "requires" a people to "declare the causes which impel them" to dissolve their political bands and assume their rightful separate and equal station. What begins as an apparently physical necessity, self-preservation, ends as a moral necessity, an obligation, because the Laws of Nature and of Nature's God establish the context for human history. *Rightful* sociality transcends mere opinion; the Signers did not merely respect the opinions of mankind (these could be erroneous or malevolent); a people are obligated to pay a *decent* respect, nothing less. The Declaration is not propaganda. Its authors would despise the immoral, or amoral foundation of pure propaganda or opinion manipulation, which implies a view of human nature that would at best reduce men to the 'state of nature,' although perhaps without hope of escape. As the 'state of nature' can be a state of war, so propaganda is the speech of war, passion its 'soul.'

The Declaration is nevertheless rhetorical. While as speech it cannot seek to compel, and it does not seek to deceive or impassion, neither does it seek to question, to invite its readers to a Socratic inquiry. "We hold these truths to be self-evident': the phrase asserts, it does not wonder, or argue. It provides a foundation for reasoned argument, and thus for a nondogmatic politics which, owing to its nondogmatic character, lessens the need for the resort to war, that threat to civil society and individual life. By not wondering, but equally by not foreclosing wonder, the Declaration encourages thoughtfulness without paralyzing action; it exemplifies thoughtful political action or statesmanship, which aims at a just peace.[43]

"All men are created equal" means "they are endowed by their Creator with certain unalienable rights..." The Signers broke with Lockean philosophy and its derivatives; the Creator-God is the God of Scripture, not the God of the philosophers. "Nature's God" comports well with the Enlightenment and its 'natural theology'; the Creator-God does not. The Declaration thus represents a politic and political combination of Scriptural and modern philosophic principles, acceptable to such Christians as James Wilson and Charles Carroll, to those who privately questioned the divinity of Jesus of Nazareth — Benjamin Franklin and Thomas Jefferson — and to those whose religious convictions were not Christian.[44] Nature and Nature's God give laws to peoples. The Creator-God endows individuals with unalienable rights.[45]

The significance of this combination for the issues of war and peace cannot be overestimated. Both Scripture (especially Christian Scripture) and modern political philosophy seek peace. In practice neither had succeeded in achieving it by 1776. In the centuries before the American founding, the regnant forms of Christianity had resulted in bitter factional strife and religious warfare — the factions' physical, forceful acts to enforce a spiritual, invisible standard. Modern, Hobbist philosophy scorns that standard and defends despotism as the best enforcement of visible human equality, on the grounds that in despotism all are equal but one, and that anything less than unquestioning obedience to a powerful sovereign will result in civil war.[46] The Signers agreed with Christian dissenters and modern philosophers who held government incompetent to enforce the invisible; human being itself, however – the natural equality of each individual human being *in* his nature – does have a reliable visible manifestation. We recognize at sight our fellow-human. If, by introspection, we also recognize certain unalienable rights to life, liberty, and the pursuit of happiness, we will eschew the forceful deprivation of those rights through aggressive war, or through the Peace of War, despotism.[47] The universal character of the American regime does not itself guarantee genuine peace; neither Christianity nor modern political philosophy alone had done so, and both asserted "the *unity* of the human race, and the universality of its rights."[48] Universalist claims as easily lead to militant fanaticism as to peace. Rather, it is the character of these universalist claims – unalienable rights to life, liberty, and the pursuit of happiness – that gives the American founding the possibility of achieving peace.

To achieve that possibility, human beings must act to *secure* their unalienable rights by instituting governments.[49] Thomas Hobbes teaches as much, advocating strong and unquestioned governmental authority to secure natural rights. But Hobbesian despotism yielded not peace but the Peace of War. The Signers broke with Hobbes, and also rejected in advance the philosophies of historicism such as those of G.W.F. Hegel and Karl Marx, by insisting that governments "deriv[e] their just powers from the consent of the governed." This doctrine of consent puts the axe to the root of Machiavellianism, government by force and fraud. It places the peaceful rule of reasonable speech over the warlike rule of soldiers and propagandists. It affirms the distinctively *human* rule of speech and reason.[50]

Government by consent provides the only practical means to combine justice with power. Justice is not identical to consent; justice is the securing of unalienable rights. Government should secure those rights; that is its purpose. Consent enables government power to serve government's rightful purpose; it does not guarantee the rightful use of power. Consent is 'necessary' but not sufficient for justice. Consent brings power to the government; force and fraud aim at mere assent, obedience or zealotry. Consent implies moral *choice*. Unlike the historicist nationalism of later centuries, national consent does not allege a 'right to national self-determination'; reason, not impassioned will, (individual or collective), governs here.[51] In asserting 'itself,' impassioned will can assert anything. It 'makes war.' It makes the securing of unalienable rights a matter of chance again, a captive to battlefield fortune. Typically, when impassioned men assert their 'rights' they make them absolute in practice, wholly embodied in the course of human events or 'history'. Because in practice rights will conflict somewhat, this absolutizing of the impassioned desideratum of the moment must yield war. The Signers did not succumb to this folly. Jefferson wrote that the natural right of self-government, "like all other natural rights, may be abridged or modified in its exercise by [the people's] own consent, or by the laws of those who depute them, if they meet in the rights of others."[52] Reasoned, prudent compromise enables men to govern one another and find the maximum practicable security for their unalienable rights.

The Signers distinguished government from sovereignty. A *people* are entitled to a separate and equal station among the powers of the earth. A government is not. A government's just powers derive from the consent of the sovereign people, securing their unalienable rights. Therefore, "whenever any Form of Government becomes destructive of these ends, it is the Right of the People to alter or abolish it, and to institute a new Government..." The Declaration does not dogmatize on the question of governmental form. Monarchy, aristocracy, mixed regime, democracy: any of these can secure a people's rights, any can assault them. Those who claim that the Declaration bespeaks democracy miss this point; the Declaration inclines toward a certain form of government (not a pure democracy), but does not rule out the legitimacy of any but despotism.[53] Unlike some utopians up to and including Karl Marx, the Signers did not imagine government could ever disappear altogether. A people should reform an unjust government or even abolish it, but only to replace it with a new form of government, "laying its foundation on such principles and organizing its power in such form, as to them shall seem most likely to effect their safety and Happiness." Such revolution does not destroy civil society; it reaffirms it by securing unalienable rights threatened by the previous government. This revolution ends the government's war upon the people.[54]

"Laying its foundation": one of the rare metaphors in the Declaration, comparing the founding of a government with the construction of a building, by its very artfulness reinforces the suggestion that the original political act is a matter of art not nature. God endows human beings with various sentiments, some inclining us toward society and others inclining us to abuse society. God endows us with reason, and with unalienable rights. The human being thus by nature needs government. Neither nature nor God directly supplies us with governments. To institute just governments, men need to use their reason and experience to found their governments on sound principles. Foremost among those principles for the Signers was popular sovereignty. But — and here the Signers separated themselves from pure democrats before and since — the purpose of this sovereignty is not the exercise of popular will for any purpose whatever. Rather, its purpose is to effect the safety and happiness of the sovereign people. Whereas life, liberty, and the pursuit of happiness are unalienable rights, common to each individual, safety and happiness (*not* merely its pursuit) are the purposes of government. Individual rights *secured* bring safety and happiness, goods conspicuously absent from the Peace of War. *Human* rights secured become *citizen* rights. Notice that this formula leaves out liberty; government does not *effect* liberty as it effects safety and happiness. The people effect liberty under a good government or against a bad one. Liberty is one thing an individual must 'do for himself.' *Citizen* rights require duty before liberty, duties that defend liberty and all other unalienable rights.

In what form shall the powers of government be organized? The form of government and even the principles upon which it is founded in practice require a choice by the people. This means that the people can make mistakes, as any group of would-be founders who intend to institute a new form of government in the world should candidly admit. The Declaration leaves that debate for another day, although not without hints.

An appeal (no matter how measured) to unalienable rights (no matter how self-evident) may encourage a politics of absolute claims and uncompromising assertions. Consent provides one guard against such extremism; unalienable rights and popular consent limit governments to forms for which statesmen can realistically win consent, and limit the people to actions that secure unalienable rights. Consent entails prudence and experience. Prudence "dictate[s] that Governments long established should not be changed for light and transient reasons." In the forty-ninth *Federalist* Madison would argue against Jefferson's proposal to make Constitutional conventions relatively easy to convene, using this same Jeffersonian insight, and amplifying it. "Frequent appeals" to the Constitutional revision process "would, in a great measure, deprive the government of that veneration which time bestows on everything, and without which perhaps the wisest and freest governments could not possess the requisite stability."[55] Experience has shown "that mankind are more disposed to suffer, while evils are sufferable, than to right themselves by abolishing the forms to which they are accustomed." No matter how self-evident unalienable rights may be, men seldom act to secure them. This habitual deference to established forms, this conservatism, has a valuable prudence to it. The Signers to some extent respect it, share it, even as they perhaps view it with a touch of irony.

"But when a long train of abuses and usurpations, pursuing invariably the same Object evinces a design to reduce them under absolute Despotism, it is their right, it is their duty, to throw off such Government, and to provide new Guards for their future security." John Locke teaches that the way to see the invisible standards and intentions of men, so politically problematic in civil Christianity, is to observe their actions. When Legislature or Prince "act contrary to [the people's] Trust" by making themselves "Arbitrary disposers of the Lives, Liberties, or Fortunes of the People," the government forfeits its legitimate power. Locke assures his readers that this teaching will not bring instability. "Quite the contrary, People are not so easily got out of their old Forms, as some are apt to suggest." Only "a long train of Abuses, Prevarications, and Artifices, all Tending the same way, make the design visible to the People..." The government itself, not the people, is then guilty of rebellion.[56] To overthrow despotism, to prevent a manifest design to establish despotism by overthrowing the government that so designs: here right and duty intersect, as both each individual as a human being, and the people as a citizen-body, a civil society, find themselves at risk. Jefferson himself individualized matters further by considering right and duty two aspects of human individuality, perceived by the moral instinct: "[N]ature hath implanted in our breasts a love of others, a sense of duty toward them, a moral instinct, in short, which prompts us irresistibly to feel and succor their distresses..."[57] This "moral instinct" corresponds to the Christian concept of conscience. Insofar as the Declaration reflects Jefferson's views, it makes resistance to tyrants a matter of conscience. This point could not be more crucial, since Christianity regards obedience to magistrates a matter of conscience.

In Romans xiii, Paul wrote, "Let every man be in subjection to the governing authorities. For there is no authority except from God, and those which exist are established by God." Governing authorities, as ministers of God, avenge Him for men's evil practices, "wherefore it is necessary to be in subjection, not only because of wrath, but also for conscience' sake." Very pointedly, given the Signers' circumstance, Paul went on to write, "because of this you also pay taxes..." To this teaching of conscience and Scripture, the Signers replied, *true* government secures God-given unalienable rights; a government that assaults that right is no true government.

The individual conscience that perceives unalienable rights, and the political and perhaps individual conscience that perceives duties, require the overthrow of false government and the establishment of true government, both actions to be governed by prudence. In commending prudence as in following conscience, the Declaration follows Scripture; Jesus Himself sends His disciples "out as sheep in the midst of wolves; therefore be as prudent as serpents, and harmless as doves" (Matt. 10:16). The Declaration silently rejects pacifist or nonresistant Christianity, not on the grounds of absolute fidelity to moral principle – Christianity no less than the Signers requires that human actions be governed by prudence – not in deference to governing authorities – Christians do not consent to obey evil-doing rulers – but with respect to the proper response to evil. Nonresistant Christianity turns the other cheek, personally and politically. The Declaration does not extend the precept "Resist not evil" to political matters, to the actions of peoples.

The Signers understood Christian and conservative inclinations to defer to authority. They cited "the patient sufferance of the Colonies" – the people's Christian virtue, so to speak – while repeating a principal idea from the Declaration's first sentence: "Such is now the *necessity* which *constrains* them to alter their former Systems of Government." The Signers made the Lockean necessity to establish and maintain civil society as consistent as possible with the Christian moral necessity to obey governing authorities. In this way they could deduce a right to revolution from a doctrine of conscientious deference. To nonresistant Christians who act peaceably, the Signers might reply that political nonresistance to evil results in the Peace of War, that martyrdom ("patient sufferance") has rightful or conscientiously perceived limits.

"The history of the present King of Britain is a history of repeated injuries and usurpations, all having in direct object the establishment of an absolute tyranny over these States. To prove this, let facts be submitted to a candid world." Carl L. Becker rightly observed that the word 'Parliament' never occurs in the Declaration, "a most significant omission, considering that the controversy of the preceding decade was occasioned, not the acts of the King, who plays the leading role in the Declaration, but by the acts of the British Parliament." The very existence of that body comes to sight only in vague hints. This "must have been intentional." Nor does the Declaration mention "the rights of British subjects," a major part of the Colonial argument up to the decision for independence. Becker explained these near-silences by reference to the Declaration's intended audience, the "candid world," uninterested in the conventional laws enacted by Parliament or the conventional rights of British citizens, issues the world would likely judge to be none of its business.[58] Unalienable human rights, not conventional British rights, would interest mankind. More than this, a candid — an unbiased, unprejudiced — world, will reject political Pharisaism, "the respectable opinion that to be just is to be law abiding." For "it is precisely this identification of the just with the legal that would lead the generality of mankind," insofar as they are not candid, "to regard the Declaration, or the act of its authors, as treason."[59]

Rhetorically, to concentrate the audience's attention upon the British King and his tyrannical designs makes the issues clearer to foreigners who cannot feel the sting of Parliamentary oppression, and perhaps would prefer even the severest acts of the British Parliament to the worse depredations of their own kings. Americans too may benefit from this concentration. The Signers did not want to appear to denigrate the rule of law or the legislative function itself. (This is why the Declaration from this point on will read like a legal indictment). They knew that whatever new form of government Americans would make, monarchy would not be it. The Signers reasonably foresaw some form of government that empowers the legislature. To discredit Parliament does not logically discredit legislatures as such, but a reasonable people is not at all times a strictly rational people, and the establishment of new forms will remain difficult enough without blackening the British legislature as much or more than the British executive. Behind this mode of arguing lies a simple if unstated insight. The executive potentially threatens unalienable rights more than the legislature does, whatever recent actualities may be. The speed and coordination with which an executive branch can work, usually far exceed the capacities of a deliberative, not to say talkative, legislature. Execution *is* action; legislative business by nature involves speech (debate) in order to beget speech (laws). The executive fights the wars, endangering civil society even when successfully protecting it. The executive more easily may decide not to protect civil society than a legislature may, given the legislature's greater reliance on popular approval.

The facts submitted to a candid world are therefore selected facts. They divide into three categories: the King's unjust attacks on American institutions; injustices committed by the King with assistance from the British legislature; and overt acts of war by the King.

By refusing "his Assent to Laws, the most wholesome and necessary to the public good," and by forbidding American colonial governors to pass needed laws without his assent, the King interferes with the very executive branch he himself has staffed, in effect willfully neglecting his own duties. At the same time he attacks the colonial legislative and judicial branches of government.

He has attempted to obtain popular assent to relinquishment of "the right to Representation in the Legislative," a right "formidable to tyrants only"; he has effectually dissolved colonial legislatures, thus exposing "the State...to all of the dangers of invasion from without, and convulsions within" − the dissolution of civil society itself into a state of war.[60] By refusing his assent to laws for establishing judicial powers, and by making judges "dependent on his Will alone, for the tenure of their offices, and the amount and payment of their salaries" he cuts the second root of the rule of law. To replace the colonial executive legislative, and judicial authorities, he has "erected a multitude of New Offices," sending "swarms of Officers to harass our people." Machiavelli advises that a Prince bent on revolutionizing a government should not so much destroy old offices as establish new ones; the King outdoes Machiavelli. Finally, "He has kept among us, in times of peace, standing Armies, without the Consent of our legislatures...affect[ing] to render the Military independent of and superior to the Civil power." This is the Peace of War: Tyrannic will, armed — the opposite of government by consent.

The second category of facts listed in the Signers' indictment concern the King's collaboration with 'others' — i.e., the Parliament. These two branches of government have attempted "to subject us to a jurisdiction foreign to our constitution, and unacknowledged by our laws." The acts of the British executive and legislative branches amount to an attempt to conquer America, attacking natural rights and legal rights under the British Constitution. Because Americans have not consented to these acts in the legally proper way these are "Acts of pretended Legislation" only, not laws at all. A combination of executive and legislative power tyrannizes over less powerful governments and the people protected by them. This is the nucleus of the United States Constitution's system of balanced, separated powers and of federalism — both systems intended to help 'keep the peace.'

The list itself consists of one sentence, the longest in the Declaration. The charges ascend from fundamental to comprehensive matters. By "quartering large bodies of armed troops among us" and protecting those troops "by a mock Trial, from punishment for any Murders which they should commit on the Inhabitants of these States," the King threatens the most fundamental if not the highest unalienable right. By "cutting off our Trade with all parts of the world" and imposing taxes without Americans' consent, he attacks property rights, the right to the means of securing the right to live. By depriving some Americans of trial by jury and by "transporting us beyond Seas to be tried for pretended offenses," he denies Americans their unalienable right to civil liberty. By "abolishing the free system of English Laws in a neighboring Province, establishing therein an Arbitrary government, and enlarging its Boundaries so as to render it at once an example and fit instrument for introducing the same absolute rule into the Colonies," the King threatens to deny not only unalienable but also English rights. By "taking away our Charters, abolishing our most valuable Laws, and altering fundamentally the forms of our Governments," the King does more than provoke revolution; he makes revolution. By "suspending our own Legislature, and declaring themselves invested with power to legislate for us in all cases whatsoever," the King eliminates the legal means to reestablish the legal foundations of their rights. He leaves Americans with conventionally unlawful effective alternatives: insurrection or the acceptance of tyranny.[61]

The final section of indictments again concerns the King alone, as the Signers turned to his overt acts of war against Americans. "He has abdicated Government here, by declaring us out of his Protection and waging War against us." In Lockean theory, the state of war far exceeds the ordinary state of nature in its rigors; the state of war, not the state of nature, goads men to establish civil societies. A king who wages war against his own subjects dissolves the very reason for his own existence, namely, the protection of civil society. Under the English Constitution the King protects the realm, enjoying rights and obeying duties consonant with that responsibility.[62] Warring against his subjects, he abdicates his authority in fact and in law. By "transporting large Armies of *foreign* Mercenaries, to complete the works of death, desolation and tyranny [contrasting, respectively, with life, property, and liberty], already begun with Circumstances of Cruelty and perfidy scarcely paralleled in *the most barbarous ages*, and totally unworthy [of] the Head of a *civilized* nation," the King violates 'Englishness' and attacks civil society itself. This accounts for the Declaration's well-known denunciation of the King's efforts to "bring on the inhabitants of our own frontiers, the merciless Indian Savages, whose known rule of warfare, is an undistinguished destruction of all ages, sexes and conditions." Foreignness and warfare against civil society itself characterize the King's worst acts against Americans. Their petitions "answered only by repeated injury," the Signers concluded that "A Prince, whose character is thus marked by every act which may define a Tyrant, is unfit to be the ruler of a free people."

A free people: Americans declare their independence not from the King but from the British. The King forms only one of the political bands connecting Americans to the English. "Nor have We been wanting in attention to our British brethren" the rightful sovereigns of England, "hav[ing] appealed to their native justice and magnanimity," to their memories of the colonists' reasons for emigrating to America, to "the ties of our common kindred," and to the desire to resume "our connections and correspondence," including trade, which war interrupts. Although the Declaration does not cry up the British people's failure to respond to these entreaties — perhaps for reasons similar to those behind its refusal to stress the actions of the People's representatives in Parliament — the Signers clearly considered this war of a people against a King a war of one people against another as well, and perhaps even more fundamentally so. Neither moral instinct, nor memory, nor shared blood, nor economic and cultural ties constitute a people. Brotherhood can bring fratricide as easily as fraternity. "We must therefore, acquiesce in the necessity, which denounces [i.e. announces] our separation, and hold them, as we hold the rest of mankind, Enemies, in War, in Peace Friends." To be just, war must be necessary. Not only a military conflict, a state of war is an action or series of actions violating unalienable rights; these actions can include military conflict, plundering, violations of international customs, even threatening moves in neighboring areas. The Declaration's list of grievances gives some of the answers to a major question of foreign policy: What is a true friend, a true enemy? By giving those answers, by showing what it means by peace and war, and by showing the direct relation of unalienable rights to peace, the Declaration prepares for a reconciliation between America and Britain after the war. It also presents the world with a principled rejection of the Peace of War.

Some forty years later, the Madison Administration still applied the principles of the Declaration to international conduct. In an essay probably edited by Madison himself, Alexander Dallas argued that the American declaration of war against Britain in 1812 bespoke "self-defense" against "aggressive tyranny." In claiming the right to board ships of foreign countries in search of British subjects, for impressment, the British "usurped and exercised on the water, a tyranny similar to that which her great antagonist [Napoleonic France] had usurped and exercised upon the land."[63] Tyranny remained a special case of the state of war.

In the second and final paragraph of the Declaration, the Signers drew the reasoned conclusion from these premises. In so doing, they revealed something of the nature of the regime they would establish to replace the English Constitution, and something of their own nature as the founders of that regime. They represented "the United States of America, in General Congress, Assembled"; a representative government, not a monarchy, not a classical mixed regime, not a 'participatory' democracy, declares American independence, and will govern Americans in the immediate years ahead. American representatives represented the states, but they did so "in the Name, and by Authority of the good People of these Colonies"; popular sovereignty with an exclusively representative form of government distinguished the American states from other states in the world, and would provide the basis of the constitutions of 1777 and 1787. At the same time, these representatives appealed "to the Supreme Judge of the world for the rectitude of our intentions." Popular sovereignty stops at the invisible. World opinion, the American people, and even their fellow-signers could not judge the rectitude of their intentions, except by the Signers' visible actions, a secondary authority. It follows that the authority of the people would not be authoritative were they not in fact "the good" people of these colonies, respectful of the invisible standard of unalienable rights. Jefferson held that Americans "may safely and advantageously receive to themselves a wholesome control over their public affairs, and a degree of freedom, which, in the hands of the canaille of the cities of Europe, would be instantly perverted to the demolition and destruction of everything public and private."[64] Therefore, "these United Colonies are, and of Right ought to be Free and Independent States."

Finally, "for the support of this Declaration, with a firm reliance on the protection of divine Providence, we mutually pledge to each other our Lives, our Fortunes, and our sacred Honor." The independence of a people depends upon their adherence to the laws of Nature and of Nature's God. Individual and political justice depends upon respect for the unalienable rights endowed by God as Creator. For the rectitude of one's intentions to obey those laws and to respect those principles, one appeals to God as Judge.

For the support of actions taken to secure those principles, one must appeal to God's Providence, to God as 'executive,'[65] and to one's fellow-statesmen.

The Signers differentiated themselves, as representatives of the people, from the people. They pledged not to God or to the people but to each other,[66] their lives, fortunes, and sacred honor. This pledge reveals their character, the character needed in representatives, that is, republican statesmen, especially in times of crisis. They pledged their lives; mere life or survival is not their purpose, as it is for Hobbes. The Signers should not then be described as egalitarians or simple democrats. They pledged their fortunes; caring for worldly success enough to mention it, the Signers also risked it. Some of them were oligarchs, but their character was not that of 'economic man.' They pledged their "sacred Honor"; aristocrats hold honor sacred. The Signers were men of aristocratic character – Jefferson's "natural aristoi," not snobs reclining upon advantageous conventions[67] – who represented the people. The people have egalitarian and oligarchic characteristics and elements, but these cannot *support* a declaration of independence from tyranny. Natural aristocrats can. They represent the virtues of the people while exercising their own.

Fully exercised, the virtues of honor-loving aristocrats can lead to war. The American problem will be to leaven a civil society protecting the life, liberty, and the pursuit of happiness of each person, with sufficient prudence and spiritedness to protect the civil society itself. For this the principles of the Declaration alone will not do. For this a people need inventions of prudence – the governmental institutions that give a regime its characteristic shape, mentions that *constitute* a regime *securing* unalienable rights.

A regime animated by the rule of law will give institutions the stability needed to secure unalienable rights. To sustain the rule of just law, the regime will need to care prudently for the education of lawyers. Thomas Jefferson accordingly proposed a textbook for law students at the University of Virginia; the anthology would contain writings by John Locke and Algernon Sidney, the Declaration of Independence, *The Federalist*, and the Virginia Report of 1799. James Madison reviewed these suggestions and agreed with Jefferson's intent: "It is certainly very material that the true doctrines of liberty, as exemplified in our Political System, should be inculcated on those who are to sustain and may administer it." For this purpose, Locke and Sidney "are admirably calculated to impress on young minds the right of Nations to establish their own Governments, and to inspire the love of free ones." The Declaration too is "rich in fundamental principles." But such statements of principle "afford no aid in guarding our Republican Charters against constructive [i.e. interpretive] violations." For this the students need to study *The Federalist* "the most authentic exposition of the text of the Federal Constitution, as understood by the Body which prepared and the Authority which accepted it" — despite subsequent party controversies. Madison added George Washington's First Inaugural and Farewell Address, to "help down what might be less readily swallowed." Law students learning about government need to understand the legal, institutional structure that secures rights, as well as the rights themselves.[68] The central essay in *The Federalist* links the Declaration to the Constitution by referring to the transcendent law of nature and nature's God, which declares that the safety and happiness of society are the objects at which all political institutions aim and to which they must be sacrificed.[69] The Founders sought to aim those institutions rightly, to avoid that sacrifice, but above all to avoid the sacrifice of unalienable rights.

The United States Constitution and the Enforcement of Peace

The Founders wrote the Constitution in the aftermath of war, during a period of occasionally violent civil discord. Discord threatened the Philadelphia Convention itself. In calling for daily prayers at the moment the Convention seemed unable to proceed, Benjamin Franklin warned that "mankind may hereafter, by this unfortunate instance despair of establishing governments by human wisdom, and leave it to chance, war, and conquest."[70] The very means of the American founding affirmed government by reason and choice instead of force and fraud.

The passions of individuals and even more the passions of groups necessitate government. The concern for personal reputation declines in a group; those who rule the group taste power, a taste that intensifies the love of power, already strong enough.[71] "The essence of Government is power; and power lodged in human hands, will ever be liable to abuse." Conscience does not suffice to restrain us, and the "favorable attributes of human character are all valuable, as auxiliaries, but they will not serve as a substitute for the coercive provision belonging to Government and Law, mildly administered." "The structure of the Government itself" serves as "the only effectual safeguard" against the abuse of power, the war against unalienable rights.[72] This structure, and the structure it encourages in society at large, originates in an insight well expressed by Hamilton: "The best security for the fidelity of mankind is to make their interest coincide with their duty."[73]

Because "the experience of the ages proves that with exceptions too few to impair the rule, men can not be held to the performance of delegated political trust without a continued and practical responsibility to those for whose benefit it is conferred,"[74] government by consent must occur not only at the time of the founding. Consent must become a means of government, even as good government itself always has consent as a proximate end.

If justice in practice requires consent, and human vice in practice requires government, government by the consent of the governed raises striking opportunities and problems. Fortunately, human nature is not simply corrupt. "As there is a degree of depravity in mankind which requires an active degree of circumspection and distrust, so there are other qualifications in human nature which justify a certain portion of esteem and confidence. Republican government presupposes the existence of these qualities in a higher degree than any other form."[75] They enable men to *govern* themselves. Government by consent is self-*government*, not merely *self*-government.

Republics had existed before, of course. According to James Monroe, 'republic' means a regime of exclusive or partial popular sovereignty with an elected executive; participatory or 'Athenian' democracy would form a subspecies of republicanism, as would many 'mixed' regimes with democratic, oligarchic, aristocratic, and monarchic branches.[76] Madison distinguished the American republic from the others in its use of representation. Representation "was neither wholly unknown to the ancients not wholly overlooked in their political constitutions. The true distinction between these and the American governments, lies *in the total exclusion of the people, in their collective capacity*, from any share in the *latter*, and not in the *total exclusion of the representatives of the people* from the administration of the *former*."[77]

America is an unmixed republic. That is, all of its governmental branches are representative — elected by the citizen-voters, or by citizen-electors elected by the body of citizens, or appointed by elected representatives. There is no purely democratic branch, no Athenian Assembly or 'participatory' democracy. There is no 'direct democracy' either — government by plebiscite or referendum. There is no oligarchic or aristocratic branch, such as the British House of Lords. The American republican government "derives all its powers directly or indirectly from the great body of the people, and is administered by persons holding their offices during pleasure, for a limited period, or during good behavior."[78] The unmixed character of American republicanism avoids the institutionalization of faction, thereby promoting civil peace. Pure democracy "can admit of no cure for the mischiefs of faction" because it provides "nothing to check the inducement to sacrifice the weaker party or an obnoxious individual." The majority, judges in their own case, rule unrestrictedly, at times without regard to individual or minority rights. Representative government moderates both the strife and the unjust majoritarianism of popular government.[79] Elected representatives "refine and enlarge the public views" by study and debate. Owing their election to broad coalitions, representatives rarely succeed as 'one-issue' candidates. They seek the adjustment of diverse interests; they avoid perpetual controversy. Even a majority faction will find it difficult to coalesce effectively, owing to the size of the republic's territory and the size and diversity of its population. Representative government thus maximizes the role of reason in politics, minimizes passion. "It is the reason, alone, of the public, that ought to control and regulate the government. The passions ought to be controlled and regulated by the government."[80] Pure democracy does just the opposite, encouraging passions and giving no voice to reason. Notwithstanding "the virtue and intelligence of the people of America," without which any popular government would be impracticable, Madison warned against "disturbing the public tranquility by interesting too strongly the public passions." Give passion the rule and demagogues, manipulators of passions, will become the real rulers. "The countenance of the government may become more democratic, but the soul that animates it will be more oligarchic. The machine will be enlarged, but the fewer, and the more secret, will be the springs by which its motions are directed."[81]

America is also a *commercial* republic, unlike the military republics of antiquity, notably Rome. Commerce guards unalienable rights by promoting what David Hume calls "parties from interest" and discouraging "parties from principle."[82] By parties of principle Hume refers primarily to the violent and uncompromising factions that fought civil wars in seventeenth century England. The Founders too recognized this problem and extended it to purely political strife; that most ardent defender of commerce, Alexander Hamilton, very nearly begins *The Federalist* with a criticism of fanatic wars.[83] A regime that guards the unalienable right to property by leaving citizens at liberty to engage in commerce, thereby encourages them to direct their attention and energy to a form of peaceful competition regulable by law. Parties of principle, whether religious or political, tend to despise law and break it. While based upon an unalienable right, commercial life looks to compromise and amelioration; it may cheat but it will not violently overthrow.

At the same time, by affirming the unalienableness of the right to property, commerce puts definite limits on the tendency to oligarchy or to aristocracy that wealth brings. This point remains one of the most-overlooked of the Founders' insights. John Locke associates the right of property with the right to life; you keep the results of your own labor. Madison quietly admitted that slavery, the systematic denial of that right, could not be republican. The slaveholding states in fact were "aristocracies."[84] It remained for Abraham Lincoln to draw the logical conclusion publicly and forcefully. Labor being "prior to, and independent of, capital, [it] deserves first consideration in civil society." The Civil War occurred because slaveholders attempted to place capital "on an equal footing with, if not above labor, in the structure of government."[85] To slaveholders, liberty means the right "for some men to do as they please with other men, and the product of other men's labor"; for genuine republicans, liberty means the right "for each man to do as he pleases with himself, and the product of his labor." Slaveholding means the enforced perpetuation of dependence by a faction among a people who had declared their independence on the basis of the laws of Nature and of Nature's God, and of Creator-endowed unalienable rights.[86] This contradiction could not long endure, and, owing to the rashness of the slaveholders' representatives – a rashness perhaps issuing from an excessive degree of 'aristocratic' spiritedness – a bloody war for peace destroyed the last major American vestige of the Peace of War.[87]

Famously, Hamilton and Jefferson differed on the issue of manufacturing versus agriculture. They did not differ so much on the issue of commerce, in practice; Jefferson realistically saw the commercial inclinations of his countrymen, much as he regretted the loss of self-sufficient agrarianism. He hoped commerce would remain primarily agricultural as long as possible. Along with Madison, Hamilton and Jefferson recognized the stabilizing character of a large middle class, "neither servile like the poor, nor arrogant like the rich."[88] With the promotion of world trade, this commercial, therefore middle-class regime would tend toward civil and international peace. Its one civil war would erupt over its most anti-commercial feature, slavery.

Wholly representative government and commerce both contribute the American republic's *extensiveness*. Madison wrote, "Americans can claim the merit of making the [European] discovery [of 'the great principle of representation'] the basis of unmixed and extensive republics."[89] With no need to assemble the mass of citizens in one place, with no religious establishment and no requirement of universal adult participation in military exercises to enforce unity of spirit among citizens, the United States government can encompass a large, diverse population on immense territories. Size strengthens stability when stability depends less on force than on reasonableness in the face of diversity. Those factions that do arise can seldom rule; if they rule, they never rule for long.[90] The people thus avoid the Peace of War. They also avoid imperialism, with its wars of conquest, while enjoying the advantages of population and territory on (potentially) imperial scale. Inducements to consent, instead of 'imperial' force, make this possible.

Unmixed, republican government over a commercial civil society with extensive population and territory, make the oppression of the people by popular factions unlikely. The Founders also addressed the potential for oppression of the people by the government. They instituted a *compound* republic, one separating the powers of its government into executive, legislative, and judicial branches, then balancing them. This system of 'checks and balances,' familiar to every American student in the days when 'civics' courses formed part of public school curricula, prevents factions within the government (whether or not they reflect factions among the people) from seizing control of more than one branch, and prevents any branch from utterly dominating the others.[91] The Founders also instituted a *federal* republic, "a system without an example ancient or modern...a system based upon popular rights, and so combining a Federal Form with the Forms of individual republics, as may enable each to supply the defects of the other and to obtain the advantages of both."[92] This "constitutional equilibrium between the general [Federal] and the State governments" guards the unalienable rights of the people from those who would tyrannize. The people's rightful possession of arms (and "advantage...which the Americans possess over the people of almost every other nation") reinforces the federal equilibrium, as the "subordinate governments" or state governments appoint the militia officers; the national government does not. "[T]he people are attached" more closely to the government of their state of residence than to the federal government and, through the militia system, the people retain the power to guard that attachment from any attempt by the federal government to injure their unalienable rights.[93]

The unmixed, commercial, extensive, compound, federal republic, founded upon consent and the rule of law, secures unalienable rights. To the Founders, peace finally meant justice, the securing of those rights. Unjust peace, the "Peace of War" whereby tyrannical men assault the rights of their fellows, can have no legitimate place in the American regime. Defensive war does have a place, primarily and perhaps only because other powers of the earth are structured in ways that give too much scope to tyrannic passions. American republicanism settles the question of war and peace among the American people. If other peoples adopt and adapt this republicanism for and to themselves, they will solve that problem among themselves, and with other peoples who live in 'American' republics. The history of the past two centuries confirms this hope.

The American Civil War appears to present the one massive refutation of the peaceful-republican argument. Less than fourscore and seven years after the Declaration, and only seventy-seven years after the Philadelphia Constitutional Convention, the American regime nearly dissolved in the blood of a fratricidal war far worse than the War of Independence. In its structural or governmental aspect, the Civil War concerned issues of sovereignty, the limits of the right to dissolve the Union. In its civil-social aspect, the war also concerned sovereignty, sovereignty as seen in the 'peculiar institution' of slavery, the individuals right to the fruits of his labor. The character of the unity of the United States depended upon how citizens conceived the regime's Americanness, and their own Americanness.

The distinctively American regime separates government from sovereignty. In the United States, Madison wrote, "The people, not the government possess the absolute sovereignty. The legislature, no less than the executive, is under the limitation of power" – limits set by law in the federal and state constitutions.[94] James Monroe gave this separation its fullest exposition in his book, *The People the Sovereigns*. "There are two great principles in government," he began, "in direct opposition to each other."[95] One recognizes the sovereignty of the people (democracy); the other asserts the sovereignty of the one (despotism) or the few (hereditary or conventional aristocracy). Mixed regimes, combining these sovereignties in one government (as did the Roman Republic and the British monarchy), rest not on principle but on compromise (in the pejorative sense) and on fortune; the people would not freely consent to relinquish any part of their sovereignty, but do so only if forced by conquest, machination, or circumstance.

Monroe did not foolishly wall off government from sovereignty. "A King without power is an absurdity," and so is a powerless legislature or judiciary. The government has power, but not sovereign power over the people.[96] Rather, the government serves as "the agent which executes the compact between the citizens," that is, the *constitutional* laws. In other kinds of government, there is always someone above the law. American *self-*government means that the people agree to a fundamental system of laws, their federal and state constitutions, which their representatives then execute; thus republican governors obey the people's laws even as, and by, governing the people.[97] The separation (but not isolation) of government from sovereignty makes the rule of law possible to an extent hitherto impossible.

This combination of popular sovereignty with representative government makes the American regime "altogether different from the others."[98]

This regime conduces to peace. If the people have sovereignty and directly exercise government, "many of the objections which apply on principle to despotism itself, in its worst form, are equally applicable."[99] Civil war not civil society or peace will quickly occur. Monroe saw this in the French Revolution, part of which he had witnessed as the American minister to France in 1794-96. The French revolutionary Convention of 1789 was not "a calm and deliberative assembly, acting according to its own judgment," as the 1787 Philadelphia Convention had been. Passions ruled there. As a result, "the government was in effect united with the sovereignty in the people," for such 'strong democracy' arises from the impassioned desire to take sweeping actions immediately. Without safeguards against popular tyranny, the French regime generated Robespierre, "a leader who yielded to the worst passions which could animate the breast of an ambitious competitor to power." Once aroused, passions that meet no institutional checks can only be controlled by exhaustion. The moderates, "cut off" from power (some literally), had to wait for the death of Robespierre and near-anarchy in order to restore order. Representative government began to take hold. But military leaders who defended the Republic from foreign attack won the impassioned homage of the people, and the result was Napoleon's despotic imperialism. The rule of passion led first to the Terror, then near-anarchy, then to a form of military dictatorship.[100]

The sovereign people "must be protected from themselves," that is, from their own passions. If not, oppression of the people and overthrow of their government "will be inevitable." The people's selfish and "more lofty motives," and the motives of their representatives, must be made "the instrument of [the government's] preservation, rather than its subversion."[101] Monroe called virtue a "visionary basis" for government, criticizing Aristotle for thinking that virtue can find institutional expression in political life.[102] As for institutions themselves, Aristotle and the other classical political philosophers "seem to have been guided more by the comparative wealth of the parties, and merit or demerit of those who held office, and exercised its powers, and by the manner in which they were exercised, than as a just regard to principle."[103] By "principle" Monroe meant the form of government – an emphasis he avowedly took from the modern political philosopher Montesquieu.[104] However, Monroe also argued that Americans can elect men of "virtue and talents" to represent them, and that when "high honorable sentiments" prevail in government they are "infused among the great body of the people" in a sort of moral synergy.[105] In all of this Monroe followed Madison, who emphasized government's structure, and the way it rechannels interests and even passions, without abandoning the quest for citizen virtue and for statesmanship.[106]

The Founders met the problem of justly governing a sovereign people not with moralism but by lending institutional support to the moral virtue, reasonableness. Passions unite *and* divide citizens (and their representatives) into factions. This intense unity and divisiveness – closely-knit social groups at loggerheads with others, and ultimately subversive of civil society itself – imitates militarism. In the twentieth century, certain groups have proudly called themselves 'militant,' perhaps without seeing the implication. At their worst, factions cause civil war. Representative government expresses popular opinion, whether factional or just, and provides scope for the exercise of ambition. But representative government with separated and balanced powers slows the expression of popular opinion, while still expressing it. Representative government physically removes the representative from his local meeting-halls, and encourages a broader view. It brings representatives into discussions with other representatives of an extended, diverse country. Representative, federal government dilutes passions, allowing the government to express "the cool and deliberate sense of the community."[107] This reasonableness itself will tend to divide factions. "When men exercise their reason coolly and freely on a variety of distinct questions, they inevitably fall into different opinions on some of them. When they are governed by a common passion, their opinions, if they are so to be called, will be the same."[108] Reasoning yields divisions, even more than passions. But these are governable divisions, divisions that, when settled, can yield governing decisions. A prudent fear of faction itself (because faction can lead to "anarchy...as in a state of nature, where the weaker individual is not secured against the violence of the stronger")[109] will supplement this reasonableness, will help to secure self-evident unalienable rights.[110] The naturally strong but dangerous bonds of passion will ease, allowing prudence and law to rule, for the sake of the Peace of Justice. American republicanism makes visible the invisible standard of reasonable virtue in the structure of government. For those who do not choose to look at that standard, the regime channels citizens' actions in ways that calm the rush of passions, permit the steadier flow of reasonable speech and deliberation.

Popular sovereignty, based upon unalienable rights, finds security in representative government. The Founders recognized another form of sovereignty, founded upon the people's sovereignty: the sovereignty of states, the powers of the earth governed by the laws of Nature and of Nature's God. State sovereignty means authority to guard the independence of one people from another, and the authority of a superior government over a lesser government within the same constitutional system. Sovereignty's "marks," Madison wrote, are a common treasury, common troops, a common coin, and a common judiciary.[111] American state sovereignty's most vexing problem was to be federalism, or the problem of union.

Federalism meets a need analogous to the need for civil society. "As the weaknesses and wants of men naturally lead to an association of individuals under a common authority, whereby each may have the protection of the whole against danger from without, and enjoy in safety within the advantages of social intercourse, and an exchange of the necessaries and comforts of life; in like manner feeble communities, independent of each other, have resorted to a union, less intimate, but with common councils, for the common safety against powerful neighbors, and for the preservation of justice and peace among themselves."[112] Madison of course saw the potential problems, as anyone familiar with the Articles of Confederation must have done: the states within the federal system may restively strain against the bands of union. The United States Constitution attempts to take a middle way between a weak confederacy of entirely sovereign small states — which risks internecine war, or at least persistent discord — and a national government — which threatens citizens with the Peace of War.

The sovereignty of the federal government as constituted in 1787 extends beyond the constituent states to individuals, as Madison and

Hamilton agreed. A "sovereignty over sovereigns, a government over governments, a legislation for communities, as distinguished from individuals, as it is a solecism in theory, so in practice it is subversive of the order and ends of civil polity, by substituting *violence* in place of the mild and salutory *coercion* of the magistracy."[113] By defining the federal government, the Constitution both establishes and limits the government's powers, "leav[ing] to the several states a residuary and inviolable sovereignty over all other objects" not enumerated in the Constitution. The Supreme Court adjudicates jurisdictional disputes, a function "essential to prevent an appeal to the sword and a dissolution of the compact."[114] "The authority of the Union" should extend "to the persons of the citizens – the only proper objects of government." It should not stop at the level of the constituent states, as secessionists later claimed, nor should it extend to citizens' minds, as religious establishmentarians claimed and as political totalitarians later did. Legal coercion cannot affect other *sovereign* states; only military coercion *and* diplomatic persuasion can do that. A federation of sovereign states, no true government at all, "must substitute the violent and sanguinary agency of the sword to the mild influence of the magistracy."[115] Not only the rule of law among the states but the rule of law within them will depend upon the success of federal union, as Washington argued in his Farewell Address. With union, the constituent states "will avoid the necessity of these overgrown Military establishments, which under any form of Government are inauspicious to liberty, and which are to be regarded as particularly hostile to Republican Liberty."[116] Not only a military government, but a militarized citizen-spirit would then corrode American republicanism.

The struggles over ratification and then secession in the first fourscore and seven years of United States history testify to the severe problems of establishing federal, republican peace, even as subsequent years have testified to its feasibility. At the Philadelphia Convention, James Wilson read aloud from the Declaration of Independence to prove that the colonies took their independence unitedly, not individually.[117] In his report, "Vices of the Political System of the United States," Madison cited violations of the law of nations and internecine violence as the reasons for "a political Constitution by virtue of which [the states] are become one sovereign power" rather than "a league of sovereign powers."[118]

Although equally a defender of the states' limited sovereignty throughout the 1790's, Madison strongly resisted the doctrine of "nullification' advanced by John C. Calhoun and others, which would entitle the constituent states to cancel certain acts of the federal government. The United States Constitution, a unique "mixture" of "confederated" and "consolidated" government, was "formed by the States — that is by the people in each of the States, acting in their highest sovereign capacity"; deriving from the same source as the state constitutions, "it has within each State, the same authority as the Constitution of the State." One state cannot annul the federal Constitution, any more than one state could have blocked its initial ratification. The people of each state, in ratifying the federal Constitution, constituted themselves as "One people for certain purposes," just as they had for the purpose of making the Declaration of Independence. To make the states the sovereigns in settling jurisdictional disputes, "would speedily put an end to the Union itself," as "a uniform authority of the laws, is in itself a vital principle." Popular elections and the Constitutional impeachment provisions will check federal power. "And in the event of a failure of every constitutional resort, and an accumulation of usurpations and abuses, rendering passive obedience and non-resistance a greater evil, than resistance and revolution, there can remain but one resort, last of all, an appeal from the cancelled obligations of the constitutional compact, to original rights and the law of self-preservation." Unalienable rights constitute "the ultimo ratio under all Government."[119] To simultaneously claim a *Constitutional* right to nullify a federal law, while claiming still to adhere to the federal Constitution, would be "a fatal inlet to anarchy."[120] In the case of an abused *unalienable* right, "the final course to be pursued by the minority, must be a subject of calculation, in which the degree of oppression, the means of resistance, the consequences of its success must be the elements." For Madison, then, prudence or reasonableness will be the final arbiter of union, a prudence obedient to the Declaration's standard, "an authority above the Constitution...the law of nature and of Nature's God."[121]

The slaveholding states failed the tests of prudence and of unalienable rights. They very nearly confirmed Hamilton's prediction, that the first America civil war, if it ever came, "would probably terminate in the dissolution of the Union" because, "When the sword is once drawn, the passions of men observe no bounds of moderation."[122]   Only the statesmanship of Abraham Lincoln prevented the destruction of the American republic. Lincoln too fought a war for peace against a Peace of War.

Echoing Madison, in his first Inaugural Address Lincoln told his countrymen, "the central idea of secession is the essence of anarchy." In rejecting the decision of a constitutional majority, secessionists invited anarchy or despotism.[123]   Lincoln had applauded Senator Henry Clay's prudence in refusing to call for slavery's immediate abolition; that "wise men" saw no way to abolish slavery "at once...without producing a greater evil, even to the cause of liberty itself" — namely, the destruction of the United States Constitution and of consent, a moral basis of political liberty.[124]   Lincoln understood the issues as Madison did: American republicanism tested the *human* capacity for self-government, not only the American.[125]   Victory in the civil war "will be a great lesson in peace; teaching men that what they cannot take by an election, neither can they take it by a war — teaching all, the folly of being the beginners of a war."[126]   Lincoln's very delay in abolishing slavery expressed his commitment to constitutionalism. To avoid the degeneration of the war "into a violent and remorseless revolutionary struggle," he "thought it proper to keep the integrity of the Union prominent as the primary object of the contest on our part."[127]   This war for peace succeeded, because a statesman of Lincoln's quality waged it, and also because the more thoroughly commercial northern states enjoyed an industrial base superior to the agrarian south, a base convertible to military purposes in a constitutional emergency.   Manufacturing and financial commerce superseded agrarian commerce, partly as a result of war and partly because it generated superior economic power in peacetime.

As the country's isolation from the world ended, American republicanism more frequently needed defense from external dangers. The Founders foresaw this and prudently feared it. Hamilton considered "safety from external danger" the "most powerful director of national conduct." "Even the ardent love of liberty will, after a time, give way to its dictates."[128] Madison added, "The means of defense against foreign danger have always been the instruments of tyranny at home."[129] John Jay argued that a strong federal union would afford the people "the best security that can be devised against hostilities from abroad," giving fewer just causes to provoke war or to invite it. The federal government would draw better men into public service than individual states could do, and better judgment would prevail more often. Treaties would "always be expounded in one sense and executed in the same manner." Fewer merely local circumstances would interfere and tempt statesmen; sectional passions and interests will influence the government less. The federal government, superior to the constituent states in moderation, prudence, and power, would earn more respect, and deter unjust wars.[130]

The more realistic Founders saw that the state militia would not defend the country well, that a standing national army was dangerous but necessary.[131] Under the name "Pacificus," Hamilton argued nonetheless that the Constitutional powers of war-and treaty-making rank as executive power.[132] Madison replied that commentators in the past fixed "their eyes too much on monarchical governments, where all powers are confounded in the sovereignty of the prince." Even Locke and Montesquieu make this error, out of their "admiration bordering on idolatry" for the English constitution. Madison defined a treaty as a law, therefore a function of the legislature. A declaration of war in effect repeals all those laws "inconsistent with a state of war," substituting for them "a new code" for the executive to follow; with peace this reverses.[133] War, "the true nurse of executive aggrandizement," pours money, honors, and fame onto the fires of executive ambition. "The strongest passions and most dangerous weaknesses of the human breast; ambition, avarice, vanity, the honorable or venial love of fame, are all in conspiracy against the desire and duty of peace." Declaration of war and the ratification of peace treaties belong in the more numerous hands of the legislative branch, where moderation and prudence will more likely prevail. The Constitution assigns those duties to Congress, for that reason.[134] The conduct of war necessarily remains in executive hands, fewer and therefore more able to act with speed and coordination.

For the American Founders, the questions of war and peace never ceased to be questions of political regimes. Political power being an ineluctable reality of human life, the Founders sought the best way to structure power, to direct human ambition and interests in such a way as to support public and private virtue. Regimes that meld sovereignty to the government itself, make tyranny and war more frequent. The only regime that separates sovereignty from government, unmixed commercial republicanism, tends toward peace on earth. Other regimes, whose rulers sense or perhaps fully understand this tendency, resist and seek to destroy 'American' republicanism. They wage protracted war against it, and, knowing that war empowers the executive, may force upon republics a damning choice: maintain republican institutions and risk defeat in that conflict, or wage the war, empower your executive, and risk revolution from within.

For their part, 'American' republicans must hope James Monroe was right. Social requirements for popular sovereignty – intelligence, possession of some property, independence and morality – characterized modern Europeans more than they characterized the ancient peoples who first attempted to sustain republicanism. "Nothing that has occurred [e.g., the French Revolution] can be considered as decisive against [the Europeans], or ought to be discouraging, provided that those who take the lead, act with moderation and humanity. Violence and cruelty will be sure to defeat any attempt that may be made."[135] In Europe and in to every part of the world, the course of events has confirmed Monroe's optimism, and his warning. While utopians cannot bring themselves to acknowledge the perennial character of the political problem, 'American' republicans do. "Of one thing alone we may be assured. The contest between despotic government and free institutions will continue to be waged to the end of the world."[136]

CHAPTER TWO

Towards an American Pacifism

American Christians who fought the Revolutionary War understood political institutions. Their kind of Christianity and the kind of politics prevalent in their time made political prudence necessary. For the most part, their Christianity was Protestant, sensitive to the problems of ecclesiastical power. Politics involved governmental sovereignty, threatening and sometimes assaulting the rights of men as citizens and as Christians. American revolutionaries learned in church the language of natural and unalienable right, and of constitutionalism. One historian asserts, "There is not a right asserted in the Declaration of Independence which had not been discussed by the New England clergy before 1763."[1] During the war with the French in the 1750's, the clergy had praised the English Constitution, with its rule of law, balanced government, and well-defined limitations of power; during the war with the British, clergymen used their influence and learning to "help in forming the new political institutions."[2] Clergymen justified citizens' defensive war against tyranny as the wielding of God's sword against injustice. A tyrannical king rebels against God indirectly, but as surely as an evil angel of light. "Resistance [to tyrants] thus became a sacred duty to a people who still were, on the whole, a religious people."[3]

Forceful resistance to tyranny imitates the just forcefulness of the Protestant God.[4] This spiritedness animated 'liberal'-Lockean and 'conservative'-evangelical clergy alike;[5] in fact it predated and survived them, too. As early as 1678, the Reverend Samuel Nowell quoted Exodus 15,3:

"The Lord is a Man of War." Abraham, "the first religious general" led 318 of his trained men to rescue his captive brother, proving that "the highest practice of Piety and practice of War, may agree well in one person."[6] Abraham did not fight at God's urging but received God's blessing after the victory, having fought not "for gain or advantage" but for the liberty of his brother; in this one might say Abraham reverses the practice of Cain. "To take up arms for the defense of friends and allies is lawful." So is defense of one's land, "a gift of Providence."[7] Nowell thus defended political union against destruction, inculcating citizen spiritedness ("A Soldier may be and should be a holy man, and the more fit he is for a Soldier")[8] and rulers' prudence ("none made greater preparation for War than Solomon did," and the wise Solomon enjoyed peace throughout his reign).[9] Civil rights and liberties of citizens, the religious rights and liberties of Christians, and the "the Law of nature, which teacheth men self-preservation," all require military self-defense. So does Scripture. Jesus tells his disciples to sell a cloak and buy a sword (Luke 22:36); in the last days, Christians must be prepared for the battle of Gog and Magog. "Whatsoever is needful for our defense, is our duty."[10] This necessity encompasses both moral and physical need: Military strength "is the proper and only means for our preservation."[11] Christians make the best soldiers because they enjoy "peace of conscience" and therefore do not fear death.[12]

The clergymen of the "Great Awakening" carried this austere Protestantism into the middle of the eighteenth century. The Rev. Gilbert Tennent, a disciple of Whitefield, wrote several vindications of "defensive war," one of them published by Benjamin Franklin during the controversy over the institution of a militia for Pennsylvania, where the Quaker tradition of pacifism remained strong. Tennent also cited Exodus 15,3, argued that nature requires self-preservation, and contended that the goods of Providence deserve protection. "I know not that a defensive war was ever questioned by any of the human Race till the Christian Institution strictly so called commenced, that some from a wrong Apprehension of several passages of Scripture, have scrupled it, and have been thence induced to oppose themselves, to the Common Sense, Sentiments and Suffrage of Mankind...."[13] Nonresistance "would be so far from promoting *Peace*, that it would rather contribute to the utter Ruin of the human Race," and "he that suffers his Life to be taken from him, by one that hath no Authority for that Purpose, when he might preserve it by *Defense*, incurs the Guilt of *Self-Murder*" – rebellion against God's government of man.[14] Jesus came to fulfill God's law, natural and revealed, not to overthrow it; like Nowell, Tennent cited Old Testament practices as authoritative. New Testament adjurations to love enemies and neighbors add nothing to the Old Testament: Proverbs 25,2 commands the gift of bread and water to an enemy; Leviticus 19, 18 requires love of neighbor and the eschewal of revenge. Yet Jewish law also permits war, thus showing that war need not revenge, and may comport with the law of love. Restraining enemies from evil does them good, expresses Christian love.[15] Human nature as first created was good, peaceable; the subsequent presence of sin has required effective means of self-defense from unjust attack, as when the sick take medicine. To expect protection from God is "vain Confidence"; Jesus did not cast Himself from the mountain at Satan's goading.[16] Failure to resist forcefully only "encourage[s] the Wickedness of the Wicked."[17] "*Religion* is one thing, and human society is another; the former is spiritual, the latter temporal; and therefore spiritual weapons are suited in Nature and kind to the one, and temporal to the other."[18] Jesus did not come to assert authority over civil matters at all. While Christians may not war *after* the flesh, they must war *in* the flesh.

The liberal clergy also committed themselves to the vindication of defensive war against tyranny, though emphasizing natural prudence somewhat more, and Scriptural sources somewhat less, than American Calvinists did. Jonathan Mayhew observed that tyranny (civil or ecclesiastical) "degrades men from their just rank, into the class of brutes."[19] Obedience to magistrates has its limits, as do all the Scriptural commands, as "common sense" tells us; one need not always obey the magistrate, any more than wives need always obey husbands or children parents. Only genuine magistrates, husbands, and parents must be obeyed. "Rulers have no authority from God to do mischief," and "it is blasphemy to call tyrants and oppressors, *God's ministers*."[20] Anticipating the argument of the Declaration of Independence, Mayhew found no duty to obey. Indeed men have a duty to resist "those who forfeit the character of rulers" — "not God's ministers, but Satan's."[21] Such resistance

> ...is not criminal; but a reasonable way of vindicating their liberties and just rights; *it is making use of the means, and the only means*, which God has put into their power, for mutual and self-defense. And it would be highly criminal of them, not to make use of this means. It would be stupid tameness, and unaccountable folly, for whole nations to suffer *one* unreasonable, ambitious and cruel man, to wanton and riot in their misery."[22]

Mayhew's successor in his Boston congregation, Simeon Howard, stood more obviously on the foundation of Lockean rationalism. He reversed the Calvinist stance on Jewish law, citing Galatians 5,1: "Stand fast therefore in the liberty wherewith Christ has made us free" — free from the "slavery" of obedience to the letter of Jewish law. He drew a political parallel, asserting the unalienable natural rights of individuals and of nations. When others attack the civil liberty founded upon these rights, "try gentle methods" — reason, persuasion. "But the experience of all ages has shown, that those, who are so unreasonable as to form designs of injuring others, are seldom to be diverted from their purpose by argument and persuasion alone."[23] If such men's designs are manifest, "we may, in order to avoid the blow they are meditating against us, begin the assault"; preventive war is a form of defensive war.[24] Howard shared with the Calvinists an insistence upon political union, the "peace among [our]selves" of "a well governed society," upon which strength, honor, and happiness depend. Tyrants divide subjects in order to rule them, and Howard trusted in the assurance that a political house divided against itself will stand no better than a spiritual house divided.[25] "Manly resistance" to tyranny serves Christian faith because "the destruction of civil liberties is generally fatal to religions."[26] Like Nowell, Howard called religion "a necessary qualification of a good soldier," combining the love of liberty, and the fortitude to meet death with "rational composure," and magnanimity."[27]

The Anglican clergymen of the American South more than shared the New England clergy's esteem for martial virtue. The Reverend Samuel Davies of Hanover County, Virginia may be taken as representative. In sermons delivered during the French and Indian War, Davies praised reason and cited (mostly Old Testament) Scripture, but appealed primarily to spiritedness in its individual and its public forms: manliness, patriotism, courage, religious fidelity, the purgation of guilt. One hundred years of liberty and security left Virginia "sunk in a deep Sleep: A stupid security has unmanned the Inhabitants," narcotized by "an effeminate, cowardly Spirit."[28] While first using fear and shame to concentrate Virginian minds,[29] Davies then took care to arouse courage and to moderate it. "Prudence is of the utmost Importance in the conduct of an Army." Courage is not "a savage ferocious Violence — Not a fool-hardy Insensibility of Danger, or headstrong Rashness to rush into it — Not the Fury of enflamed Passions, broke loose from the Government of Reason." "Rational courage" — "steady, judicious, thoughtful" — is "the courage of a Man, and not of a Tiger." Courage and prudence combine to make manliness, with which Christians may "scourge a guilty world" and "save Nations on the Brink of Ruin."[30] Guilt, "naturally timorous," will dissolve not in pride but in repentance, reconciliation with Jesus, and dutiful action in defense of "British liberty," property, "the pure religion of Jesus," and Virginia families.[31] "We have no Method left, but to repel Force with Force"; cowardice and "supine Neglect" of God's providence betrays ingratitude worthy of God's curse.[32] While Davies acknowledged that "the Contagion of Vice and Irreligion is perhaps nowhere stronger than in the Army," that "School of Vice", he sobered the men by reminding them of death's nearness and the calming effect of a clear conscience. He thus attached the soldier's desire to be (and to seem) courageous with Christian virtue. Serve God and country instead of yourself, he urged, and you will be real men, free men not slaves.[33] As for military leaders and rulers, Davies held up the example of King David, "a Man characterized from the highest Excellency to which human Nature can arrive, *Conformity to God* the Standard of all Perfection."[34] Public spirit — service to one's generation — and religious spirit — service to God — complement one another. "Without...a regard to the divine Will," acts of humanity and public spirit "form but a monstrous, atheistical Patriotism, and an un-creature-like irreligious Benevolence."[35]

The American Christian statesmanship envisioned by the Protestant clergy of the colonial and founding eras has had no better exemplar than John

Jay. Author of the 1771 New York state constitution; New York delegate to and President of the Continental Congress, serving on its Committee of Military Affairs; colonel in the New York militia; author of several of *The Federalist* papers; United States Secretary for Foreign Affairs; Chief Justice of the United States Supreme Court; and in later years the president of The American Bible Society: Jay was a man "of profound piety and unbreakable religious faith, unbending in patriotism, endeavoring always to keep an independent and evenly balanced political outlook."[36] A political realist, he worked to strengthen reason and moral virtue without supposing they could prevail unsupported by force; he was a firm anti-utopian.[37]

Jay addressed the question, "Is all war prohibited by the Gospel?" in two letters to the pacifist John Murray, Jr. As did the American Calvinists, Jay emphasized the moral authority of the Old Testament: "The moral law is exactly the same now that it was before the Flood"; the Gospel "extends and perfects our knowledge of it," and "also enjoins on *all* mankind the observance of it," but does not change it. The moral law was perfect from the beginning, needing no amendments.[38] The Jewish moral law commands retaliation against evildoers, but not personal retaliation; magistrates rightfully retaliate. Jesus rebuked Peter's use of the sword in the Garden of Gethsemane (Matthew 26, 52) because Peter had no lawful authority. Jesus's spiritual sovereignty over a spiritual kingdom has no need of a temporal sword. Temporal authority does.[39] Domestic war against murderers and robbers "has constantly and universally been deemed just and indispensable" (as in Romans 13. "It certainly is as reasonable and as right that a nation be secure against injustice, disorder and rapine from without as from within."[40]

"The most effectual way of producing [a pacific disposition among all nations] is by extending the prevalence and influence of the gospel." American republicanism hardly provides the only vehicle for this extension, having arisen centuries after the firm establishment of Christianity. Nonetheless, American republicanism can make evangelizing easier. Americans find themselves in the providential position of enjoying sovereignty with representative institutions. "It is the duty as well as the privilege of our Christian nation to select and prefer Christians for their rulers."[41] Such rulers in turn will conduct themselves so as to encourage Christian *conduct* domestically and abroad — most emphatically not the same as a state establishment of religion. Such conduct does not entail military defenselessness, which would only "produce new excitements to the gratification of avarice and ambition" by Mediterranean pirates and "the successive potentates of Europe." "Even just war is attended with evils," and so "is the administration of government and of justice: but is that a good reason for abolishing either of them? They are the means by which greater evils are averted."[42] Someday nations will no longer learn war. "In the *meanwhile*, and *until* the arrival of that blessed period, the nations will not beat their swords into plowshares," and Christians should take prudent measures of self-defense. Although Christians can take actions, even political actions, to extend the Gospel's influence, "no created being can either accelerate or retard" the arrival of the Apocalypse itself. "It will not arrive sooner or later than the appointed time."[43] Prudential reason perceives the limitations nature imposes upon human aspirations, good and evil: Scripture enables us to perceive limitations imposed by God's Providence. Thus Jay found prudential and spiritual support for the doctrine of just war.

First Pacifist Regime: Penn's Founding and the Principles of Quakerism

Against a religio-political ethos of just-war pacifism, American pacifism must attempt to show itself equally or more realistic than an exceptionally realistic doctrine propounded by statesmen and clergy of uncommon candor and probity. While a good historian can write, "America has drawn from Pennsylvania the lineaments of her great democracy," another reports that most "American Quakers supported neither the war for independence — which their doctrine forbade — nor even independence itself."[44] The "Free Quakers" and others who disagreed with the majority of Quaker loyalists, found themselves expelled from their congregations, 'disowned.' Understandably, "general odium" fell upon the Quakers for their stance, misinterpreted by Patriots as Toryism.[45] "Unable to accept the transition from monarchy to republicanism," some Quakers left for Canada.[46] Those who remained sometimes endured typically American reprisals — not the martyrdom of death or injury, but the confiscation of property.

This Quaker ambivalence toward 'America' and 'America's' ambivalence toward Quakers to some extent reflects the tension between Quakerism and politics as such. From the beginning, "the social impulse of Quakerism was...essentially religious rather than political," issuing "from an inward law of equity in the heart," not from an impulse for political levelling.[47] In seventeenth-century England Quakers "exasperated Puritan judges" by contending that the Holy Spirit alone guided the righteous, who were therefore beyond human law.[48] The first Quakers' reading of Romans 13 emphasized the teaching that magistrates terrify evildoers, somewhat at the expense of the teaching that Christians must obey magistrates, too – not out of terror but out of conscience. "Early Quaker thought was Apocalyptic, viewing the era as the climax of history," and thus "formulat[ing] no political doctrines." Yet – and here complications ensued – Quakers also "said that if God's justice were to be enforced, it could and must be done by men under the Spirit"; they rebuked magistrates "who refused the Spirit's leading."[49] While denigrating human laws and institutions, Quakers refused to really separate religion from politics, and worked for a politics of supreme *spiritual* ambition: "the Lamb's War."

James Nayler proclaimed "The Lamb's War Against the Man of Sin," a spiritual war against "the god of this world."[50] Some forty years later, Thomas Taylor still insisted, "the true *Israel* of God is now coming up out of the Spiritual *Egypt* indeed, to possess the true Land of Promise...."[51] And even a century after Nayler, the American Quaker Anthony Benezet wrote, "There is no distinction in Christianity between civil and religious matters," and that the martyrdom that must "in a great measure" follow from this denial should be a cause for rejoicing, not grieving. "I know human nature will in this case make strong appeals to reason and vulgar opinion, in defense of its judgment and its interest, but it cannot judge in the present case, [as] it has neither faculties, nor organs, to see into the deeply humbling mystery of Divine love."[52]

Nonetheless, although Christians can meet martyrdom with joy, particularly in times that seem apocalyptic, protracted martyrdom may require a divinity beyond the spiritual resources of human beings, however perfected by the Holy Spirit. The first Quakers soon began to cultivate the institutional means of civil peace. Edward Burrough commended the rule of

law and Christian government by the consent of the governed.[53]   But it
remained for Isaac Penington to consider the question of political regimes,
examining the link between regimes and the public good.   "Absolute"
government, or "government not accountable to the people," offers
considerable if hypothetical advantages. *"Laws* cannot fully answer the needs
and necessities of men," of circumstances; if rulers "be men of knowledge and
integrity, whose Judgments and Consciences are not liable to be deceived or
perverted," they can exercise prudence in a way no system of laws can do.
They can frame and dispense laws of righteousness "freely, purely, and
swiftly." *"Absoluteness* is best in itself...." Unfortunately, given "the corrupt
estate of Man, who is too apt to bend all aside to his own advantage with the
prejudice of others," absolute government yields "Slavery instead of Liberty,
Oppression instead of Ease, swallowing up the good and happiness of the
People instead of nourishing and preserving it;" the people's "liberties, yea
their very lives [are] subjected, not to righteousness in another, but to the
corruption of another."   Limited government is "safest for the present
condition   of   man."   Penington   thus   formulated   an   embryonic
Madisonianism.[54]

Like the American Founders, Quakers addressed the problem of
union and faction. "The terrible religious wars which had devastated Europe
before the Peace of Westphalia in 1648 left men keenly alive to the perils of
division in matters of religion and zealous for a sternly imposed uniformity" –
imposed in England by military rule.[55] The zealous heterodoxy of Quakers,
including their refusal to take oaths designed as legal enforcements of union,
combined with their principled defenselessness, tempted authorities to acts of
persecution, a temptation to which they succumbed all too often.[56] Quakers
interpreted militarism and persecution as symptoms of anger; unlike most
other Christians, who give a place to righteous indignation (as did Jesus in the
Temple, overthrowing the tables of the money-changers), Quakers found "no
good" at all in anger, one calling it "the Parent of Murder" and "the directest
opposite to Love" and therefore to God. "No man is angry for God's sake, but
it is for our own will." Whereas political and religious thinkers alike have
associated spiritedness with courage and self-defense (and also with rashness

and aggression) a Quaker insisted, "Love contains the whole Armour of God."[57]

Christian love bears a heavy load in Quakerism, both providing for the common defense and serving as the chief bond of religious and even social-political union. Instead of guarding and uniting the country by force, Quakers propose religious toleration; as the founder George Fox said, "let him be Jew, or Papist, or Turk, or Heathen, or Protestant, or what sort so ever, or such as worship sun or moon or stocks or stones," each individual shall enjoy freedom of worship.[58] Nonetheless, force does support even Quaker civil society. The theologian Robert Barclay, while insisting the magistrate has no right "to force the consciences of others," added: "[O]n the other hand we are far from joining with or strengthening such libertines as would stretch the liberty of their consciences to the prejudice of their neighbors, or to the ruin of human society." Precisely because they are not anarchists, Quakers must seek to show why toleration and nonresistance will not ruin civil society; typically, they seek to show why those principles will strengthen it. Barclay therefore distinguished religious toleration from moral license. While the magistrate must not be "the church's hangman," citizens must not *do* anything contrary to the moral and perpetual statutes generally acknowledged by Christians; in which case the magistrate may very well lawfully use his authority."[59]

Two problems arise here. First, as John Locke understands, religious toleration easily slides into religious indifference. If the blood of the martyrs is the seed of the Church, then what is toleration to the Church? One Quaker historian writes, "In thirty years the intolerance of Church and State [in England] had effected a greater advance in the rights of conscience than was gained by the next hundred years of toleration."[60] Once persecution as it were awakens Christian conscience and love, and establishes religious toleration, the atmosphere of toleration may lull conscience and love to sleep. This is why Barclay decried games, sports, and theater as sternly as any Puritan; these peaceful activities mitigate or make one forget fear of God.[61]

In America this problem came to light in the legend of the pilloried mouse. The Philadelphia Quaker Anthony Benezet lived by Fox's precepts of toleration. As a teacher, he began an evening school for Afro-American children, judging claims of their inferiority "a vulgar prejudice, founded on the pride of ignorance of their lordly masters"; he also enjoyed excellent relations with American Indians, about whom, his biographer writes, "no man in that day knew more."[62] One day two of his students built a miniature pillory, inserted therein a live mouse, and placed them on Benezet's desk. Benezet pretended the boys had shown mercy to the mouse (they hadn't put it to death). Discovered, the boys stood "trembling" at the punishment they anticipated. Benezet only kept them after class and their behavior improved afterwards.[63]

Benezet believed this showed the beneficient effects of mercy and Christian love. It does, in context. The context, however, was not love but fear, "trembling." If the boys had not feared punishment, would Benezet's mercy have moved them so? Christian mercy makes sense when the faithful remember a just and vengeful God, and anticipate hellfire for those who forget Him. In civil society, religious toleration needs the strongest bonds of love to bring union. To punish moral transgressions alone while leaving religious heterodoxy untouched, will lead to questions with respect to the grounds of moral consensus, questions that may weaken moral consensus. Why should American Indians not practice ritual torture on young members of the tribe? Why should Mormon men not have more than one wife at a time? Why should Moslems not kill blasphemers? Does the enforced imposition of Christian morality make sense without Christian belief? It could, but only if some foundation other than Christianity could be found for it. At this point such phenomena as Jefferson's 'moral sense' begin to proliferate, with more or less success in maintaining civil peace.

The second problem Quaker love poses, concerns the maintenance of international peace. Quakers refuse to disavow Christian political responsibility, and also disavow war.[64] Barclay argued that war, like frivolous recreations, distracts men from the fear of God, albeit in an entirely different way. War distracts men from their fear of God by arousing spiritedness; in this Quakers dissented from the argument of Samuel Davies, that war-sermons can make soldiers humble by reminding them of death. "Fighters are in the lust," Fox insisted, "and all that would destroy men's lives are not of Christ's mind, who comes to save men's lives"; Zion "needs no such helpers." (One may wonder: Does *England* need them, however?) He told Oliver

Cromwell, "with the carnal weapon I do not fight, but am from these things dead, from him who is not of the world."[65] Benezet contrasted civil government's just punishment of evildoers with the "vain esteem of warriors," a quest for glory that shunts aside the Golden Rule. He told Benjamin Franklin that this lust "is the root of that unreasonable and irreligious assertion so common in the mouth of Politicians, that there is no other way to preserve the liberty and happiness of mankind by any other means but that horrid destruction and corruption which War occasions." In place of war Benezet commended "patient suffering;" he resisted supposing that nations will cultivate it. He rather saw "the great cycle of the history of men": "War is the offspring of the inseparable union between the sensual and malignant passions; War protracted to a certain period, necessarily compels peace; peace revives and extends trade and commerce; trade and commerce give new life, vigor and scope, to the sensual and malignant passions; and these naturally tend to generate another War." Only divine grace can end this cycle, as "human nature, left to itself, has no power but that of producing mere evil," as a consequence of the Fall.[66]

After its initial apocalyptic optimism, Quakerism hoped for the gradual overspreading of grace through the nations. Penington sought to envision how this might unfold. He conceded that the adoption of nonresistant methods might "seem to be a weakening of the strength of the Magistrate, and of the defense of that Nation, wherein God causeth the virtue and power of his Truth to spread in the hearts of people; yet in truth it is not so, but a great strengthening." For "the seed of God [is] the support of the earth." To those who call this "an Utopian state, or a world in the Moon," Penington replied that "the principle of God," now hidden "in the hearts of men...shall be raised and come into dominion. Christian love is not the human love of Christians; it is Christ's all-powerful love operating in and through Christians, making peace possible in an otherwise evil world. Not human efforts but God will preserve the first Christian nation and all the others to come. Meanwhile, "whoever desires to see this lovely state brought forth in the general, if he would further his own desire, must cherish it the particular," and promote nonresistance here and now.[67]

The best attempt to cherish a Quaker union of Christian love "in the particular," occurred in America. "The problem of the pacifist magistrate was faced by Friends only in the New World"; elsewhere they were excluded from government. In 1681 William Penn received a royal charter to establish a colony in Pennsylvania, a "holy experiment" in nonresistant Christian politics.[68] A fellow-student of John Locke at Oxford and son-in-law of Isaac Penington, Penn shared with them a commitment to the rule of law through government by consent; this "Christian legislator" was "unusual among Quakers in shifting so easily back and forth between God, conscience, reason, nature, and private interest" – sufficiently prudent to integrate English liberalism into a Quaker framework while also becoming a confidant of the Catholic monarch, James II.[69]

Penn wanted a genuinely Christian government. "It is too undeniable a truth, where the clergy has been most in power and authority, and has had the greatest influence upon princes and states, there has been most confusion, wrangles, bloodshed, sequestrations, imprisonments and exiles," the result of "outward" religion, an amalgam of pride and avarice. Ambition, "the lust of pride after power," causes wars.[70] Temperance or moderation "is not only religiously, but politically good: it is in the interest of good government to curb and rebuke excesses: it prevents many mischiefs; luxury breeds effeminacy, laziness, poverty, and misery: but temperance preserves the land." Penn strove to reconcile moderation with government by consent, telling prospective colonists, "you shall be governed by laws of your own making, and live a free and, if you will, sober and industrious people." Exercising "a tender care in the government that it be well laid at first," Penn encouraged a civil society composed of farmers, handicraftsmen, such "ingenious spirits" as agricultural researchers and inventors, younger men with small inheritances, and "men of universal spirits" to govern the others.[71] Given this population of rural Christians untainted by urban luxury and ambition, consent would prevent corruption in government. For its part "good government...is a constitution of just laws, wisely set together for the well ordering of men in society, to prevent all corruption or justly to correct it"; "founders of governments" should establish a "frame of government that shall preserve magistracy in reverence with the people and best keep [magistracy] from being hurtful to them." Government serves three ends: the virtue, peace, and prosperity of the people.[72]

It was on the regime question that Penn hesitated and to some extent foundered. In framing the Pennsylvania constitution, Penn consulted the political philosopher Algernon Sidney, and they quarreled over the issues of nonresistance and the increasingly oligarchic cast of the successive drafts. Penn may have been somewhat indifferent to political forms: "Let men be good, and government can't be bad; if it be ill, they will cure it. But if men be bad, let the government be never so good; they will endeavor to warp and spoil it to their turn." Penn therefore emphasized the need for "a virtuous education" of youth. A Provincial Council would have "a Committee of Manners, Education, and Arts, that all wicked and scandalous living may be prevented, and that youth may be successively trained up in virtue and useful knowledge and arts."[73] The Provincial Council was one house in a bicameral legislature, the other a popularly elected Assembly. The Governor and the Council, not the Assembly, would prepare laws for ratification by the legislature and final approval by the Governor. Penn did not permit the Assembly to initiate legislation until 1701. Penn founded a classical mixed regime to serve a Christian civil society. In contrasting the Pennsylvania Constitution with the 1787 United States Constitution, it would be tempting to note the latter's lack of any system for education, particularly moral education. But this would obscure the different functions of the two constitutions: the 1787 Constitution constitutes a *federal* government, that is, a system whereby Pennsylvanians and the peoples of other states may govern themselves as Americans; the Federal government presupposes the vigorous conduct of moral education within each of the united states. The 1787 Constitution does not neglect moral education; it builds upon it.

The major contrast between the Pennsylvanian and the United States constitutions concerns the regime question: a mixed regime as against unmixed republicanism. The 1683 Pennsylvania Assembly quickly set out to modify Penn's constitution, beginning a series of factious quarrels that eventually led to the relinquishment of power by Quakers less than seventy years later. Such quarrels typify mixed regimes, as the 1787 framers knew. Religious toleration in some respects hastened this decline:

A State founded on universal toleration attracted to it an amazing number of immigrants and, as its prosperity increased, many entered who had no sympathy with its foundation principles. If Quakerism had retained the white heat of its early convictions, the newcomers might have been convinced of the truth, not of an isolated principle, but of the whole body of Quaker doctrine."[74]

Be that as it may, non-Quakers eventually exploited politically the increasingly unpopular nonresistant convictions of Quakers. Those convictions themselves declined as prosperity increased; Quakerism could not fully withstand the very prosperity Penn encouraged. Religio-political faction — insufficiently controlled by the mixed character of the regime and paradoxically, exacerbated by toleration — finally ended Quaker rule.[75] Would a purely republican regime have succeeded, or does the principle of toleration make faction and the abandonment of pacifism inevitable no matter what the regime?

The problem of union also emerged, somewhat less directly, in Pennsylvania's rejection of war.[76] One Quaker historian concedes that "built into the very foundation of the Quaker commonwealth was the element of dependency on a higher authority [the British Crown] that had by no means renounced the use of force in international relations," and thus cannot be said to have been "a reliable testing ground for the political responsibility of the pacifist precepts of the Sermon on the Mount."[77] Nonetheless, the great success of Quaker nonresistance in Pennsylvania was in relations with the Indian tribes. Penn's ambitious hopes for widespread religion conversions did not materialize, but peace did prevail almost without exception. The Quaker's fellow-Americans proved far less amiable. Penn quickly became embroiled in a territorial dispute with Lord Baltimore, who held the royal charter to Maryland. "Each governor accused the other of deceit, hypocrisy, and fraud, and both exhibited a bad-tempered stubbornness that prevented any choice of a compromised settlement." In 1684 a border war broke out, and eventually several counties in southern Pennsylvania seceded. "By the time he departed for England in August 1684, [Penn] knew that his utopia would never be."[78] Again, the problem was union; a nonresistant government could not enforce it, and did not inspire it.

By the 1740's, Pennsylvania Quakers began to seek a new *modus vivendi* with non-Quakers. John Smith replied to one of Gilbert Tennent's sermons on just war, first by vindicating traditional Quaker doctrine. He reaffirmed that the "divine Light and Truth" in genuinely Christian souls delivers them "from all Sin" in this world. He averred that "if any Nation or People were fully persuaded in their Minds that the Almighty required them to forbear the use of Arms, he could, if he pleased, prevent such Misery happening to them" as happens to others. *Contra* Tennent, Smith held that nonresistance is no suicide because it lacks the will to suicide; Smith thus replaced prudence with Providence. As for Old Testament wars, God allowed them because He had at that time chosen a single nation to bear His spirit in the world. After the advent of Jesus, all nations "were invited to become the People of God" and war became unreasonable — an argument that perhaps too readily assumes the invitation's universal acceptance. All this notwithstanding, Smith offered a concession roughly along Penington's lines:

> ...whenever the Magistrate is convinced that the Doctrines of Christ forbid War, it will be as much his Duty, as any other Man's to render Obedience to those Doctrines. However, the People called Quakers do not undertake the condemn our Superiors engaging in War, in the present unhappy State of human Affairs: We rather think it probable, that as they have shewn a noble and Christian Disposition, in granting Liberty and Protection to such as are of tender Consciences, it may please God to bless their Arms with Success, and reward them for their Kindness to his People... Smith thus foresaw a time when non-Quakers would govern Pennsylvania, and recovered the prudence he had seemed to forget.[79]

For and Against the American Regime: Pacifism in a Pacificist Order

David L. Dodge founded the first political organization dedicated to the achievement of world peace by exclusively peaceful means. His New York Peace Society began in 1815, as the public reacted against the War of 1812. Sustained progress proved difficult. Years later Dodge remembered:

> In fact the great barrier to our progress was the example of our fathers in the American revolution. That they were generally true patriots, in the political sense of the term, and many hopefully pious, I would not call in question, while I consider them as ill directed by education as St. Paul was when on his way to Damascus.[80]

A peaceful regime that nonetheless practiced just war: not only the memory of 'our fathers' but the endurance of their principles, secured by the political institutions they founded, encouraged pacifism while limiting it. Pacifists responded in several ways.

Some proceeded as if politics were irrelevant or nearly so. Peace would come through Christian evangelizing, not politics. The earliest statement of this type, after the American founding, came from the Quaker John I. Wells. Wells sharply contrasted "the rational mind," which he associated with "the spirit of war," to faith in God, the peaceful Gospel-spirit of "universal love." Turning away from the love of God – often an effect of "a state of prosperity," which "incline[s] toward a forgetfulness of the great beneficent author of our blessings" – brings "the forfeiture of divine protection" and the consequent attempt at self-defense. "All those who rely on human invention must suffer loss," whereas "the spirit of the Lord will enable thee to overcome and crown thy endeavors with ultimate success," in Heaven if not on earth.[81]

David Low Dodge entitled an 1809 essay *The Mediator's Kingdom Not of This World, But Spiritual.* He went so far as to claim that Providence arranged for Jesus' disciples to carry swords at Gethsemane precisely to give Jesus the occasion to remonstrate against their use. Dodge too demanded firmer reliance on Providence by Christians: "The great difficulty with the subjects of the Mediator ever has been, and still is, a want of faith in the promises of God."[82] To an anonymous critic who defended political life, citing Romans 13 and observing that under republican institutions "Christians may now live unpersecuted,"[83] Dodge replied that even Satan's power is under God, that government is not good in itself but is "over-ruled by God for the good of his children" – an elegant distinction whose practical significance he failed to elucidate, and whose 'theoretical' truth he failed to prove from Scripture. On persecution, Dodge admitted its decline while remarking a concurrent decline in the "spirit of living '*godly*' in Christ Jesus.'"[84] Dodge particularly tried to show that war violates Jesus' injunction to prudence as much as His injunction to harmlessness (Matt.10:16); even "the spirit of defensive war is folly," provoking war more often than it saves peace, destroying more property than it protects, "hazarding *eternal*, to defend *temporal* interest," and generally failing to defend the warrior or his country.[85] War endangers liberty by organizing society along military lines and by "inflaming the most destructive passions." Glancing at the example of Rome, he observed that republics "have generally lost their liberties in consequence of the spirit and practice of war." War fails to fulfill its expressed end, a lasting peace with liberty.[86] Aside from these very general political observations, Dodge had almost nothing to say about the American regime itself. To achieve peace on earth, Christians should evangelize and move closer to God than they have been; the Holy Spirit, as the real Evangelist and Jesus Christ, as the ultimate Judge, will do the rest.[87]

Apolitical pacifism in America did not always entail optimism about the practical efficacy of Christian love. True to the traditions of his church, the Mennonite Daniel Musser combined nonresistance with sturdy political realism:

> There is but one way in which non-resistants can be consistent. That is, by entirely separating the Kingdom of Christ and that of this world.... Law is the means by which government acts, and it implies the presence of power, and power consists in the sword. Law, without the sword, would be worthless.... Civil law is only an arm of the military power, and when we threaten a man by an appeal to the law, we point to the sword, and threaten him with vengeance.[88]

Musser envisioned no human government based upon 'peace principles.' Nor did he deny the human need for government, which properly prevents the "unjust, immoral and dishonorable" from "bring[ing] ruin and destruction" upon the "moral, just and honorable."[89] Government is the natural means, ordained by God, to restrain natural man, fallen from grace. "It is very evident, that Christ did not come into the world to improve its political condition, to advance worldly wisdom, to favor external interests, or in any way to improve the material condition of man."[90] His disciples obey those governmental commands and laws that do not compromise their conscience. His disciples, governed by Him, do not 'need' human government except for protection from evildoers. His disciples do not attempt to govern evildoers, leaving that task to human government and to God. In the New Testament, Christians' "*duty to the government* is especially dwelt upon, but never a word about their duty *in the government.* This, in connection to Christ's commands, is conclusive evidence, that Christ never designed they should occupy a place there." The best governments give power to non-Christians of natural virtue. To determine justice is difficult, but the Gospel is for simple people; hence God chose His children *out* of this world.[91]

Musser had no quarrel with the American regime. "True non-resistants admit the authority of the government of the United States, admit that it is God's ordinance for good." Musser did not commend the regime for its defense of natural right; "a pilgrim and stranger has no rights, and does not belong to the country or kingdom where he stands in that relation." He commended it simply for its toleration of Christians, and prays for those in authority.[92] He would have commended equally the English government Americans overthrew. He criticized the American revolution: "I question whether one of the clergymen, who preached up the duty of Christians to support the Revolution, ever once quoted Romans xiii"; here he was seriously mistaken in the fact, although perhaps less so in principle.[93] Musser went so far as to shrug at prudence, claiming that a Christian will not even "pray for the success of any measure or policy of the government, or...pray for the success of the army" — in his day, the army of the Union or the Confederacy. "God sees not as man sees," and therefore the true prayer in such matters is, "'Thy will be done.'"[94]

Among apolitical Christian pacifists, none disputes the power of the Holy Spirit or the wisdom of God in His Providence. The dispute turns on differing estimates of God's willingness to change hearts to a degree that would justify optimism in putting nonresistant methods to good practical effect. The 'optimists' — usually Quakers or else non-Quaker moral reformers like Dodge — believe God will act soon, or is acting now, to change hearts in numbers that will make war obsolete. 'Optimists' also tend to rank human efforts, man's 'co-creation' with God, quite high. Noah Worcester, whose 1815 tract, *A Solemn Review of the Custom of War,* precipitated the formation of the 'peace societies,' held that "waiting for the millenium to put an end to war, without any exertions on our part...is like the sinner's waiting for God's time for conversion, while he pursues his course of vice and impiety."[95] 'Pessimists' — usually traditional Mennonites — see no signs of an imminent or immanent coming of the Kingdom, and do not think human beings will do much to help God usher the Kingdom in.

By ghastly coincidence, Worcester judged that war could be eradicated in a century – this, almost exactly one hundred years before the onset of World War I. The pessimism of American Mennonites proved nearer the truth.

Without compromising their Christianity, other pacifists sought to think politically. Of these, Thomas S. Grimké, Francis Wayland, Joshua P. Blanchard, Charles Sumner, Charles K. Whipple, H.C. Carey, and, most impressively, John M. Washburn took principles of the American regime as the foundation for a genuinely America pacifism.

Grimké founded this 'American' pacifism. Writing in 1832, he contrasted the politics of the ancients with the moderns. Among the ancients, "War was the master passion of the people, the master spring of government." This passion cannot serve "the rational and valuable ends of society." He speculated on how the world would have benefited, had commercial Carthage defeated militarist Rome; the recent defeat of Napoleon's France (its symbol the Roman Eagle) by commercial England had provided an opportunity for peace not seen in centuries. For "the spirit of commerce is essentially peaceful."[96]

Thanks to Christianity and commerce. societies have become more peaceful since the days of Rome. But governments remain warlike. Here the American principle of popular sovereignty, united with representative government, can powerfully conduce to peace. A Christian, commercial civil society will "exercise a wholesome authoritative control over rulers." Grimké emphasized the centrality of education to the success of pacifism: "EDUCATE FOR PEACE, NOT FOR WAR." This means a Christian education, "imbued deeply, vitally, extensively, with the spirit of the religion of peace," and opposed to the "impious, vile, unnatural and ruinous...union between pagan and christian influences in education" whereby we "water the fruits and flowers of paradise, with waters from the sea of Sodom." The world cannot endure half-Christian and half-pagan; classical education in the works of pagan antiquity must go. Children must learn to exalt martyrdom over heroism.[97]

Grimké criticized the American Founders in order to redeem them. "Their banner should have been the DOVE, meek, gently, compassionate, faithful; not the EAGLE, fierce, sanguinary, the monarch of birds of prey, the ensign of conquerors and tyrants." Grimké proceeded to rewrite the Declaration of Independence in pacifist terms, retaining the God-endowed unalienable rights of equal creation but ending with a pledge of lives, fortunes, and sacred honor "in the spirit of christian martyrs, not of patriot warriors!" So armed and disarmed, the Founders "must have conquered" the British; for "the truth, beauty and power of the principles of peace, are invincible as a band of angels." More realistically, Grimké speculated that ties of nationhood and religion would have moderated the British response to a peaceful American declaration of independence.[98]

Be that as it may, Grimké tellingly contended "Our whole system of education is the very reverse of the maxim, 'KNOW THYSELF,'" as "it is fitted, to make us neither Christians nor Americans." American youth studied Cicero's Oration on Catiline more than *The Federalist*. "Who ever heard of studying an American speech as a part of education; and yet I cannot doubt, that an intimate acquaintance with the best American speeches, from the revolution down to the present time, is incomparably more valuable to the American, whether as a private or a public man, than a thorough acquaintance with Cicero or Demosthenes." Grimké called for an American education roughly consistent with the philosophic and religious dimensions of the Declaration of Independence.[99]

Francis Wayland showed what the specific content of this education could be. A professor of moral philosophy and eventually president at Brown University, Wayland conceived *The Elements of Moral Science* as a textbook in competition with that of the English theologian William Paley, which contained a just-war argument. Wayland taught that conscience, habituation to virtue, the rational observation of nature, and revelation necessarily supplemented each other — an insight closer to the doctrine of the American Founders than Quakerism.[100] Taken together, these three sources issue in the knowledge that "the relation which men stand to each other is essentially the relation of *equality*; not *equality of condition*, but *equality of right*," the "self-evident" right to use one's own God-endowed characteristics. That "EVERY

MAN HAS A RIGHT TO HIMSELF" is the foundation of liberty and of property.[101] The self-evident equality of unalienable right comports with the sociality of human nature, which produces the social contract that enables us to redress wrongs and protect rights. The social contract confers no rights. It secures "the enjoyment of rights already bestowed upon [man] by the Creator."[102]

"The best form of government for any people is the best that its present moral and social condition renders practicable." War is generally wrong. "[T]he cause of civil liberty has always gained more by martyrdom than by war," and "no one can for a moment suppose that this work of universal destruction is in harmony with the precepts of the Prince of Peace."[103] Although "Christianity has nothing to do with the *forms* of government" − Romans 13 commands obedience to a civil magistrate of the Roman Empire − it does cause "a tendency to free institutions" by teaching "universal equality of right." It "is intended, however, to improve the condition of civil society, not by revolution and bloodshed, but by instilling into our bosoms a spirit of piety towards God, and of justice and mercy towards men. While Christianity is doing this, it is rendering good government necessary, and bad government impracticable."[104] Wayland capped his argument with a statement of the doctrine of noninterference in the internal affairs of foreign countries:

> We have no right to interfere either by force or by intrigue with the religious sentiments or political institutions of another nation. If we possess this right, every other nation possesses, and may exercise it as freely as ourselves. The result of such an admission would be to declare the innocence of universal war...[105]

Wayland here misapplied Christian universalism. To say that a generally peaceable, Christian nation must not claim the right to interfere in the political and religious affairs of another nation, because the latter nation equally could claim that right, overlooks the question of whether the other nation really is peaceable and Christian. Noninterference may be a prudent general rule, but it can only be sustained morally on the basis of some principle, not as a hedge against the possibility of retaliation.

Joshua P. Blanchard, a truer pacifist than Wayland, imagined that Wayland-like moralizing could have a practical effect that Wayland did not envision. "If we would not make a war, even for a just claim, which our safety did not require, why should we suppose − in a similar case − [other nations] would make war upon us?" (Blanchard had unknowingly answered this rhetorical question two pages earlier by remarking, "men love *power*.") He retreated to safer ground by calling war a form of "soul-suicide" evincing lack of love for both neighbor and oneself.[106] He too built upon a critical selection of 'American' political principles, observing that the United States Constitution "does not assert its basis to be on any superhuman delegation." Established by the people, only, it deserves no more, or less, obedience than any human institution.[107]

The American Revolution "rose before the world on a basis of political purity, undiscerned in the speculations of heathen philosophy, or the vaunted intelligence of European civilization." Despite the problems of slavery, "martial desolation, machine politics and its spoils system," and excessive taxation, "we are improved" since the Revolution in religion, literature, and science. "Extending commerce has bound us to our race [i.e., the human race] in a humanizing chain of brotherhood," and the reform spirit quickens more hearts every day. The United States Constitution fails to fully embody the principles of the Revolution because the Framers interpreted the Declaration's self-evident truths "from a heathen, and not from a Christian criterion"; the Framers "looked back to the fascinating republics of Greece and Rome for guidance to the security of their asserted rights," a "delusion [that] still continues." For the ancients and for the Framers alike, "patriotism was the paramount virtue."[108]

Blanchard was almost entirely mistaken in his ascription of ancient or classical political principles to the Framers; the United States Constitution embodies the Declaration's principles much more fully than he believed. Despite these errors, which caused him seriously to underestimate the Constitution's indebtedness to Scripture and to modern political philosophy, Blanchard called our government "the best that wisdom has ever yet devised." He prudently warned his readers not to expect that "the principles of the Revolution can ever be entirely and effectually carried out." To end the practice of war, permitted by the Constitution, he commended arbitration of international disputes by disinterested third parties, "a new revolution" that would vindicate the principles, and preserve most of the institutions, of the American revolution.[109] The hope for an effective system of international arbitration proved delusive; the new revolution failed to revolutionize. But an even more serious and immediate dilemma arose at mid-century, the dilemma faced by Quaker Pennsylvanians: How can pacifists maintain political union?

The rhetorical peregrinations of United States Senator Charles Sumner, remain a measure of the pressures this dilemma produced. In his celebrated 1845 oration, "The True Grandeur of Nations," Sumner had asked,

> Can there be in our age any peace that is not honorable, any war that is not dishonorable? The true honor of a nation is conspicuous only in deeds of justice and beneficence, securing and advancing human happiness. In the clear eye of that Christian judgment which must yet prevail, vain are the victories of War, infamous its spoils.

The Hobbesian war of all against all must be replaced by international law, a vast social contract among Christian nations, replacing the subhuman (because irrational) custom of war, "organized murder." "Not that I love country less, but Humanity more, do I now and here plead for a higher and truer patriotism," animated by the "Law of Love" instead of the "ancient Law of Hate."[110] This hope is not utopian, for "Christianity is the Religion of Progress," of the gradual fulfillment of the Law of Love. Commerce, the Law of Love, treaties, international organizations, and propaganda will together produce a "Unity of Nations...over independent sovereignties and states." Peace is "rational, humane, and cheap. Above all, it is consistent with the teachings of Christianity."[111]

But Sumner and the other pacifists opposed slavery as well as war, and that brought on their dilemma. What can a pacifist do, if slaveholders deny the self-evident truth of God-endowed unalienable right, and move to dissolve the political union based upon that principle? Sumner chose to call their bluff. As late as October 1860, he predicted that the slaveholding states would not secede, because this would void the Fugitive Slave Law requiring free states to return runaway slaves, and because extension of slavery into the western territories would become impossible.[112] This reasoning should have been seen as flimsy at the time. How could *pacifist* abolitionists prevent eventual conquest of the territories by the slaveholding states? Why would slaveholders immediately concern themselves with fugitives and extension, if they anticipated a frontal political assault on slaveholding itself? When the Confederacy declared itself, Sumner, like many American pacifists of the time, abandoned his pacifism for a defensive-war stance. Secession was an act both of rebellion and war, therefore doubly criminal; the Union ought forcefully to undertake a police action to bring secessionists to justice. The "Rights of War," though "harsh and repulsive" nonetheless derive "from the overruling, instinctive laws of self-defense, common to nations as to individuals." Months later, Sumner upgraded these instinctive laws to a "sacred cause," namely, "defense of country" against the "Satanic audacity" of "Rebel Slavemongers." "Thus do I, who formerly pleaded so often for Peace, now insist upon liberty as its indispensable condition — clearly because, in this terrible moment, there is no other way to that sincere and solid peace without which is endless war." A lasting partition of states "must involve the perpetuation of armaments and break out again in blood" — the argument of *The Federalist* 1. "Give me any peace but a liberticide peace."[113] On the necessity of liberty for peace, Sumner cited Cicero's second Philippic, one of those productions of pagan antiquity hitherto spurned by American pacifists. He might more aptly have cited Locke on civil government, or any number of the American founders.[114] The statesman Sumner thus repeated the thought-process of the theologian Wayland, rediscovering by experience what his forerunner worked out in thought.

Confronted with the dilemma of secession or disunion, pacifism failed in either of two ways. Some pacifists held to strict pacifism, rejecting war but finding no plausible way to sustain political union nonviolently. Others saw that disunion meant the perpetuation of war, that peace depended upon the sustenance of equal, unalienable rights including liberty. These pacifists eventually adopted just-war pacifism, reconfirming the logic of the Founders.

These dilemmas called forth the most politically profound theoretical book ever written by a pacifist in America. Seven years after the Confederate surrender at Appomattox, the Reverend John M. Washburn, a Presbyterian from New York City, published *Reason vs. the Sword*. "When the storm-cloud of war burst upon our country," he recalled, "it filled the writer with amazement and confusion. The idea of fighting, to him was abhorrent; the idea of dividing the nation was painful; the institution of slavery was odious." Nonresistance, union, and justice: Washburn addressed himself to what had been the three incommensurables of American pacifist thought, and attempted to effect their reconciliation.[115]

God forbids war and ordains government. Therefore, Christian self-government must eschew war and somehow sustain itself. "[T]here must be some principle which, when reduced to practice, would render government permanent, and relieve the world of the scourge and horrors of war." This principle, the Fatherhood of God and consequent brotherhood of man, implies the "natural equality of man in rights and privileges," a principle "theoretically recognized in this country from the beginning of our present form of government." Slavery and the warmaking power contradict this principle, and ought not to enjoy Constitutional provision.[116]

God-created, rational human beings should neither kill nor be killed by other human beings. The combination of Christianity and republicanism, or Christian self-government as it should culminate in the American regime, rests on the principle that "all men have the unalienable right to maintain self-government, free from the terrors of the sword."[117] Christian republicanism perforce revises Romans 13 by taking the sword out of the hand of the magistrate, who is no longer pagan.

The American Founders would have agreed that all human beings have the inherent right to self-government free from the terrors of the sword. However, they would have asked Washburn, 'What happens when a man violates the republican social contract, thereby refusing self-government?' Self-government remains his unalienable right, even as it is for the willing slave, but how does civil society respond to one who refuses to *govern* himself, but prefers passion to reason, hatred to love? How does civil society respond to another nation that refuses or fails to *govern* itself? What should be the Christian-republican response in practice to the willful denial of the self-evident truths of God-endowed unalienable right? The American regime's

Scriptural basis never entailed a sectarian-Christian basis, and thus admitted just-war Christians, Jews, and even those of dilute religiosity to self-government. This enabled the American republic to defend itself forcefully against enemies foreign and domestic. If a more restrictive definition of Christianity gains favor, and if America is to become a Christian republic in that purer or perhaps narrower sense, how will political union endure? And if one seeks, not political union but spiritual union, if one seeks to overcome human-being-as-political-animal with spirituality, then have we not confounded country with church? Are we entitled to claim that we human beings can do this, absent a returned Messiah? Washburn divided his book into three parts discussing the theological, political, and moral aspects of his thesis respectively.

Salvation is human life's "true object." War occurs out of excessive attachment to this world, weak attachment to the better one. Although unassisted reason can dismiss the vanities of this life, one needs revelation of the "endless life God only can understand," and of "real duty" in this life. "And if before man sinned there was no death in the world, it escapes the wariest research to discover how the sinful act could invest the sinner with the prerogative of inflicting death upon another sinner!" Rather, "the life forfeited would immediately revert to the giver."[118] To the objection that men may rightfully act as God's instruments in taking certain self-forfeited lives, Washburn replies that the Law of Christ superseded the Law of Moses. God "has not told what [His] reasons were" for commanding "the Jewish wars"; in principle we cannot decipher those reasons, and so cannot apply them to our own.[119]

No divine command actuated the American Revolutionary War. Lusts did; the war itself, as distinguished from the revolution, was not "founded in principles essentially different from those of Alexander, Charlemagne, or other military captains." Human beings have by nature the right to revolution, but not the right to make revolutionary war. In forming a new government, by contrast, the American Founders did for the most part obey God, Who gives men scope for their prudence. God's ordination or *exousia* calls for government 'in the abstract'; God ordains *"that there should be civil government."* Men's ordination or *archon* calls for a concrete government "as their wants and wishes suggest," with "the single limitation, that they shall not violate His revealed law, nor the dictates of justice"; government is a mediate creation by God through man. Washburn strained to contend that the sword of Romans 13 merely represents the fact of forceful political power, not an authorization by God of its use. Washburn associated war with tyranny; "war is the tyrant of tyrants." The American Founders ordained and established "the most beautiful and desirable form of government in the world," namely, "free self-government" − the very opposite of tyranny and therefore the very opposite of the war-spirit.[120]

Good government seeks to fulfill the legitimate wants of fallen human beings. It therefore rests on the consent of the governed. Ancient governments and the governments of modern Europe disregarded consent. Interests, not force, form the true bonds of government; interests are those things and actions that gratify bodily and mental wants − as distinguished from passions.[121] Washburn attempted to distinguish the regulation of these wants, political government, from moral government, the province of Jesus Christ. Washburn acknowledged that many actions compound political and moral elements; drunkenness, for example, interferes with both the morally and the politically attained goods, and may be regulated by political as well as by moral means. Washburn would have agreed that if men were angels no government would be necessary, adding that political government employs human reason to satisfy man's physical and mental wants, that the moral government of Jesus Christ employs its means to satisfy man's spiritual neediness. The confusion of political with moral government results in coercion, the human use of God's rightful means, or the rule of unreason.

Thus Washburn, while applauding the Declaration of Independence, preferred the words "wants" and "interests" to the more moralistic language of unalienable rights, except when it came to the right of self-government. He agreed with the Founders that the "axioms of political liberty" are true by nature, that is universally, "for all people." Yet Washburn also introduced a hierarchy not assumed by the Declaration. Whereas men rightfully deny the right to life only by God's command (as in the Torah) the right to liberty may be abridged without God's command, if one violates "the liberty of others." Why is life not forfeitable when it contradicts the right to life of others − as, for example, the life of an insane tyrant? Alternatively, why is liberty forfeitable when life is not − particularly as liberty's abridgement prepares the assault on lives? Because, Washburn insisted, life's termination "extinguishes the possibility of enjoying any of the other [rights]"; further, "a wrong done to life, is irreparable forever." This argument curiously inverts Washburn's initial argument on salvation, which upheld the all-importance of the afterlife, and thus presupposed the opinion that no wrong done to life could be irreparable, except in this world. Washburn might reply that this world is the only province of political government, anyway. He did argue that no human being has the right to take his own life; that governments derive their just powers from the consent of the governed; therefore, government can have no just power to take lives, as this amounts to suicide internally, murder externally, and results in tyranny − as "*all* war must do," including the recently concluded Civil War, which has resulted in military occupation of the Southern states. Self-government precludes the sword.[122]

Washburn admired the theory of American government while deploring its practice, which he called inconsistent with that theory. Abraham Lincoln suffered from "confusion of mind," holding "the right of self-government as a mental conception, but den[ying] the right to reduce it to practice"; he "made *right* dependent on *power*," and thereby "assumed the harmony of two propositions, which no genius can reconcile − that men can be free and yet be coerced."[123] Washburn thus overlooked the distinction between freedom as 'doing as one likes' and freedom as self-*government*; the Southern secessionists admittedly did as they liked, but whether they governed themselves in doing it, exercised reflection and choice rather than passion and impulse, is another matter.

"What is the privity of relation, or the logical connection, between *moral* obligation and the edge of the sword?" If there is none, and political government extends to "no force beyond the *pleasure* of the people" as limited by God's laws, then political union rightly ends when that pleasure ceases. Human force cannot intervene, either morally or politically.[124] "Allegiance extorted by force, is the allegiance of fear. That is essential slavery. Slavery is right ruled over by might."[125] This argument unfortunately does not tell us what wrong ruled over by might is. But that is the crux of the problem. Were the Southern states demanding disunion for the sake of better providing for innocent or lawful wants and pleasure, disunion might have served the good. Washburn himself admitted that secessionists could not honestly say so.

This renders questionable Washburn's optimistic view of the practical sufficiency of interest as the bond of government. "To urge that government cannot be sustained by considerations of interest addressed to reason, is equivalent to urging that men cannot be influenced by reason; and what is this but putting them on a level with irrational beasts?"[126] But to sustain government, reason would have to be more than influential; it would have to be decisively influential – for long periods of time. To deny this does not degrade humanity to bestiality. The presence of Washburn's *non sequitur*, particularly at this point in his argument, itself confirms reason's limited influence; so does the imprudence of Southern secession. Washburn's Christian rationalism led him to overestimate the power of education, to claim that "Forty-nine fiftieths of mankind are, through education, just what they are taught to be."[127] His four-point programme for reform betrays this overestimation. He urged the election of unwarlike presidents, followed by the abandonment of all military institutions and the use of military funding for 'peace education,' culminating in the instruction of the masses. As the election of unwarlike presidents in a republic would require a citizenry already convinced that unwarlike presidents are needed, the project cannot even begin. Were it attempted in reverse order, it would require an (unrepublican) elite of professional education-ideologists and/or educator-clergymen gradually to seize control of classrooms nationwide – an ambitious if not inconceivable project by no means guaranteed success, especially if all other powerful countries failed to follow the American example.

Washburn denied the political and the moral necessity of war. The argument from necessity, based upon the observation that all men are not good Christians – and that, therefore, "war and judicial murder [i.e., capital punishment] are necessary to preserve the state and protect society" – should "be regarded as moral poison." In Romans 3:8 Paul teaches that doing evil so good may come, deserves condemnation. Politically, Washburn denied that war can bring peace, erroneously predicting more civil wars in the United States within the next fifty years. While it may be true that "*revelation* shows these acts [of war] to be *impious*," it is not simply true that "*history* and *experience* show them to be unwise."[128]

Washburn did acknowledge the limits of Christian rationalism, admitting, "Whether men will follow the course of conduct dictated by reason, is another question" than that of whether they should. He called it "unjust" to blame reasonable peace-principles for the actions of warlike men, but if the adoption of such principles actually embolden such men (as history and experience show they sometimes do), why would one not blame those principles, or at least their imprudent misapplication?[129]

Washburn completed his argument with an appeal to morality, "as tested by the laws of Jesus Christ, the only law-giver for conscience." Whereas Jesus commands love of God and neighbor, "it is one of the first duties of the great [military] captain to sear the conscience and reduce to silence the voice of the generous impulses of the heart"; "war implies complete forgetfulness of the soul," lost in the "love of dominion, ambition, avarice, and lust," submerged by calls for revenge and retaliation.[130] But political heresy or treason no more deserves forceful punishment than religious heresy does. Even self-defense bases itself in "*feeling*, and not reason," as only God has the right to save our lives. The command, 'Defend thyself' has no place in Scripture.[131] Washburn innocently failed to see that innocent nations, as well as innocent persons, might be destroyed maliciously by a revolutionary conqueror, a tyrant desiring the institutionalization of war. "No form of civil government can be instituted that men will not demolish so soon as it fails to accomplish the end which they think it ought to accomplish," he insisted, despite the contrary evidence of history, and experience.[132] By denying that political regimes affect the moral character of citizens,[133] Washburn underestimated the moral effects of the habituation of citizens into certain channels of conduct. By thus denigrating institutions that secure unalienable rights, which he tended to reduce to such nonmoral categories as "wants" and "pleasure," he could defend those institutions. Providence replaces institutions altogether. Washburn would have American principles without any forceful defense of the institutions designed to secure those principles.[134] To Washburn, forceful defense of unalienable rights means the immoral defense of non-moral though not immoral, wants and pleasures; to Washburn, this means the human use of the destructive prerogatives of God to defend, ineptly, this-wordly concerns of man. The spirit of war is thus the spirit of atheism, of weak faith in divine providence, God's provision for our wants.

Political pacifism based upon the principles of the American founding added to Christian love the God-endowed unalienable rights of the Declaration and its corollary, self-government by representation and by peaceful commerce. It attempted to find in these principles a substitute for the appeal to force. It therefore relied upon both rationalism and providence far more than the Founders did.[135]

In the 1840's, as the last members of the revolutionary generation died, another kind of political pacifism developed in America. This pacifism deliberately rejected the principles of the founding. Without pejorative connotation it may be called anti-'American' pacifism.[136] William Ellery Channing, a pacificist who collaborated with Noah Worcester in the Massachusetts Peace Society, anticipated some of its themes as early as the 1820's.

Channing praised the American "social order" — "without a soldier and almost without a policeman." He distrusted all government, claiming, "Liberty would be the best police officer."[137] However, he deplored the American tendency toward warlike spiritedness, asking "Has Christianity no power over us? Can a people never learn the magnanimity of sacrifices to peace and humanity?" He denied the peaceableness of commerce; wealth brings overpopulation, which breeds vice, and power, which gives scope to vice. Only "the Christian spirit can avail against war."[138]

Even and especially republicanism aggravates war-spiritedness:

> It is the distinction of republican institutions that, whilst they compel the passion for power to moderate its pretensions, and to satisfy itself with more limited gratifications, they tend to spread it more widely through the community, and to make it a universal principle.... The despot's great crime is thought to be that he keeps the delight of dominion to himself, that he makes a monopoly of it, whilst our more generous institutions, by breaking it into parcels and inviting the multitude to scramble for it, spread this joy more widely. The result is that political ambition infects our country, and generates a feverish recklessness and discontent which to the monarchist may seem more than a balance for our forms of liberty.[139]

As did Hamilton in *The Federalist* 6-8, Channing separated commercialism from republicanism, thereby enabling himself to deny the peacefulness of both. The rarity of commercial republics at the time Channing wrote, and the consequent difficulty of predicting what their relations with each other would be, make this error understandable.

Henry C. Wright cut deeper. Citing John Locke's definition of political power ("a *Right* of making Laws with Penalties of Death, and consequently all less Penalties, for the Regulating and Preserving of Property, and of employing the force of the Community, in the Execution of such Laws, and in the defense of the Commonwealth from Foreign Injury, and all this only for the Public Good" [*An Essay [on] Civil Government*, II,I,3]), Wright called force in politics tyrannical and anti-Christian. "Until we can *shoot our love* into the hearts of men, or thrust it in upon the point of the sword or bayonet, christians can have no use for carnal weapons." As for tyranny, it "is not an *abuse* of the man-killing power, but its essential element." As tyranny is no true government, the real anarchists are the "man-killers"; Christians require Christian government; insofar as the American regime rests on Lockean principles, it falls short of Christianity's true government. Wright thus approached an apolitical pacifism.[140]

In what was perhaps the first 'peace education' text for American grammar school students, *A Kiss for a Blow*, Wright dismissed the Revolutionary War: "Two hundred thousand men butchered for the sake of a tax of three pence and a pound upon tea."[141] In his *Evils of the Revolutionary War*, published prudently (that is to say anonymously) in 1846, he engaged in no such trivializing distortions, confining himself rather to thinking through some of the techniques of nonviolent resistance that would be practiced systematically only in the next century. Wright conceded, "I take it for granted that [the British] would not attempt to put to death the great mass of the population" – a fair assumption – but then went on to confuse Englishness with human nature itself:

> Can it be imagined, is it consistent with the attributes of human nature to suppose, that such a persevering and undaunted defense of principles so just would fail of working conviction in the hearts of a people like the English?...[M]oral might is *always*

on the side of justice, and...governors are *never* destitute of the feelings and sympathies of men.[142]

Even in England, mankind seldom has had it quite that good.

Wright forced such optimism upon himself by adopting a purist view of human life generally and of government in particular. "There are two antagonistic principles, on either of which all human institutions must be founded": love and violence. Given this near-manichaean premiss, this refusal of complexity, he could only strain his readers' credulity, if not his own, when commenting on Romans 13. He brought himself to argue that magistrates wield swords but may not use them, because swords are human contrivances, even though magistracy is divinely ordained.[143]

Adin Ballou stood as the most conscientious and thoughtful of the anti-'American' political pacifists in the nineteenth century, the one who tried to design a practical alternative to the American regime, which he called "radically, fundamentally ANTI-CHRISTIAN" because it authorized war. If two-thirds of Americans were non-resistants, he claimed, the military could be eliminated; moral resistance and "benevolent [i.e., non-injurious] physical force" would suffice for national defense.[144] "We should rely on preventive, rather than deadly force."[145]

Christianity regards perfect love as "the supreme virtue." This sets it apart from all other systems, which countenance "maxims or instructions expressly authorizing and justifying retaliation and pitiless vengeance towards exceptional classes of offenders." A true Christian cannot govern in any regime that authorizes war; "sword-sustaining" or "man-killing" governments "cannot sustain their independence and authority without taking human life."[146]

> Every man who rejects Christian non-resistance falls back on the world as it is, and on bloody violence as the great dernier resort of all persons, parties and nations, for the final arbitrament of human controversies. There is no middle ground. There are only two opposite principles — only two sides — and every person takes one or the other.[147]

The *militia Christi* held up by nominally Christian governments "is the sort of Christ for whom the proud and vindictive Jews were looking." But "God can do nothing that is not benevolent."[148]

Be that as it may, Ballou recognized that men can do things that are not benevolent. "There is nothing at which unregenerate and spiritually undisciplined human beings so revolt as at the doctrine that they must not fight with some sort of carnal weapons in defense of themselves and their friends; in support of liberty and human rights; and that they must not fall back upon organized governmental agencies backed by the strong arm and weapons of carnal warfare for the resistance, punishment, and subjugation of evil-doing men." Ballou thus tacitly denied the teaching of Romans 13, although he did acknowledge the moral necessity of Christian obedience to governmental commands that do not conflict with conscience, and he recognized that such governments constitute "the nearest approaches which the mass of men in their present low moral condition are capable of making to the true ideal." Perhaps by "fall back upon" governments, Ballou meant participation in them in order to avoid martyrdom: "Is it so dreadful a thing for the christian to be hurried to heaven − to be sent to eternal life a little before his natural time − to have all his pains of dissolution crowded into a moment?"[149]

At the moment Christians enter government, morality and piety divorce. Violence, at home in the form of persecution, and abroad in the form of war, overtakes them; "it is astonishing to think that with all the boasted progress in religious conceptions and ideals, the nations of Christendom constitute today the most belligerent and warlike portions of the earth."[150]

Jesus commanded no particular political regime. "He was not anointed to prescribe forms of civil government, autocracy, monarchy, aristocracy, democracy, or any imaginable compound of these ocracies; nor to superintend the political, military, financial, and such like institutions, necessary to any form of civil government; nor to teach any governmental science, economy, or policy, whether national or international." "Human genius" guided by Providence must establish and care for these inventions of prudence.[151] As a human invention, government should neither be exalted nor despised. Christians should expect neither too much from government nor too little — neither assume that government can be Christianized easily nor that it can never be Christianized at all. Jesus "knew very well that the administrators of existing civil government would not and could not obey the law of perfect love, or exemplify the specific duty springing from it, until society, in its organic form, should outgrow and abandon all dernier resorts to deadly force."[152]   Therefore, Christians should not make "moral war" on governments because those governments authorize violence.   Christians should "live above" such governments in "orderly submission" — a paradox better known as living in the world but not being of it.[153]

Ballou recognized moral differences among governments.   The criterion for judging such difference is "useful service," which forms the foundation of Christian government as distinguished from the punitive foundation of non-Christian government. Ballou insisted on the practicality of Christianity.   Indeed, without the Christian love that animates useful service, all things "become practically unfruitful" in the long run. The fruit of the tree is the test of its virtue. "We may suffer wrong, but we must not do wrong." This is not weakness. On the contrary, "in this lies the secret of our strength." To the objection that non-resistance encourages evildoers, Ballou replied, "This is an assumption incapable of proof." He asserted that violence "never converts the evil doer nor saves a human soul" but only induces more vice. "Satan cannot cast out Satan. Only Christ and the Gospel can do that." This severe dichotomy caused Ballou to overlook the possibility that injurious force might prepare the evildoer's soul for conversion by concentrating his mind on the worldly futility of his course.[154]

For this reason Ballou had to call non-resistance "the true method of self-preservation" in worldly terms. Human sociality, "the intense workings of the law of rational harmony," universalized, alone will bring self-preservation. Ballou sought a kind of Christian version of Enlightenment, whereby the entire human race would gradually become not only wise but good.[155]

Ballou considered human beings naturally political as well as social. Christianity does not forbid participation in a government office that "require[s] no sacrifice of principle and involve[s] no personal responsibility for governmental resorts to deadly force or other unchristian practices."

Citing Jesus' "house divided" sermon (and with perhaps a glance at Lincoln's speech) Ballou called unity the fruit of righteousness, discord the fruit of evil. He sought to design and establish a "new order of Society" to satisfy "all *real* human interests" and to build a Christian government 'from the ground up.'[156]

In contrast with the American Founders, Ballou looked to small-scale communities for models of his new order, citing the achievements of Pythagoreans, Platonists, Essenes, and early Christians. His 'socialism' equally opposed communism, small-or-large-scale. "All socialism [that eschews individual property] is essentially atheistic, selfish, unprincipled, anarchical and rife with physical violence," because it requires forceful expropriation and leaves charity no concrete objects. Socialism without individual, private property sanctifies taking and prevents giving. The "practical Christian republic" is "the designed unity of the righteous." Ballou envisioned a network of such communities, gradually becoming a worldwide federation. These republics would never request the protection of existing governments, except in ways consonant with "divine principles."[157]

Ballou founded the Hopedale Community as "the first constituent body of the new social order." The Community emphasized education, which, as Ballou conceived it, began with prenatal care. "Affectional education," the training of sentiments, was to unify and perpetuate the Community. Ballou described seven techniques or "levers" of affectional education: example, habituation, association (from scenery to companions), contrast (e.g., showing children the bad fruits of vice), intimacy, the direction of thought and imagination away from the "indulgence" of "lusts" and toward "some good object of pursuit", and religious instruction ("absolutely indispensable"). In sum, the Community depended, first, upon the convincement of its members, upon unity of opinion, and, second, upon sincere, voluntary action based on that unity. Ballou's favored locution in this passage is "Let them" do this, or not do that — as it must be, absent all but the mildest force.[158]

William Ellery Channing cautioned Ballou of the difficulty "of reconciling so many wills, of bringing so many individuals to such a unity of judgment and feeling." This difficulty

> ...was always present with us, and was aggravated in our case by the preponderance of minds more or less deficient in mental and moral discipline. All meant well, and had sincere reverence for our 'great principles,' as we called them, but all had not a nice sense of order, justice, and fitness of action in little things, nor patience and forbearance with what crossed their feelings, habits, and tastes. On this account our membership was occasionally reduced by voluntary withdrawal, our doors always swinging outward as well as inward to those who at any time cast in their lot with us.

The tension between community and liberty precluded growth of the Community itself and of a larger network of communities. Economic crisis finally ended Hopedale as a commune: "My hope was too large and my economic judgment too small." The problem Lincoln saw in republicanism — union and the perpetuation of political institutions — found no solution at Hopedale. The practical Christian republic proved less practical than the American republic it was designed to supplant.[159]

Nowhere do the problems political union cause for pacifism stand out more starkly than in the writings of William Lloyd Garrison. Garrison's sharp ambivalence toward the American regime — he veered from anti-'American' to 'American' pacifism, depending upon circumstances — resembled the attitude of a strong-willed lover to a difficult mate.

Early in his career as an Abolitionist publisher, Garrison called all existing governments "Anti-Christ," and anticipated a revolution in America replacing a government of force by a government of love.[160] "The time for the overthrow of any government, the abandonment of any alliance, the subversion of any institution, is whenever it justifies the immolation of any individual to secure the general welfare" — whether in slavery or in war. "[T]he welfare of the many cannot be hostile to the safety of the few." Far from being conceived in liberty and dedicated to the proposition that all men are created equal, the American union was "conceived in sin...brought forth in iniquity," and matured to "high-handed tyranny." "Accursed be the AMERICAN UNION, as a stupendous republican imposture!" The American regime is "a libel on Democracy, and a bold assault on Christianity!"[161]

Garrison's righteous indignation aimed not so much at American principles as at the terms of union. He questioned not the self-evident truth of God-endowed unalienable rights, but the means used to secure those rights. He wanted "every government to be elective and republican," believing the union to be an impediment to republicanism. The slave states' security "lies in northern bayonets," which, Garrison imagined, protected slaveholders from an insurrection.[162] Garrison never wavered from his adherence to the principles of the Declaration of Independence. All men have "the same equality of natural rights." "The right of a human being to his own body and soul...is not a debatable question. It is to be affirmed and maintained, not argued or proved." Like Madison, Garrison criticized "the slave oligarchy"; unlike Madison, he did so acrimoniously and without qualification, calling slaveholders "more tyrannical in spirit, more hostile to human development, more barbarous in their conduct, and more shameless in their villainy, than any that [have] ever cursed mankind." Such hyperbolic denunciation separates the agitator from the statesman. Nonetheless, in principle if not in prudence these two kinds of men may agree. Madison, Washington, and Jefferson would never have exaggerated as Garrison did: "For a people, holding it to be a self-evident truth, that all men are created equal, and endowed by their Creator with an inalienable right to liberty, to be literally trafficking in the bodies and souls of millions of the human race, and bending all their energies to perpetuate this terrible system, is the most extraordinary paradox in the records of human depravity."[163] But they did acknowledge the tension between American principles and their own slaveholding practice and took it seriously.

Garrison preferred to stand entirely on the ground of principle. "If the Declaration of Independence is to be cherished, we are right; if the gospel is to be obeyed, we are right, if man is man, we are right." If slavery's immediate abolition was impossible, immediate dissolution of the Union was the only moral alternative. "What fellowship has light with darkness? and how can Christ and Belial belong to the same government, and cooperate together for the promotion of righteousness in the earth?" This purism equally caused Garrison to denounce Southern secession; although he had long advocated disunion, secession for the immoral purpose of protecting slavery was "treasonable." "[O]nly a revolutionary right, for the causes set forth in the Declaration of Independence, could justify the South in its course." When it came to preventing this secession-for-the-wrong-reasons, Garrison could only look to the military force he had always denounced. Lincoln and the Republican Party, wielding the power of the Grand Army of the Republic, were sinful instruments of God, visiting upon the nation "tribulation and woe proportional to its great iniquity," thereby demonstrating "the natural operation of the law of immediate justice."[164] This violent coming-to-justice served the abolition of slavery; had it been only to preserve the union, Garrison would have denounced it — hence his attacks on Lincoln until the Emancipation Proclamation.[165]

On what basis can Garrisonian nonresistance maintain the kind of union it would find morally acceptable? Not on the basis of the nation-state: nonresistance "is a state of activity, ever fighting the good fight of faith, ever foremost to assail unjust power, ever struggling for 'liberty, equality, fraternity,' in no national sense, but in a worldwide spirit." Thus the motto of his newspaper, *The Liberator*: " Our Country is the World — Our Countrymen are Mankind." Garrison claimed, "the cause of justice and liberty must eventually triumph, whether by or without a resort to murderous weapons; but it will not be because of those weapons, but because of its inherent goodness, and the transitory nature of tyranny."[166] Governments scourge evildoers until such time that evildoers receive "the will of God." But such government is not morally right. "I am astonished that any member of the Society of Friends could ever have felt justified in voting to uphold the Constitution of the United States, in view of his religious conviction that war in all cases is anti-christian, immoral and inhuman; for, by that instrument, the whole war system is explicitly sanctioned and provided for." To hold some kind of government to be necessary, is "the jesuitical doctrine of Rome, that 'the end sanctifies the means.'" As late as 1858, Garrison deplored the growing "warlike spirit" among Abolitionists; "just in proportion as this spirit prevails, I feel that our moral power is departing and will depart."[167]

But by 1862 Garrison could insist, "Liberty goes with Union." Disunion for the purpose of perpetuating slavery offended him as much as union (allegedly) for that purpose. Garrison silently abandoned his chimerical assumption of thirty years before, that union kept slaveholders in power. He now contended that disunion actually threatened liberty in the North.

> Be not deceived; this rebellion is not only to eternize the enslavement of the African race, but it is also to overturn the free institutions of the North. The slaveholders of the South are not only opposed to Northern Abolitionists, but to Northern ideas and Northern institutions. It is to establish an oligarchic, slaveholding despotism, to the extinction of all free institutions.

There was no inconsistency here. Garrison saw that "the Government may now constitutionally do what until the secession it had not the power to do": abolish slavery. For this purpose, it could use its army. With the freeing of the slaves, it might not even need to; Garrison continued to imagine that the slaves could liberate the South by themselves. "I do not believe in war," he reminded himself, "but I do say that, if any class of men, being grievously oppressed, ever had the right to seize deadly weapons, and smite their oppressors to the dust, then all men have the same right," and "no people living would be so justified before heaven and earth in resisting unto blood as the Southern slaves."[168]

By July 1864, after the Emancipation Proclamation, Garrison saw that Lincoln's primary duty as President was indeed to save the Union. This was "not the evidence of a callous heart or a pro-slavery disposition," as Garrison had previously charged, "but indicates the man of integrity...honesty, patriotism, and ability." For years after the Union victory, Garrison scarcely mentioned the war-power clauses in the United States Constitution; the abolition of slavery had been his primary goal.[169]

The Quaker historian Peter Brock writes that American pacifists of the nineteenth century "ultimately failed to resolve...the problem of squaring the quest for international peace with the attainment of justice and freedom within the national community."[170] This is accurately but perhaps too abstractly put. Pacifists in the nineteenth and other centuries have not found an effective way to establish and preserve political union on pacifist terms. Pacifism's emphasis on love and harmony obscures this fact from pacifists and nonpacifists alike; union would seem to be the least of the problems a doctrine like pacifism would suffer, with its admiration for the communal virtues and its hatred of violence and tyranny. Yet admiration for a set of virtues, or even the conspicuous display of them, does not always suffice. In practice the controlled use of force promotes peace better than the exclusively peaceful cultivation of peaceful virtues. Pacifism by definition cannot avail itself of certain kinds of force necessary to the preservation of peace.

'Progress' does not solve this dilemma. Twentieth-century American pacifists face essentially the same problems as Penn did in the eighteenth century and Garrison in the nineteenth. The number of genuine pacifists who seek peace through 'American' principles has dwindled, but their writings remain instructive. (Of the numerous internationalists who seek to extend the principles of the American regime throughout the world, almost none would forgo all use of injurious force).[171] Guy F. Hershberger continued the Mennonite tradition of Christian pacifism combined with political realism, yielding a sharp distinction between church and state. Hershberger contended that if there were a truly Christian nation, no government would be necessary − a rather more optimistic formulation than Madison's, but expressing the same general notion. Quaker Pennsylvania's failure "show[s] that nonresistance and the coercive functions of the state can not go together."[172] Nonresistant Christians shall not govern; they shall pray for those who do. Hershberger strongly upheld the "difference between good and bad government" and condemns totalitarianism.[173] Similarly, Church of the Brethren writer Herman A. Hoyt observed that contemporary religious pacifists "oppose the war efforts of their own nation"; they illogically suppose that because Christians should not war, neither should America. "God permits the nations of this world to exercise force during this present evil age."[174] While not sharing the Christian just-war convictions of the American Founders, Hershberger and Hoyt refused to interfere with the exercise of those convictions precisely because they refused to mix religiosity with politics, as both just-war and 'activist' pacifist theorists usually do.

Nearly alone in this century, Martin Luther King, Jr. sought a pacifist politics generally along 'American' lines.[175] It probably was not coincidental that King earned far more political success than any other pacifist of the twentieth century; Americans saw him as one of their own.

To be sure, King adapted one novelty to American political life: "The Gandhian method of nonviolence."[176] But this was no more than a method. Each of the principles King served by that method, affirmed the American

Founding. "True peace is not merely the absence of tension; it is the presence of justice" — words with which every one of the American Founders would have concurred. All of them shared King's respect for Christian morality, and many of them shared his adherence to it. All of them would have agreed that "morals cannot be legislated, but behavior can be regulated," and that "the law itself is a form of education."[177] When King spoke as a prophet, he did not only envision the future; he called Americans back to "that sublime principle" of the Declaration of Independence, equality of unalienable rights.[178]

In his most widely-read book, *Why We Can't Wait*, published on the centennial of the Emancipation Proclamation, King called for a national rededication to "that noble journey toward the goals reflected in the Preamble to the Constitution, the Constitution itself, the Bill of Rights and the Thirteenth, Fourteenth and Fifteenth Amendments." He described God-endowed unalienable rights as both Scriptural and Constitutional. And while conceding that "nonviolent direct action did not originate in America," he argued it had "found its natural home in this land, where refusal to cooperate with injustice was an ancient and honorable tradition and where Christian forgiveness was written into the minds and hearts of good men." Without minimizing the strong "frontier tradition" of an "eye-for-an-eye," King cited the American colonists' peaceful boycotts and protests, our forefathers' first resort against tyranny, as precursors of his own tactic. He cautioned that "direct action is not a substitute for work in the courts and the halls of government," as the American Founders well knew. Like them, he called conventional law unjust if "not rooted in eternal law and natural law"; like them, he required that lawgivers obey their own laws, not exempt themselves from the laws as segregationists did. Finally, he thought about the problem of political union and took the American Revolution as his model for its solution.[179]

> Unity has never meant uniformity. If it had, it would not have been possible for such dedicated democrats as Thomas Jefferson and George Washington, a radical such as Thomas Paine and an autocrat such as Alexander Hamilton to lead a unified American Revolution.[180]

Although he did not solve the problem of union — merely to invoke the Founders while subtracting their appeal to forceful revolution does not solve anything — and although he did not seriously address the problem of union under a pacifist *government*, as distinguished from a pacifist political movement, King avoided the purism of many American pacifists, which had effectually prevented any long-standing political union at all.[181]

King's intellectual hostilities were almost as revealing as his affinities. While troubled by the "need for a better distribution of wealth," he rejected Marxism on three grounds, all consistent with the principles of the American regime. He objected to the materialism that rules out Providence; he rejected the moral relativism that claims the end justifies any means; he rejected totalitarianism and the "deprecation of individual freedom." He warned, as had de Tocqueville, that "capitalism can lead to a practical materialism that is as pernicious as the materialism taught by communism" — a point the American Founders understood and guarded against by advocating not merely commerce but commercial republicanism designed to secure the unalienable rights endowed by a Creator-God. With equal firmness, King rejected the critique of 'America' from the right in its most impressive formulation, Nietzsche's.[182]

King understood that "the conflict which we witness in the world today between totalitarianism and democracy is at bottom a conflict over the question 'What is man?'" To Marxists, man is "merely an animal"; to Americans, "man is a child of God," with "the unique ability to have fellowship with God" thanks to the capacity for spirituality, within which King includes reason. Marxists unrealistically deny the fact of human spirituality and what goes with it, the tendency to sin.[183]

King criticized pacifism itself in a way the American Founders would have applauded. "All too many [pacifists] had an unwarranted optimism concerning man and leaned unconsciously toward self-righteousness." King too saw that men were not angels. "I came to see the pacifist position not as sinless but as the lesser evil in the circumstances." He "tried to arrive at a realistic pacifism."[184] In this of course he parted with the American Founders, who would not have agreed to call any pacifism thoroughly realistic. Thinking of America, King argued:

> Violence often brings about momentary results. Nations have frequently won their independence in battle. But in spite of temporary victories, violence never brings permanent peace. It solves no social problem; it merely creates new and more complicated ones.[185]

The American Founders too never believed "violence" or injurious force *alone* would bring "permanent peace," or that it alone could solve any social or political problem. They disagreed with King in his contention that violence "merely creates new and more complicated problems." American independence, for example, was won on the battlefield between 1775 and 1783. The more complicated problem of slavery was not new, not created by that war; it preexisted it. Slavery itself ended in war; the more complicated problem of racism again was not new, not created by the Civil War, but preexisted it. Wars do indeed help to solve problems; for example, the Second World War helped to solve the problem of rightist totalitarianism as a world-historical force. American dependence upon foreign states, racism and slavery, and totalitarianism 'right' and 'left' remain in some sense perpetual problems, evils that could recur if not prevented by more intelligent means than those of war. But this does not make war dispensable.

In the last years of his life, perhaps responding to the pressure of political activists opposed to American participation in the Vietnam War and impatient with the stubborn realities of poverty and racism, King began to criticize the American regime much more harshly. While acknowledging its "miracles of production and technology," the "system" may have had an "inner core of despotism." He called for "a change as far-reaching as the American Revolution." Had he been spared an assassin's bullets, King might have elaborated on the character of this change and related it to 'American' principles. He had yet to abandon those principles, saying rather that Americans had failed to "follow through on the revolutions that we initiated."[186]

The near-uniqueness of Martin Luther King's 'American' pacifism in the twentieth century points to a radical change in pacifist doctrine. Most American pacifist writers no longer much appreciate the principles of the American regime. Often they reject those principles and call for a revolution not only in laws and institutions but for a transvaluation of values. While King rejected Nietzsche and Marx, calling for a "revolution of values" that would have reaffirmed the original 'American' principles and provided "our best defense against Communism,"[187] the new pacifists pride themselves on giving a radical critique of the American regime. They would strike at its roots, not merely prune its branches.

CHAPTER THREE

'German' Pacifism in America: The Historicist Turn

Although critical or anti-'American' pacifism dates almost from the founding period itself, the twentieth century has seen a new strain, one that typically cannot distinguish between republicanism and other political regimes, even tyrannical regimes. During the First World War, a college professor said

> I cannot believe that this present war is a war of democracy against dictatorship. It is rather a war of one imperial system [the British and French]...against a nation [Germany] determined to build a like system in a like manner."[1]

After two world wars, the American Friends Service Committee could not yet perceive the distinction between American republicanism and its most powerful totalitarian rival. Both the United States and the Soviet Union exhibited lust for power, denied human dignity by encouraging industrialization and technology, worshipped secularism, and maintained a cult of violence. Any differences between the United States and the Soviet Union were mere "accidents of history and geography."[2] And during the height of United States participation in the Vietnam War, a pacifist could claim that the 1956 Soviet invasion of Hungary and the ongoing war in Vietnam "have proven that each of the opposing ideologies of the world is murderous at its core." More, "any political or economic system which can preach an ideological crusade against the poor, punctuating it with napalm and TNT, or can tolerate worms in the stomachs of children, deserves not allegiance but uprooting." The murders of Martin Luther King and Malcolm X revealed the truth about American "values," which "seem to have established [America] as the Pontius Pilate of our age."[3]

War provokes passions in warlike and peaceful souls alike and passion by nature often looks foolish after the fact and at a distance. But the tendency to moralize about 'imperialism,' 'accidents of history,' and economics, to the exclusion of the regime question, and the resulting blindness to the real moral consequences of real political differences, emerges from a deeper well. Expansionism, history, and economic life share one feature: all of them focus the mind on change not structure, "the course of events" instead of self-evident truths. Historicist thought employs metaphors of organicism – 'growth,' 'development' 'decadence' – not metaphors of permanence – 'balance,' 'foundations.' Historicist thought produced what Jane Addams called the "newer ideals of peace," ideals she was the first to elaborate and to contrast with both earlier pacifist doctrines in America, and with the pacificist regime of the American Founders.

Published in 1907, *Newer Ideals of Peace* remains among the most thoughtful statements of the new pacifism. Addams identified "two great lines" in the older pacifist doctrines: first, a modernized version of Christian compassion, appealing initially to "imaginative pity" but finally making an "appeal of dogma," a command; second, an "appeal to the sense of prudence," citing the economic costs of war and arguing for the utility of international law and dispute arbitration. This dual recourse to religion and to reason paralleled the moral foundations of the Declaration of Independence. Addams rejected both moral command and the appeal to prudence – the first as too dogmatic, the second as ineffectual.[4]

Addams formulated "the new dynamic of peace," the "newer, more aggressive ideals of peace, as over against the older, dovelike ideal." Appeals to compassion and to prudence would be "totally unnecessary" if pacifists tapped an historical force, namely "the cosmopolitan interest in human affairs with the resultant social sympathy that at the present moment is developing among all the nations of the earth." Addams sought these sentiments not in the American ethos, in populations whose moral and political life the regime had shaped, but in "the poorer sections of [the] cosmopolitan city," where "many nationalities which are gathered there from all parts of the world," having "sundered social habits" and "renounced [the] customs" of their native countries, now felt "an unquenchable desire that charity and simple justice shall regulate men's actions."[5]   Historical change, animated by "aggressive ideals" and fueled by the will to novelty and the desire for a secularized form of Christianity, aiming to "carry onward the progressive goodness of the [human] race": Addams' historicism would revolutionize any *regime*, that is, any stable political order.   This will-to-revolution depends upon believing all 'values' to be relative to their own 'time.' Addams warned:

> We continue to defend war on the ground that it stirs the nobler blood and the higher imagination of the nation, and thus frees it from moral stagnation and the bonds of commercialism. We do not see that this is to borrow our virtues from a former age and to fail to utilize our own.   We find ourselves in this plight because our modern morality has lacked fibre, because our humanitarianism has been too soft and literary, and has given itself over to unreal and high-sounding phrases.[6]

The softness of modern morality contradicts instead of reflecting modernity.   Such moralism harkens back to "the a priori method of school men."   It must give way to the modern "scientific method of research" into the lives of "real people," particularly the newly arrived, urban immigrants in America, whose poverty and deliberate eschewal of Old World conventions forced them to face life as it is, and to find practical ways to cope with it.[7]

The principles and institutions of the American Founders impeded the progress Addams envisioned.   The governments of cities had failed, owing to "the inadequacy of eighteenth century ideals" and to "the breakdown of the machinery" those ideals animated.   Addams claimed that the Founders' "idealism" was "doctrinaire," based upon fear of experience.   The Founders' mere "theories concerning 'the natural man'" shielded their eyes from "the difficulties and blunders which a self-governing people were sure to encounter," and made them insist that, "if only the people had freedom, they would walk continuously in the paths of justice and righteousness."   Addams disdained the "crudeness" of the Founders' unprogressive view of human nature, with the "empty dignity of its 'inborn rights.'"[8]

Addams further claimed that the Founders "timidly took the English law as their prototype" and thus guarded property rights more than "the spontaneous life of the people," a phrase she left undefined and undefended. Ignoring her own sentimentalism, she charged the Founders with "moral romanticism" for failing to believe "in the efficiency of the popular will." "In spite of a vague desire to trust the people, the Founders meant to fall back in every crisis upon the old restraints which government has traditionally listed in its behalf" – namely, "penalties, coercion, compulsion, remnants of military codes." These old restraints, made to appear virtuous by the success of the Revolutionary War, often bound Americans more tightly than the despotism they overthrew. Faced with immigrants from continental Europe, this "century-old-abstraction" of unalienable rights, a "dogma of the schoolmen," dissolves entirely; "we have no national ideality founded upon realism and tested by our growing experience."[9]

In sum, it would be hard to imagine a more embarrassing farrago of inaccuracies than the one Jane Addams served as food for thought on the American Founders. The regime's success in integrating diverse nationalities rests precisely on the Founders' institutional "inventions of prudence" designed to secure those supposedly abstract and platitudinous unalienable rights of individual human beings. Addams sought to undermine the American safeguards for *individual* liberty and the property rights that support it, replacing this with *group* rights supported by a government empowered to eliminate 'capitalism.' She failed to see that the government's insistence on securing individuals' property rights, would guard immigrants, too, as they acquired property – that Lockean property rights are based upon the right of keeping the fruits of one's own labor to secure self-preservation, liberty, and the pursuit of happiness.

Thus she preferred "a more passionate human creed" than the Founders' encouragements to reasonableness would support. This creed was "the modern evolutionary concept of the slowly advancing race whose rights are not 'inalienable,' but hard-won in the tragic processes of experience...." What began with a sort of urban Rousseauism, which discovered the innately good 'fundamental man' in the immigrant neighborhoods of American cities, quickly became a call for the use of "the historical method" by "the moralists and statesmen of this dawning century" – a method that conveniently reinforced a "passionate creed," synthesizing the abstractions of both science and moral fervor. By the grace of this 'science' and this passion, "human kindness" would replace all coercion, and a pacifist regime would flourish.[10] Addams took a strictly historicist position on war: War did nurture certain virtues at one time, but it and they were now atavistic. She called instead for a "progressive patriotism."[11]

Addams looked to Germany for a political model. "The inherited instinct [of Americans] that government is naturally oppressive, and that its inroads must be checked, has made it a matter of principle and patriotism to keep the functions of government more restricted and more military than has become true in military countries." By contrast, Germany, supposedly more militaristic than America, "is gradually evolving into a Government logically fitted to cope with the industrial situation of the twentieth century," while America lags behind, "retaining eighteenth century tradition."[12] This extraordinary bad prediction silently disappeared from the writings Addams published after the First World War. She did not however abandon the ideology that made her vulnerable to such illusions. In her 1922 book, *Peace and Bread in Time of War*, Addams hoped "that the world could be organized politically by its statesmen as it had been already organized into an international fiscal system by its bankers." She continued to reject the possibility that the war, or any war, could contribute to the advancement of democracy: "It seemed to me quite obvious that the processes of war would destroy more democratic institutions than [President Wilson] could ever rebuild however much he might declare the purpose of war to be the extension of democracy."[13] This was factually untrue; the number of commercial republics in Europe immediately after the First World War exceeded the number at any time before.

Still, the war sobered Addams, moderating if not excising her ideological passion. "Whereas nationalism thirty years earlier had seemed generous and inclusive, stressing likenesses, it now appeared dogmatic and ruthless, insisting upon historic prerogatives quite independent of popular will." She noticed that Soviet communism and communism generally "had become...absolutely militaristic."[14] She did not see that Marxism started out militaristic to the core, as had modern nationalism. She thus remained captive to German ideology.

German ideology animated other pacifist intellectuals and social activists in the early twentieth century, none more so than Randolph S. Bourne, who sought to represent "the younger intelligentsia" of the time."[15] Influenced by the historicist philosophies of John Dewey, William James, and Josiah Royce, and by the historicist economic determinism of the historian Charles Beard, Bourne described "German ideals" as "the only broad and seizing ones that have lived in the world in our generation." As did Addams, Bourne deplored attempts to sustain principles defended in previous eras; this "would be simply to expatriate ourselves from the modern world."[16] The American republic is "the direct descendent" of "early English monarchy," because "the same State functions and attitudes have been preserved essentially unchanged." Bourne called the State − any State − "armed power, culminating in a single head, bent on one primary object, the reducing to subjection, to unconditional and unqualified loyalty of all the people of a certain territory." The essence of the State is war, including the peace of war or tyranny; monarchies and republics equally make war against other peoples and their own. Less thoroughgoing an historicist than Addams, Bourne defended the Declaration of Independence and its statement of unalienable rights; his villains were rather the Framers of the 1787 Constitution (a document "manufactured in secret session by the leaders of the propertied and ruling classes"), who overthrew popular sovereignty.[17] Bourne never thought through this tension between historicism and principled American populism, and his anarcho-populism was far more naive than anything Addams ever entertained in public.[18]

'Germany' did not go unopposed by contemporary intellectuals, pacifist and nonpacifist.[19] In rejecting the extremes of militarism and pacifism, the philosopher Ralph Barton Perry called for a public rhetoric "that shall take the middle ground." He criticized the German moral philosophy of "self-realization," individual and collective, because it made moderation and prudence impossible; in the quest for self-realization a man becomes "a menace to any neighborhood" because "when spiritual exaltation reaches a certain height it becomes necessary to use handcuffs and a straightjacket."[20]

By founding the government upon popular sovereignty, modern republicanism makes nationalism in some form inevitable, thus making restraints on national fervor all the more necessary. "There is nothing less picturesque and compelling than moderation" – and nothing more necessary. German philosophy, which believes nature mere appearance and contends that "the substance and ordering principle in reality is the mind which receives the appearances, or in which the contents lie," cannot on principle sustain moderation in action, as it 'reshapes' nature, including human nature, in its very epistemology.[21] German Idealism culminates in Hegelianism, which effectually 'nationalizes' this Kantian epistemology, making it into historicism, and taking moderation out of politics.

Against this, Perry insisted that so-called 'values' are facts – permanent interests that inhere in human nature itself. Commercial republicanism, particularly in its "principle of representation," recognizes and guards "all the interests which [the government's] policy affects," ensuring "these interests shall have facilities for making their claims effective."[22]

The encroachments of 'German' or historicist ideology in American intellectual life began well before the First World War. The academic study of politics had been historicist for nearly half a century,[23] as had the ideology of prominent intellectuals dating back to Emerson. Addams and her successors shared political and philosophic assumptions that prevailed without qualification in other countries, with bad results. Historicism prevailed in America (and in England) only with what might be called saving qualifications imposed by the regime. One may consider pacifist historicism historically – examining its roots, as historicists like to say, in doctrines predating it by a century.[24]

Pacifying Hegel: How Pacifists Appropriated Historicism

The philosophy of G.W.F. Hegel would seem singularly uninviting to pacifists. Napoleon's admirer, a forerunner of bourgeois-baiting radicals 'left' and 'right', sharing with them a confidence in war as the antidote to commercial peaceableness or decadence, harshly pointing to the slaughter-bench of history, Hegel would not seem congenial to those horrified by carnage.[25] Nonetheless, Hegelianism turned out to be hostile to pacifism rather in the way imperial Rome was hostile to Christianity — hostile, indeed, but susceptible to conversion.

Hegel proceeds from the premise of the Enlightenment, adjuring philosophy to "relinquish the name of love of knowledge and be actual knowledge." Organicist metaphors illustrate his means for acquiring knowledge; philosophers now can know, and not merely wonder, thanks to "the progressive development of the truth" in the history of human thought. Philosophies contradict one another only as the fruit "contradicts" the flower; the fruit supplants the flower, but develops from it.[26]

Force forms the core of Hegel's universe.[27] His "Absolute Spirit" is nothing other than the most comprehensive force in the universe, creating and destroying in the 'organic' or 'dialectical' manner. On the level of human life, the name for this process is History, "the process of becoming in terms of knowledge, a conscious self-mediating process — Spirit externalized and emptied into Time."[28] Despite the term "Spirit," rather reminiscent of Christian theology, there is nothing 'spiritual' about this. Human beings 'become' human by asserting and resisting domination. The slave attains his freedom "solely by risking life; only thus is it tried and proved that the essential nature of self-consciousness is not bare existence." Thus "each must aim at the death of the other"; despite Christianity's precepts, Hegel sees no peaceful solution to the conflict between master and slave. This willingness to kill and to be killed, to *dominate* 'mere life' *means* freedom. Therefore, "war is the spirit and form in which the essential moment of ethical substance, the absolute freedom of ethical self-consciousness from all and every kind of existence, is manifestly confirmed and realized."[29]

Freedom and "the Idea of right" coincide. Right is Spirit objectifying itself into institutions, in conditions of mental and sometimes physical conflict. "Self-determination" is "thinking reason resolving itself into finitude," specifically, the finitude of human institutions.[30] To set human rights against "the universality of the state "is one of the commonest blunders of abstract thinking"; citizenship in "a good state" makes "right and duty," particular and universal, coalesce.[31] The state is "mind objectified" or "the march of God [i.e., Absolute Spirit] in the world," or "the power of reason actualizing itself as will."[32]

What, then, is a "good" state? Being "the absolute power on earth," the nation-state 'wills' or particularizes the truth that is Absolute Spirit. *Zeitgeist* or time-spirit, History, is Absolute Spirit in its particular, human aspect. A good state, first and foremost, wills. It must have the institution of willing *par excellence*, the Crown, with a bureaucracy to do the bidding of the Crown. Bureaucracy 'rationalizes' human life, and thus serves Absolute Spirit/Dialectical Reason. "World history is not the verdict of mere might." It is spirit "clothing itself with the form of events or the immediate actuality of nature." The good state is the one animated by "the Germanic spirit," the "spirit of the new world," conquering nature and events and thus finally *ending* history in the thought of Hegel himself, who has achieved final knowledge of the Absolute Spirit; "the human and the divine are essentially one."[33] From now on, History will merely repeat itself, cyclically, in 'divine' German-type nation-states (bureaucratic monarchies), as philosophic history repeats itself in the mind of the 'divine' Hegelian sage.

Hegel wants a 'depersonalized' state, analogous to an organism. This state is not despotic, as despotism involves the particular will of monarch or mob. A good state must have "an inwardly developed, genuinely organic, totality." "The Idea of the state in its full development is the Crown," never subject to popular election. Elective monarchy "grounded on the will interpreted as the whim, opinion, and caprice of the Many," is "the worst of institutions." An hereditary monarch need not submit to the particularistic, irrational will of the people.[34] Hegel evidently favors a mixed regime with a strong monarchic bent.

Each state defends its freedom, its autonomy (literally, self-lawgiving) against other states. Organicism or 'totalitarianism' means the state has "absolute power against everything individual and particular, against life, property, and their rights, even against societies and associations." All are justly sacrificed to preserve state autonomy, even as the slave risks his life for his own self-determination. Totalitarianism for Hegel does not mean tyranny or despotism; it is entirely *im*personal, 'rationalized.' The very organicism, or dialectic intricacy of the state is supposed to prevent any particular will, including that of the Crown, the hereditary monarchy, from dominating it.[35]

The threat to the Hegelian state is protracted peace. Peace expands economic life, life in what Hegel calls civil society – social life 'below' political life. With peace, individuals' "idiosyncrasies become continually more fixed and ossified"; the parts overwhelm the organic whole; "in the long run, men stagnate" and the state dies. Wars reunify the state. "The seeds burgeon once more, and harangues are silenced by the solemn cycles of history."[36]

Against the state there are finally no individual rights. "Sacrifice on behalf of the individuality of the state is the substantial tie between the state and all its members and so is a universal duty." Courage, particularly as embodied in a professional military class, actualizes the state's sovereignty, displays its freedom – as in the paradigmatic example of the slaves self-liberation from the master. The professionalism of the military class, and its use of technologically advanced weapons, increases the 'rationality' – i.e., the impersonality – of the state, rather as the bureaucracy does. "The nation state is mind in its substantive rationality and immediate actuality and is therefore the absolute power on earth." Out of the "deeds and destinies" of these "national minds" arises a dialectic constituting "the universal mind, the mind of the world, free from all restriction, producing itself as that which exercises its right – and its right is the highest right of all...." The real Providence, the real Holy Spirit, is the "World Mind." "History is mind clothing itself with the form of events or the immediate actuality of nature." Hegel expects the impersonality of the state to result in more humane war-tactics, as no vindictiveness will fuel the conflict.[37]

Hegelianism thus opposes the fundamental principles of American republicanism.[38]   Ralph Waldo Emerson adapted Hegelianism to the American ethos on the 'cultural' plane; Woodrow Wilson adapted it for political use; Walter Rauschenbusch adapted it to the Christian church.

Emerson made Hegel more egalitarian, therefore less rationalistic. Emerson replaced rational dialectic with a dialectic of feeling, a process in which larger numbers can participate. A "universal soul" or "Oversoul," remarkably like Hegel's Absolute Spirit, animates "individual life," especially in the wise men allied "with truth and God." Like Hegel, Emerson would deify man, who, through the universal soul or spirit, can mold physical nature and "build [his] own world." "Let us demand our own works and laws and worship."[39] Unlike Hegel, Emerson asserted the identity of philosopher and poet; Emerson's creator-man works primarily with imagination and character, not science. The universal spirit is none other than an organized enthusiasm, whereby men can overcome the separation of art and nature.[40]

Democratized Hegelianism finds God incarnated in all men; every mind, not only the sage's mind, "must go over the whole lesson [of history] itself." The Over-Soul speaks as "one mind common to all individual men."[41] This is a modern democratism, one that insists on individuality even as it exalts the Over-Soul. It is not the American Founders' individuality, however; Emersonian individualism rejects the reality of original sin or natural corruption.[42] Divine incarnation is only partial, however. Historical relativism results. No man "can quite emancipate himself from his age and country," but is "necessitated by the air he breathes and the idea on which he and his contemporaries live and toil, to share the manner of the times, without knowing what the manner is."[43]

As does Hegel, Emerson believed "the history of the State sketches in rough outline the progress of thought." Historicism does not prevent reformism; Emerson's egalitarian and emotional Hegelianism lends itself to the passion for political reform, producing a gentle Hegelianism of the 'left.'[44] This may be seen in his writings on war. Emerson understood Hegel's argument for war, that it "breaks up the Chinese stagnation of society, and demonstrates the personal merits of all men"; war is "better" than peace for "the luxurious and the timid."[45] He conceded, in proper historicist fashion, that war was necessary in "the infancy of society," disseminating the "secrets of wisdom and art," bringing "different families of the human race together – to blows at first, but afterwards to truce, to trade and to intermarriage." But his sentimentalism made Emerson expect mankind to transcend war. "All history is the decline of war, though the slow decline," and "a universal peace is as sure as is the prevalence of civilization over barbarism, of liberal governments over feudal forms." The measure or "mercury" of a nation's "state of cultivation" is the issue of war and peace.[46]

Emerson replaced the discipline of war with the sentiment of love. "A nation of lovers" will "carry the sentence of honor and shame" before the world; "all forces [will] yield to their energy and persuasion." Emerson was the first secular ideologue to claim that love provides its own defense by the moral power of its own deliberate defenselessness.[47] Emerson 'Christianized' Hegelianism, abandoning its impersonal rationalism for a secularized version of Christian love.

Later in the nineteenth century, as American universities began to imitate German models, 'Germany' began to dominate the study of politics.[48] Woodrow Wilson had the unique chance to elaborate historicism in theory before partially implementing it at the highest level of American government.[49]

As a twenty-year-old Princeton University student, Wilson confided to his diary serious criticisms of the American regime:

> The American *Republic* will in my opinion never celebrate another Centennial. At least under its present Constitution and laws. Universal suffrage is at the foundation of every evil in this country.[50]

The United States is only "a miserable delusion of a republic...too founded upon the notion of abstract liberty!" As had several of his most prominent Southern intellectual forbears, particularly Calhoun, Wilson admired England's mixed regime; "the English form of government is the only true one."[51]

An Ivy League education turned this Burkean Southern conservative into a devotee of 'Germany.' In a book written for college students, Wilson discussed what would come to be called 'comparative regimes.' He distinguished political systems that are "defeated or dead" from "those which are alive and triumphant." Because peoples of German origin dominated the world at the time, "it is Aryan practice we principally wish to know."[52] England remained Wilson's favorite, for its gradualism of development. The United States had earned his favor by developing from English institutions. Wilson did not discuss the doctrine of unalienable rights or of American republicanism (except for federalism). He tried to account for the Civil War entirely in terms of "national feeling" based primarily upon social and economic differences.[53]

Like Emerson, Wilson democratized Hegel, though not as Emerson did. Wilson claimed democracy was the final stage of human development; its "true concept...is inseparable from the organic theory of the state."[54] Wilsonian 'democracy' bears as close a resemblance to Hegelian monarchy as it could, without ceasing to be democratic. "Properly organized democracy is the best government of the few," representative government. But — and here the Hegelian surfaces — bureaucracy or "civil service" is "but another process of representation," This science is "the latest fruit of [the] science of politics," a science "developed by French and German professors." It "must inhale free American air," but it nonetheless expresses the Hegelian "spirit of the time."[55]

Thus Wilson presented an extraordinary and revolutionary political agenda as an act of incremental conservatism. He cautiously assayed the political difficulties. Convinced that "the democratic state" as yet lacked the means for carrying "those enormous burdens of administration which the needs of this industrial and trading age are so fast accumulating," yet mindful that "it is harder for democracy to organize administration than for monarchy" because public opinion rules democracy, often in a "meddlesome" way, Wilson sought to exercise a new kind of statesmanship in order to found a new kind of regime.[56]

The new, historicist statesmanship would not so much defend the existing regime as *lead* the people to new modes and orders of life. "Society is not a crowd, but an organism, and, like every organism, it must grow as a whole or else be deformed." "Leaders of men" precipitate the "evolution of [society's] institutions" with "creative power" — the most recent example had been Otto von Bismarck.[57] The leader is a sort of secular prophet:

> Leadership, for the statesman, is *interpretation*. He must read the common thought: he must calculate very circumspectly the *preparation* of the nation for the next move in the progress of politics....The nice point is to distinguish the firm and progressive popular *thought* from the momentary and whimsical popular *mood*, the transitory or mistaken popular passion.[58]

Hegelian rationalism resists democratization. The philosopher Hegel could say this openly. The political leader Wilson could not. The new historicist statesmanship requires a new kind of prudence. The new prudence *foresees*; it is literally promethean. Jane Addams, whom Wilson cultivated as a political ally, particularly during his 1916 re-election campaign ("He kept us out of war" was the slogan), was rightly "a little uneasy in regard to [Wilson's] theory of self-government." He seemed "as if he were not so eager for a mandate to carry out the will of the people as for an opportunity to lead the people whither in his judgment their best interest lay."[59]

The best interest of the people lies in socialism, the logical result of 'democratic' Hegelianism. If society is an organism, then "the community" has "the absolute right...to determine its own destiny and that of its members," for "men as communities are supreme over men as individuals." While the "wisdom and convenience" may limit public control, "limits of principle" upon that control "there are, upon strict analysis, none." Democracy *as 'organism'* requires socialism. To achieve it, an existing political democracy needs a modern bureaucracy founded by a "leader of men."[60]

The new, socialist regime will bring peace. "Ours is a day, not of national so much as *international* and common forces," Wilson averred. "No nation any longer lives apart," and "moral progress" must obtain. "No 'people' has the right to rule as it pleases, independently of the rule of law...or independently of moral obligations."[61] As in Hegel, the dialectic of national 'organisms' produces an international order whose development the wise leader foresees and serves. In his later career, Wilson claimed that American "principles of right" had been vindicated historically, although American forms of government had not been. But because he refused to give truly independent status to 'American' principles, conceiving them as historical and socially-organic, not unalienable and natural (Creator-endowed), Wilson's political theory and practice would have the effect of transforming the principles along with the institutions of the American regime.[62] The same man who ran on the slogan "He kept us out of war," could then launch a military crusade to "make the world safe for democracy" — a war to end war — precisely because he 'thought dialectically' while leading his nation toward socialism.[63] His wartime speeches exhorting Europeans to practice such "American principles" as government by consent — immediately qualified by a denial that he had "any desire to exalt an abstract political principle" — expressed his dilemma perfectly. The "abstract" principle had, he recognized, a decided practical effect: "Any peace which does not recognize and accept this principle will inevitably be upset," as "it will not rest upon the affections or the convictions of mankind." Without conceding the truth of unalienable right and its institutional embodiment, government by consent, Wilson had to admit the utility of the belief.[64] One imagines a smile on the ghostly lips of the "abstract, sentimental, rationalistic" Mr. Jefferson.

German theology became historicist in the nineteenth century. The American 'German' theologian who most influenced the actual tenor of life in American Christian churches was Walter Rauschenbusch, whose *Christianity and the Social Crisis* appeared in the same year as Jane Addams' *Newer Ideals of Peace*.[65] The book begins portentously: "Western civilization is passing through a social revolution unparalleled in history for scope and power," the commercial and industrial revolution. The antidote to economic and social inequalities produced by this "inevitable" revolution is a revolutionary or prophetic form of Christianity. From the beginning, "the essential purpose of Christianity was to transform human society into the kingdom of God by regenerating all human relations and reconstituting them in accordance with the will of God." Commerce and industry are good, but their competitive use is evil. 'Capitalism' does not accord with the will of God, and therefore must be revolutionized in line with the alleged economic and social egalitarianism of the Hebrew prophets and the early American colonists.[66]

Although Rauschenbusch contended that "humanity is always fundamentally the same," his definition of "humanity" does not distinguish men from beasts.[67] Consistent with historicist belief, Rauschenbusch claimed that historicism itself stems from "social movement": "The French Revolution was the birth of modern democracy, and also of the modern school of history," leading to the "new historical study of Christ." But the real engine — literally — of social change is not political at all; political revolutions are "puny" in contrast with the steam engine. Industrial technology drives economics and society, and these 'make history.'[68]

The new, historical study of Jesus of Nazareth had claimed that Jesus was "not a timeless religious teacher." Jesus "spoke for his own age,"[69] except in three respects in which he also spoke to our own: He was a pacifist, He was an historicist, and He was an egalitarian.

> Jesus had the scientific insight which comes to most men only by training, but to the elect few by divine gift. He grasped the substance of that law of organic development in nature and history which our own day has at last begun to elaborate systematically. [70]

Jesus' historicism or organicism may be seen in his use of organic metaphors, as in the parable of the mustard seed (Matt 13:31). By calling for the "organic growth of the new society...cell by cell," Jesus anticipated historicist social science.[71]

Christian organicism is egalitarian. "All human goodness must be social goodness," not individual, and "love is the society-making quality." Pride makes social distinctions whereas "love equalizes." Rauschenbusch approvingly quoted "one of the spiritual leaders of the French Revolution," Camille Desmoulins, who called Jesus "Le Bon Sansculotte."[72] Rauschenbusch appeared to substitute an Hegelian Church for the Hegelian State, writing, "The State is the representation of things as they are; the Church is the representative of things as they ought to be" — democratic, with "communistic ideals."[73] However, evidently mindful of certain passages in Revelations, Rauschenbusch quickly added:

> The primitive attitude of fear and distrust toward the State has passed away. We do not regard the existing civilization and its governments as hostile to Christianity. The ancient feeling that demon powers inspire the State has vanished with the belief in demons.[74]

Sounding rather like Wilson, Rauschenbusch defended his political optimism as based upon "the power of public opinion"; sounding rather like Marx, he claimed that the work class had embarked on "a great historic class struggle." This struggle would end and this opinion would endorse peaceful, Christian communalism.[75]

To different degrees, Emerson, Wilson, and Rauschenbusch 'pacified' Hegelian doctrine. They shared Hegel's 'organic' conception of human life, which relativizes the thought and actions of each age to the whole sweep of human history, conceived as having ended recently (in Hegel himself) or to end soon enough to see the whole by now (as in Marxist communism). They tended to depreciate political life in favor of such putatively 'deeper' or stronger forces as economics and social customs, as Hegel does. For them, statesmanship was leadership. The statesman is the prophet or sage who brings his people to the Promised Land.

The Americans tended to democratize Hegel, to make Hegelianism egalitarian. 'History's' dialectic tended to become more materialist and less rationalist in American hands. It thus became more Marxian, with a very telling difference: It remained somewhat moderate, that is (within the revolutionizing context of historicism), more gradualistic, less apocalyptic than Marxism. In this, the American regime shaped American historicists well.

The moderation of the Americans' historicism inclined them toward pacifism, as in Emerson (up to the Civil War) and Rauschenbusch, or toward pacificism leading to a pacifist 'end of History,' as in Wilson. A respect for, if not strict adherence to, Christianity also endured. All of these Americans were socialists who sought to revolutionize the American regime, although never by means of violent class warfare.

Jane Addams' historicist pacifism – the first historicist pacifism to be fully elaborated in America in conscious opposition to the principles of the regime – thus participated in a cultural, political, and religious movement that attracted many of the most prominent intellectuals throughout the world in the nineteenth and twentieth centuries. This movement challenged the principles and institutions of the American regime, whose virtues historicism tends to obscure. The combination of 'prophetic' imagination and obscurantist thinking resulted in serious errors of political judgment.[76]

False Prophets: Why 'German' Pacifists Make So Many Mistakes

Historicism, which believes human nature almost infinitely malleable, has itself proven more malleable than human nature. It lends itself to extremes, whether of pacifism or bellecism.[77] When seemingly moderate (as in Wilson) it is merely restrained, gradualist. For these reasons, it often confuses deliberation and desire, missing the lasting things in its quest for change. Whether secular or Christian, 'German' pacifists put great emphasis on the prediction of 'History's' movements and also make very bad predictions. Their ideology requires them to predict, then blinds them to reality.

Among the secular 'German' pacifists in America, Eugene V. Debs and Kirby Page may be taken as representative. Debs opposed the American form of government and society, calling instead for "industrial and social democracy." He nonetheless wrote, "I believe in the Constitution of the United States." The contradiction was only apparent. By the Constitution he meant only the Bill of Rights, particularly the rights of free speech and press — that is, the instruments he hoped would enable him to effect socio-economic change. As an historicist, he compared the Bolshevik revolutionaries to the Americans. He blamed capitalism for both modern wars and for the modern instrument of oppression, the prison. He could not foresee the more formidable warmaking and prison-building capacities of Marxism-Leninism.[78] He imagined the future, and saw no private control of the means of production: "Capitalism has had its day and must go. The capitalist cannot function as such in a free society."[79]

Kirby Page not only ignored leftist totalitarianism; he equally overlooked the rightist regimes. He blamed the First World War on militarism, nationalism, and imperialism — 'world-historical' categories that allowed him to make no reference to political regimes. "The military mind revealed the same characteristics in the different countries," he claimed: "the idea that war was inevitable;" the belief that war was necessary for the defense of rights, prestige, and interests; the belief that war was beneficial; the (contradictory) claim that "armed preparedness constituted the safest guarantee of peace"; the conviction that the end justifies the means; the insistence that war comports with Christianity; cynicism with respect to treaties.[80] By ignoring the regime question, Page could avoid considering how such mental characteristics might express themselves in different countries, and in the interrelations among those countries. He simplistically ascribed war to a combination of "economic competition" and "the emotions and dogmas of nationalism."[81] While deriding reports of preparation for military aggression in a rightist despotism, and assuring his readers that the only existing leftist despotism did "not believe in international war," he could seriously worry about the potential "threat to world peace" posed by a commercial republic.[82] As a result, Page's "strategy of national defense" had an almost entirely apolitical character: the strengthening of the League of

Nations; "education for peace;" the relinquishment of "exclusive sovereignty" and of "imperialistic coercion;" remedying international injustice; "tear[ing] down the war system" — all without reference to the political content and form of specific kinds of education, nationalism, imperialism! internationalism, and war systems, as parts of different kinds of political regimes. Page could then ignore the different kinds of and uses for education, nationalism, and internationalism. He could even ignore the different kinds of imperialism and war systems.[83]

Christian pacifists in America reacted strongly to the churches' support of United States intervention in the First World War; more, many Christians turned toward pacifism in repentance for their own wartime bellicosity.[84] Perhaps the most influential and thoughtful pacifist in America who sought to integrate historicism with Christianity was A.J. Muste. The Biblical patriarch Abraham, Muste wrote,

> ...stands at the beginning of both profane and sacred history because in obedience to divine command he left the city of his ancestors. Unquestionably, this represents a great turning point in man's history. It is in one sense the greatest revolution of all, since it is the father of revolutions and of the revolutionary concept of history as the expression of God at work. History and the daily life of man are, therefore, real and not illusory. If God is to be found at all, he must be found here. Men become co-workers, co-creators, and they are in movement toward a goal.[85]

What is fixed, Muste claimed, is unreal. Flux alone is real on earth, until the Second Coming of Jesus. In modernity, "Human beings are physically in motion again" — "rootless" both psychologically and spiritually. For Muste as for Marx, "Mankind has to become a 'new humanity' or perish."[86]

Muste worked for "the realization of the ancient prophetic dream of the kingdom of God on earth." To arrive at the Kingdom of God, only peaceful means will suffice. Because it is "quite possible to use 'nonviolent techniques' in a spirit of violence and hate," only peaceful means undertaken in a spirit of peace will suffice to co-create the kingdom of God, with God.[87] Muste combined an apparent utopianism of ends and means with clear-sighted realism about human motives. He had studied not only Emerson and Marx, but the Bible and Lincoln.[88] Historicism, Christianity, and even some appreciation of the American Founding tugged at him, leading him to mirages and to vantage points, unpredictably.

Muste had his Marxist phase in the late 1920's, when he argued that the existing order originated in and itself produced violence; let no one proscribe violence by the working class unless he identifies himself "in spirit with labor." Revolutionism is prior to pacifism; pacifism retains its validity only insofar as it generates the most effective techniques of class warfare. Throughout his career Muste accepted the Marxist-Leninist belief "that imperialistic capitalism leads to war and must be abolished."[89] In typical left-historicist fashion, he denied any substantial, moral difference between Nazi Germany and England or France in 1940; the latter were merely "satiated powers," the former not. In the 1920's he could see no distinction between Joseph Stalin and the British parliamentarian Ramsay MacDonald (Muste was then a Trotskyist). He admired Marxists for their activism – their "commitment" and "vision," or prophetic activism. When he returned to Christianity, he carried many of these historicist convictions with him, retaining many historicist blind spots.[90]

Muste envisioned a revolutionary coalition of Christian and Jewish congregations, "workers' movements" (trade unionists, Socialist and Communist Party members), and individuals "genuinely concerned about the adaptation of democratic concepts to modern needs and conditions." All these groups, he claimed broadly, originated in the Jewish and Christian prophetic faith. Contemporary tyrants saw the affinities among these groups, as Hitler and Stalin (by 1940, distinguishable from Ramsay MacDonald) had attacked religious believers, workers, and democrats in their own countries. To remain democratic democracy must now renounce war; fascism and war are synonymous.[91]

Unlike a thoroughgoing historicist, however, Muste founded this argument firmly on a conception of *human* nature. "[I]n the final analysis the problem of society is the problem of the nature of man." If human beings are beasts, then dictatorship is the essence of politics. "Only if the human being is the creation of spirit, a being capable of making moral decisions and therefore of governing himself, is the dream of a free democratic society capable of fulfillment." Government by consent requires the capacity for choice.

Without that capacity, one only rules with the lash, as self-government would be impossible. "[I]t is only those who bow the knee to God who do not bow the knee to man."[92] War forces, overrides consent. War is therefore despotic or fascistic not only in effect but in essence.

Free democratic society had been only a dream. "The pacifist who thinks that war can be abolished while everything else remains unchanged, and especially his own comfortable, middle-class existence in the U.S.A., is rapidly becoming extinct." Muste called for small-scale communities, citing Gandhi's example. But although he decried Americans' complacency or pharisaism, he did not denigrate all 'American' institutions. "Those who reject the way of violence will insist that it is precisely the movement for social change which has most to gain by using to the full such, admittedly as yet imperfect, democratic machinery as men have developed."[93] He listed four "profound ties" between democracy and pacifism: the foundation of governmental powers upon consent; the acknowledgment of an objective moral law "above both the individual and the state"; mutual love or brotherhood as essential to human nature; acknowledgment of "the human being as human, not [of] this or that breed or class."[94] Muste claimed that "so-called democracies can wage war and engage in the exploitation of other peoples" because they are not democracies at all; they are "economic oligarchies" that mold a divided or self-contradictory soul, "forever shrinking from war and yet forever tangled in war." The American Founders recognized this by seeing "no need of any army to police a people who are free to discuss and to settle differences in a democratic fashion." With enough such regimes, an international authority or "federal world government" could keep the peace, with the help of a police force.[95]

Muste's concurrence with many of the basic principles of the American regime, coupled with his historicist demand that the institutions designed to secure those principles be used to revolutionize those institutions, accounts for his equally ambivalent feeling toward the Marxist regimes. Muste of course deplored the violence of Marxist class warfare, rejected the messianic conception of the proletariat that he had once shared, and criticized the dictatorship of the Communist Party in the Soviet Union. Consistent with his pacifist assumptions, Muste placed much of the blame for Soviet totalitarianism on the Red Army, not so much on Lenin or Stalin, or even the secret police. He substituted a dialectic of pacifist versus bellecist/militarist for the Marxist dialectic of proletariat versus the bourgeoisie.[96]

Militarism, in its Soviet form as in any other, implies materialism, Muste claimed.[97] The Leninist Communist Party aped the Christian Church — lacking, by grace of its materialism, the real God and a genuinely moral teaching. "[S]uch a party is always in danger of becoming a supreme instrument of tyranny."[98] The true 'International,' the true Church is — the Church![99] Muste nonetheless would not relinquish his hope for converting Marxist-Leninists into political allies on the basis of their own historicism, and his: "We all go back in one way or another to that labor and socialist movement of the later nineteenth and early twentieth century, that remarkable combination of mass power, prophetic idealism and utopian hope."[100] Muste did not appreciate the extent to which historicism lends itself to totalitarianism because he had 'synthesized' his own historicism with nonhistoricist convictions. Both his historicist and his nonhistoricist convictions blinded him to that part of history wherein war serves justice. He imagined that "two world wars have proved that war does not stop Communism" but rather "gives Communism its chance," without even hesitating over the elementary fact that neither world war was fought by its winners in order to defeat Communism.[101]

Muste's central nonhistoricist conviction, and his only principal nonhistoricist conviction not shared by the American Founders, was his belief in the political efficacy of Christian love. This belief issued in his major diversion from the Founders' institutions — his preference for small communes instead of extended, commercial republics. Concurrently, Muste doubted the efficacy of reason:

> Character is built by action rather than thought. Contemplation does not beget virtues.... The god of philosophy is an abstraction. The God of experience is Personality, Power, and Love.[102]

The "central truth" that makes pacifism right and workable is, "God is love, love is of God." Love not reason provides the basis for the unity of mankind. Love is "the most real thing in the universe, the most powerful, the most permanent"; love "holds the atoms and the suns together." In commending love, the Bible is "starkly realistic," because "gentleness, selflessness, non-aggression, fearlessness" – the results of Christian love or *agape* – are the only means that work "in the training of animals, in contacting primitive peoples, in the education of children, and in the treatment of criminals and the mentally sick." Love is not sentimental; it is a command. Aggressors break this command, often reacting to those who also break it. Love is a fearful command, because those who break it are responsible to God, even if they were injured first.[103]

The injured must not blame the injurer, but himself. "[Y]ou suffer because you have sinned....Therefore, you must repent, change yourself," and replace hate for your enemy with love for your enemy. If in loving your enemy you are martyred, you have not failed; you have triumphed with God, who is love and who is supremely powerful.[104]

Those American Founders who were Christians would have agreed with all of this. They would have denied that the power of Christian love could unify a country for any appreciable length of time. The Founders thought that Christian love cannot serve as the basis of politics. Muste disagreed. Muste wanted to reunite Church and state. But this time, both would eschew physical force except in police work. "What is the verdict of history upon this religious-political strategy?" The Jews survived; the Amorite, Hittite, Egyptian, and Babylonian empires disappeared. The Christians survived; the Roman Empire disappeared. More, "I find no good reason for supposing that any army could be gotten to invade a people which flatly renounced war." War "only leads to more war, violence begets violence." Where justice prevails, violent force need not enter; the conditions that provoke labor violence, and totalitarian political movements, and gangsterism do not exist, within a nation or among nations. "Struggle is basically spiritual and spiritual weapons alone prevail in the end."[105]

The Founders might reply that while the ancient empires disappeared, the ancient peoples survive to this day, as much as Jews and Christians. The ancient Jewish and modern Christian empires have disappeared as completely as any of the others. While there may not be a *good* reason for invading a pacifist nation, armies or their leaders might discover any number of bad ones, and act upon them. War demonstrably does not always lead to more war; violence does not always beget violence. Where justice prevails, violent force need not enter, but often it does, because men are not invariably satisfied with their just proportion of goods. While spiritual weapons prevail in the end, we do not live in the end-time, and spiritual weapons may need physical auxiliaries precisely because the human soul finds itself inside a mortal body.

Muste committed the error of supposing that because wars are fought between nations of men, not between nations of angels, these imperfect men are merely "misguided."[106] He ascended to stronger ground in arguing that different nations are misguided or indeed sinful in different degrees, and that one must not go to war over differences of degree. France and England in 1940 were less sinful than Nazi Germany, but Muste conceived of war as violence, and of violence as mortal sin; a Christian may not do evil even to cause good. Too, the evil of violence cannot cause good, cannot defend democracy because it is radically anti-democratic.[107]

This argument unwarrantedly assumed that an undemocratic or even radically anti-democratic action could not preserve democracy. There are many examples of such actions preserving, even winning, democracy: wars have preserved democracies; dictatorships or near-dictatorships in times of crisis have preserved democracies.

Muste in effect admitted the limited efficacy of pacifism. "The pacifist must be ready to pay [the] price," and the Cross stands at the center of Christianity. But he did not really think Christianity would fail humanity, though it might, in this life, fail the martyr individual or the martyr nation. The "sole alternative" to the "demonic" power of nuclear weapons "is the love that absolutely refuses to destroy." The intellect cannot prove this. "That conscience is a response to a moral order you can prove only by making moral decisions and acting conscientiously." One apprehends the God of love "only by loving Him and His creatures."[108] Muste wrote these words in 1947, two years after the invention of nuclear weapons. In terms of experience − the terms he chose over reason − he thus far has been proved wrong. The nations have survived without much loving God, or each other. Worldly-wise policies founded on fear (deterrence) and prudence, courage, and moderation have carried the nations for some time. This does not mean that such policies will always suffice. It does mean they can suffice, for generations.

Muste's 'prophetic' Christianity yielded other, riper fruits by which it could be better known. His form of prophetism tended to replace prudence. Muste often prophesied. In 1940, he predicted that another world war would "set back [the clock] for generations, if not for centuries," owing to the increased destructiveness of military technology. He predicted that unless mankind stopped making war, democracy would be "quenched in one land after another." He predicted that until war's abolition, "the whole movement for social justice is halted." In 1941, he predicted that a victory over Germany would result in the same circumstances as resulted after the First World War, with Communism more likely to prevail; only Christianity could prevent that victory, he claimed. But the 'peace' settlement would be just as punitive as in 1919, and just as disastrous. He predicted that a victorious United States would seek "to do what we condemn Hitler for trying to do" – "world domination." In 1947, he predicted that "the next war...if and when it comes" for the United States, would be a nuclear war. He claimed that the Allied occupation of Germany was failing, and only "the message of pacifism and reconciliation" could redeem it. He predicted that small, 'primitive' countries with dispersed industrial bases would build nuclear weapons and threaten the United States. (All this meant that "those who died in [the Second World War] died in vain"). He predicted that no international organization could prevent war; neither could the commercial republics 'contain' communism with a combination of military, political, and economic means. In 1950, as the Korean War flared, Muste predicted that continued reliance on warfare would result in either "global war and chaos" or "the general triumph of totalitarianism." In 1952, he predicted that the practice of military conscription would gradually 'nazify' the United States. In 1965, while Americans fought in Vietnam, Muste predicted that a cease-fire would not likely result in a purge by Vietnamese Communists; the Communists would likely respect the cease-fire.[109]

"God is my witness that I do not want that to happen," Muste wrote on the prospect of a Communist purge in Vietnam. But it did. Almost all of his major historical predictions were wrong. It would be hard to find a man so consistently wrong, a would-be prophet so often and impenitently false. Real prophecy melds true predictions with moral laments and warnings; real prophecy gives a clear vision of history, neither merely historical ('scientific') nor moralistic. Muste was a bad prophet because his predictions were merely didactic.[110]

Muste was a fine moralist. But historicism tempted him to predict as well as moralize. Following the misleading lights of moralism and historicist analysis, he failed. He did not fail as a Christian moralist. Such exhortations as, "Now is the time for the American people to stake their safety on God's grace and their own good consciences and on that measure of common sense and humanity which even our enemies possess," lie on moral bedrock, not sentimentality: "So long as we are still afraid of death we can be bought off. We are not yet hard enough to overcome evil."[111]

Historicist-Christian Pacifism Reconsidered: Norman Thomas and Reinhold Niebuhr

After a brief Marxist excursus, A.J. Muste returned to a Rauschenbusch-like synthesis of historicism and Christianity, refining his arguments into an impressive moral case against war. Two of his contemporaries shared Muste's attraction to the Social Gospel, but eventually turned away from pacifism. For each, the regime question finally overrode repugnance for war as such.

For several decades, Norman Thomas was the most prominent democratic socialist in the United States. Influenced by Rauschenbusch's writing, he had become a socialist after seeing the effects of poverty in New York City, and after being convinced that the First World War "was an imperialist struggle, to be accounted for in terms of socialist analysis."[112] His pacifism consisted of the example of Jesus's life; the Christian precept, "You cannot cast out Satan by Satan" and its corollary faith in divine providence; the refusal to grant governments the right to do what individuals may not do; and the conviction that war will end if socialism replaces capitalism.[113] His Christianity saved him from unqualified Hegelianism. He rejected the "doctrine of the divinity of the state," a doctrine that would abrogate the individual's right to conscientious objection to war and exemption from military service. Thomas recognized that the United States enforced a generally lenient policy toward conscientious objectors, but failed to see the full implications of this leniency with respect to the differences among regimes; he often wrote indiscriminately of 'the state.'[114]

Thomas did see the sharp distinction between democracy and totalitarianism. He associated democracy with peace and war with totalitarianism, tacitly rejecting the American Founders' emphasis on commerce and representative government as agents of peace. Opposing Communism, he still preferred it to Fascism; he falsely predicted that if another world war occurred democracy would perish and the "communist salvation" would be "the best we can hope for."[115] He went on to concede that the very pacifism that might save democracy "requires for its success a rarer quality of courage and personality than violence" – a quality "the average man and certainly the crowd" usually lack.[116] Since democracy depends upon the average man, only the radical transformation of the average man, through socialist revolution, could save democracy. "The way to fight Fascism is to build Socialism."

Thomas conceived of Fascism in the manner of most 1930's-era Marxists: "the last stage of disintegrating capitalism," capitalism "with a new mask on," or "state capitalism," of which Franklin D. Roosevelt's 'New Deal' provided a "tolerably liberal" example. "The Marxian prediction of the collapse of capitalism by forces inherent in it was longer postponed than some of its believers had anticipated, but it is being astonishingly fulfilled before our eyes," Thomas imagined. To prevent the triumph of Fascism as a response to this apparent disintegration, Thomas urged the nonviolent "capture of the political state" by socialists, as the prelude to economic revolution. In the United States, Thomas judged the Constitutional separation and balance of the Federal governments powers to be "archaic"; he advocated proportional representation, a unicameral legislature with an executive subordinate to it, and sufficient legislative power to "pass all needful social and economic legislation" – that is, the effective abrogation of property rights.[117] Socialist parliamentary rule would replace commercial republicanism, which Thomas misleadingly styled "our capitalist-nationalist government." A United States socialist government would unilaterally disarm: "We have to *wage* peace, and risk something for peace."[118]

Totalitarianism turned out to be even worse than Thomas had thought. By the time of the Spanish Civil War in 1937, he saw that totalitarianism would bring "new cycles of war and new dark ages of oppression," and judged it "unrealistic and mad to say that it does not matter who wins in Spain if only the guns are stilled."[119] By 1941, his mood combined a slightly self-defensive nostalgia ("Modern totalitarianism was no part of the dream of the revolutionaries of the early twentieth century, whether or not they regarded themselves as Marxists") and mild disillusionment ("when I consider how many proposals of the social workers, whose ranks I joined as a very green youngster in the fall of 1905, have since been fulfilled in New York City and the nation, I am divided between satisfaction over the achievement and disappointment that it has added so little to the sum of human happiness"). After twenty years, he finally admitted that Fascism "is not capitalism at all": rather, Hitler "has proved once and for all that social purpose and social planning can successfully accomplish prodigious results," despite Hitler's "destructive immediate purpose." The Leftist totalitarianism of Communism, though based upon the "madness" of "class war," an "enormous evil," nonetheless and equally demonstrated the bankruptcy of "capitalism." If the United States were to go to war in Europe, "I think the defeat of our democracy [would be] all but sealed."[120]

By the Second World War, Thomas' pacifism "had become a far more relative thing" than that of "the sincere conscientious objector." He did not analyze the reasons for this shift, but it seems fair to note the paucity of specifically Christian appeals in his later writings, along with his increasing sensitivity to regime questions. *Democratic* socialism "is the only form worth having," and he did not reject the use of force to keep that hope alive against predators 'left' and 'right.'[121]

Because the bedrock of pacifism in America has always been Christianity, the defection of theologian Reinhold Niebuhr, who had allied himself with Social Gospel pacifists in the 1920's, reverberated longer, deeper, and more extensively than that of Norman Thomas, primarily the leader of a secular political movement. At first glance, Niebuhr appeared to desert pacifism only for a more exclusively secular historicism – initially, he deemed only class war, not international war, justifiable.[122] But even his early writings contain some key arguments radically at odds with historicism.[123] His writings over a thirty-year period trace a slow rediscovery of the political thought not of Marx or Hegel, but of James Madison.

Niebuhr had rejected war on three grounds: that "history has so vividly proven its worthlessness as a method of solving social problems"; that in itself war allows no impartial arbitrator, because the parties to the conflict also settle the conflict with force; and that war destroys life, especially innocent life. Dismissing international peacekeeping organizations as necessarily partial, and acknowledging that "weakness invites aggression," Niebuhr had still insisted that a "strategy of love" could harness a nonviolence force that "creates its own victories," victories "greater than would seem possible from the standpoint of the merely critical observer."[124] No intelligent man could long find such vague stuff satisfying, and Niebuhr did not. In *Moral Man and Immoral Society*, probably his best-known work, he displayed serious ambivalences about pacifism and historicism. The book's principal thesis was quite un-Hegelian: Niebuhr argued that individuals generally behave more morally than do nations or other groups. Reason, self-transcendence, and conscience, though far from powerful in individuals, enjoy relatively greater power in individuals than in groups. In society, reason, self-transcendence, and conscience simply lack the force that they can wield in the individual soul; they are not virtues that can be *organized*, and in society organization yields power.[125] "All social cooperation on a larger scale than the most intimate social group requires a measure of coercion," but "the same force which guarantees peace also makes for injustice" because, in the necessary absence of effective, organized virtues of the highest order, coercive force will be abused. Among nations, the problem becomes acute; "the power which prevents anarchy in intra-group relations encourages anarchy in intergroup relations," as the selflessness of citizens' patriotism yields "national egoism" and the hypocrisy that cloaks self-aggrandizement in appeals to universal principles, from 'civilization' to improved sanitation.[126]

Rationalists blame ignorance for social conflict; religious idealists blame selfishness. Niebuhr rejected both those forms of 'Enlightenment'

120

doctrine: "All men cannot be expected to become spiritual any more than they can be expected to become rational." Reason and spirituality can be "a leavening influence in social life," they cannot form the foundation of "the political structure of society."[127] This sounds rather like the tenth *Federalist*, but Niebuhr at this point disliked the Founders' defense of property, and claimed that Madison falsely attributed social and economic inequalities to difference in the natural faculties for acquiring properties. He attributed republicanism's commercial character merely to the class interests of its founders. In America "privileged groups" rule as "self-appointed...guardians of peace and order," but these groups will fall as "the full maturity of American capitalism will inevitably be followed by the emergence of the American Marxian proletarian." While endorsing Marxist social and economic *analysis*, Niebuhr rejected Marxist (and especially Leninist) pretensions with respect to the motives of proletarians and the revolutionary elites that lead them. Class egoism no less than national egoism will yield hypocrisy and violence. Only because he believed "rigorous equalitarianism" to be "the ultimate rational ideal of society," and that proletarians seek this goal with somewhat more sincerity than oligarchs do, did Niebuhr prefer leftist 'movement' politics to any other. Marxist politics aims at "equal justice," the "most rational possible social goal."[128] The rationality of equality as a social goal comes not from the putatively logical unfolding of 'History' – whether conceived as 'Spirit' or as a material dialectic – but from the minimization (not the utopian elimination) of coercive relationships, which will leave reason and conscience as free as possible.

A similar ambivalence pervaded Niebuhr's discussion of pacifism. "Nothing is intrinsically immoral except ill-will and nothing intrinsically good except goodwill." Therefore, even violence is not intrinsically immoral. Further, once one admits the social and political need for some coercion, and the human need for civil society and politics, "we cannot draw any absolute line of demarcation between violent and non-violent coercion;" for example, a peaceful boycott of goods may cause the malnourishment of infants. Increased social equality will bring less injustice, and thus less coercion; the goal of "greater social equality" is "a higher goal than peace," because it will yield a more lasting peace. This resembles the American Founders' distinction between "the Peace of War" and genuine peace; Niebuhr's concept differs in being much more radically democratic or egalitarian.[129]

Yet Niebuhr declined to concede the possibility of a "War for Peace" or just war. "If reason is to make coercion a tool of the moral ideal it must not only enlist it in the service of the highest causes but it must choose those types of coercion which are most compatible with, and least dangerous to, the rational and moral forces of society." He found the best form of coercion in Gandhi, who advocated not nonresistance to evil but non-violent resistance. By "enduring more suffering than it causes," nonviolent resistance gives evidence of goodwill and diminishes resentment on both sides of the conflict. It is not to be confused with genuine Christian love, which may or may not animate Gandhian activists. But nonviolent resistance is the least egoistic and violent means of social coercion.[130] As of the early 1930's, then, Niebuhr's slogan – had he been given to such simplisms – might have been 'Christian love in individual relations, Christian Gandhiism in social and political relations.'

The mid-1930's saw Niebuhr engaging in a critique of 'liberalism,' subtly in *Reflections on the End of an Era* 1934, more polemically in *Doom and Dawn* 1936. He described "the liberal culture of modernity" as "quite unable to give guidance and direction to a confused generation which faces the disintegration of a social system and the task of building a new one." His critique of liberal "commercial and industrial civilization" resembled that of historicism's more romantic wing: Liberal civilization is "mechanical rather than organic in it structure," veiling real social relations behind an impersonal money-economy that fails to see its own coerciveness. Commerce "suppresse[s] and obscure[s]" the "human factor in every social relation" by replacing the personal economy of bartering with the money economy. Although it is not easy to see why an economy based upon the principle, 'I like you/I don't like you, so I will/will not exchange with you' can be held morally superior to 'Your money is as green as anybody else's,' Niebuhr was right to suppose that the barter economy gave more scope to morality (and to immorality) than modern commerce does. The same might be said for Niebuhr's critique of commercial republican politics; he derided the principle of the consent of the governed, claiming that "all democracies turn into oligarchies," but that modern oligarchs differ in enjoying no personal loyalty. This impersonality exacerbates class conflict, and will result in fascism as a last gasp before the proletarian revolution.[131]

Niebuhr thus shared the apocalyptic illusions common to 1930's intellectuals ("our western society is obviously in the process of disintegration") and badly underestimated the realism of the American Founders.

> The world [liberalism] envisaged was one in which self-interest was either no peril at all or in which reason would quickly bring the potential anarchy of competing egoisms under control. This dream was one which grew naturally out of the illusions of traders and academics.[132]

Niebuhr here confused the principles of the American Founders with the new liberalism of a Woodrow Wilson, which was really a progressivist historicism. He therefore ignored the function of institutions, understood by the Founders as capable of promoting stability without causing stasis, by channeling the course of passions and (therefore) of events. For Niebuhr, 'liberalism' meant rationalism plus commerce and a vague consent-of-the-governed 'republicanism' masking oligarchy. 'Liberalism' "fondly imagine[s] that moral ideals are inevitably applied to the political world, once they are generally accepted": a telling criticism of the more sentimental versions of political and religious progressivism, but largely irrelevant to the American regime.[133]

Still, Niebuhr saw that modern politics needed a spot of liberalism. While finding political and religious liberalism too optimistic, he considered Christian orthodoxy at once too pessimistic and too complacent. Disallowing Christian participation in the "unredeemed and unredeemable" natural world to which it "consigns the world of politics," yet sanctifying "social injustice" by calling the magistrate God's minister, Christian orthodoxy expects and does too little in politics. It provides no "ethical distinctions of the historical level" to guide Christians in reforming or revolutionizing bad regimes.[134]

Such standards had been provided by Christian natural law or, more rarely, by the Christian adaptation of Jewish law (e.g., the American Puritans). But Niebuhr wanted neither reason nor 'legalistic' revelation as a guide. He classified political life not as part of nature, but as part of 'History,' preferring the 'dynamic' or revolutionary politics to a stable political order, which he believed *necessarily* unjust, given the necessary narrowness and egoism of whatever class rules. At the same time, he saw the danger of radical political action "seek[ing] to level centers of power in the interest of justice," and generating more cruelty than justice. "The liberal spirit therefore remains a needed resource in building and preserving a community."[135]

As its title implies, *Doom and Dawn* expressed a more apocalyptic mood. Niebuhr clarified his reason for rejecting natural law as a moral standard. "Sin is the spiritualization of the anarchy of nature"; nature is the war of all against all, as the ancient atomists and the modern Hobbes supposed, providing no moral standards whatever.[136] This rather incautious or one-sided assertiveness characterized much of the book, written during the nadir of the Great Depression and evidently reflecting fashionable (and understandable) assumptions of the time. This assertiveness may be measured in such claims as, "The *anarchy* of contemporary civilization proves that *all* the presuppositions of modern culture were and are wrong"; "we live in a warlike world *because* each nation in the world community, particularly each modern nation, is organized on the basis of an *economic* system which makes mutuality among nations *impossible*"; "*every* analysis of economic and political problems points to the *fact* that life *cannot be made sufferable* in a technical age upon the basis of the present property system."[137] Human *nature*, like all of nature, is fundamentally anarchic; leftist radicals "imagine that capitalism is the essence rather than the aggravation of human anarchy," and pacifists − even more optimistic than leftists − fail to see that "life is of its nature more perennially violent" than pacifists wish. Only Christian love can heal this fundamental flaw in nature; it alone can bring the dawn to civilization otherwise doomed to night.[138] The persistence of human civilization − of life itself − for decades after this book was written sufficiently refutes the claims Niebuhr made in it, errors of a mind too inclined to make much of contemporary trends, assigning cosmic causes to passing dislocations.

By the Second World War, realism had strengthened its grip on the would-be prophet. *Christianity and Power Politics*, published in 1940, attacked "perfectionism" in its Christian and in its secular forms as "unable to make significant distinctions between tyranny and freedom because it can find no democracy pure enough to satisfy its devotion; and in any case it can find none which is not involved in conflict, in its effort to define itself against tyranny." Perfectionism fails "to distinguish between the peace of capitulation and the peace of the Kingdom of God."[139] Stated in this manner, the distinction Niebuhr drew must be dismissed as polemical. What "perfectionist" Christians could not distinguish was the peace of capitulation or the Peace of War from civil peace, a peace that can be defended by a just war or War for Peace. "Perfectionist" Christians, influenced by progressivist historicism, dreamed of a world where neither tyrannical peace nor mere civil peace would obtain; both would recede before the Kingdom of God, brought on by exclusively nonviolent means.

Niebuhr criticized Christian perfectionism, with its pacifism, for reducing the Gospel teaching to the Law of Love (Matthew 22:37-40) and then urging Christians into political life. Niebuhr saw that earlier forms of this perfectionism − Mennonism, for example − prudently eschewed politics refusing to suppose political life capable of sustaining undiluted Christian love. Modern perfectionism foolishly assumes human nature to be essentially good. It is pacifistic *because* it rejects the sober and sobering concept of original sin. It therefore allies itself with a pacifist rationalist, Bertrand Russell, and a pacifist mystic, Aldous Huxley, with whom it shares a utopian confidence in fundamental human goodness. Such beliefs blind pacifists to the necessity of coercion in human life. Because they abhor all coercion, they cannot see the importance of limited coercion − of decentralized power or democracy. Alternatively, pacifists may reify 'peace,' confusing tyranny or the Peace of War with genuine peace. The failure to make such relative distinctions can only lead to the breakdown of civil society itself. Niebuhr took the Law of Love not as a principle of indiscriminate criticism that distinguishes between forms and degrees of imperfect justice. Only this conception of the Law of Love will save Christians from self-righteous folly.[140]

Secular perfectionism amounts to the faith of the faithless, the willed effort of "modern man" to "escape despair." The new liberalism exacerbates the republican and democratic tendency to react slowly to foreign threats; the modern democracies feature "a confused pacifism, in which Christian perfectionism and bourgeois love of ease have been curiously compounded." Capitalism, "not wholly on the side of democracy," wants to use Fascism as a counterweight against Communism and indeed against democratic social revolution. In its complacency, "bourgeois civilization...simply unable to envisage the possibility that a resolute foe might be intent upon its annihilation or enslavement."[141]

Despite all this, Niebuhr continued to miss the pervasiveness of historicism in contemporary Western civilization, republican and totalitarian. He believed Germany to represent a "pessimistic corruption" of Christianity, arrayed against the "optimistic corruption" of Christianity seen in the republics. Nazism, he believed, was Lutheranism gone mad; the darkest pessimism about human groups had yielded a call for brutal coerciveness, a call the Nazis only glorified.[142] This interpretation overlooks the wild optimism of Nazism, its belief that the coercion of natural history or evolution could breed a super-human race, free of the genetic 'impurities' that make for decadence. Nazism differs from Communism primarily in this emphasis on a (chimerical) natural history. Both differ from the progressivism typical of historicism in commercial republics mostly in their impatience, miscalled radicalism, and their consequent abandonment of simple decencies left over from the 'old' order. Commercial republics influenced by historicism, as Niebuhr did understand, find Nietzschean or Marxist morality almost inconceivable, partly because extremist historicism believes the simple decencies utterly contemptible; at the same time, the optimism progressivism shares with all historicism makes it fascinated by the *élan* of extremists, hopeful for reconciliation with them. After all, do we not share the same goals of justice and fraternity?

> A non-violent expression of the claims and counter-claims of politics is important precisely because political arguments are never merely rational arguments. The threat of force against recalcitrant minorities is always implied in them. If this is not understood, the liberal is in danger of betraying the essentials of a democratic civilization for the sake of loyalty to democratic principles, that is, for the principle of arbitration with the foe. If the foe happens to represent a civilization which incarnates war as the ultimate good, the liberal may sacrifice the institutions of peace for the sake of a peaceful settlement with a foe who intends to destroy them. Thus peace is lost for peace's

> sake, because it is not understood that there are moments in history when the covert threat of force which underlies all political contention must be brought into the open.[143]

For the first time, Niebuhr praised the "wholesome realism" of James Madison, "and the concept of checks and balances which entered into our American constitution." The Founders recognized "the perennial influence of interest upon political ideas, of the character of politics as a contest of power, and of the necessity of balancing various centers of power in government against one another in order to prevent tyranny." Niebuhr also now considered the function of reason in politics as Madison did: not as the rule of rationalism, but as "a transcendence of reason over force sufficient to regulate, equilibrate, arbitrate and direct the play of force and vitality in social life so that a maximum of harmony and a minimum of friction is achieved" – recognizing that the maximum will be modest, the minimum substantial.[144]

Niebuhr's socialism, then, did not aspire to putting an end to 'History.' It aimed at limiting concentrations of economic power, and thereby the capacity of oligarchs to commit sinful acts. In the realm of economics, Niebuhr wanted to use unMadisonian means for Madisonian ends.[145] In his 1944 book, *The Children of Light and the Children of Darkness*, Niebuhr misread the tenth *Federalist* as a critique not only of factions but of groups as such. He therefore mistakenly condemned the Founders for excessive individualism, a fault he imputed (with rather more justice) to "liberalism" generally.[146] "The ideal of individual self-sufficiency, so exalted in our liberal culture, is recognized in Christian thought as one form of the primal sin," a sin that would make family and civil society impossible. For this reason Niebuhr retained a foolish sympathy for historicist organicism, asserting that "Marxist collectivism was, on the whole, a healthy and inevitable revolt against bourgeois individualism." He 'explained' the social stability of the United States and Holland, particularly their resistance to proletarian ferment, by observing "the bourgeois ethos" was "powerful" in those regimes – a rather circular explanation.[147]

Because he was both more optimistic and more pessimistic than Madison – more optimistic with respect to the power of Christian principles and the attractiveness of democratic-socialist communitarianism, more pessimistic with respect to commerce and republican institutions — Niebuhr called for a much higher-toned politics. "The preservation of democratic civilization requires the wisdom of the serpent and the harmlessness of the dove" — a requirement hitherto commanded only to those who intended to proselytize for a persecuted and defamed Christianity.[148] Commercial republicanism, to be sure, had been persecuted and defamed for much of the twentieth century, and on the issue of regimes Niebuhr now had things straight. Citing Abraham Lincoln on the impossibility of the United States enduring half-slave and half-free, Niebuhr applied this to world politics; "only an [international] order which implicates justice can achieve a stable peace." Looking at the principal Allied powers — Great Britain, the United States, the Soviet Union — Niebuhr saw that "of these three Russia will have the greatest difficulty in establishing inner moral checks upon its will-to-power."[149] Such a commonsense perception may seem unexceptional, until one measures the hard-traveled intellectual distance it marked.

Human beings have the freedom to transcend the limits of nature. "It is precisely because of the essential freedom of man" — to plan and do both good and evil — "that he requires a contrived order in his community" — customs, institutions, laws.[150] Niebuhr clarified and also subtly changed some of his previous opinions on history in his 1943 Gifford Lectures, published as *The Nature and Destiny of Man*. He contrasted "historical religions" with other forms of human thought and belief, particularly "idealism," "mysticism," "naturalism," and secular historicism. "Idealism" equates the "self" with universal reason; Niebuhr's examples are Plato and Hegel. "Mysticism" seeks nonrationally what idealism seeks rationally; union with the One, striven for by the Self's own powers. "Naturalism" or materialism denies the "self's" freedom, as in Lucretius and Hobbes. Secular historicism, seen in Darwin and Marx, recognizes that history is 'going somewhere' (not merely in circles) but believes this destination unmitigatedly good. Historical religions share idealism's conviction that the self consisting of body, mind, and spirit combined, and thus involved in the necessities of nature but not determined by them — can transcend itself and its circumstances of time and place. Unlike idealism, historical religions effect self-transcendence not through reason but through imagination and the conception of "changeless principles" through faith and devine revelation. Historical religions are prophetic-messianic; they expect a Christ, who will fully disclose at the end of history truths that are only partially disclosed during history.[151] Historical religions expect the fulfillment of history, unlike idealism and mysticism, which seek to transcend history.[152]

The human ability to see that oneself, one's nation, and one's civilization "cannot be the end of history" serves as the natural *ground* of revelation. However, Niebuhr contended (contra Hegel), one cannot by nature or reason discover or even foresee the *end* of existence. For this human beings need divine revelation, whereby we are judged for our intellectual and our moral inadequacies – the latter freely committed, the former committed partly due to our natural weaknesses, partly due to our sinful inclination to becloud our own minds. God "perfectly combine[s] power and goodness," unlike any creature; "power is the product of spirit" with "an alloy of physical force," but always more than physical. Thus God alone creates and judges perfectly; of creatures, human beings create and judge in flawed ways, subject to divine correction and in need of divine mercy.[153] No historicist would say, with Niebuhr, "the meaning of human life transcends the meaning of history."[154]

Love enters history (thus making pacifism plausible) because the Messiah who promised the completion of history, willingly suffered for man, with a spiritual force that has and will triumph over evil. The triumph and glorification of suffering – the power of suffering love – are absent in Judaism, where one does not sacrifice the innocent for the sake of the guilty, and in paganism, where one does so sacrifice, but merely to propitiate the gods. Although divine love has entered history, it has yet to end history; divine love "must remain suffering love in history." Love will grow, but so will evil – hence, the wars and rumors of wars, and the appearance of false Christs culminating in the anti-Christ. "The perfection of man is not attainable in history"; the love that seeketh not its own "is not able to maintain itself in historical society." Liberal Protestantism, Marxism, and progressivism all "fall into the error of regarding the transcendent norm as a simple possibility," failing to see that sin corrupts, and will continue to corrupt, "all forms of political justice and social organization." History "must remain under the judgment of God."[155]

Modern political ideology often issues in fanaticism because it sees no evil in itself or its proponents, and fears no divine judgment. In discussing the quest for justice, whether reasoned or fanatical, Niebuhr revised his previous opinion, now associating justice with nature.[156] Divine love or *agape* "is both the fulfillment and the negation of all the achievements of justice in history," anticipating their goodness while judging their inadequacies. Although initially Niebuhr appeared to continue to insist on the strict historical relativity of all political arrangements, and even of all natural law philosophies, he finally resisted the historicist attempt to collapse natural law into a highfalutin form of conventional law, with no real noetic content. Citing Paul's acknowledgment that Gentiles obey, by nature, some of the Law's commands (Romans 2:14), Niebuhr conceded that reason can discern "transcendent principles of justice." The mistake is to suppose that reason discerns all such principles, fully, and that abstract principles can be fully realized in history. Conventional or 'positive' laws represent compromises between these imperfectly conceived and partially followed principles of justice and existing civil-social powers. "No possible refinement of social forces and political harmonies can eliminate the potential contradiction to brotherhood [the social embodiment of *agape*] which is implicit in the two political instruments of brotherhood – the organization of power and the balance of power."[157]

The intractability of human limitations and sinfulness, particularly as seen in politics, poses a serious problem for any *political* form of pacifism. Historicism attempts a too-easy solution to this problem. "The spread of the pacifist movement in modern liberal Christianity, particularly in the Anglo-Saxon countries, to the point where it seemed that the perfectionist hopes of the small sectarian churches would be shared by the whole of Protestantism was undoubtedly due, primarily to the substitution of the idea of progress in liberal Christianity for the truth of the Gospel."[158] It is one thing to disavow political power and take responsibility for the consequences of refusing to secure unalienable rights by forceful means. Those consequences may well include martyrdom. Also, nonviolent resistance, as distinguished from nonresistance, has merit as one political technique among many; "it is well to explore all methods of achieving justice and maintaining peace, short of violent conflict." To make of nonviolent resistance "a moral and political absolute," however, brings only "moral and political confusion," because this will invite aggression.

> The implicit and explicit aversion of the democratic world to violent forms of dispute was a factor upon which proponents of 'total war' calculated. If increased the probability of their success and therefore the certainty of their venture.[159]

Although this serves as a sound rebuke of pacifist optimism, Niebuhr's criticism should scarcely faze a pacifist who did not expect to win, but simply sought to do as much as he could. The real moral question would be, To what extent should a pacifist *interfere* with normal governmental activities on behalf of unalienable rights, including the use of military force? Assuming that a pacifist could be sufficiently detached from his own understandable enthusiasm for pacifist techniques to prudently calculate probabilities of success, including success in war, the pacifist would then have to decide whether or not to actively work to impede war preparations and war-fighting in a given circumstance.

Years later, Niebuhr addressed another question that pacifists address with difficulty, the question of political union. Written some eight years after the invention of nuclear weapons, *Christian Realism and Political Problems* succinctly refuted the notion that the very existence of such weapons might serve as a goad to the founding of a world government ending international war: "There is no record in history of peoples establishing a common community because they feared each other, though there are many instances when the fear of a common foe acted as the cement of cohesion."[160] The attempt to present weapons themselves as 'the enemy' remains as fatuous in the nuclear age as in any other, and cannot answer the question of political union. Even established governments "have only limited efficacy in integrating a community," as "even the wisest statesmanship cannot create social tissue." On this Burke was right.[161] "Free societies" or commercial republics "are the fortunate products of the confluence of Christian and secular forces" — the latter including 'capitalism,' with its ability to coordinate mutual services without political coercion. Christianity also contributes to decentralized civil-social cohesion, because "the toleration which democracy requires is difficult to maintain without Christian humility"; excessive secularization brings moral relativism, inviting the disunifying assertions of fanatics secular and religious.[162]

Contrasting class conflict in continental Europe with the lesser tensions seen in England and the United States, Niebuhr suggested that "more adequate formulae of justice" did not account for the difference. Rather, the various interest groups in England and the United States shared a sense of justice, a disposition to practice justice, and loyalty to "the national community." The "spirit of justice is identical to the spirit of love" – a formulation differing from Niebuhr's earlier account of natural justice. Such principles as liberty, equality, and loyalty to covenants "are no more than the law of love in its various facets."[163] Unalienable rights exist by God's creation; their recognition exists by God's grace. This prepares a way for revivifying the religious dimension of the Declaration of Independence.

Niebuhr did not quite manage to do this, because he too simply equated the principles of the Declaration with those of Thomas Jefferson. *The Irony of American History*, published in 1952, approached this matter by noticing two conflicting idealisms in American political life, idealisms familiar to readers who take up the book decades later: "Our idealists are divided between those who would renounce the responsibilities of power for the sake of preserving the purity of our soul and those who are ready to cover every ambiguity of good and evil in our actions by the frantic insistence that any measure taken in a good cause must be unequivocally virtuous." Fortunately, American institutions allow freedom, and therefore disagreement, concerning the ends pursued; this disagreement causes political conflicts that enable no one group an unqualified triumph, because, again, the institutions disperse power throughout many groups. American institutions rest on "understanding of the power of the self's passions and ambitions to corrupt the self's reason is a simple recognition of the facts of life which refute all theories, whether liberal or Marxist, about the possibility of a completely disinterested self." This understanding, shared by such Founders as John Adams as well as "our Calvinist fathers," saves the United States from its own utopian tendencies.[164]

Niebuhr added to this insight a persistent misreading of both the Founders and the Puritans. Both American Calvinists and Jeffersonian Deists considered America "a new beginning for mankind," removed from Europe's vices. To believe in the "American Israel," Niebuhr argues, requires "illusions of a unique innocency" about Americans, a failure to understand "the perennial conflicts of power and pride." This failure becomes acute when Americans, Puritan or Jeffersonian, imagine that prosperity betokens virtue. In fact, Niebuhr observes, passions grow even as they are gratified. This strain of the American mind "believes self-interest to be inherently harmless"; it is "blind to the lust for power in the motives of men." The Declaration of Independence too optimistically aims to happiness, which human sin always renders problematic. "[T]here is a deep layer of Messianic consciousness in the mind of America," a belief in America "as the darling of divine providence," chosen to lead the world to good government. This betrays "moral pride."[165]

Without minimizing Americans' moral pride — to seek righteousness almost inevitably involves one in self-righteousness, a fact that should moderate but not end the seeking — it must be said that Niebuhr exaggerates. When New England Christians, Puritan and others, called America the new Israel, they did so among a people well aware of the old Israel's numerous sins and failings. In the figure of an American Israel righteousness mingles with self-righteousness, but also with responsibility and even humility; a Bible-reading people could have it no other way.[166] Although much more optimistic than the Puritans, and more optimistic than many of his colleagues, Jefferson's lively sense of human depravity and responsibility cannot be doubted, particularly with respect to the issue of slavery, so closely linked to the issue of tyranny — and therefore to the Declaration of Independence, which in its original, Jeffersonian version condemned slavery and went so far as to blame its presence in America upon tyrannical Britons.[167] Jefferson's well-known description of Americans having a wolf by the ears, accompanied as it was by a warning of divine retribution, did not lack the sense of human sinfulness.

Niebuhr's error or exaggeration concerning the dimensions of American messianism committed him to three additional errors. First, he could not distinguish between Franklin Roosevelt's progressivist historicism and Thomas Jefferson's doctrine of unalienable right; Niebuhr supposed that Roosevelt, following Wilson, had simply invented a new kind of Jeffersonianism, one that used governmental power more confidently.[168] But it is the very distrust of governmental power that best reflects the Jeffersonian distrust of human conduct. Second, Niebuhr had to claim that "an unconscious or inherited wisdom," a "pragmatic approach to political and economic questions which would do credit to Edmund Burke," has "saved" Americans; "common sense" not "abstract theories" has prevailed, and this is "primarily the wisdom of democracy itself," the "ironic triumph of the wisdom of common sense over the foolishness of [modernity's] wise men."[169] This point perfectly captures the virtues and vices of the United States as governed by historicist progressives, but it obscures the real prudence of the Founders who, after all, enunciated the principles of the Declaration and devised the republican constitutional arrangements that secured those principles.

Finally, Niebuhr had to distinguish sharply between the "presuppositions" of the Declaration and of the Constitution, claiming that James Madison "combined Christian realism in the interpretation of human motives and desires with Jefferson's passion for liberty."[170] In fact the combination of Christian or more accurately Biblical realism – the acknowledgment of a Creator-God, the accusation of tyrannical depravity, and the acceptance of both popular and statesmen's responsibility – with the self-evident truth that all men are created equal, with an unalienable right to liberty, already occurs in the Declaration.

This notwithstanding, Niebuhr had finally come to appreciate America's "moral and spiritual resources," as originating in the founding and in Christianity.[171] He saw that "modern communist tyranny is surely as wrong as the slavery which Lincoln opposed," and that "the Communist danger is greater than the Nazi," in part because more subtle in its strategy – less dependent upon sheer military force – and in part because its "idealistic pretensions" resemble those of America's home-grown progressives.[172] Americans' "prudent self-regard," neither idealistic nor cynical, will serve them best in this struggle.[173] Wilson's "abstract universalism," obscuring the power of the United States from Americans themselves, will only mislead, not least because it will confuse the domestic procedures of liberal progressivism with foreign policy.[174] This too-nearly-pacifistic pacificism (issuing, coincidentally, from the mind of a statesman who led his people into war after praising himself for keeping them out of it) forgets the occasional need to secure forcefully the kind of political union that secures rights.[175] "Democracy is neither a universal panacea nor, at the other extreme, merely a cultural monopoly of the Anglo-Saxon and Scandinavian worlds" – neither *simply* universal (its universality to be extended by 'historical' progress) nor a specimen of 'Eurocentric' political and cultural 'imperialism.'[176] Republicanism needs force to defend itself. It also needs more than mere force. Republicanism involves sin, yet resists it more effectively than other forms of government. When properly conceived, republicanism rests on the human understanding of human sin, as well as the appreciation of human virtue.

Pacifist Rejoinders: Moralists

The rise of modern totalitarianism, which caused some pacifists to abandon pacifism, concentrated the minds of those who remained pacifists on the issue of political realism. Niebuhr's substantial critique stung. Pacifists were roused to answer it.

Several distinguished pacifists responded with traditional moral arguments. A.J. Muste called Niebuhr's dichotomy of moral man and immoral society "entirely out of harmony with the prophetic world view, which rules out also a dualism between political and religious behavior." Perhaps because this "world view" would logically entail theocracy, Muste emphasized the moral point: "The attempt to split a person up into several beings subject to a variety of moral laws can only result in schizophrenia and moral disintegration.[177] This ignores Romans 13, which does not require individuals to obey different moral laws, but recognizes that non-Christian magistrates and Christian subjects will not obey identical moral laws, and need not to so for mundane purposes. This in no way denies the unity of moral law; Christians obey a more comprehensive moral law than pagans do, not an entirely different one.

The matter becomes problematic only when Christians wield political power, as for example when a Christian or predominantly Christian people establish a republic. In this case, Muste was right to ask, "Just what is the workable compromise between the prophets and Machiavelli?"[178] One might be tempted to reply: "The wisdom of serpents and the harmlessness of doves." However, harmlessness does not always maintain the political union that secures unalienable rights. Can there be, then, a workable compromise between the prophets and, say, Aristotle (who formulated the doctrine of the just war) or between the prophets and the tradition of natural law? Muste did not believe there is a genuine harmony between the Gospel and any doctrine or tradition that justifies war. Grace can overcome sin, not entirely but for the most part; Muste candidly admitted humbly that few pacifists had been so blessed.[179] Pacifists seem to stand in need of divine forgiveness.

Because Muste believed that love serves as the principal bond of civil society, and because he took the Gospel to teach absolute nonviolence, he insisted that Christian peoples should live as almost no individual can live — gracefully.[180] But if *Christian* love could serve as an effective civil social bond, Christian societies would endure longer than others. No Christian civil society adhering to Mustean principles has endured as long as Sparta, as long as republican or imperial Rome, as long as many of the Chinese dynasties, or as long as the American republic. Experience shows the fragility of pacifist Christian communities, their need for divine intervention to bring an end to mundane history.

Charles E. Raven attempted to overcome Niebuhr's criticism by simultaneously denying the charge of utopianism and admitting the necessity of martyrdom. "The world" called Jesus' promises utopian — the world of the Pharisees and the Sadducees, and of Pontius Pilate, the world of "evil in its most respectable and authoritative guise," the guise of "social orthodoxy and political security." "[Y]ou can overcome evil, but only on Christ's terms, and by Christ's way, and at Christ's cost," martyrdom. Emphasizing the fact that Jesus did not flee from His persecutors, Raven overlooked Jesus' advice to His disciples to flee during the last days (Matthew 24:15). Raven also misinterpreted Niebuhr as denying that human beings in groups "can produce creative results which immeasurably transcend the sum of what those individuals severally can accomplish"; Raven unwarrantedly jumped to the conclusion that political "democracy" can duplicate the real successes of some small groups, which Niebuhr did deny.[181] Raven mistakenly claimed that a theology that sharply distinguishes the divine from the human, "repudiate[s] incarnational philosophy" by "deny[ing] that there can be any real union between the divine and the human"; Niebuhr instead denied that this union was possible without a Second Coming of the Messiah. Unlike Socrates, the second Isaiah, and Prometheus, Jesus on the Cross proved martyrdom victorious in history by His resurrection and by changing "the course of history" with agapic love, revealing and releasing "the infinite energies of God."[182] Raven thus wrote imprecisely, as Jesus' victorious martyrdom released infinite energies in definite − that is to say finite − ways. These ways did not obviate the necessity for civil society and political life as practiced before and since Jesus' Advent. Given the real historical achievements of the early Church, Christian communalism should not be "dismissed as utopian"; Raven cited his own experiences on committees and teams as proof of this, without seriously considering the narrowness of such experiences with respect to politics.[183]

The Quaker Cecil E. Hinshaw acknowledged, with Niebuhr, that "the translation of ideals into institutional and organizational form is an extraordinarily difficult task," given the conflicts among principled men owing to the contradictions between their principles, and given the size and complexity of modern societies. Still, pacifists should not withdraw from this society, "this prison of a dying age," to form some new monasticism, retreating to "the double standard of morality" familiar in much of Christian history.[184] Pacifists should "see man as he is neither better nor worse, for errors either way can be fatal"; the belief in the natural goodness of men is not the foundation of all pacifism. "The Calvinist and the Quaker agree rather well on the depth of human sin, but they disagree as to whether divine power could triumph over that sin in this earthly life."[185] Hinshaw recognized the existence of evil "in ourselves" as Christians and in our avowed enemies. No listing of the misrepresentations in time of war fever and hysteria can do away with the hard fact that there have been times of terrible and unjustified aggression by peoples and nations," aggressions that, "as a nation, inadequate though we are in ideals or the practice of them [we] are morally required to oppose" when "evil is directed at us or against those for whom we have some degree of responsibility." Hinshaw commended Gandhian nonviolent resistance for this purpose, as well as persuasion — two "weapons of love." He cited the example of Danish and Norwegian resistance to Nazi Germany, and East German resistance to the Soviet Union in 1953.[186]

> ...it is remarkable in those instances how *little* killing did take place. These cases tend to show that human nature cannot become so depraved and mechanized that it is completely impervious to the appeal made by passive resistance.[187]

After an enemy conquest, Americans, inspired by "the simple truth that the soldier of the occupation army, even when he acts brutally, is a human being, made in God's image" but conditioned "by the environment in which he has lived, the training he has had, and the pressures of the dictatorship upon him," would act as a nation of well-disciplined Christian psychologists. Their "knowledge of the enemy would undergird a nation-wide therapy directed toward the invaders that would be rather like the therapy we now use in mental hospitals."[188] Hinshaw did not consider the limitations of therapy used in mental hospitals, particularly in view of the circumstance he described, where the lunatics, so to speak, would be running the asylum.

Culbert G. Rutenber made the best moralist's answer to Niebuhr. The title of his book *The Dagger and the Cross* refers to a wooden crucifix seen by the English literary critic John Addington Symonds while touring Italy. The small dagger concealed within the crucifix symbolized for Rutenber "the confusion of the Christian Church in its efforts to live in both worlds at once"; in crises, individuals and groups abandon one or the other, "revealing the true center of loyalty in commitment." Since the Roman Emperor Constantine announced his conversion to Christianity in the fourth century, Christians' "confidence in worldly power has absorbed our trust in spiritual power." These powers can be reconciled, but only after the Second Coming, as in Revelations 5, when the Lamb achieves "blessing and honor and glory and dominion forever and ever." Rutenber did not expect the harmony of secular and divine powers until that time.[189] Rutenber agreed with Niebuhr that many twentieth-century pacifists shared "a rather starry-eyed view of human nature." Worse, "pacifists' tendency to minimize the seriousness of the challenge of a country like [Nazi] Germany or [Soviet] Russia makes them appear either blind or uninformed." Rutenber asked, "Is it possible to undergird pacifism with a more biblically grounded theological foundation than liberalism provided?"[190]

Although Rutenber occasionally tried not so much to make pacifism appear practical as to make war appear futile, he found a much less assailable foundation for pacifism than any argument about practical consequences could provide.[191] Realistically denying "that love must always triumph," he concluded that Christian pacifism if it emphasized no consequences but obedience to the will of God. "Consequences aside, says the Christian pacifist, I am a pacifist because God wills it." Political life cannot depend upon agapic love; political life must emphasize "justice rather than love." Political life cannot be as personal as private life. To personalize political life excessively will make political life impossible.[192]

Rutenber then claimed that warfare in the twentieth century violates justice. Even judging the justice or injustice of a particular war has become nearly impossible, as propaganda has made claims and counterclaims harder to assess. Modern technology involves mass destruction of innocent lives, eliminating the possibility of just means of warfare. A Christian soldier would have to take orders from his commanding officers, relinquishing his obligation to moral choice.[193] Such arguments weakened his real position, however. Morally, a prudent citizen need only consider the information he has or can obtain, not the information he cannot have; modern technology need not destroy innocent lives, and many wars require no weapons of mass destruction; a Christian soldier need not take all orders, and under the United States military code, he can conscientiously refuse to obey an illegal command. Rutenber's final argument was simpler:

> God's will is supreme. It is the essence of Christian faith to believe that if one is really doing God's will, somehow God will take care of things."[194]

Indeed, "the temptation to lower our standards because of the involvement of others in ensuing pain" − the courageous desire to protect family, friends, and country from attackers — "is a most subtle temptation and most understandable."[195]

While advocating nonviolent resistance to military attack, Rutenber sensibly asked, "How successful can pacifism be?" Recognizing that totalitarianism "is not a mere dictatorship," and that 'progress' is no realistic faith; seeing moreover that "the influence of Christianity has declined," thus vitiating the will of the people to practice principle nonviolent resistance steadfastly; remembering that "even Jesus did not succeed" in convincing the Roman magistrates; and noticing that the very impersonality of modern war (and, he might have added, of modern Hegelian-bureaucratic politics) makes the personal appeal of Christianity less powerful; Rutenber honestly answered that pacifism is not likely to succeed. Although "the habit of thinking in terms of calculated chances of success may be a dangerous thing," a friendly critic might note that the habit of not thinking prudently may be a more dangerous thing. Rutenber was left with his core argument: pacifism fulfills the will of God; it always succeeds as an act of Christian witness.[196]

The Christian moralists' response to Niebuhr cannot finally depend upon the question of consequences except in the Biblical sense that the wages of sin is death. Niebuhr's prudential arguments may be qualified and of course the debate over what is the prudential course in a given circumstance never ends in unanimous agreement. But Niebuhr's insistence on prudence is unanswerable in political terms. The Christian moralists' argument depends upon the accuracy of their interpretation of divine command. Niebuhr forced American pacifists back to the Bible.[197]

The Pacifist Response: Prophets

As might be expected in an ethos saturated with historicism, most pacifists did not criticize Niebuhr primarily from a moral perspective, returning to the Gospels for a renewed sense of God's commands. Many preferred to try revivifying the prophetic tradition, the tradition historicism secularizes. Post-Niebuhrian 'prophetic' Christian pacifists have wanted to synthesize Niebuhrian pessimism with an historicist critique of existing socio-economic and political orders. To make this synthesis plausible, they must emphasize the apocalyptic aspect of Christian doctrine. The existence of modern technology (in particular mass-destructive weapons) appears providential in this respect, lending itself to apocalyptic rhetoric.

Thomas Merton adopted the familiar Marxist claim that "the whole social structure" of the modern world in general and the United States in particular yields violence. The modern social structure, "outwardly ordered and respectable," has the "psychopathic" inner core of Hegelianism gone mad: "Violence today is white-collar violence, the systematically organized bureaucratic and technological destruction of man" seen in Nazi genocide and modern warfare. Although Merton conceded that "violence must at times be restrained by force," it is not clear that he classified warfare (and surely not modern warfare) as legitimately forceful in any circumstance, that is, capable of restraining violence. He clearly preferred nonviolent resistance, "the only really effective resistance to injustice and evil."[198]

Merton agreed with Rutenber in finding "the chief difference between non-violence and violence" in their different loci of dependency. Nonviolence "depends entirely on God and on his Word;" violence depends "entirely upon its own calculations." But Merton was far more optimistic than Rutenber in calling nonviolent resistance "realistic and concrete," a "willingness to suffer *a certain amount* of accidental evil in order to bring about a change of mind in the oppressor." Rutenber would agree with Merton that "Christian meekness...refrains from self-assertion and from violent aggression because it sees all things in the light of the great judgment"; Rutenber would not agree that violence can be abolished when "a new way of solving it...become[s] *habitual*." For Rutenber, the technique of nonviolent resistance cannot *solve* anything, because habituation is not the real issue. The 'problem' of human conflict will be solved only by the Second Coming.[199]

Rather like Muste, Merton offered penetrating moral analyses of violence. "A violent man cannot begin to look at truth," Merton wrote, because he fears excessively the 'other,' the stranger who differs:

> If I, as a Christian, believe that my first duty is to love and respect my fellow man in his personal frailty and perplexity, in his unique hazard and his need for trust, then I think that the refusal to let him alone, the inability to entrust him to God and to his own conscience, and the insistence on rejecting him as a person until he agrees with me, is simply a sign that my own

faith is inadequate.... Claiming to love truth and my fellow man I am really only loving my own spiritual security, and using the Gospel as a gimmick for self-justification.[200]

Merton added to this moral analysis some lucid cultural-political criticism beyond Muste's usual range. Merton saw that modern political philosophy – "thought patterns that began to assert themselves in the Renaissance, and which assumed control at the French Revolution," – had resulted in "outright nihilism" both in the liberal democracies and in communist regimes. Because modernity has so strengthened itself in human minds the world over, the Christian Church must seek new ways to appeal to people, to open them to the Word. Merton had very considerable reservations about democracy itself. After the French Revolution states required "larger armies," and the Church "protected her institutional structures in potentially hostile countries [by] support[ing] the nation in its wars." Thus "God was drafted into all the armies and invited to get out there and kill Himself." The second half of the twentieth century has seen existentialism among the elites and "pseudo-spirituality or...outright nihilism of mass-man."[201] Merton very acutely noticed that modern unbelief is not so much rejection of faith as indifference to it, "a subjectively sincere and total lack of interest in the very idea of a God who speaks...a cool and often bored acceptance of that awful autonomy by which man can indeed make or destroy himself, but in which he is not summoned by anyone to do anything special." In the United States as elsewhere, 'God' serves politics, and modern politics insists on security above all.[202]

The modern political philosopher who most emphasizes security is of course Thomas Hobbes, for whom civil society amounts to a means of escape from the natural war of all against all.[203] Merton correctly argued that Hobbes presents a Machiavellianism "propounded with an air of respectability," that Hobbesian 'natural law' contradicts Ciceronian and Thomistic natural law. Merton, however, endorsed the error opposite to that of Hobbes, praising the belief Pope John XXIII expressed in the 1962 encyclical *Pacem in Terris*, that human nature is "radically good," and that peace may therefore be had on earth through human efforts.[204] This unwarranted optimism, combined with a very dark pessimism about modern thought, yielded an apocalypticism whose hysteria betrayed the fears it sought to overcome.

Merton's well-known mysticism and his prophetism were but two aspects of the same quest to open himself and his fellow-moderns to divine grace. "There is no real love of life" – and hence no firm rejection of violence – "unless it is oriented to the discovery of one's true, spiritual self, beyond and above the level of mere empirical individuality, with its superficial enjoyments and fears." Mysticism cures modernism – or, rather, leads to the cure, which is divine grace. Whereas the Social Gospel, a sentimental variant of humanistic modernism, had sought to reconcile man with man, Christians must seek reconciliation with God as well. Merton's mysticism issued not in passivity but in participation in history; "the Church is Christ present in the world to reconcile the world to Himself." In the historicist manner, Merton described the interaction of Church and world as dialectical. "If we foresake this forward movement toward eschatological fulfillment, then we plunge into the interminable circling of the world upon itself," and the "essentially pagan" vices of historical cyclicism described by Niebuhr. "Openness to God" and the receipt of His grace does not only entail personal salvation; it also entails engagement "in the historical task of the Mystical Body of Christ, for the redemption of man and his world."[205]

Because this historical task shaded into an historicist task of a world revolution that proceeds 'dialectically,' Merton committed false prophecies similar to those of Muste, though less numerous. He wrongly assumed that racial violence in America would escalate out of control; that American violence in the Vietnam war would only worsen (the war "cannot be won by either side"); that "we are on the edge of a revolution, perhaps even a limited civil war" to end in a "police state." "The American ideology of freedom and democracy is now largely discredited everywhere, even among a significant proportion of Americans." Further, "nuclear deterrence has proved to be an illusion, for the bomb deters no one," as seen in Korea, Indochina, Laos, and the Congo.[206] Inasmuch as American nuclear strategy always aimed at deterrence of Soviet invasion of Western Europe and Japan, and at deterrence of Soviet nuclear attack, not at deterrence of Soviet backed wars by Soviet trained forces in other parts of the world; inasmuch the so-called

"American ideology," was not discredited much, or for long; and inasmuch as no revolution or police state arose in the United States, one is entitled to call Merton a false prophet, and to locate the source of his error in his distinctive 'synthesis' of hope and pessimism, which caused him to make imprudent political judgments. Merton claimed that American nonviolent civil rights advocates and war protestors were "being driven to the Marxist position by a sort of self-fulfilling prophecy"; police violence was 'radicalizing' them and, once radicalized, they would be 'fair' game for outright destruction.[207] The 'prophecy' turned out to be not 'self-fulfilling' but just plain wrong, a specimen of left-historicist illusion.[208]

Some 'prophetic' Christian pacifists have exercised one kind of prudence; they have avoided making falsifiable predictions. In one of his earliest published essays, the Church of the Brethren scholar John Howard Yoder directly confronted Niebuhr's justification of war. Yoder denied that war is "less harmful to civilization and moral values than tyranny," without considering that tyrannies usually last longer than wars, thereby perpetuating the evils they cause more effectively than wars do. Yoder argued that "slavery may be 'worse than war' in the sense that it is more unpleasant for me; but in war the sin is mine, in slavery it is not" – an argument that overlooks the ability of clever tyrants to rig circumstances to require sinful acts,[209] and shirks the responsibility not to increase the temptation of evil men to commit evil acts. Yoder criticized Niebuhr for neglecting the role of the Christian Church and the Holy Spirit whose power is "a working reality within history and especially within the Church." Yoder convicted Niebuhr of an "un-Biblical assumption of responsibility for policing society and for preserving Western civilization."[210] Yoder's criticisms appeared to coincide with the traditional Mennonite view shared by the early Christian Fathers and by Paul, that Christians shall not govern, but shall be governed by God and by just magistrates.

But as Yoder's convictions developed, he moved toward a more historicist Christianity. He called traditional Mennonism "a pacifism of cultural isolation," vulnerable when the isolation ends. He called Mennonite dualism – nonresistance for genuine Christians, just-war pacifism for others – an implicit denial of "both missionary and ecumenical concern."[211] Yoder's preferred pacifism, the pacifism of "the Messianic community," "does not promise to work," and avoids the self-righteousness of "prophetic-protest pacifism."[212] Messianic-communal pacifism may appear to be apolitical, but political considerations nonetheless consistently intrude upon it. For example, Yoder called "programmatic political pacifism," which he sought not to imitate but to appropriate for use in his own analysis, "the wisest and most honest view of the political scene available," despite its admitted collapse in the 1930s "with the rise of Hitler." While this political pacifism "counts too much on the goodwill" of rulers, Yoder wrote, "militarism" is far worse. Militarism places "enormous trust in the good intentions of its own leaders." Yoder belittled "prudential calculation" in warfare as less likely "to produce the desired outcomes" than political pacifism is.[213] Yoder's failure to give any reasons for this extraordinary judgment did not improve its plausibility. Yoder's observation, "What made peace possible, or war impossible, between Pennsylvania and New Jersey, was not that one of them finally won a war against the other" – an observation that overlooks the example of the conflict between Pennsylvania and Virginia at Gettysburg – did nothing to enhance that plausibility.[214]

While appropriating parts of the analysis of politics offered by political pacifism, Yoder rejected regime analysis, or tried to. "Mary's praise to God is a revolutionary battle cry," and Jesus' "primary agenda item" was to attack injustice. The Christian attack on injustice requires "the institution of a new way of life, not of a new government"; Jesus had "low esteem for the political order." Jesus, the Head of the Church, is the Lord of History, ruling over magistrates and harnessing their vengefulness for the sake of an order that "give[s] room for the growth and work of the Church." The Emperor Constantine mistakenly tried to make Christian morality "workable for all society," and ended by making Christianity subservient to politics. Politics should serve Christianity. Yoder noticed that certain kinds of political order do modestly assist the Church in its work by tolerating Christianity, "as the democracies of Switzerland, England, and the Netherlands show us."[215]

He also noticed that the Christian ethos affects governments. "Christianized morality seeps into the non-Christian mind through example and through the education of children who do not themselves choose radical

Christianity, with the result that the whole moral tone of non-Christian society is changed for the better and there are honorable and honest men available to run the government before the church is numerically strong enough for 'responsibility' to be a meaningful concept."[216] This process brings regime considerations back, as it were with a vengeance. Because the military defense of oneself and even of others is not Christian − 'one's own' is not to be loved more than the enemy; the aggressor's life is worth no less than the life he threatens; killing is never loving; allowing evil to happen is less blameworthy than committing evil (if it were blameworthy, God Himself would stand condemned); to calculate the 'lesser evil' is impossible, given the complexities of human history; in practice, 'self-defense' always 'justifies' any war − the Christianization of governments renders governments themselves problematic. If governments can serve Christianity, and if Christianity nonetheless injures governments, problems arise. Therefore, the only thing that makes Christianity morally responsible in socio-economic and political life is the far greater danger of politics, particularly in its 'Constantinian' form. "[W]orldly power is intrinsically weak." As Niebuhr saw, even at the height of their power, governments cannot guarantee justice. Violence is "the outworking of idolatry"; killing others puts "another value" − "democracy or justice, or equality or liberty" − ahead of God and one's neighbor, whom we are commanded to love as ourselves.[217] Governments finally do not secure unalienable rights. They end in self-defeat. With Rutenber, Yoder called "egocentric altruism," justifying oneself "in the form of duty to others," the highest, most seductive temptation, as it seems so necessary to the securing of justice.[218]

Yoder shared Merton's distaste for modern democracy, which has "increased the space for demagoguery." "[I]t often appears that the involvement of the masses in decisions about patriotism and war does not provide for a better defense of the real interest of most of the people."[219] No political regime secures justice. Only "Messianic communities," Christian communes governed only by Jesus, might secure justice. They can do so because Christ is the Lord of History; He can and will bypass the governments He has hitherto used. Yoder resembled leftist historicists by anticipating the withering away of the state, while rejecting historicists' secular explanations for that withering. He suggested no timetable for the replacement of governments and nations with Messianic communities. His prophecy thereby gained in irrefutability what it lacked in sense.

Stanley Hauerwas formulated a similar teaching in a more prudent way. Troubled by the obscuring of Christian truth by political accommodation to the American regime, Hauerwas firmly distinguished the Church from the world, and therefore from all worldly institutions. Whereas the American regime sanctions defensive war, the Church does not. "The church is our alternative to war," even as commercial republicanism was the American Founders' alternative to militarism, including Christian militarism.[220]

Hauerwas went so far as to claim that the Church, the community that maintains the Christian "tradition of moral wisdom" across time, is more fundamental than the individual's belief in Jesus Christ. He thus ignored the Gospel emphasis on faith rather than community, and risked a spiritualized version of sociology.[221] Further, he rejected natural justice or natural law, calling Christianity a story or narrative, within which our own life-stories occur.[222] But while the Christian holds that the Holy Spirit's word tells an authoritative story, one must notice, as Hauerwas does not, that no story can make sense without abstractions, principles. The story of Jesus would make no sense if such words as 'resurrection' and 'salvation,' 'good' and 'evil,' did not punctuate it. The inevitability of abstraction in human thought requires the reconsideration of natural justice and natural law, if only because no mere narrative can mean anything without these abstractions or abstractions that replace them – e.g., divine justice and divine law.

Given his simultaneous exaggeration of the social character of Christianity, and depreciation of natural law, Hauerwas underestimated the utility of commercial republicanism (which he tended to reduce to "liberalism") in the quest for securing unalienable rights and thereby obtaining peace. In today's world, he warned darkly, "the sword of Constantine has passed to new hands," and "the evidence is still out" on Americans' toleration of Jews – or, for that matter, of dissenting Christians. Accordingly, the Church should "give up the security of having its ethos enforced or at least reinforced by wider social structures, trusting rather in the power of the Holy Spirit to be its sustainer and guide."[223] This advice is only prudent so long as the Church acknowledges that the regime of commercial republicanism more than allows the Church to proselytize, more than tolerates religious life; commercial republicanism insists on the Christians' unalienable right to proselytize and systematically secures that right. Because the everyday life of commercial republicanism may also distract or even seduce Christians from a Christ-centered life, Hauerwas' requirement of trust in the Holy Spirit as primary to Christian life is of course well taken. But his either/or warning is unsubtle, not well taken. "Scripturally there seem to be no good grounds to associate the Kingdom of God with any form of political organization"; historically, Christianity has endured a variety of regimes.[224] But it is also historically accurate to say that in modernity, pacifist Christianity has best endured in commercial republics.

Hauerwas imprudently denied that "a choice must be made" between 'America' and 'Germany' — or, more concretely, "between America and that bearer of totalitarianism, the Soviet Union." Whatever the political regime, "no state will keep itself limited" if no "body of people separated from the nation" insists on those limits. To prove this, Hauerwas claimed that the protection of *individual* rights has become "no less destructive for 'intermediate institutions' — notably the family — than the monistic state of Marxism." By viewing the foundations of all associations as private and "arbitrary," liberalism undermines them, drains them of real purpose and legitimacy. Whereas "the Russian lives in a social system that claims to achieve freedom by falsely investing all authority in the power of the Party, the American lives in a social system that tries to insure freedom by trying to insure that each individual can be his or her own tyrant." Hauerwas thus confused contemporary, relativistic liberalism, a variety of historicism, with the principles of the American Founding. He did so precisely because he depreciated natural law. For the Founders, private associations including the family deserve protection because they are *not* "arbitrary" but rightful, and because to regulate them too strictly would involve government in nice judgments government is ill-suited to make.[225]

Hauerwas back-handedly recognized this in preferring the United States over the Soviet Union. Modern America inherited "social and moral perspectives from the past that have successfully qualified some of the excesses of pure liberalism." He did not see how these inheritances cohered with the nature of the American regime itself. Instead he called the United States a "democratic state," which "can be just as tyrannical" as totalitarianism and therefore "continues to wear the head of the beast." He sought to substantiate this by citing democracy's command "to take up arms and kill not only other human beings but other Christians in the name of relative moral goods." He did not notice the protection given to conscientious objectors, a protection seldom recognized by regimes that are not commercial republics.[226] Hauerwas' political obscurantism allowed him to call the conflict of the Church and the world "the overriding conflict of our time," not the conflict of republicanism and totalitarianism. This either/or purism may be seen in his claim that "the church is the only true polity we can know in this life," the only one with "the courage to form its citizens virtuously." These formulations do not acknowledge that even subordinate principles are still principles, that derivative worth is still worthy.[227]

"The debate between pacifism and just war thinking is a theological issue of how we are to read and interpret history," Hauerwas claimed. Hauerwas read history as eschatological. The Church embodies the only genuinely peaceful way of life, horrified not at the thought of dying but at the thought of killing. Christian peace is the only peace that does not seek survival in this world. Without the Christian eschaton, "the demands to forgive our enemies push us beyond what we normally think to be humanly possible as long as we assume that the world in which we exist will go on indefinitely." Christianity calls for a limited Apocalypse now, within the Church, anticipating the complete Apocalypse of the Second Coming in time's fullness.[228] Hauerwas' reading of history depended not on the accuracy of his own 'prophetic' predictions — he made none — but on the accuracy of the prophecies of Jesus.

Democratic Political Peacemakers: Before and After Niebuhr

Niebuhr brought pacifism to the bar of realism and left it there. The distance between pre- and post-Niebuhrian pacifist thought on American politics may be seen by contrasting the writings of Gene Sharp, a productive scholar active in the 1970's and 1980's, with the prominent turn-of-the-century statesman, William Jennings Bryan.

Though not himself a pacifist, Bryan's just-war pacificism came extraordinarily close to pacifism. He resigned as President Wilson's Secretary of State in protest of war preparations in 1916, calling military force nearly obsolete. He looked forward to the practicability of pacifism in the near future.[229]

Early in his career, Bryan recognized the importance of military force in sustaining political union:

> Other armies have been inspired by love of conquest or have fought to repel a foreign enemy, but our armies held within the Union brethren who now rejoice at their own defeat and glory in the preservation of the nation which they once sought to dismember. No greater victory can be won by citizens or soldiers than to transform temporary foes into permanent friends.[230]

Even later, during the First World War, he reserved the right to make war in case of invasion of United States territories or in case of the "actual invasion of the rights of [our] own citizens." He had already cautioned, "Force can defend a right, but force has never created a right"; he never denied, however, that a right can be defended or secured by force.[231]

Bryan strongly opposed most wars, however, including most of the wars the United States, with belated imperial ambition, undertook during his lifetime. The American regime's commitment to government by consent should prohibit any war of conquest. The United States should "remain a homogeneous republic," not "become a heterogeneous empire." Americans should practice "the arts of peace rather than the arts of war."[232] Bryan envisioned a gradual progress toward pacifism among nations, a progress inspired by the example of the United States and also by the Holy Spirit. The world, he believed, was "moving" towards the "social ideal" of peace and democracy. This ideal "would be weighted down rather than aided by the armor and weapons proferred by imperialism." Christian nations should lead in "the promotion of peace," hastening "the day when human life − which when once destroyed cannot be restored − will be so sacred that it will never be taken except when necessary to punish a crime already committed, or to prevent a crime about to be committed." Humanity shall gradually perfect itself, leading the world to "universal brotherhood."[233]

Bryan's republicanism approached the boundary of pure democracy as closely as his just-war pacificism approached pacifism. Representatives should, in his view, express the thoughts and wishes of those who elected them, and not exercise independent judgment. An enthusiast of direct democracy in the form of referendum, which he believed (with unMadisonian zeal) the perfection of the government by consent, and commended as the best means of deciding questions of war or peace. He evidently held to the optimistic belief that the people would be less war-inclined than Congressmen.[234]

Militarism, the "modern Mars," is "nothing less than a challenge to the Christian civilization of the world," a threat to the progress of democracy and peace. In opposing President Wilson's war preparations, Bryan claimed that military force "represents the old system – the system that must pass away; persuasion represents the new system – the system that has been growing, all too slowly, it is true, but growing, for 1,900 years." The European war exemplified "the frightful follies" of the old, pagan system of "alternate retaliations and competitive cruelties." In Europe, "Christ and Pilate again stand face to face...striving for mastery and domination" of the world.[235] Bryan made the familiar pacifist claim that military force and even military preparedness provoke war instead of preventing it by inspiring hatred, while admitting that such force can work in the short run. He opposed any League of Nations whose charter would include an enforcement provision, for that reason. He called instead for an international court, national referenda on war and peace for all League members, and armament reductions. He cited George Washington's advice against entangling alliances. He claimed, *contra* Machiavelli, that it is better for a nation to be loved than feared. "Why not test the friendship plan among nations," and abolish war, as duelling and the codes of chivalry were abolished? To William Howard Taft's criticism, that chivalrous men "gave up weapons when they could rely on the police, exercising the force of the community, to protect them against violence," and that national armament stockpiles would be relinquished only after the establishment of an effective means of international policing, Bryan replied that international law could never be enforced without an international standard of morality. "The real difficulty with Europe is that the governments reject the moral standards that regulate individual life."[236] This reply left unanswered the question of whether, without enforcement, international moral standards would obtain — any more than they would obtain without enforcement within the borders of the nations.

Bryan's hopes, though not historicist, partook of the optimism of the high noon of historicism and shared its progressivism. Optimistic in his own way, Gene Sharp nonetheless proceeded with far more caution. For Sharp, peace will require the most assiduous work by citizens armed with Gandhian techniques. His own work began with a "comprehensive attempt" to "examine the nature of nonviolent struggle...including its view of power, its specific methods of action, its dynamics in conflict and the conditions for success or failure in its use." Success requires the non-utopian acknowledgment that power must be used, not rejected or somehow abolished. While concurring with the claim that "violence against violence is reinforcing," Sharp viewed nonviolence as a means of "political *jiu-jitsu*" that "tends to turn the opponent's violence and repression against his won power system, weakening it and at the same time strengthening the nonviolent group."[237]

Sharp was a more extreme democrat than Bryan, even, and entirely a pacifist, which characteristics made his post-Niebuhrian concern with realism all the more impressive. Calling political power "pluralistic" and "fragile," he criticized defenders of war for conceiving of political power as monolithic — proving that he had never studied Clausewitz with much acuity.[238] By the plurality and fragility of political power, he meant simply that governments depend upon consent, and "obedience to a ruler's command, though usual, is not inevitable." By "consent" Sharp meant mere volition; if you point a gun at me and I obey your order, I 'consent.' On this basis Sharp can as it were coerce Machiavelli himself into agreement with the thesis. Because "Western civilization" fails to understand that 'consent'-based nature of political power, governments and citizens alike overestimate the efficacy of violence, which they mistake as a sure foundation of authority. This is why we fail to see the efficacy of nonviolent resistance, which calmly refuses to consent, particularly in response to violence.[239] In his elaborate classification and discussion of types of nonviolent resistance, Sharp never quite got round to admitting that violence or force has the notable advantage of physically destroying or immobilizing one's political opponent. He did admit that nonviolence is not safe, but seemed to believe it the safest response to violence.[240]

Without explicitly acknowledging the power of violence, Sharp did allow that "the use of nonviolent action against totalitarian systems requires separate discussion," owing to the secrecy of those regimes and their "more probable" use of "extreme brutalities against the nonviolent activists."[241] Tyrants atomize their societies. Tyrants destroy the social, and political, and economic structures 'between' individuals and the tyrant, making the operation of tyrannical power more direct. Sharp therefore much preferred "liberal constitutional regimes" to tyrannies. "If effective means are not soon found to destroy dictatorships, and to alter the conditions which make them possible, the task of preventing and resisting them will rapidly become more difficult." He recommended study by Americans of nonviolent techniques of 'destabilizing' totalitarian regimes by "encourag[ing] deliberate inefficiency, laxity in carrying out duties, and perhaps eventual mutiny among the system's officials, bureaucrats, administrators, police, and soldiers."[242]

Within the commercial republics themselves, nonviolent resistance or civil disobedience should not replace speech and other "existing constitutional means" of influence. Here too, consent remains central to Sharp's doctrine. Nonviolence should be used only as "a democratic means of expressing extreme dissent" that otherwise could only issue in violence.[243] There was little in Sharp's recommendations of "the introduction of the right to organize civil disobedience" that did not already exist in the United States after the Second World War. He did not explain why would-be violent dissenters would choose nonviolence.

Sharp advocated not only direct but participatory democracy in the United States. He wanted to combine small-scale Jeffersonian 'ward republics' and communal social structures with nonviolent direct action campaigns to undermine and drastically limit state power. This, he assumed, would eliminate the use of violent coercion by government, and establish what might be described as nonviolent militia to resist any invader — "the change from one 'weapons' system for defense to a very different 'weapons' system."

Although many readers might not take this as a sign of realism, one must consider it in contrast with other pacifist doctrines, which are apolitical. Sharp insisted that a moral equivalent of war would not suffice; a country needs a political equivalent, too. Many pacifists, he observed, ignore or evade the reality of political power, particularly the many "cases of military conquest without provocation."[244]

Although Sharp therefore can be said to have appreciated the lessons of history, he did not appreciate its silence. History affords no example of a nonviolent overthrow of a totalitarian government, or of successful nonviolent resistance to a conqueror. There have been forceful revolutions and defenses against tyrants. Also, in his calls for "popular empowerment" he did not fully appreciate governmental checks and balances as a means of preventing tyranny. He thus exaggerated the political power, or potential political power, of society.

The interaction of pacifism with historicism, and of each with the principles of the American Founding, brings out questions concerning pacifism and the political order as such. To what extent can Christianity be said to strengthen commercial republicanism? Or does Christianity more properly call commercial republicanism to account, or even to judgment? Can there be a genuinely Christian politics? To what extent do modern political philosophies strengthen pacifism? Does any modern political philosophy conduce to peace, particularly when confronted with modern technology?

To examine these questions, it may be best to proceed analytically, that is, to consider the Scriptural and the secular components of 'American' regimes in isolation. The Second Part of this book concerns Scripture, especially Christian Scripture; the Third Part concerns modern political philosophy in relation to the wars and weapons of modernity.

SECOND PART

PACIFISM AND CHRISTIANITY

•

Love is even more powerful than other forms of force, could we only discover its strategies.

Harvey Seifert

The Kingdom of God has its own statesmanship, which it is for Christians to try to practice.

Gilbert Porteous

CHAPTER FOUR

God's City: On the Justice of War

CHARACTERS

Philip Soffron
Simon Liteson
Unnamed boy
Kip Falos
Andrew Docksman
Christopher Falos, Sr.
Nicholas Hendé
Kalir Menasheh
Joseph Chardim
Demetria Falos
Lydia Falos
Beth Liteson

Soffron: I went to the Wall yesterday with Simon Liteson, a young theologian, to see men praying there for the first time in nineteen years.[1] Although of course we did not approach the Wall ourselves, we prayed from a distance. This city will now permit a diversity of prayers and not only in private.

As we began to hurry back, Mr. Falos saw us from a distance and gave a coin to a little boy who ran after us and pleaded for us to wait. Simon cheerfully agreed, and soon we were greeting Falos, who was accompanied by Simon's wife Beth, their new friend Andrew Docksman, also a theologian, and some people who evidently had been praying at the Wall. Falos invited us to share the considerable hospitality of his home and table, where we could "lift a glass to the liberation," as he put it. "Also, there will be several young people there, and I know you share my interest in talking with them." Simon and Beth were eager to go, and I came with them.

At Falos' apartment we found his sisters Lydia and Demetria, who help him run his extensive commercial and philanthropic enterprises. Also, there was Nicholas Hendé, who evidently functions in political and business circles as a sort of consultant, Joseph Chardim and Kalir Menesheh, both natives of this city.

Falos's son, Kip, was at home, having just completed his sophomore year at Harvard University. He greeted me with awkward enthusiasm, happy to see me but restless and preoccupied. I asked him how America had seemed to him.

"God, what a country!" he exclaimed, trying to seem worldly but not quite hiding a certain fascination. "There's racism and class injustice. There's the puritanical attitude toward sex. There's the war in Vietnam and the threat of nuclear war with the Russians — a military-industrial complex basically runs the country. Yet despite the fact that this may be the last generation on earth to have a chance to save the human race from total destruction, most Americans don't have consciousness of the need for radical action. The professors and Pusey, the University president, are mostly just the sort of so-called decent liberals who got us into this mess in the first place. To them, everything is 'gradual.' But the kids are different. Sometimes we sit up for hours, telling about how to change things, really change things. And you know what? We're going to win!"[2]

I was filled with wonder at what he said, and urged him on. "Kip, do you get criticisms from people who charge that you and your friends say these things only because you have lived comfortable, leisured lives, and you feel guilty for your unearned advantages and fearful of losing your very lives in war?"

"Absolutely, we hear it all the time. Mostly from Establishment types feeling a little guilty about their own complacency. Look, we don't have to commit ourselves to changing society. We could spend our time at debutante balls or something, then get into a job in the family business, if that was what we wanted. Some people do."

"The reason I asked was that I've noticed that you never seemed overly fond of money. From your own experience with your friends, you may have seen that people who make money themselves tend to rate money very highly, and to take pride in it, calling themselves self-made men and so forth."

"That's right. In America, the Kennedy family shows the difference between new money, as they say, and the values of the next generation."

"So the advantage of wealth is to free the mind from the love of money?"

"I guess you could say that. The main thing is that society should be set up so that nobody has to worry about scarcity, and no one pursues wealth as an end in itself. Consumer society is dehumanizing. It reduces people to the status of things, and when you do that, you get wars, which are the ultimate expression of dehumanization, of using people as objects and making them into objects, dead objects."

"Justice is a sort of love of persons?"

"Exactly. Persons are infinitely precious, possessed of unfulfilled capacities for reason, freedom, self-cultivation, and creativity. I feel that each individual is unique, and the way to bring out that unique value is through a community of fraternity and honesty. A real democracy, a participatory democracy, would eliminate all violence from human relationships by making them truly inter-*personal*. Wars only come about because old men want to use young men as instruments to perpetuate their own privileges; they manufacture 'threats' to 'national security' in order to block meaningful change in the social order."[3]

Kip jumped up and walked quickly toward the door. Then he turned around abruptly and said, "If we don't act now, violence will finally be met with violence. In America I've become convinced that the universities are the place to start, because we can think things through there, and build a base for an assault upon the real powers not only in American society, but through the whole world."[4]

"I wonder if I understand what you are saying. Tell me, do you fall in love with all the girls you meet?"

Kip laughed, a little self-consciously as I thought, but he also relaxed a little. "Not really. It only looks that way."

"Then you love some more than others?"

"Yes."

"All beloved persons are not created equal?"

"No, not exactly."

"And there are even people you really feel nothing at all for, even if they like you? And there are even some girls (rare ones, I am sure) who like you less than you like them?"

This met with silent assent.

"Similarly, in a commune or kibbutz, there are bound to be tensions, arguments, particularly when love is involved, I suppose. Love may even lead to rivalry, or so I have heard. You have seen this sort of thing."

"Yes, I have," Kip said, seriously.

"Tell me another thing. There can be no brothers without fathers and mothers?"

"No kidding."

"Parents are needed sometimes to make peace between even the most fraternal brothers, yes?"

"Yes, but I'm talking about grownups, not little kids."

"I understand. But I didn't mean this parenthood quite so literally. In maturing, as you now can see, a person comes to find a certain pattern to live by, wouldn't you say? A pattern that gives him direction?"

"Yes, we must create our own values and then have the courage to live up to them."

"But who is the 'we' who is creating the value?"

Kip hesitated. "I'm not sure what you mean. *We* are the 'we' who create."

"Yes, but if a child creates his own pattern, it could only be childish, unless he sees something beyond his own childishness, and wills it for some reason. If, by creating values, we are only saying 'I will,' will we not will only what we are, albeit more and more vehemently? And would this not lead inevitably to the most violent conflict?"[5]

Kip hesitated again, perhaps torn between thinking and action.

"Maybe that's where meaning must be created. But listen, I mean, I can't talk here forever, there's too much to do, and as soon as I can, as soon as this insane blood-shed stops, I'm going back to the U.S., where I can do the most good." He left, without saying where he was going.

Mr. Falos cleared his throat. "Kip's a fine young man, and I'm proud of him." This met with some murmurs of assent.

"Yes," I agreed. "He may not always know what his immediate next step will be, but he does know the step after that. As for the ultimate destination, I was wondering if you understood him to say that justice is love of people who most deserve love, and anger with those who refuse to make themselves worthy of deserving love?"

"Yes. And we have to learn to know the difference between a true friend and a false friend, a true enemy and an enemy who can be made into a friend."

"In your experience, how can we make enemies into friends?"

"By sincere goodwill, backed up by generosity. There are very few who will not respond to those two things, taken together."

"Few, indeed. But would not false friends who refuse to become real ones make up, so to speak, for all the others? What I mean is, that in order to be generous, one needs the means of generosity. Yet false friends specialize in separating the generous person from his means. We can discuss this frankly, inasmuch as we are among true friends today."

"Indeed we are, thank goodness," Mr. Falos said, in an expansive tone.

"But it is obvious to me that we have not really answered the question we raised," I said, "because we haven't settled the question, Who is a true friend? What qualities make a person worthy of our love?"

Before Mr. Falos could answer, Nicholas Hendé interrupted with an elegance, a formal courtesy, that well masked the fact that he *was* interrupting. And in truth his interruption was not altogether unanticipated, as I had noted a certain irony, alternating with impatience, in his manner, as if he were determined to laugh at everything we said.[6]

"Certainly, I must confess to a certain surprise, I should not say astonishment, at the *direction* in which Monsieur Soffron has been leading this little discussion. Our friend Christopher has been altogether too kind. As a successful man, a man of realism, he knows how surreal your comments have been; his indulgence to us, his friends, has no bounds and wants none. Yet I must defend him, as it were, from his own indulgence."

"Please do so, so that we may learn from you," I said.

"I shall overlook your sarcasm and proceed. In the real world, great love leads to unbridled acquisition, not to great friendship. Above all, we must not concern ourselves with the sentimentalities of the imagination but ready ourselves to act decisively. If we let go of what *is* done for what *should* be done, we will find ourselves defenseless, impaled on the sword of necessity.[7] A prudent man will know how dangerous it is to fail to revenge an injury, for old injuries can never be cancelled by new benefits.[8] By all means we must observe the most strict justice – that is, a just proportion between our own force and the force of others.[9] Fear, not friendship or sentimental affection, rules the majority of men. And while, in everyday life, we can afford to act like humane beings, assigning our severity to the rule of law or some other necessity, to fail to understand this, to so fundamentally misread human psychology, is to invite us to our ruin, to nothingness.[10] It is to be led astray by a false interpretation of our religion, enfeebling us and fitting us only for a life of suffering and masochistic humiliation."[11]

Mr. Falos seemed attentive but uneasy. Mr. Hendé, taking due note of this, hastened to continue. "Certainly, all the greatest virtues of men are to be admired and practiced. Whenever possible when we acquire property, whether in business or in war, we should distribute it generously to our people. Such generosity enables us never to exploit them.[12] Prudence or practical wisdom is a great virtue, and it counsels us never to repeat an injury, and to give no injury that need be repeated. We will only be able to do this if we adhere to the rule of law, nationally and even internationally. Of course, these laws must be good laws. And as there are not good laws without good arms to defend them, and as no good things can be safely left to the care of people who do not need them for their own safety, we must always insist on using our own arms. I can think of no greater sin for a man of responsibility than to depend on some other person or persons for ensuring the well-being of his people.[13] Those who are responsible for others must therefore diligently study and practice the arts of defense, so that things may be ordered in such a way as to encourage the unifying faith of the people.[14]

"Fear, it has been said, is the beginning of wisdom," he continued. "There are many ways to teach such healthy fear.[15] In revealing the Law of Moses before the Law of Love, God taught us nothing else than the priority of healthy fear to wholesome love. Love, taken by itself, is held in place by the chains of obligation and affection – weak chains easily broken. Fear, by contrast, truly binds. Love is someone else's to give or return; fear is yours to give, as liberally as need be. This is how we make true friends, and earn glory, moderately avoiding that easy familiarity that breeds contempt, as well as the hatred that inspires murderous, wicked rebellion.[16]

"In a world of struggle against evil men, we must of course appear merciful, faithful, honest, humane, and respectful of religious values. To survive in this world, you must know the realities. To know the realities, you must not judge by mere appearances – as do those who believe only what they see on the surface – and not by hearsay – as do those who believe whatever is told them. You must know how to grasp, to feel the truth with your own hands. Without this 'feel' for reality, you will not know whether to use your hand to caress or to strike.[17]

"Now, to renew my argument for a third and final time," Hendé said, "let me say that my remarks, at once cautionary and, as I hope, inspiriting, should never be said to contradict the hopes for democracy we all cherish. Indeed, I am a great friend of good government. In republics, I say, there is greater life.[18] In politics as well as religion, poverty or at least a modest living most conduces to virtue.[19] In addition to modest living, one must have unity. Because factions result from idleness or peace, and the insolence it spawns, a responsible governor of a republic will seek unity through great and risky actions, none being greater than war.[20] Of course, much depends upon the character of your people. A spirited people will expand, or they will tear each other apart; for a tranquil people, such as the old Venetians, on the other hand, expansion is poison.[21] What is truly incoherent is the dream of making a people both expansive and tranquil.[22]

"Even more than the character of the people, however, their good discipline determines success. Civil and military life are very close. Not some sort of gift from nature but good discipline – art and industry – shape a virtuous citizenry. The philosopher Aristotle was very far from the truth in this as in so much else, for certainly it is the art of discipline that makes men courageous (that is, fearful only of realities, but therefore prepared to counter them) and unified. Left with no alternative but to conquer or die, a people will master their fate and bring to themselves true security and satisfaction.[23] It would be a most wicked thing if our religion could be interpreted in such a way as to make us indifferent to our very survival, effectually worshippers of blind fortune. Where would justice be then?"[24]

Having delivered himself of this extraordinary address, Mr. Hendé prepared to bask in the glow of triumph, like some lion who has roared in domination over his pride. However, at the risk of feeling his claws, I decided to respond. "Are you saying, Monsieur Hendé, that justice is triumph in war, that any war is just, so long as it is successful?

"If I had meant to say it so, I would have said it so."

"But perhaps saying so would have proved you a poor warrior, one without strategems? I for one could not dream of improvising such a long, elaborate, and in some respects comprehensive speech; I find that I must make do with short, unimpressive speeches. Therefore, I must say, that I did not ask if you meant to say it *so*, but if you meant *such-and-such*, namely, that a successful war is always just?"

"Perhaps sycophants will deny it, but that is the way the world thinks, although very few will admit it, even to themselves."

"But the world's secret convictions, though revealing the world's true mind, need not be true to the facts?"

"They need not be. But they are. In their hearts, men know I am right, though they will not always admit it, even to themselves. They are childish when they tell themselves charming stories, but, like children, they know make-believe from the real world."

"What, then, is a successful war?"

"Why a victorious one of course."

"But if victory were not advantageous?"

"Victory is always advantageous."

"Surely not to the loser? And perhaps not even to the victor, if he is saddled with an unruly people more trouble than they are worth to him."

Mr. Hendé hesitated, as if calculating how far he should go. "An unruly people can be made peaceful, by a man of understanding."

"Peaceful, perhaps, but is this advantageous, in view of the dangers of peace you mentioned a few minutes ago?"

"In that case, a new struggle can be used to unify their hearts with that of their new ruler; then the conquered may share the prospects of ruling too."

"This does not end the problem, it extends it. Your justice at first only extends disadvantage more and more widely with every triumph. Eventually there would be none left to conquer − only the world in the grip of a tyrant with all remaining humanity as his accomplices. Men will be no less oppressed but far more guilty than ever before."

"Yes, by God, Philip," Mr. Falos said, "most clearly so."

Kalir Menasheh interrupted. "It is not at all so clear. The true Ruler of the world, the very opposite of the tyrant, the very Bestower of the rule of law, nonetheless commands defense of this city and aids His people in battle when they are righteous. We see this in many places; the Book of Nehemiah recounts but one instance.[25] And because the true test of a prophet's words is their confirmation in time,[26], we must say that there can be truth in conquest for both conqueror and conquered. Both sides have 'succeeded' by fulfilling Providence, as we see time and again in Scripture.

"The Law leaves no place for sentimentality. After all, one of the first human dialogues resulted not in peace, not in mutual understanding, but in murder.[27] The very name of Israel itself was bestowed after violent struggle with evil.[28] While the Lord hates the one who loves violence, He can as easily command his people to beat their plowshares into swords.[29] He need not directly command His people in battle for them to war justly, their victories to be celebrated in song by our women, by our mothers most of all.[30]

"This is not to condone militarism. The Law rules warfare, neither extolling nor adjuring it. Inside Canaan, we were to destroy enemies who refused to adhere to the seven Noachide commandments, the universal laws of morality; although those nations have disappeared, the seed of Amalek, of tyranny, live on.[31] The Law *is* life, in the fundamental sense that life itself is lawful, regulated by the Lord of Creation. Torah is the link between Creator and created; the very existence of the created depends radically upon the will of the Creator.[32] Far from burdensome, as some religionists suppose, the Law liberates men; by conforming their wills to the will of their Creator, men find genuine peace, fullness of being.[33] And, contrary to what philosophers suppose, there is no such thing as theory. The only genuine 'theory' is the Law.[34] Philosophic theory brings intellectual wars, just as the desire to 'free' oneself from the Law brings religious warfare. Far from some sort of disputable mysticism, Revelation is thoroughly rational; our reasonable faith in Revelation rejoices in man's scientific discoveries, which enhance our understanding of Torah, of life.[35]

"Judaism abhors death.[36] Jews sanctify life, including the defense of life, in sharp contrast to the prototypical philosopher, Socrates, who chose death, and also unlike Nietzsche, who wanted to choose life but rejected the true Law of life, confusing this with the law of the jungle.[37] This choice of life, this fear of death, brings with it the fear of God's righteous anger, which is the beginning of wisdom and the obverse of hatred of evil − of pride, arrogance, perverted speech.[38]   Righteous fear and hatred inspire Jews to speak fearlessly against powerful evildoers. Nathan censures David, the King anointed by the Lord, while the philosopher Xenophon makes his poet Simonides attempt to convince the tyrant Hiero that wise men and tyrants can be friends.[39]

"Unlike modern secularists who prattle of 'creativity,' meaning the imposition of their own eccentricities, the man of the Law's indomitable will serves the community of the Law, and thereby serves God. The man of the Law sees that creativity requires obedience to the national will that desires God's law. God's law makes this nation − not the other way around.[40] The realm of the community of Law, the life of the community of Law, is above all in speech, in hearing, in prophecy addressed to the community.[41]   This community at times allowed itself to be ruled by kings, at times not. The kings were in some respects suspect, too much like the rulers of other nations.[42] But in any event the Sanhedrin or supreme court truly ruled the nation; in Greek terms, the true Israel was and is an aristocracy, an aristocracy of interpreters of the Law.

"The *herem* should not be confused with the Christian holy war or the Moslem *jihad*. It does not aim at religious conversion or even at imperial rule.[43] We war upon our enemies and drive them away not because we are virtuous but because our enemies are evil.[44] This refusal to succumb to self-righteousness enables us to help our enemies, but helping enemies in no way contradicts lawful warfare.[45] Magnanimity toward evildoers and converting their ill-will to good will when possible is a national obligation.[46] Nonresistance to evildoers is not.

"Therefore, I reject the contention of the theologian who claimed that Judaism has 'nothing more to say to mankind.'[47] Nor do I take the ancient loss of this city as punishment for a certain kind of disbelief, as Origen did.[48] The truth was stated by the prophet Micah, who cites unbelief, bloody-minded predation, unlawful war, and many other immoral acts, as the causes for our expulsion.[49] Although religionists condemn what they believe is the latitudinarianism of the Law,[50] the history of the world only confirms that disasters ensue when men dismiss the Law either as too low or as too lofty."

"But this is not what Nicholas was saying," Mr. Falos objected. "He did not measure advantage by law, but law by advantage. Philip was asking 'Whose advantage?' and 'What is advantage?'"

"It seemed to me that Mr. Hendé said that one element of advantage, perhaps the heart of advantage, is victory," I said.

"Yes, and true victory does not saddle a man with disadvantages," Mr. Hendé added. "To win a war and gain a multitude of pains on that account is no real victory. God save us from such victories."

"True advantage inheres in true rulership?"

"Yes."

"True rulership represents genuine caretaking, however, does it not? An abused and degenerate people will only afford their ruler a multitude of pains, while a well-tended people will honor and defer to the authorities?"

"You must have been born yesterday to imagine so. A well-tended people will incline to insolence, and can only be made useful by being compelled to do battle for their country. A ruler must therefore be 'unjust,' to use your language, while enforcing justice upon his people. Justice is nothing but a high-minded form of innocence; the real virtue, the real prudence, lies in knowing how to be unjust. war teaches this even better than peace."

168

"War teaches the need for national unity, does it not? For a faction-ridden country will fight itself more than its enemy?"

"Indeed so: War itself is a great unifier of men."

"But not always: the Germans owed their defeat in the First World War in part to internal faction, yes?"[51]

Mr. Hendé admitted this, somewhat grudgingly I thought.

"And a man divided against himself − a man who seeks out his neighbor's wife, yet must do so in secret, for their discovery would ruin his reputation, which forms the basis of his power, and his power and prestige are perhaps what makes him so attractive to women in the first place − would not this underhanded overreacher live in constant tension, or self-faction?"[52]

At this Mr. Hendé paled slightly, and seemed to grope for words. I continued: "Surely such an unjust man would finally paralyze himself, lacking a truly coherent character? And an unjust country would fail in its wars, for the same reason?"

"I suppose this is your way of raising a glass to the liberation, Monsieur Soffron," Mr. Hendé said.[53]

"In my own small way, Mr. Hendé. A liberation is only as good as those who are liberated, after all."

ii

At this point, I was indeed ready to reach for some wine. But Simon Liteson was not satisfied with ending the discussion here.

"Philip, do you wish to persuade us truly that justice can coexist with war? If so, you must show not that successful war requires some minimal degree of justice, nor even that war might sometimes serve justice. You must prove that war can be right in itself, choiceworthy in itself. For while I am ready to concede that war may have its virtues, I say its vices far outweigh them. And while war may sometimes serve justice, it does so all too seldom and, in any event, does so in ways no Christian can allow. God, who sees all and into all, will see and condemn the sins of any warrior, 'just' or unjust. 'Just war' is a figleaf, a convention, an instance of sinfulness trying to make itself invisible."

Before I could reply, Andrew Docksman leaned forward. "My good friend Simon, do not value justice in war so lightly. Our Lord does not condemn all war, and our tradition upholds the duty to engage in just wars. As Legnano teaches us, war is a contention arising from something discordant to human desire; desire then attempts to exclude the discordancy, that is, to make peace. War is either spiritual or corporeal. Spiritual war can be heavenly, as when Lucifer led the assaulted upon God, or human, as when an evil man tempts a good one, or a man confronts the evil within himself. Corporeal war can be universal, as when the divinely established powers on earth that tend toward good take lawful actions aimed at securing peace in the world. Corporeal war can also be particular − as in the protection of one's life and the lives of family and neighbors.[54] In the words of Suarez, war is 'opposed to an unjust peace, for it is more truly a means of attaining peace that is real and secure.'[55] Given the fact that sovereigns (whether consisting of one man or of every man) have no earthly superiors, and yet some sovereigns and would-be sovereigns are depraved, war is a kind of ultimate appeal by means of action to a just Providence."[56]

"I am sure that all Christians recognize the depravity of man," Simon replied. "The question is, how shall we treat this depravity?[57] Is war a sort of dangerous countertoxin that cures disease,[58] or is it a symptom of disease? The New Testament makes no distinction between just and unjust war, defensive and offensive wars; this is a distinction without a difference. The military spirit seizes the public mind in opposition to the Holy Spirit.[59] The military spirit is the spirit of Satan, of evil, of destruction. War is the concentration of all human crimes; whatever nation wins, Satan gains the real victory, extending his kingdom of darkness."[60]

I asked, "You do not dispute, however, Andrew's contention that there can be human *spiritual* war?"

"I affirm it. Christian warfare is spiritual to the core. It's a war of peaceful actions and of words that express *the* Word.[61] It can be, as Andrew said, either social or individual − a conflict of two or more wills or a conflict within one soul. Christian warfare is, as the early Friends used to say, the Lamb's War of peaceful soldiers, a conflict of evil against goodness symbolized by the Cross. We must follow Jesus to Jerusalem, where He became subject to the spiritual powers that rule the world, and take up the Cross ourselves.[62] The Cross symbolizes self-sacrificing love of neighbors, and of enemies perhaps most of all.[63] To the historian who asks, 'Why do so many saintly men become soldiers?'[64] I answer that religious zeal or even 'saintliness' − if that is what it is − will not suffice. Knowledge of the Gospel is also needed, that intimate knowledge beyond mere recitation of words, a knowledge that issues in unswerving, self-sacrificing actions.[65] Those in whom the Holy Spirit has already subdued sin covet no worldly kingdoms; much less will we fight for them.[66] Our own suffering inflicts wounds on the conscience of our enemy.[67] In this conflict Christians recover some of our true nature, reconquering not merely Jerusalem but Eden.[68]   And this reconquest foreshadows the still greater triumph promised us in the Book of Revelation ."

"I am less interested in the fact that many professing Christians become soldiers as in the fact that many early Quakers had been soldiers."[69]

"This goes back still further. The early Church appropriated and spiritualized the battle songs of the Old Testament."[70]

"Indeed. Perhaps because both Jews and Romans were fighters, and a certain spiritedness remains in spirituality?"

"Perhaps. But if so this is rarer today. Among Friends, there is concern that the activists are spiritually shallow, the spiritual regrettably quietist."[71]

"A comment on the character of modern politics, no doubt. Returning to the subject of what Legnano calls corporeal wars, would you say that wars are occasioned by the love of money, a love occasioned by love of the body?[72] That war arises when the city oversteps the bounds of the materially necessary?"[73]

"The latter, yes. As for love of the body, it is natural and good. The purposes for which God created human beings may be seen in their bodies; we are unfeathered bipeds, as the joke goes, but more important we are unclawed, unfanged ones, endowed with speech and reason, dependent upon our parents longer than any other creature.[74] War originates in hunting, as men descend from vegetarianism to killing animals then to murdering harmless men, using artificial tools, weapons, to destroy their own true nature.[75] Not love of the body but lust and pride tempt men to war; the more complex the civilization, the greater the temptations and the more powerful the weapons.[76] All the arts are perverted to this end − ceremonies, music, even children's toys incite militaristic feelings."[77]

"If these feelings are in fact artificial," I said, "they seem to be of surprising longevity. If we can take Homer as a sort of guide to war, we do see the results of lust and pride, or perhaps simply love and honor: Paris dishonors Menelaos, who seeks justice or perhaps revenge; Agamemnon dishonors Chryses, a priest of Apollo; Achilles accuses Agamemnon of greed; Agamemnon returns Chryseis to Chryses, satisfying Apollo and his priest, but then dishonors his accuser Achilles in exactly the same way; Achilles' mother, Thetis, intercedes with Zeus, thus putting him in conflict with his consort Hera; Achilles, meanwhile, kills many of the sons of Troy's Priam, dishonoring his son Hektor. These cycles of dishonor and revenge stop in two ways, one divine, the other human. Questioned by Hera, Zeus threatens her with physical injury, 'wrenching her heart to obedience' because Zeus is 'far too strong for any.' Achilles and Priam, by contrast, overcome their anger by magnanimity, a kind of large-souledness that forgives out of supreme strength of character."[78]

"Yes, but the 'human' way of Homer rests upon a sort of pride. Human beings need and can take a divine way of kindliness. This human *and* divine way, first embodied in Jesus, the Son of Man, finally works more effectively than the 'divine' tyranny of Zeus."[79]

"But surely the effectiveness of the Son also owes something to the prospect of eternal punishments devised by the Father?"

Simon shifted uneasily. "Such punishments are for God to devise and implement, not men. Christians, as human beings not gods, replace pride with humility, selfishness with love of neighbor, revenge with patience − love of world with love of God.[80] Warriors mistakenly attempt to overcome the fear of death with anger. Their anger grows so great it even overcomes fear of God, as Homer himself saw, when he made Achilles wrestle with a god."[81]

"Still, punishments and rewards imply a choice for an end, not an end in itself. Would anyone obey the laws of a god who bestowed rewards and inflicted punishments arbitrarily?"

Simon could not in good conscience disagree. I continued, "At first glance, the question of *human* rule or self-government seems to involve the problem of combining some of the force enjoyed by Zeus with some of friendliness of Achilles. Given the possibility of war — even an austere nation may find itself threatened — there will be some need of a class of men who knew how to fight. These, one hopes, will do good to their friends, their fellow-citizens, and harm only real enemies. To identify real enemies, they will need some prudence, yes? To avoid making mistakes?"

"If such a class of men were necessary, this would be true."

"And human beings may wage war not simply out of vice but because they are rational creatures who may judge resistance morally preferable to submission?"[82]

"*Reason* may bring them to this conclusion, although the Law of Love cannot."[83]

"And, again simply in human terms for the moment, war may actually compel men to be just and moderate, while the good fortune and leisure of peacetime can make them arrogant?"[84]

"Monsieur Hendé said so."

"I recall that he preferred the word 'discipline' to justice and to moderation."

"True."

"And the nature of each thing tends to oppose those things that are against its nature, to as it were hunt and/or evade whatever threatens its own nature?"[85]

"Yes, although there are many different ways to hunt, or shall I say fish, for men."[86]

"And the actual consequences of corporeal wars range from continued animosity and renewed war to reconciliation and peace?"[87]

"No, I really see war breeding war, violence begetting violence. Peace after war lasts only until the conquered party regains its strength. Defeated nations build up their strength with exercises fueled by the spirit of vengefulness. And to counter this, the victor can only impose another kind of war, the war of the tyrant on his subjects."[88]

"This is indeed a great danger, but is it necessarily the case? Almost every existing nation-state shows the results of lingering animosities *and* enduring reconciliations − else those states could not survive for long. And while *continual* warfare endangers political freedom, as the history of the Roman Republic makes clear,[89] perhaps the inclination to wage war continually is rather a pre-existing defect of the regime? And the pressure of war may bring out unsuspected defects?[90] Perhaps we should look to the character of the regime to see if it promotes reconciliation after war, and properly channels aggressiveness during peacetime?"

"War must be avoided altogether. First, it is at bottom nothing better than a gamble, as even that great warrior Julius Caesar admitted.[91] Second, while it may exalt the rulers, its hardships fall mostly on the people, whether or not they sought it.[92] Finally, war itself combines fear with bloodlust; the joys it seems to offer are like the glitter of brittle glass.[93] War, as Barth has written, reveals the fundamentally chaotic character of the political will-to-peace, the inability of would-be self-governing men to be masters without becoming at the same time slaves, to preserve themselves without destroying themselves."[94]

"Is war any more a gamble than nonresistance, or nonviolent resistance?"

"In its worldly affects, perhaps not. But nonresistance keeps our own hands clean of blood, and that may be of inestimable value spiritually."

"Salvation depends first on faith, not on works?"

"Yes of course."

"Then a faithful warrior will be no more a gambler than a faithful nonresistant, in body or in soul? And war need not combine fear with bloodlust, but may spur men to overcome their fear, and to cherish life more deeply?"

"War is sweet to those who have not tried it − and to those who have tried it too often."[95]

"I have never asserted the sweetness of war. And with respect to its hardships, I suppose an insurance broker would not always charge lower premiums to a peasant than to a king, though the soldier's premiums would be highest of all."

"What must still be justified is not the courageous endurance of war's hardships but the willful infliction of them.[96] Why is murder less immoral for being widespread?"[97]

"Logically, war need not involve killing, yes? If scientists developed a usable weapon to temporarily weaken soldiers without harming them, a war could be won that way?"

"Yes, but this is dreaming."[98]

"No, this is theorizing. We are trying to isolate the essence of war, and we have now established that killing is not its essence. Overpowering or physical compulsion is the essence of corporeal war. Killing is only the principal means used in order to compel, throughout history so far. As for the equation of killing with murder, my understanding is not that warriors condone killing because it is widespread – a warrior might also condone capital punishment, which need not occur frequently. Nor could the social acceptability or legality of war truly justify it. There must be some other justification?"

"The justification today is usually 'self-defense,' although that justification is hypocritical nine times out of ten."

"Whether it is hypocritical or not is irrelevant to the argument, however? In view of the hypocrisy of many professed Christians, whose hypocrisy is no reflection on Christianity itself?"

"Granted."

"Self-defense or, more ambitiously, the promotion of justice may require killing under some circumstances?"

"The point is, defense of the body by killing other bodies perverts the soul from its true function, which is loving kindness toward God and neighbor, self and enemy. Killing may sometimes defend successfully, even promote justice very occasionally. But to want to defend your own body and the bodies of family, friends, and neighbors so much that you destroy other human bodies to do it is to give way not to measured, natural love of the body but to lust, unregulated love of body. It is to exalt bodily love over Godly love."

"You supremely loving man, do you propose to take this love into the world?"

"We are obligated to do so. The search for peace has been a wandering without end, peace itself tantalizing, to be had finally only when Jesus Christ returns.[99] But even Augustine, who sought to justify war, acknowledged that peacemaking is more blessed than war not only in personal but in political life.[100] History, as superintended by God, has itself taught men no lesson more insistently: To spurn the Gospel of Christ leads to nothing but destruction.[101] But to live the real substance of religion is to harmonize fully principle with practice.[102] Peace stands for a way of life, a way pursued, as Joan Fry once wrote, 'in our own souls, in our family life, in our business relations, our public life, and finally in the great world of nations.'"[103]

"If this were so, then the strongest international agreements are those involving the least compulsion?"

"As is the case: without mutual consent, treaties are nothing but pieces of paper."

"But is this not *also* because there is not always effective enforcement — as there is, for example, when individuals sign a contract within civil society? Even if I agree that what Americans call a 'handshake deal' can be the strongest, what about the middling situation, where most of our public life tends to take place?"

"Christianity requires more than middling virtue."

"No doubt, but how often does it get it?"

"Whenever Christians are truly Christian."

"Then principle and practice meet only with difficulty?"

"Only with the assistance of the Holy Spirit."

"And, given the failings of even sincere Christians, this assistance is not a constant?"

"Only because the human will is inconstant."

"The human will's inconstancy then makes the union of principle and practice less than likely on many occasions?"

"Compulsion is also less than reliable on many occasions, as the Romans learned when they tried to eradicate Christians."

"They did so in no prolonged, comprehensive way. In Japan authorities repressed converts successfully. On the Fiji Islands, Christians were nearly eradicated until they ceased being nonresistants.[104] This is not to say that we should confuse victory or survival with virtue,[105], but rather that principle and practice do not always cohere as tightly as we might like. We need to think about how to respond to this regrettable fact. We need to consider what kind of education is fitting for the Christian warrior. A young person must be cared for with respect to his opinions, as they will crystallize and often remain unchanged – or else violently break."

Andrew, who had been listening to our conversation with great attention, agreed with this. "Over the centuries, the Christian Church has acknowledged the need for such education, based upon sound theology."

I replied, "And Christian theology firmly teaches that good things come from God, evil things from wills turned away from God; that God is eternal and does not change because He acts and is not acted upon; that only the truth sets us free and that Satan is the prince of lies. These teachings form the basis of the Christian warrior's education?"

"I agree with you completely."

iii

"About theology, then, Andrew," I said, "did I understand you to say that both Scripture and Church tradition upheld the possibility of justice in war?"

"The New Testament does not deny it, the Old Testament confirms it, and our tradition elaborates on that possibility."

"Church tradition consists primarily of reasoning upon Scripture and the lessons of experience over nearly two millenia, both guided by the Holy Spirit?".

"Precisely."

"But many different men claim guidance of the Holy Spirit, and some are lying or deluded?"

"Yes."

"And the lessons of experience will appear very different, not only depending upon experience but upon how one thinks about experience?"

"Necessarily."

"So therefore the bedrock, so to speak, of tradition is the Word as recorded in Scripture?"

"Yes. That bedrock was created by the Holy Spirit."

"And we know this first of all from Scripture itself, its self-explanation as it were?"

"Yes."

"Then in order to know how to educate Christian warriors on the subject of war, we must consider Scripture with conscientious care. Perhaps we should proceed to do so, as you and Simon evidently understand the Scriptural teaching on war in very different ways."

They assented to this, although Simon cautioned that the Holy Spirit's influence is decisive; "without it we will run into a legalistic reading of Scripture with no real life in it. The comfort and truth of the Holy Spirit was promised to the Apostles by Jesus, for the time after Jesus returned to the Father.[106] This promise was spoken to give peace and courage to the Apostles, and, by extension, to all of His disciples in future ages.[107] This is especially important when we try to think about war, because the New Testament has so little to say explicitly on the subject.[108] We must look not only to the letter of the Scriptures, but to their principles and spirit, which condemn not only contemporary evils but our own.[109] Although I admit the New Testament contains no direct command against participation in war, its overall meaning is pacific.[110] Christians fight not against flesh and blood but against the spiritual hosts of evil who rule evil men; the gospel of peace arms us with the shield of faith, the sword of the Spirit, and the helmet of salvation for battle against the Father of Lies and of Murder.[111] In this battle we do not fear evil, even loss of life, because we risk our lives for Jesus' sake, whose love sustains us.[112] The modern call for 'self-preservation' or survival is utterly unChristian; both the notion of physical survival at all costs and the illusion of self-preservation, or peace as anything other than a gift from God, are repugnant.[113] The peace of Christianity is identical to the Hebrew *Shalom*, meaning completeness, the completeness that can only come through unity under God, obedience to the Creator who formed us and all else; it has nothing to do with *shalvah*, mere rest or ease and supposed security, which leads to destruction."[114]

"But in that case," Andrew said, "a just war is an act of peace, because the Creator commands His people to fight just wars."

"But the Son commands otherwise. Christians do not emulate the manly soldier; they humble themselves as children, forgiving their brothers not once, not three times, but seventy times seven, that is, beyond practical calculation."[115]

"Brothers are one thing; not all are true Christians. When soldiers came to John the Baptist and asked 'What shall we do?' he did not tell them to abandon their arms. He told them to 'Intimidate no one nor accuse falsely and be satisfied with your pay.'[116] Pacifists who argue that war involves intimidation, ergo, John is prohibiting war, ignore the obvious point that John addresses the soldiers' police functions and not their warmaking."[117]

"They are not necessarily ignoring that point. They may be affirming that regulated, lawful, police functions are licit, whereas warfare, which is scarcely regulated, is not. Also, John the Baptist worked under the Mosaic code; I am concerned solely with the new dispensation of Jesus, which extended and perfected that code.[118] When John baptized Jesus, God's spirit came down from the heavens as a dove, the only bird allowed as a sacrificial offering in Levitical law, and thus a symbol of peaceful martyrdom, not predation or war."[119]

Andrew and Simon began to discuss the character of Christian lawfulness and its relation to *halakha*, so I asked, "Am I mistaken, or was Jesus understood to be an *archegos*, or what we would call in English a founder? The word derives from the Greek *arche*, meaning both 'form' and 'origin,' and is often mistranslated 'leader' or even 'captain.'"[120]

"Yes, Jesus is 'the *Archegos* who delivers them perfect through sufferings' in Hebrews 2:10," Simon quoted. "Also, in the Gospel of Matthew Jesus is described prophetically as a governor who will 'shepherd' God's people Israel – guide, guard, and feed them. The angels told shepherds of our Lord's birth; they were men under the rabbinic ban because their isolation from the rest of Jewish society removed them from proper regulation.[121] This Founder's life, not quite inside the Jewish community, and his sacrificial death renewed the Covenant of God with Israel and extended it to the New Israel whose citizens are Christians, bringing peace among them.[122] This new or renewed law supersedes the old, as may be seen in the Gospel of Matthew when the *Archegos* raises from death the daughter of an *archon*, a ruler, whose father's authority stopped at death's door.[123] Jesus' life-giving authority spurns the temptations of the death-dealer, Satan, and points to nonviolence.[124] Only He who is without sin may cast stones, even at the guilty. He takes the place of the guilty in His sacrificial death, and, since His death, no other killing is now permissible. To ignore this teaching, to reject this sacrifice, will lead to our own rejection and judgment by Jesus."[125]

"All true," Andrew replied, "except for one detail. The Chorus of Heavenly Host sing, 'Glory in highest places to God and on earth peace among men of goodwill.'[126] Among men of bad will, and among men some of whose wills are bad and some good, peace will not obtain. *Then* the Baptist's moderate and law-abiding soldiers will prove most helpful."

"The Founder's founding speech contradicts the spirit of militarism and affirms the spirit of nonresistance. So does the example of His life.[127] On the mountain he blesses the poor in spirit. The very act of blessing, the celebration of blessedness or *makaroi*, contrasts with the pagan quest for happiness, eudaimonism; faith and love, not knowledge and spiritedness, acknowledgment of the need for grace, not self-sufficiency, conquer the very spirit of war, of death.[128] Peacemakers are to be called the Sons of God.[129] Peacemakers do not oppose evil, do not demand an eye for an eye, but turn the other cheek when slapped, give to the one who sues, go the extra mile, give to those who ask — loving enemies as well as neighbors and praying for persecutors."[130]

I said, "The concept of law implies limits. To make a law of love boundless is to convert it to a sentiment — an imaginary one at that, given the limitations of real sentiments. What are the limits of the law of love?"

Andrew was quick to offer an answer. "The law of love enunciated by Our Lord in the Sermon on the Mount refers to the interior disposition of the heart rather than to any exterior act. In our actions we must often conduct ourselves with what Augustine calls 'a sort of kindly harshness'..."

"As distinguished from what Machiavelli calls 'pious cruelty'?"

"As sharply distinguished. We need to act for the welfare of unwilling souls, not merely their bodily pleasures and pain, their bodily life or death.[131]

'Resist not evil' means, inwardly, do not take pleasure in vengeance; it does not mean that we are not to correct our erring fellow-men, forcefully if necessary.[132] If we do not do so, personal safety, private property, and finally the whole social structure, the very possibility of social structure, would dissolve.[133] What is more, a slap on the face, the loss of a coat, a walk of an extra mile, and generosity to the needy are no more than incidents of everyday personal life; they are not invasion, financial ruin, slavery or grand theft."[134]

Simon preferred a different explanation. "The law of love − to love God with all your heart, soul, and understanding, and to love your neighbor as yourself − is not a law in the conventional sense. In Galatians 3, 15-19 we learn that the Jewish law was added to the original covenant between God and Israel, some 430 years later; the law was ordained by angels, not directly by God, and was imposed as a response to the nation's transgressions. Jesus renewed the original covenant, superseding the intervening code as surely as faith supersedes knowledge of law. Thus we *are* commanded to love infinitely, never to resist evil whether it is a slap on the face or sword thrust to the belly. Jesus' own actions confirms that these were not 'idealistic' platitudes but real commands for the real world. The Cross was willed. It was a moral and political choice, which all Christians are called to imitate, in things big and small."[135]

"In so doing," Andrew replied, "they would be undermining the justice of the social order itself − which we are never commanded to do."

"Although there is a sense in which peacemaking precedes justice − namely, that we are not allowed to undertake a 'just war' supposedly for the sake of peace[136] and we are to conquer evil by good, leaving vengeance to God[137] − in the most important sense all Christians should affirm that loving faithfulness is most just. The Biblical term, righteousness, has the same root as justice. Our redemption in Christ 'justifies' us before God; faith itself is righteous or just, and this faith brings us peace with God. Peace with God may bring on spiritual war with men; spiritual war may bring physical suffering, which brings patience; patience builds character, which produces hope − itself justified as the Holy Spirit pours God's love into us. Thus we become even more than righteous or just men. A Christian becomes the good man, the *agathou*.[138] Not only individuals but nations have a conscience, a law 'written in the hearts of them' (Romans 2, 15). Although too often the nations seek only food, drink and clothing, Jesus tells the nations not to be anxious for their lives but to seek first the Kingdom and righteousness of God, after which material necessities shall be added.[139] No man of God in the New Testament ever kills, even for the very best of causes."[140]

"No man of God whose actions and words are fully detailed in the New Testament occupies a position of public authority that would entitle him to kill," Andrew said. "After becoming a man of God, Saul becomes Paul."

"Is this not revealing?"

"Yes, it is. And the same Paul writes that we should live in peace with all men *so far as this is possible.* This refers not only to the physical impossibility of peace, but its moral impossibility at times.[141] The command to make peace, if extended to nations, refers to good-faith efforts to seek peaceful settlements before going to war. It does not preclude forcefully acting on the righteous anger of love if these efforts are rebuffed.[142] We may surely distinguish between lawful killing that expresses and enforces the respect for life, and murder, which disdains life and arrogates to the murder sovereignty over it."[143]

"But the destruction of a living body precludes all correction of the soul."

"True, but this does not prohibit just execution, in civil society or in war, because the evils inflicted *and suffered* by an evil man may well outweigh, and be more certain, than the hypothetical good anticipated in sparing him."[144]

"This is to hold the divine command hostage to fallible calculation. Vengeance is not for man; Christian scripture could not be clearer."[145]

"Paul clearly permits Christians to punish disobedience."[146]

"This refers to excommunication from the Church, not death at the hands of public authorities."

"The divine law that animates the Church forbids voluntary self-destruction. If you refuse to defend yourself effectively from death, you are *de facto* a suicide. Divine law does not utterly overthrow any natural law or even any natural impulse; it regulates them. Hunger, thirst, sexual desire, and self-preservation are natural instincts not forbidden, which would be an absurdity, but governed by the law of love.[147] Our Lord sets down gradations of punishment: servants who abuse power when the master is away are to be severely punished, 'placed with the unfaithful'; servants who fail to prepare for the master's return are to be beaten; servants who do not know their master's will are to receive a light beating. Jesus brings not peace on earth, simply, but division − peace or *shalom* being completeness or unity.[148] As in civil so in international society: The author of Hebrews praises Gideon, Barak, Samson, Jepthah, David, and Samuel for becoming 'strong in war' and 'making the armies of foreigners yield.'"[149]

"Corporal punishment does not necessarily entail capital punishment. And Paul is not Jesus."

"Our Lord himself breathes not a word of condemnation in the parables in which he uses soldiers and rulers to illustrate His principles and practices.[150] And while these illustrations do not imply approval..."

"Any more than the prediction that the day of the Lord will come like a thief in the night implies approval of robbery!"[151]

"...there is no condemnation of these practices, as there is of theft in the Ten Commandments...."

"And of killing."

"...and indeed Jesus may thereby effectually commend the prudence of men who have responsibility for the good order of civil society.[152] Political responsibility may well include the lawful destruction of human lives when the character of those lives endangers the lives of others, whether individuals or the nation as a whole. While the story of the Good Samaritan is a foundation stone of our religion, Jesus does not tell us, in the Sermon on the Mount or anywhere else, what the Samaritan should have done had he arrived while the beating occurred."[153]

"No one can know. I expect he should have attempted to restrain the victim's attackers by non-injurious force, but surely not with lethal force. Had He killed in defense of the Samaritan, He would have prevented a nonfatal crime lethally, a violation of His precepts *and* of prudence."

"The point is, we do not know. And in the case of a governor or a soldier, we do know what needs to be done. One thing that needs to be done is taxation in order to raise money to support an army. Our Lord requires us to pay taxes without differentiating between the use of these revenues for peace or for war."[154]

"Nor does he distinguish between the use of the revenues by Caesar for gladiatorial sports, lavish feasts, the payment of prostitutes, or any other vicious practice.[155] We owe Caesar his coins, upon which he stamps his effigy; we owe God our whole persons, upon which He stamped *His* effigy or image."[156]

I asked, "This ignores the middle ground, the human body. Do we owe it to God, or to Caesar?"

"To 'Caesar,' Andrew said, "in the sense that we can constitute a rightful sovereignty or 'Caesar' – a civil society that needs our physical protection."[157]

"The body is created by God, not Caesar, and is therefore owed to God," Simon countered. "At the resurrection, body and soul will be unitedly saved or damned."

"In the meantime," Andrew said, "This body has needs in this world, needs that are supplied by civil society, which is by no means condemned by Our Lord. On the contrary, He requires us to support it. Even religious institutions may require forceful defense or self-defense, as when Jesus expelled moneychangers and merchants from the Temple in Jerusalem."[158]

"The force Jesus used was directed against tables and beasts. Even if He did strike any of the men – and there's no evidence he did – he never used anything approaching lethal force.[159] What is more, while there is no explicit condemnation of warfare itself in the New Testament, James and Paul do explicitly condemn the passions that cause wars. James teaches that wars and fights are caused by pleasures 'soldiering in your members,' that 'the wrath of a man does not work the righteousness of God.' Paul lists enmities, strife, jealousy, angers, and rivalries centrally among the works of the flesh; kindness is central in his enumeration of the fruits of the Spirit, and peace is among them. Those who deny the Christ are 'by nature children of wrath,' but Jesus Christ is *our peace*, who, 'by abolishing in His flesh the law of commandments and decrees, in order that out of two he might create one, in Himself – a new man, so making peace – and might reconcile both to God in one body through the Cross, killing enmity.'"[160]

"The observation that passions cause wars does not make all wars unjust; an injured or threatened nation need not fall prey to lusts in order to defend itself. Even non-Christians understand this, warning of warlike passions without condemning all war.[161] The Church in Paul's time had no public authority, nor much protection by or even from public authority. When Christians acceded to public authority, they found themselves with responsibilities that included military defense.[162] And even in the first years of our faith, soldiers were never denounced. Our Lord is far more critical of lawyers than of soldiers.[163] Paul accepts the protection of 400 soldiers, 70 horsemen, and 200 spearmen on his way to Caesarea, with not a whisper of disapproval.[164] In Augustine's words, had Christianity condemned war, 'the soldiers in the Gospel who asked how they were to be saved should have been given the advice to throw down their arms and give up military service entirely.'[165] Far from condemning one centurion, Our Lord heals his servants, commends his faith, and does not so much as murmur dissent when the centurion compares his authority to His own....'[166]

"Yes. The centurion is to his soldiers as Jesus is to diseases![167] He draws them out for their destruction."

"As I recall the centurion also compared his soldiers and his slave to Jesus' soldiers."

"Solely in faith, not in acts. It is one thing to be praised for faith, another to be commended for deeds.[168]

"And then there was the devout centurion Cornelius, a devout man sent by God to find Peter, never told to leave the military profession. Peter commends Cornelius not only as a man who fears God but as one who 'does what is right.'"[169]

"Censuring Cornelius would have been gratuitous, as he was about to be filled with the Holy Spirit. We have no reason to suppose this did not change his way of life.[170] Silence may well mean disapproval, not tacit praise or toleration: unlike the contemporaneous Zealots, Jesus never counseled resort to violent force; further, no practicing Jew could perform military service in the Roman legions on religious grounds, anyway, so such counsels would have been entirely superfluous."[171]

"Given this silence, it makes more sense to attribute the anti-military animus of early Christians to the pagan religiosity of the Roman Army.[172] Soldiers have never been refused baptism or excommunicated from the Church; indeed, historically, one is impressed by the diversity of vocations that animate the faithful.[173] The blood of countless soldier-martyrs has established a doctrine more powerful than any speculative interpretation of ambiguous Scripture."[174]

"If the practice of the professedly faithful were decisive, there could be no test of faith. If the Holy Spirit comes to a man in military service, he should leave; plurality of vocations does not entail promiscuity of vocations.[175] Jesus did not explicitly interfere with civil and political institutions, but rather inculcated principles that, by their eventual universalization by the grace of God, would revolutionize those institutions. He knew that physical force only apes real, spiritual force.[176] And indeed, how could it be lawful to make a vocation of the sword, when Jesus tells Peter, 'all those who take up the sword shall perish by the sword'? Jesus thereby prohibited killing even in the best conceivable cause, the defense of the Son of Man."[177]

"How many take up the sword and do not perish by the sword — Peter himself being the most prominent example."[178]

"Obviously, we should not take this too literally. Jesus merely prophesies future misinterpretations and distortions of the message of the Holy Spirit, and their general consequence."[179]

"Our Lord tells Peter to put his sword back in its sheath not because He objects to violence but because He wants to 'drink the cup which the Father has given me.' The best conceivable 'cause' is *too* good to be defended by the sword, and needs no all-too-human defense. Also, Peter took the sword without authoritative sanction — from Our Lord or even from temporal magistrates."[180]

"Then why does Jesus teach, 'My kingdom is not of this world; if my kingship were of this world, my attendants would have struggled so that I should not be delivered to the Jews'?"[181]

"To say that *my* kingdom is not of this world is not to say that Christians must not function *in* this world. I should think rather that Jesus implies here that war is *not* wrong, only war or violence in this particular circumstance.[182] Further, Jesus himself tells those of his men who are unarmed to buy a sword; among them they already have two swords, which will suffice as long as they are together, but each will need one for self-defense as soon as they disperse."[183]

"This passage, the subject of so much controversy, does not lend itself to such easy solution. It is as likely that Jesus' discussion-ending sentence, 'It is enough,' means 'Enough of this nonsense!' And the key point is, except for Peter, whom Jesus rebuked, the Apostles never used swords whether in defense of Jesus or of themselves, at anytime.[184] Jesus rather calls His disciples to overcome evil with good, as good acts in response to evil will heap coals of fire on an evildoer's head, burning his conscience."[185]

"Yet in the very next passage, Paul affirms the authority of magistrates...."[186]

"Think of Jesus! Think of Jesus weeping for Jerusalem! 'Would that even this day thou knewest the things for peace. But now they are hidden from thine eyes.' The chief Jewish priests and officers claimed that Jesus had deified Himself, setting Himself against Caesar, committing a capital crime. In the next breath they said *they* had no king but Caesar, an ignoble lie or a confession of faithlessness, a blasphemy in *Jewish* terms.[187] To defer to Caesar brings no security, no peace – only destruction."

I intervened to say, "Perhaps the thought should be expressed more cautiously? The ancient Spartans deferred to their magistrates, and their regime lasted for centuries. Xenophon tells us that their 'most important men show the utmost deference to the magistrates: they pride themselves on their humility.'"[188]

"What is more," Andrew said, "there is no inconsistency between Paul and Jesus. The authority of magistrates is 'by God,' and existing magistrates 'have been ordained by God.' Resisters will be judged, and the magistrate 'does not bear the sword in vain' but rather serves as 'an avenger for [God's] wrath on the one who practices evil.' Because 'all have sinned and fall short of the glory of God' all of us need redemption through our Christ. We *also* need a strong temporal authority to punish our sinful acts and, better, to dissuade us from committing them in the first place. We should defer to the authorities not only out of fear of their wrath but for conscience's sake. There is no contradiction between such deference and true freedom, as governors sent by God punish evildoers and praise those who do right, those who act freely in bondage to God. As for the kings and magistrates themselves, we are to pray for them; in turn, they are to protect us, as when Paul was saved from murderers because he was a Roman citizen. The very prophecy of the destruction of the Temple in Jerusalem teaches us that destruction will occur because 'the love of the many' for God and for each other 'will grow cold,' and it will grow cold because 'lawlessness will increase.' The fact that Our Lord refrained from punishing those He met on earth simply reflects His own purpose on earth. He did not collect taxes, either, and yet we know He commanded us to pay them."[189]

"The issue is much more complicated than you say," Simon replied. "The diversity of Christian responses to the State throughout history reflects the diversity of responses of the earliest Christians.[190] Simple obedience was not possible, for, as Tacitus remarks, Neronian Rome was 'where all things hideous and shameful from every part of the world find their center and become popular.'"[191]

"Antiquity's California?" I asked, in a helpful spirit.

"In the Book of Revelation, the Roman Empire, with its Emperor-worship, is clearly a Satanic power deserving of destruction."

"And so it is," Andrew said, "insofar as the emperor rebelled against God and deified himself. This does not mean that legitimate institutions that do not arrogate to themselves 'total' authority are to be denigrated"[192]

"To commit an act of war is precisely to arrogate to oneself total authority. In Romans 13 Paul refers to civil authority in its police function; the sword is a symbol of authority, only, in what was then a peaceful empire. We are to obey the civil authority so long as it commands nothing evil, but Christians may not kill. It is evil for human beings to kill, although God, the giver of life, may also take it away. In *this* sense, our most deferential of religions is also the most revolutionary, because Christians shall not act as pagans do, in or out of government. Christianity means an entirely peaceful social revolution. Christians know that sin lives in the human will, which is not really altered by punishment. Only the loving Holy Spirit changes the will —

only it is literally radical, getting at the root of human conduct. This is the teaching of grace."[193]

"A noble teaching," I said, "which as it were selects the classes of citizens within each country who are most fit for ruling and for being ruled."

"Simon, are you saying that Christians may not participate in government at all?" Andrew asked, with a trace of indignation.[194] "Nothing could be farther from our tradition. While it may be true that there is no such thing in history as anarchy in the literal sense, it is also true that circumstances arise in which men destroy each other like fishes in the sea.[195] Hence the need for civil government. Civil authorities should inspire not an evil fear, a fear of evil actions by the government, but a salutary fear of just punishment by public means.[196] Such fear can, in time, alter the human will. Insofar as he participates in government, a Christian is not to be meek; he is to administer God's justice and loving wrath, without oppression, over the lives, property, and other externals of his fellow citizens. He does this precisely because he lives and works on earth not for himself alone but for his neighbor.[197] Faith in Christ does not exempt us from the duty to obey civil authority, unless we are commanded to do evil. While the civil authority does not have to be Christian, it can be Christian, and Christian citizens do have the right to revolt against an unjust civil authority.[198]. Scripture tells of kings who converted to Christianity, and never suggests that they abdicated upon doing so."[199]

"I do not say that Christians may not participate in government at all. I say they must participate as Christians – as nonresistant, nonviolent men and women of faith. If they cannot rule on Christian terms they must utterly renounce the ambition to rule until such time as they can rule on Christian terms. Ruling on Christian terms will not mean attempting to enforce doctrinal beliefs. It will mean ruling morally. It will mean the legal enforcement of moral behavior.[200] Christian rulers will have no private property except necessities, no more than a sustaining salary. They will mingle freely with their fellow citizens, rejecting the Pharisaical love of money and thus teaching by example that the true ruler is himself the servant of God."[201]

iv

Andrew shook his head. "We cannot serve two masters who are opposed to one another. But we can and must serve masters who govern together. Magistrates may or may not possess personal riches; they inevitably direct the riches of the government itself. Christianity only insists that they do not love these riches, this power. Not Christians but the Donatists charged the State as such with diabolism. Realistically, if Christians refuse to serve as legislators, soldiers, police, magistrates, who will? And why should Christians refuse to share the burdens, the dangers, the injuries of the whole community, as well as its benefits?[202] Civil government is necessary to habituate citizens to virtue, to help in their development as moral persons, to protect Christian institutions, and to promote general peace and tranquility. Our pilgrimage on earth requires such helps, and those who would undermine them effectively deprive citizens of their very humanity."[203]

"Yet," I said, "there are 'two kingdoms,' one earthly, one heavenly, even when they are more or less in harmony?"[204]

"Of course: 'Entangled now, mutually intermingled until the final judgment, when they will be detached from one another.' In one is God's peace, impossible to lose; the other desires its own kind of peace. In one is true justice, the republic founded and governed by Our Lord – Abel's city, not Cain's, raised not by human plans and efforts but by divine grace. The other can be Cain's city, but more often is merely Adam's – that is, erring and needful of coercive protection, prey to the lust for mastery, *libido dominatur*. To attempt to rule the earthly city by heavenly means before God's final intervention in history would effectively set wolves onto the sheep. At its best the earthly city breeds the wolfishness out of its wolves...."[205]

"Makes them into sheepdogs?"

"If you like. This lust for mastery is so strong, and the human desire for life on any terms so great, that conquered peoples often prefer to submit to it than to continue a lost struggle. A tyrant must be vicious indeed to provoke his chattel to rebel, and then they are often too weak to succeed. We settle for a pale justice, and for the chance to educate souls, evangelize for our Church. The sword given to the magistrate to protect citizens against harm shall be used to ward off evils from within and from outside as well. To say otherwise would be to eviscerate magistracy itself. We choose warfare only to bring peace, to bring that *tranquillitas ordinis* in which each human being is assigned to his proper position in society in an ordered agreement between those who command and those who obey."[206]

"Do I recall that Augustine lists eight kinds of peace, but not peace among nations?"[207]

"St. Augustine was a highly realistic man, who knew that the command to love enemies cannot mean to disarm the honest and to give the peaceable over to plunder. Evildoers who risk death in war, preying upon the innocent, deprive *themselves* of the opportunity for repentance. By refusing to defend themselves against evil men, Christians would only restrict membership of the Church – and thereby salvation – repelling decent people who choose not to place the indiscriminate love of an enemy above family, neighbors, countrymen, and even of evildoers themselves. The Hebrews clearly distinguished between *soneh*, personal enemies, and *oyev*, public enemies – in Greek *exthroi* and *polemioi*: Our Lord tells us to love personal enemies, but never exempts public enemies from punishment."[208]

"Who can rule best for such genuine peace as the earthly city can obtain?"

"A king can act more effectively than many, to bring unity; he can also tyrannize more effectively. On the other hand, polyarchy ends in tyranny, as seen in ancient Rome. A constitutional monarchy or a mixed regime ruled by law is best.[209] For while love cannot be commanded and enforced, justice can be; else we 'will embrace an anarchy that counts the world well lost for love.'[210] It is therefore up to us to support regimes that best maintain peace.[211] In this regard we should recall that for the mature Church, the preservation of property is a necessity, conducive to the practical maintenance of the civil order. While private property should be regulated, to abolish it entirely would be an act of folly inviting the acts of injustice that lead to war."[212]

"It would seem, then, that we are prepared to affirm that war in defense of a just city is a just war, that the just war will defend the virtues strengthened by the just regime including moderation, prudence, and courage."

Simon would let us go no farther. "Nonsense. This sort of talk is the sum and substance of patriotic rhetoric the world over. Patriotism is nothing more than group selfishness dressed in a robe of purple prose. It is a kind of slavery, a tool used by governments to rule humanity by dividing us into little pieces. The worst thing is, our rulers in many cases believe their own rhetoric, imagining that they're calling us to something great and good.[213] While I would not go so far as Tolstoy in condemning the State as such (some civil order is needed, and tribal communitarianism is no longer practical) Tolstoy is more right than wrong.[214] The incitement of patriotic fervor blocks the humane feelings Christianity espouses and deforms the Christian conscience. For the true Christian, the artificial *patria* of patriotism is not the real Father, and never can be. Western and Eastern civilization alike have made poetry of war-songs, miseducating their sons to imitate military conquerors whose crimes are excused by the 'greater glory' of that overblown Egoism, the State.[215] What is good for the individual soul is good for the nation; what is bad for the individual soul is bad for the nation. We must not load our sins onto the community, as if it were a mule or a scapegoat, that will haul them away. 'Country' is not Christ! 'Country' wants not to die for our sins but to fatten itself upon them.[216] 'Country' is a fatted calf that declines to be slaughtered, but wants us to slaughter and be slaughtered for its own sake."

"I am sure we should not do what you condemn," I said. "But I am struck by one of Tolstoy's questions, or rather assertions, when he writes, 'How can an Irishman in the United States express his patriotism today' – this was in the 1890s – 'when by his religion he belongs to Rome, by his birth to Ireland, and as a citizen to the United States.'[217] In retrospect, we see that citizenship can be decisive, and removes or at least moderates the tensions if the regime is well-designed. That being the case, what sort of regime, with what sort of ruler, will mirror the Christian soul, eliminating or at least rechanneling the spiritedness of nations?"

"Magistrates and other citizens should compete with other nations not in war or in wealth but in humanity, in morality," Simon replied. "It is true that a nation loves to imitate its leading citizens. Therefore let magistrates replace oppression with consent, fear with charity, personal power with the public good. The atmosphere of the armed camp is no nurturer of Christian souls. The glare of campfires reflects the anger of the souls gathered round them.[218] Christian morality is in very poor condition, if its continuance depends upon military defense. This 'defense' talk is nothing but a sham designed to increase the power of rulers. The decent Christians who join such governments only give them a moral authority they don't deserve.[219] I agree that, unlike the early Christians, we cannot leave public responsibility to others. We should not walk away...."[220]

"Cannot or should not?" I asked.

"Mostly should not. To protect justice we can *and* should use only just means. Military might is not a just means. If the means are morally low, how can the moral value of the victory be high?"[221]

"Presumably that depends upon the moral losses that would be incurred by defeat?"

"My point is, we can build a regime based upon neither materialistic eighteenth-century capitalism nor materialistic nineteenth-century communism. We can bring together the sphere of religion and economics to rule as one. Lenin on the Left and Mussolini on the Right founded economic institutions much like the old guilds, but without the spiritual foundation of redemptive love that is absolutely necessary to guide cooperation. Christianity is the religion of incarnation. We must learn to incarnate Jesus in ourselves and in our institutions. Only then will we have true peace."[222]

I was about to ask for further information about this attempt so to speak to institutionalize Christian grace, to make a synthesis of two spheres of life that usually remain distinct.[223]. But Andrew was dissatisfied with Simon's characterization of patriotism.

"Although the Greeks defined politics in terms of disparate parts of the human soul — timocracy institutionalizes spiritedness, democracy the appetites, and so on — St. Augustine defines politics in terms of love. Each regime is animated by the love of something. These things are merely worldly; in political life, nothing is sacred. But they *are* loved, not always merely coveted, and they *can* be goods, although not invaluable goods.[224] A Christian may well love his country, that community bound together under one regime. Both Jesus and St. Paul loved their country – else why weep for Jerusalem? Patriots will defend their country against enemies foreign and domestic, against the tendency of governments toward despotism.[225] If earthly peace obtains between men of good will, and good will requires sound religion, and sound religion is strengthened by sound government, this confirms the teaching of our tradition, which holds that Our Lord came not to destroy the natural law the just regime respects, but to complete it. Thus St. Augustine teaches that Rome grew not by vengeance but by pardoning the sins of the nations it conquered. Force is one thing, violence another. Force is that measure of power necessary and sufficient to defend justice. Christians must not believe as the ancient Sophists did, that we can rule by speech alone. Force is also necessary."[226]

"What kind of ruler will be needed in order to maintain the distinction between force and violence?" I asked. "Dante at first leads us to suppose that only a world-ruler would be just. The argument goes as follows: The root of injustice is greed or lust, that is, untrue love. A world-ruler by definition would possess everything. There would be nothing left for him to lust after. The only desires remaining would be good ones; the world-ruler would desire only the good for himself and for others. Yet Dante quickly adds that the world-ruler needs a charitable soul, and his regime would need law. So the question must not be so easily answered as it appears."[227]

"No, of course not. The good Christian king Saint Louis exercised Christian magnanimity in his reign, comprehending all the cardinal virtues: courage, moderation, love of truth, and love of the people, particularly the poor.[228] Still, he initiated a military crusade. And King Solomon, whose name means 'peacemaker,' was a type or foreshadowing of Our Lord; while no other ruled Israel more peacefully, dangers remained and so did the need for arms. Law-abidingness is needed, but it is not always sufficient; prudence will require forceful defense of the country, and points the Christian sovereign to prayer, to acknowledgement of his dependence upon God's providence – more needed than either dead books or live heads, as Martin Luther observes."[229]

"I believe Luther also writes that 'since the beginning of the world a wise prince is a mighty rare bird, and an upright prince even rarer.'"[230]

"He believes the world such a wicked place that it deserved no better. I am not quite so pessimistic. At any rate, these are the attributes of the ideal sovereign, whether composed of one, a few, or of many persons."

v

"Such a ruler is very good," I said. "But given the rarity or at least the exceptional character of the ideal, perhaps we should examine the forms bad character take in men and in nations so we will know what to look out for, and prepare for it."

Christopher Falos had a different idea, and whispered something to Simon.

"I agree with you," Simon said to him, aloud.

"What is it?" I asked.

"We feel that you are neglecting a whole section of the argument. There's a big difference between the way I understand Christian love and the way Andrew understands it. This makes us react in opposite ways to the issue of war, and I wish we could induce you to discuss this more fully."

"Do you agree, Andrew?"

"All of us agree, Philip," said Mr. Hendé. "And I am sure we speak for the ladies present, as well," he added with gallantry. I myself had noticed an attentiveness among them, particularly when Andrew spoke of loving defense of country.

"Well, then, I shall yield to this collective ardor. But I am concerned that we may be in for some complications, as love is rarely so simple on the inside as it appears from the outside. It is rather a maze, sometimes with a monster at the center – we can never know for sure until we get there."

"Lead on, then," Simon urged. "Bring us inside. We are well armed with the weapons of faith."

"Very well. One complication seems to be this one: love seems to be a double-edged sword. The lover seeks his own well-being and the well-being of his beloved. Sensing that two individuals will have somewhat different natures, love seeks the union of lover and beloved, to make them into one being instead of two. This sometimes works. But the larger the number of lovers, the more difficult union becomes, the more problematic the reconciliation of diverse natures. However, the desire for one's own well-being remains as strong as ever, no matter how attenuated the communal bonds. With even the best intentions, communal feelings will then fray, and conflict ensues. How much truer this is in relations between countries, where few strong ties exist in the first place. Perhaps it was for this reason that the ancient Greeks paired Aphrodite with Ares, knowing that love and war secretly attract each other, leading one or both to disaster, or at least embarrassment. Is there, then, a way to manage love, a way to save communities from its defects, and from war? Simon, perhaps you can rescue us from this maze?"[231]

"This is where irreligious love must always lead. Look at Homer: his whole rhapsody of bloodlust, the beginning and end of both the *Iliad* and the *Odyssey* is − a woman.[232] Christian love is completely different. Paul defines Christian love, *agape*, primarily in negative terms, as Jewish writers define God. Love is not jealous, not boastful, not provoked; it 'does not reckon the evil, rejoices not over the wrong.' Unlike prophecies, speaking in tongues, and knowledge, it 'never fails.' Positively, it 'suffers long' and 'rejoices in the truth.' It is greater even than hope and faith.[233] It is not *philia*, a word associated more with family and friendship; it is not *eros*, a word that doesn't appear in the New Testament at all.[234] The ancient pagans complain that Christians love each other almost before they know each other.[235] We can do this because we do not love each other as 'personalities' but as Christians, and for Christians love is a word of the will, not a word of the heart.[236] Our intimacy is with Jesus, only secondarily with each other. Because it gives instead of taking, it is unlike erotic love or desire, and therefore provides a foundation for a communalism unthreatened by individualistic demands and untroubled by warlike passions.[237] Christianity does not sacrifice the innocent for the sake of the guilty, as paganism did, nor does it sacrifice the guilty for the sake of the innocent. It sacrifices the godly for the sake of the guilty, because only the One of supreme value is worthy of sacrifice, a true sacrifice. Strictly speaking, the proper human response to this true love is not love of God but faith, *pistis*. For *we* have nothing of our own that is valuable, worthy of sacrifice; it is for us to trust God and be grateful. Love of neighbor is founded upon God's love for us; Christians incarnate God, and are chosen by God to incarnate Him. No personal merit is involved.[238] The Christian centers his life on God, not on himself or even on other people. The Christian's love of his enemies reflects God's love for sinners, which all of us are.[239] This love improves or 'perfects' us, without freeing us altogether from sin.[240] It does free us from sin sufficiently to tame the urge to retaliate against wrongs."

"What is the relation between love and the virtues, as for example justice?"

"Love is prior to justice. To establish justice, we must love first."[241]

"How then do we know that we love justly?"

Andrew broke in. "Because virtue is the 'due ordering of love,' as St. Augustine expresses it. Genuine love articulates, modulates, *defines* the virtues. Love of neighbor means not to yield in evil things but only in good things.[242] This is how Our Lord can speak of the *law* of love, summing up all of Judaic law in the twin command to love God and to love your neighbor as yourself. 'Love is the fulfillment of the law'"[243]

Simon picked up his own thread: "And this law of love precludes war, inasmuch as war stops where love begins. Justice *grows out* of love, not the other way around. Nonresistance to evil is the result of love, and the only force we may employ, if any, must be in such form that prepares the way for the redemption of the enemy's soul. War seeks to kill, not to redeem, and therefore cannot be loving. Killing always says, 'I love you less than I love myself and my own.' 'Thou shalt not kill' is an integral part of that law summed up in Jesus' Law of Love."[244]

"Can this be expected of a government that tolerates diverse religious opinions, particularly if diverse persons share in governing?" I asked.

"Expected, no. Urged, yes, just as we urge our fellow-citizens to be Christians, or to be better Christians. Many citizens are animated less by Christian love than by erotic love in both its physical and spiritual forms. So were the ancient pagans. Personal happiness is the highest good of all 'erotics,' ancient and modern. They seek to 'fulfill themselves,' satisfy their natures, or even, in modernity, to 'realize themselves,' fulfilling 'laws' of their own making. In either case they *desire*, moving toward some 'end' or *telos*. At best, their souls move upward toward beauty and goodness. However high-toned, this love is finally egocentric, seeking its own good. But human beings can never draw near to God by their own efforts, however energetic and refined. God is too powerful, too far removed for that strategy. There is no ladder to God that man constructs, nothing that he can climb through his own efforts. God must extend the ladder. God only can give man the strength to climb it. *Human* strugglings and strivings are utterly vain in this. Only God has the power to bring man to Himself, to make something worthy of Himself from the 'nothingness,' even destructiveness, of sin. The result of this love in the human soul is not mere happiness but the divine gift of joy. Because God's power is infinite, Christian love never fails, even when it leads to martyrdom on this earth."[245]

"Erotic love at its best is not infinite but measured, like music, yet in principle infinite in its persistence?"[246]

"Yes. And much of Christian theology has consisted of efforts to synthesize this natural love with Christian love."[247]

"So you would say that the popular slogan, 'Make love, not war' identifies the wrong kind of love?"

Andrew answered before Simon could: "The kind of love it alludes to is better regulated than maximized."

"And that's because it will lead to war sooner or later," Simon agreed, "or at least fail to prevent war."[248]

"Yet erotic love is necessary for life, clearly?"

"Granted."

"And it will need a shield? The old-fashioned, manly concern to protect women and children is not entirely groundless, not merely romantic?"

"Of course not," Andrew interjected.

"And in order to defend the community, some kind or ordering or rank will be needed?"

"Yes," Andrew said.

"And Christian love can order things, or rank things in this way?"

Andrew replied, "Yes, because Christian love, God's love, bestows worth instead of judging it.[249] It makes the unworthy worthy and it exposes 'worthies' as unworthy.[250] At the same time, it denies the pagan belief that love and majesty do not go well together."[251]

"And yet that majesty does need to undergo some metamorphosis, an incarnation in human form? To induce your creatures to feel a kind of pity for you – is this not the supreme triumph of a god?"

"Yes. My point is, that Christianity recognizes that not everyone is a commander, or need be. Each in his own rank will rule or defer to rulers, as is fitting.[252] Christian love can work through structures, through well-ordered institutions that conduce to union while preserving differences of individual natures.[253] Christian love is orderly, else it could not create nature, create the cosmos, in the first place."

"Love also created Hell?"

"Of course – as Dante teaches when he makes Hell speak:

Justice moved my Maker on high:
    Divine power made me,
    Supreme wisdom and primal love.[254]

War is indeed a Hell on earth, and it serves the same purpose: to castigate the morally corrupt. It also tries the righteous, who, though righteous, still love earthly life too much."[255]

Simon objected, "War is nothing more than a denial of Christian love. What sort of love runs enemies through with a sword, or blows them to pieces with a bomb? I now see why Tolstoy said, 'Love is a very dangerous word.' Once you permit killing and maiming in the name of God, you open a Pandora's box of evils. And while I know that generations of preachers have been little more than Bible bullies, dogs who bark at their masters' enemies-of-the-moment, the sanctification of vengeance and slaughter is just plain vile. Even worse is this cold-blooded love that very charitably slits throats, ostensibly to save souls. This isn't love; it is hatred and hatred's slaveowner, fear. Worse still, it can be indifference."[256]

I asked Simon how far he wanted to go in the argument that soldiers feel either hatred or no real emotion at all: "We have the testimony of soldiers who claim that the range of feelings in war is wide, and not always incompatible with love."[257]

"I distinguish between more or less innocent confusion and rigorous examination of one's conscience in the light of the Holy Spirit. The average Christian might well say, 'Strike, and spare not' if there seems no other way.[258] But I am speaking of the most thoroughgoing Christians, which is what all of us should strive to become."

"Defending our families and neighbors is not innocent confusion," Andrew replied. "It is one form of Christian love. St. Ambrose teaches us that war preserves our country and defends the weak, with the courage, justice, prudence, and moderation that love animates.[259] To wage war in love does not require no killing at all, but rather to make war while hoping for peace, for reconciliation, with no lust for personal revenge, while at the same time recognizing that the worst thing for sinners is not death but success, victory, which only confirms them in their sins. Given the mysteriousness of God, the hiddenness of His reasoning, we must leave the questions of life and death to Providence, while remembering that Moses punished some with the sword in love, not cruelty."[260]

"Murder is the opposite of forgiveness. Christian love issues in forgiveness. Therefore, Christian love never murders. It is not conditional on good behavior. It is unconditional, radically unjustified, undeserved."[261]

"Christian love often expresses itself in forgiveness. But it need not express itself in that way alone. One might kill *after* forgiving, in order to prevent the commission of evils forgiveness alone is likely to fail to prevent. The conventional association of killing with hardness of heart is demolished by the Holy Spirit."

"If we kill all sinners, who will be left alive? What enemies will there be to love?"[262]

"We will have numerous enemies — the many persons who start vicious rumors, who seduce the innocent, who harass us at court. The seven deadly sins will find numerous outlets short of capital crime and warmaking. In these circumstances, Christian forbearance, patience, and loving kindness will be most appropriate, and will often prevail."

I said, "One of the old historians recounts an incident involving the Persian King Xerxes, who refused to kill some heralds as the Spartans had done, out of respect for 'the laws which all men held in common' and 'true greatness of soul,' *megalopsychia*.[263] *Megalopsychia* can overlook injuries by reason of its sheer size and strength; retaliation is beneath it. While overlooking injuries, this kind of soul can also recognize the political need for consent. A philosopher advises that it is better to be loved than feared because love strongly motivates others to consent; fear is a weak and dangerous motive of obedience, as men hate whom they fear. The natures of the lion and the fox are 'both of them certainly very unworthy of a reasonable creature.'[264] And a statesman contends, 'If you would win a man to your cause, *first* convince him that you are his sincere friend'; his heart 'is the high road to his reason'[265] Another statesman said on his deathbed, 'If you do good to your friends, you will also be able to punish your enemies.'[266] Thus the political man, who needs to concern himself with the love and hatred of others, will serve primarily as a benefactor, secondarily as a punitive agent. Those who seek no political office need not strain to benefit or injure others. Some such men can live as aliens or strangers in many civil societies. They will share the truth with truth-loving friends, and the truth shall set them free — free, most notably, of passions, of the need for passions. For truth can be shared without loss or diminution of the sharer's portion, as no other good can be. I was wondering, Simon, if you suppose that these two human types, the political man and the thoughtful man, can somehow be combined?"

"It is not thoughtfulness that needs to be combined with action, but Christian love. Love doesn't will knowledge of the other. It wills his conversion through the Holy Spirit expressed in our trust and our charity. Reasoning searches for causes, patterns, but love is free of causality. It does not so much matter if I am loved or feared. What matters is that I love or fear the other. What is more, there are many times when love of God and man provokes the annoyance, even the contempt, of men."[267]

"Christians need not dim their eyes," Andrew rejoined. "Paul teaches that some men are hateful; we also love our enemies, equally after the example of God and His Son. We hate the sinful will but love human nature, which was created to be good. 'An eye for an eye' and 'Turn the other cheek' do not contradict each other. Both regulate anger. Neither one prohibits anger, or war. If guided by reason, anger will support courage, and reinforces reason against timidity, thus enabling man to fulfill his nature."[268]

"You underestimate the power of God as it acts through the love of Christians. This is a love that overflows the bounds of law, ultimately even the physical laws of causation, for it is the ultimate force behind the universe. We don't seek superior physical force. We serve as conduits of God's love for his enemies; this love is a force that convinces their wills. Each Christian has himself experienced the power of the Holy Spirit over his own soul, and he knows it can never be resisted finally, when God chooses to exercise it – in His time, not ours. If Jesus was wrong in this, He was wrong on the Cross itself. Far from indicating a preference for tyranny over war, the Cross and the Resurrection are God's answer to both tyranny and war. The Resurrection proves the power of God that animates the supposed folly and weakness of the Christian life. A loving God is the supreme sovereign, the universal King and Lord.[269] What is needed politically is a nation with the courage and the faith to disarm militarily, and to let the power of God work through their moral example.[270] The tragic cycle of violence that prevails through so much of human history can only be broken by forgiveness, not by the retaliation that fuels it."[271]

"So you are saying that, for example, if the Soviets struck the Americans with nuclear missiles, and the Americans refrained from retaliating, this would break the cycle of violence?"

"For Christians death is not the ultimate tragedy."[272]

"But would it break the cycle of violence?" I persisted.

"Perhaps yes, perhaps no. History is in God's hands, not ours."

"This requires a kind of supreme self-forgetting?"

"Absolutely."

"And yet we are warned of Judgment and Hell if we do not forget ourselves?"

"The absoluteness of divine love comports with absolute Judgment. The question the Holy Spirit poses to each and every one of us is very simple: Yes or No? Do you accept my gift, or do you not? Will you yield to me, be transformed and saved? Or will you resist, try to create your own moral (or immoral) law, and lose your soul? Love can come as liberation or as judgment. It's up to us."[273]

202

"If so, then we should choose what is of benefit to us, and will do so, if we are wise?"

"Ultimately, as Denck has written, the one who truly loves God would accept damnation itself for the love of God, knowing that God is wholly good."[274]

vi

"This, then, is what it means to be a good soldier of the Holy Spirit," I said. "And should we not consider this soldier a kind of nonviolent manhunter?"[275]

"Yes, we are invited to be fishers of men."[276]

"And their teaching must not only contain the truth but win over the souls of many persons?

"Yes, not out of natural speaking ability so much as the grace of God, whose Spirit forms their persuasive words."[277]

"And, as that great nonresistant, Origen, taught, Christian knowledge of divine intentions as found in Scripture is not irrational − else it would be hard to see how it could be called 'knowledge' at all − but rather rests on faith for most persons, and on careful study beginning with faith but ending in knowledge, for others?"[278]

"All of us start in unreason − even philosophers."

"Where else can humans start? And many of us remain there.[279] How then do we shed our ignorance and know, and thereby share legitimately in God's rule?"

"Not by human reason alone and unaided. Reason would enable us to understand creation, to some extent, but not the Creator. And to misunderstand the Creator is to misunderstand His Creation. The man of reason alone may understand what is not − may criticize incoherence and sense his own ignorance − but he cannot attain the power of saying what is. And therefore such a man cannot be truly good, truly wise, and achieve the happiness he seeks in this life or the next. His prudence in speech conceals not truth but his own secret vices. He is miserable, his soul at war with itself as any soul not touched by grace must be. He is only, ultimately, a source of political disorder and war, never peace, as he cannot truly create.[280] To avoid warring with God, His Creation, and particularly with his fellow-creatures, man must accept the truth. The truth is not the disembodied *logos* of the philosophers, with their abstract ideas, but the embodied logos, Jesus Christ. Human history acts in response to His *person*, and other persons such as Caesar and Satan, and is to be comprehended 'personally.' Not 'objects' in 'nature,' not 'types' and categories, but particular, individual persons yield knowledge and ignorance. *We* becloud our own minds, or demons do, or Satan; God is the only source of knowledge."[281]

I wondered at this Logos, with its tempting synthesis of supreme power and supremely true speech. "Yet it is surely true that some knowledge of nature can come through reasoning and observation unaided by the Holy Spirit? That there are regularities well expressed in logic?"

"Granted."

"And morality, which involves choice, rests to some extent on human nature, and must take account of those 'givens' and even express them to some extent?"

"To some extent, of course."

"The Machiavellian project to make external nature submit to man's inner passions is the opposite of this, yes? For I am speaking of logical or scientific union with intelligible nature, with moral control of inner passions?"[282]

"Yes."

"And such moral control is seen, if perhaps to a lesser degree, in some non-Christians, and was therefore discovered by men more or less unaided by revelation?"[283]

"All right. Pedestrian decency is within the moral compass of non-Christians. But the one thing needful for salvation, and for the fulfillment of the moral law, is not. And that thing is grace."[284]

"Still, given the frequency of the absence of grace among our fellow-men, pedestrian decency is no small thing? And would you agree, blessed man, that for those who are ignorant of God, the quest for that degree of truth that *is* humanly available will require fairly considerable virtues, such as courage combined with intelligence?"[285]

"Yes, and also the highest form of erotic love."

"So it was not surprising that the young philosopher Vattel reportedly 'spent his time studying and calling on ladies'?"

Simon laughed for the first time.

"Nor is it surprising that he quickly died as soon as he was forced to go to work? For a philosopher needs his leisure?"[286]

"I suppose so."

"And that when we see a buzzard high overhead, sharp-eyed, comprehending the whole yet descending to the particulars, unflinching at the sight of death, vigorous in love, omnivorous, not much wanted but not much preyed upon either — do we not see the very type of the philosopher?"[287]

"Perhaps so, but doesn't the buzzard gloat at the prospect of death and war?"

"Some stern moralists say so.[288] However, can there be any doubt that the buzzard is by nature the most useful of all the animals as well as the wisest, always observing the conflicts of man and beast, never causing any, and removing the traces of error wherever he finds them?"[289]

Simon hesitated, not knowing quite what to say, or, perhaps, how to say it.[290]

"And can we say that the philosopher, who seeks a fully completed life, will never be careless about conflict?"[291]

"No doubt."

Andrew Docksman was troubled by all of this. "At the very birth of an infant, we hear crying, not laughter. Philosophy, which may be the highest form of fallen human *nature*, cannot end the civil war of the soul's passions, and thus cannot bring happiness, no matter what it promises. Philosophers resist correction by Christ out of pride. They see nature, with its cycles of birth and death, genesis and destruction, and therefore gyrate endlessly without ascending to God, producing nothing but fruitless wrangling. Far from not causing war, it was vain erudition that introduced conflict to Christendom, despite the best attempts of the Church Fathers to turn their own substantial learning to the service of God.[292] Philosophers at worst become frivolous eccentrics, and even at best they give no real help to their country, but are like flies who pester a horse by sucking its blood."

"I see what you mean," I said. "But consider that this may be because so many citizens can see no use for them. These citizens seek to preserve their bodies and, some of them, to *save* their souls. They do not always think of improving their souls, although some do attempt to improve their bodies through exercise. They treat their souls less well than their bodies, thinking of their souls as 'selves' or 'identities' to be preserved intact at all costs, as they would seek to preserve their bodies in some emergency. As for their rulers, too often they fear philosophers because philosophers perceive the secrets of their rule; at the same time, philosophers distinguish between good and bad desires, whereas tyrants do not so distinguish, as tied to the body in their own way as those whom they tyrannize.[293] The body tends to resist the soul, and the rational part of the mind, while perceiving necessities, cannot forcibly change them.[294] Thus the philosopher is particularly vulnerable to ruled and to rulers alike, yet many countries do great injustices to philosophers, and especially to potential philosophers whose natures are often corrupted, or made restless and impatient, by the things proffered by their countrymen. Now it seems to me that the answer to this problem may be found in the great Origen, who criticizes the philosophers of his day for not recognizing that Jews possess greater wisdom than they, who, 'in spite of their impressive philosophical teachings fall down to idols and demons, while even the humblest Jew looks only to the supreme God.'[295] If potential philosophers see the many in the light of the One, the particulars as representatives of the species, the kinds, and these kinds in the light of the whole, they will not fall prey to confusions and seductions."

"What is the need for that?" Simon interjected. "Jesus states the truth openly, and Gospel truths are hidden only to those who *will* not see because God has blinded their minds. The mind of the flesh is death, the mind of the Spirit is life and peace, both foreordainedly. All-too-human tradition, at its best philosophy, only obscures the truth. Jesus' love excels human knowledge; love builds men up, while knowledge only inflates our pretensions. Fear of God is the beginning of wisdom, not idle curiosity, because the power of God is not human wisdom but a wisdom mysterious to men; no one comprehends the thoughts of God except the Spirit of God. We must put on the mind of Christ, which is the peace that surpasses human understanding, not the flesh-mind that only wars with itself and others, out of folly. Philosophers' wisdom is worldly and wordy, with no real power. Philosophers' wisdom is impotent and impudent folly, which, when it fumbles for the power it lacks, only abets tyranny and war. Christians, however, cultivate piety, righteousness, philanthropy, faith, and hope, turning the sword and spears of passion into the ploughshares and pruning hooks of fruitful peace."[296]

"And yet the Gospel record itself requires interpretation, as Origen teaches. Apparent contradictions need to be searched out and reconciled, sometimes by considering each speaker and the audience of each speech, sometimes by means of reasoning, and historical research. Origen calls for a presentation of Scripture 'as a connected whole,' and has recourse even to allegory in making the connection."[297]

"Without divine guidance, any interpretation will be vain."[298]

"As Origen remarks, Jesus of Nazareth is Logos, Reason, 'because He takes away from us all that is irrational, and makes us truly reasonable.' A reasonable interpretation of Scripture accounts for the body or letter of the text, its soul or imagery and metaphors, and its spirit, the symbolic meaning of the letter and images.[299] And so, Origen says, in ancient Israel 'it was possible to see an entire nation studying philosophy; and in order that they might have leisure to hear the divine laws, the days called Sabbaths and their other feasts were instituted.'[300] And this confirms human nature instead of denying it, for, as Augustine writes, 'We may appreciate how great is the love of knowledge implanted in human nature, and how unwilling that nature is to be deceived, by noticing that everyone prefers to be sad and sane rather than glad, but at the same time mad.'[301] And it is the nonresistant Christian Clement of Alexandria who teaches that the greatest of all lessons is, as philosophers have said, to know yourself, and to coordinate one's soul in accordance with the rule of reason, which he associates with Christian doctrine, over spiritedness and the appetites.[302] Only then can we *see* clearly, beginning with necessary trust in common sense perception, rather than in illusory images and figures of speech, and rising to knowledge of the good."

"Quite impressive," said Andrew, with a trace of irony he picked up I know not where. "But how do these philosophic Christians or Christian philosophers propose to defend themselves?"[303]

"A philosopher can remain silent, drawing no attention to himself.[304] And even in wartime, when governments and nations give themselves over to suspicion, a man who laughs is never dangerous, as the saying goes.[305] Also, as Augustine teaches, the untainted stream of philosophy is best 'guided through shady and thorny thickets, for the possession of the few, rather than allowed to wander through open spaces where cattle break through, and where it is impossible for it to be kept clear and pure.'"[306]

Simon Liteson intervened. "But Augustine also warns how dangerous concealment is. He criticizes Varro for refusing to reveal the falsity of Roman gods, calling them demons in disguise.[307] Christians must not remain silent. We must evangelize. There must be no double standard, no concealment of the truth."[308]

"Double standards are of course ruled out for all Christians," I agreed. "Clement of Alexandria observes that, unlike the Gnostics, Christians have no secret doctrines. However, the same Clement also warns that 'there is great danger in divulging the secret of the true philosophy to those whose delight it is unsparingly to speak against everything, not justly.' While philosophy does not directly declare the Logos, he continues, it does teach what he calls 'probable arguments' and rigorous logic prevents Christians from falling into heresies. He cites the example of Moses, 'a prophet, a legislator, skilled in military tactics and strategy, a politician, a philosopher.'[309] In this Clement only follows Jesus of Nazareth, who advises the apostles to exhibit the prudence of serpents as well as the innocence of doves, and therefore, as Paul sees, to be all things to all men.[310] Perhaps this is why Christendom has made a home for philosophy within it, while other more legalistic religions are often less hospitable. Augustine can therefore call the New Testament 'a truly liberal book,' pointing us toward the truth that sets us free.[311] Despotism injures philosophy, as Tacitus and others knew.[312] This is why one of the first nonresistant Christian theologians, Justin Martyr, told the Emperor Titus that the truly pious and philosophical oppose violence and tyranny, which are against reason. Justin blames the execution of Socrates on demons who called themselves gods, angered at the philosophic challenge to their power. Alluding to a saying of Socrates, Justin writes, 'Unless both rulers and ruled philosophize, it is impossible to make cities blessed.'[313] This need not mean that all citizens will philosophize, or that all will philosophize to the same degree. It does mean that political liberty will reduce the philosopher's vulnerability to his enemies, and even help to convert those enemies into friends or at least render them tolerant. Philosophers, who strive for a degree of independence from opinion, yet recognize their practical dependence upon opinion, can live in such a regime."

vii

"As long as your philosophers understand that they have no excuse to deny God, they will walk on earth in justice," Simon replied. "Since their creation, human beings have seen the invisible power of God in created things. But too many have worshipped the created instead of the Creator. This deification of nature leads to unnatural acts – to sodomy, murder, strife, slander, and the invention of evil. Sinful men deserve punishment because their own unguided reasonings have darkened their hearts."[314]

"If I am not mistaken," I said, "Augustine establishes the justice of Hell by claiming that, while the punishment of unbelievers will be eternal, the intensity of punishment will not be infinite. Each soul will be happy or wretched according to the tendency of its own will, the measure of all its acts and deserts.[315] Thus Hell will not be a state of tyranny or of unjust war. Heaven, by contrast, will be the place of clear-rightedness, distinguished not only from Hell but from our life on earth, where we see things dimly, as mere reflections."[316]

"As a person, God is not without anger or kindness. He is alive. He moves. Without God's activity, He could not reward or punish. He would lack authority.[317] The oneness of God conduces to peace as well as to authority, for Christians deny that the universe was created in that battle of the gods that polytheism makes possible.[318] This combination of divine activity and oneness revolutionized the ancient empires, and will revolutionize the empires of today as well."

"Then in some sense Christianity is not merely political, not concerned with gaining the approval of king or crowd, but supremely political, adjuring us to seek the approval of the supreme King?"

"Yes."

"Although it even more closely resembles a family than a country? The Creator, God, resembles a parent more than a king. When Jesus of Nazareth speaks of bringing not peace but the sword, he describes one result of his intention to convert members of pagan and Jewish families into the Christian family.[319] Or am I mistaken?"

"Not at all."

"In a way, the Logos is a kind of educator?"

"Yes, an educator not in carnal war but in peace. Jesus is Logos-become-flesh, that is, Logos made practicable for all, the most authoritative law. This Educator has many means of instruction, in words and in action. Although piety is the only command that is universal – Christians may marry or not, hold offices or not, raise children or not...."[320]

"To wage war or not?"[321]

"...The Logos will make souls peaceful, if they open themselves to the teaching; they will become warriors of the Holy Spirit. The carnally warlike 'self' will break down and, many times, God will reward us with peace on earth as well. If not, we will be sacrificed, gladly, even as Jesus died to reconcile man to God. Insofar as Jesus' mind, heart, and spirit live within us, we are incapable of carnal war. To claim, as so-called 'realists' do, that our sin prevents us from this is to deny the Incarnation itself."[322]

"Would it not be more accurate to say that in no human being this incarnation is perfect, as in Jesus of Nazareth? That human beings can only imitate Him, and not *be* Him?"[323]

"Be that as it may, we *can* surely refrain from carnal warfare and accept the Cross if needs be.[324] Nonviolence makes sense as a way of life and not just as a tool, only if we accept the Cross-bearing Jesus as central to our own lives, our own faith and conduct. Otherwise, we will fall back on either religious legalism or recourse to nature – the legalism of natural law, perhaps.[325] And in doing so we'll abandon nonviolence."

"Nonviolence would also make sense as a way of life in some forms of Hinduism, Buddhism, even Taoism? Perhaps it would be better to say that undiluted nonviolence requires some form of absolute spiritual sanction, not necessarily Christian?"

"All right."

"And this raises the question of the specific character of *Christian* nonresistance, yes? If I am not mistaken, Maimonides expressed serious reservations on this point, on the status of Jesus as a prophet?"[326]

"Jesus praised his Father for hiding the future punishments from wise and intelligent men and for revealing His intentions to children. 'No one knows the Father except the Son and he to whom the Son wills to reveal the Father.'[327] And when Jesus says, 'a prophet is unhonored in his native town and his house' he refers first of all to Joseph, his non-father.[328] 'The Son *wills*': This is a command, not an erotic invitation as we see in Eastern mysticism. The 'commanding' character of Christianity goes with its familial character."

"How do you judge its noetic claims, beyond commands?"

"Jesus teaches that those who do not believe Him do not really believe Moses' writings, either. From the 'human' side, knowledge itself is strictly a matter of willing. '[I]f any one wishes to do the will [of God], he will know whether [my] teaching is of God, or whether I speak for myself [only].'[329] Even Saul, the persecutor of Christians, Saul on the road to Damascus, earnestly wished to do the will of God, and was therefore open to the instruction of the Holy Spirit."

"The forceful instruction."

"Forceful, but not lethally so. Only his pride was hurt, as they say. What philosophers and scientists fail to see is that to know Jesus *is* to know nature, and to know nature is to know Jesus — sometimes without knowing it! Jesus is 'the first-born of all creation.' *In Him* all things in the heavens and on earth were created, and, as Paul writes, 'in Him all the fullness of God was pleased to dwell, and through Him to reconcile all things to Himself, making peace through the blood of the Cross.'[330] It is because all of us, even Jesus Himself, are God's creatures that we have — 'built into' us, so to speak — a susceptibility to God's grace, which *alone* conduces to peace, because it alone is in accord with our true nature. This peace, this *shalom*, this fullness of being, is rare because obedience is rare, although God's grace is so abundant and powerful that it can transform warlike into peaceful men, once they consent to it.[331] Conversely, heretics, who fall away from God, fall into war.[332] It is this combination of free will, divine grace and God-created nature that makes divine judgment righteous. We *are* able and *should* be willing to accept God's grace, which is in turn 'empowering,' as we say today (founding, as it does, a new regime for renewed human beings), but is also the most powerful judgment against us if we fail to accept it."[333]

"Therefore, there is finally no tension between wisdom and genuine authority, although there can be tension between wisdom and consent?"[334]

"Exactly."

"And God may use war to punish and to reward human beings, providentially?"[335]

"Yes, although the same wars occur *also* because of human disobedience to God."[336]

"God sees this disobedience before it actually occurs?"

"Absolutely. To deny divine foreknowledge is to deny the Biblical God."[337]

"God then created the human will, endowed it with freedom, and foresaw exactly the results of that freedom, the choices we would make, including the choice to conduct wars?"[338]

"Yes, and there is no contradiction, because time does not exist *for* God, only *by* God. Creation, foreknowledge, and providence are all one *to* God. This is the meaning of the Tetragrammaton, 'YHWH,' from which is derived the word 'hayah,' meaning 'to be.' 'I am that I am' also means 'I shall be whom I shall be.'"

"But they are not 'all one' to the human beings who actually make the choices God foresees and therefore permits while readying punishments both temporal and eternal?"

"We are not God. His thoughts are not our thoughts."

"But Jesus was His true intermediary?"

"Yes."

"And Jesus will rule with God, judging human beings after the greatest war, the one described in the Book of Revelation ?"[339]

"Yes. These are 'the days of *ekdikeseos*,' often translated 'wrath' or 'vengeance' but, as is clear from the Greek, *dike*, justice is central to it. While the *kingdom* of God is one of righteousness and peace, the *coming* of that kingdom is one of righteous warfare. Jesus will rule the nations 'with a staff of iron.' After the Dragon, Satan, is bound for one thousand years, he will be 'loosed for a little time,' waging another war. Then finally the kingdom will come to stay, after the day of judgment."[340]

"In the last days, God will send an 'operation of error' or 'deluding influence' to confuse the minds of those who have not *received* the *love* of truth?"[341]

Simon hesitated, as if suddenly unsure. "Now with respect to those last days," I continued, "they will begin when the world believes itself to be at peace, secure? And Jesus of Nazareth will return 'like a thief in the night'?" And while He denies that there will be any observable sign of the Kingdom's coming, vultures will be a sort of emblem?"[342]

"Yes."

"And the Book of Revelation, as I recall, prophesies that Jesus will come 'soon.' Jesus of Nazareth prophesies that some standing before Him will 'by no means taste of death before they see the Son of Man coming in His Kingdom.' Evangelists will not have gone through all the towns of Israel, before He comes. Do I recall correctly?"[343]

"Yes. Most of these statements refer to the Transfiguration and the Resurrection, after which Jesus' kingdom *did* come, as seen in the manifold increase of His followers. When Jesus says 'all these things' will come to pass before 'this generation' passes away, He refers to the destruction of the Jerusalem Temple and related events, not to His 'Second Coming.'"[344]

"You are a faithful man," I smiled. "I am not sure that the context of these prophetic statements supports this interpretation, which in any event does not account for the passage in Revelation ...."

"But the concept of a purely future coming is not Biblical, anyway. The problem of the delay of the Parousia has been imported into the New Testament by later scholars...."[345]

"Perhaps because they *are* later, and the Parousia has yet to arrive?"[346]

Simon looked uncomfortable. "Be that as it may, to this day Christians care about the meaning and direction of history, and take their part by guarding the kingdom here and now, and working for its expansion."[347]

"Do you agree that the delay of the Parousia, and the lawless history of mankind, with its many wars and vices, may dangerously incline the young toward lawlessness and moral relativism, bringing them to lead whatever life pleases them most immediately?"

"Absolutely. This is a great danger. And insofar as we remain sinful, the threat of war persists — so the relation is reciprocal."[348]

"For non-Christians, we must hope at best for *just* wars?"[349]

"It is now too late for that. We are in one of those times when apocalypticism is true sanity. The spiritual and providential laws that Christians affirm are as solid for us as are the laws of dialectical materialism for the Marxist."[350]

"The question then becomes, are they more true than the scientistic myths of Marxism? Otherwise, we may forget the injunction of Jesus of Nazareth to cultivate prudence, yes?"[351]

"When all is said and done, the true prophet is the one who proclaims God's Logos, not the one who foretells the future. The law of love provides Christianity's animating spirit, not eschatological predictions."[352]

"I see. Jesus of Nazareth is a founder of a new *politeuma* or regime, the anticipation of which will effect what we consider prudent here and now?"[353]

Simon conceded this, a touch reluctantly.

"Then perhaps I now better understand Jesus of Nazareth's command to 'Become as children.'[354] I imagine they will be, say, ten years or younger, although it is impossible to tell for sure. But historically, would it be fair to say that in social and political terms the early Church in effect constituted what sociologists call a 'new class' within the existing order?"[355]

"Yes, but not just another social class."

"Of course not. And Christian nonresistance, again historically, has been either the faith of minority sects within Christianity — sects that were sometimes a majority in a given, small, political order or that the faith of groups integrated in some way into a larger, nonpacifist Christian sect?"[356]

"Yes. Our moral and eschatological vision has not yet united all Christians."

"One reason for this is the perceived political difficulty of rejecting lethal force in self-defense?"

"No doubt. This is why we have repeatedly lifted our critique of existing institutions beyond rationalistic philosophy, to prophetic witness.[357] We speak not for some new ideal or organization, but above all for a spiritual *movement*. We want to eliminate the rigidities of structure and imitate the actions of the Holy Spirit, ever-present, ever-changing yet permanent in intention.[358] The most deeply committed Christians will always undertake 'crusades.'[359] The only question is, will the Christian warrior use authentically Christian methods?"

"In order to enforce the conscientious use of those practices, without using force, one needs excommunication, I take it?[360] If translated into political terms, this would mean exile or at least disenfranchisement?"

"Yes, I suppose it would."

"You do intend that Christians wield political power?"

"Yes. We can't reject all direct responsibility for politics."[361]

"Yet in the modern world theocracies have disappeared, among Christian nations, and moral crusades will tend to have still greater difficulties in attaining the political authority they seek. The very foundation of religious tolerance, consent, has made unanimity of sentiment less likely?"[362]

"Still, we are obligated to try, and pray for the assistance of the Holy Spirit, which alone can make this happen."

"In trying, would it be helpful to make the prophetic content of our utterances as accessible as possible to fellow-citizens who do not entirely share our own understanding of morality? To appeal to their reasoning consciences?[363] And perhaps thereby to avoid confusing prophecy with predictions?"

"What do you mean?"

"For example, I have seen some Christians equate faith in disarmament with faith in metaphysical questions. This can and has led to serious miscalculations.[364] And I have seen some who take the Christian injunction to 'remove the beam in your own eye' before complaining of the mote in your neighbor's eye as an invitation to overlook the mote in the neighbor's eye altogether. But the reverse of hypocritical complacency is justice — not self-denigration or exaggerated guilt?"[365]

"True enough."

viii

"Then," I said, "we have reached the point where we should consider justice and the other virtues as they relate to war. For you will agree, Simon, that, far from being somehow beyond good and evil, war is to be judged, just as all human activities are, and will be judged in accordance with the virtues and vices warriors exhibit?"[366]

"Yes, virtues and vices — fruits of the spirit and sins — as defined by God's Law and made possible by His Spirit."

"And when we think about virtues and vices so identified, we quickly see virtues are strengths, vices weaknesses, yes? And weaknesses come from a sort of extremism, as when a man's anger at injustice runs to persection or vengefulness on the one hand, or retreats to timid indulgence on the other?[367] Whereas the best men and women stay in the center, so to speak?"

"That's a reasonable way of putting it."

"A reasonable way of putting things looks not so much to public opinion but to the way things really are, whatever people might way about them?"

"Of course."

"And this is true of justice?"[368]

"Absolutely."

"For the most part, returning kindness for evil will be good, but there will be times when another kind of good, namely, loving coercion, must be returned?"[369]

"Agreed. The problem arises with killing in war. The 'just war' tradition begins not in Christianity but in pagan antiquity.[370] It survived in Christendom in part because theologians split personal from political conduct. But there is absolutely no Scriptural basis for this. Christianity gives us one morality for individuals *and* for nations, and promises a day of judgment for individuals and for nations."[371]

"The purpose of sound morality is to attain peace in the fullest sense, is it not? That is, it is to achieve fullness of being thanks to the exercise of all the virtues?"[372]

"Absolutely."

"And some ancient writers understand this, too, do they not? They even insist that countries should undertake wars only for the sake of peace, that statesmen should 'legislate the things of war for the sake of peace'?[373] And, if I am not mistaken, they do this because a good country seeks the nation's happiness, which it can attain by itself if self-sufficient; therefore, conquest cannot be the final purpose of a good country, but only instrumental at most. These thinkers emphasize the use of war not as a mere instinctual spasm, but as an exercise of reasoned foresight and preparation, primarily in self-defense.[374] The very concept of political rule, for these thinkers, involves the principled choice of policies directed toward the fullness or completion of human being. This contrasts sharply with simple coercion, so often the symptom of anger, which, unchecked, yields tyranny. Rulers are not mere agents of other persons, nor are they pawns of 'fate,' nor are they 'dictators' barking at cringing 'masses.' They are actors of deliberate choice.[375] And this includes the choice for war."

"All very interesting. But none of it Christian."

"Some of it surely is. Augustine may 'revalue' the Roman virtues, but the virtues remain recognizable. For example, he says that people without justice do not have a regime, no 'gathering of men united in fellowship by a common sense of right and by a community of interest.' Without this fellowship, there is not a people, only an agglomeration of persons; without a people, there can be no people's estate, no regime. But he quickly relents, saying that if we define a people simply as 'a large gathering of rational beings united in fellowship by their agreement about the objects of their love,' Romans *are* a people with a regime, albeit one with bad love-objects. He then goes still farther, admitting that a wrong-minded people will love 'a peace of its own, which must not be rejected.' He only insists that this peace will not last because it will be wrongly used. Nonetheless, the merely secular peace of the merely secular regime is good in Christian terms − not good enough, but good, worthy of preservation.[376] Warfare, while not fully just, does in

Augustine's view serve the short-lived demi-justice of the peaceful regime, yes?"[377]

"Augustine tells Christians to assume wide responsibility for the endurance of secular peace. The early Christians did not. We may of course pursue justice insofar as the law of love allows. But no farther. If stealing, lying, anger, and insult are wrong, how can killing in war be right? Jesus Himself was sacrificed by the Sanhedrin for reasons of false prudence, the desire to maintain existing institutional arrangements. For Christians only obedience to Jesus is worth more than life; any other sacrifice — as for example to a political regime — is sheer idolatry."[378]

"Augustine, if I am not mistaken, refers responsibility for public affairs ultimately to God. Human responsibility is mediate — not more, not less. Stealing, lying, anger, and insult generally disturb civil peace; war may serve to defend civil peace. Civil peace requires institutions, principles, and habits that conduce to it. If those institutions are not defended effectively, even more lives will be effectively sacrificed. This is why some pacifists distinguish between just and unjust wars; deploring both, they deplore unjust ones more.[379] And this is why some pacifists also distinguish among regimes more or less capable of preserving peace and upholding justice."[380]

"Tyranny is not prevented by war. Tyranny is fed by war, by the recourse to brute force that war is."[381]

"Sometimes yes, sometimes no. This is universally true only if life itself is essentially warlike. If 'war is the father of all,' then 'good and bad are the same' and 'strife is justice.'[382] But even Heraclitus calls war an 'attunement of opposite tensions,' which means that when he sees war he sees the conflicts within it as part of a unity whose elements are somehow balanced. Therefore he does finally distinguish justice from injustice — an example of which is *hybris* or pride, even as in Scripture. If, however, he really does mean to say that *conflict* is the father of all, that the tensions and not their attunement are what matters, then it becomes hard to see how he could know this to be true.[383] Would his own mind not also be part of the conflict, unable to pull back from it even to see where it was? The evident fact of human knowledge points toward the likelihood that stability or peace provides the context of war, not vice-versa. This enables human beings to establish political regimes.

'Ideally,' as they say, such regimes would be structures of voluntary rule over voluntary subjects; in practice, many regimes are voluntary rule, with some violence, over involuntary subjects. That is, they are defective regimes.[384] Thus the greatest factional split in politics may be between virtue and depravity, one conducing to peace, the other to violence. Given this fact, statesmen must understand military things and design the regime so that no one faction can achieve military predominance.[385] Augustine understood this, making the analogy of life to peace and again to war; there can be life and peace without pain or war, but no pain or war without life and peace of 'some sort.' War is waged by persons; persons have a nature, a nature that needs 'some sort of peace to hold it together.' Peace is foundational, war instrumental. This leads to his concept of the *tranquillitas ordinis*, which may require war to defend itself."[386]

"War can't defend peace. It ends it."

"Surely you do not suppose that courts of justice and just laws and voting will be sufficient to maintain a peaceful regime?[387] Or even the various means now called 'nonviolent resistance?'"

"No."

"And if political life has a voluntary character, whereas tyranny has a predominantly violent character, then war is a sort of temporary tyranny, rather like the office of the dictatorship in republican Rome, or the presidential emergency powers in today's French constitution?"[388]

"A tyranny that threatens to overthrow the regime. As your Augustine asked, 'If justice is left out, what are kingdoms except great robber bands?'"[389]

"Nothing else but. But if force is left out − including, occasionally, the force of war, what will be left of justice in practice? Augustine knows that 'there is no other place but this life for correcting morals.' Therefore 'we have the institution of the power of kings, the death penalty of the judge, the barbed hooks of the executioner, the weapons of the soldier, the right of punishment of the overlord, even the severity of the good father,' all to protect the good and to frighten the wicked, whom it is merciful to punish, and cruel to pardon."[390]

"War substitutes violence for justice. It is a moral inversion, an act of contempt for both the living person and for justice."[391]

"If that were the case, how could any justice come from it, or occur within it? Force in itself is not evil, any more than human flesh or sexual activity are evil. All are needed in order to obtain human goods, and all can be used in an evil way. Civil society, essential to human good, requires forceful defense from internal and external enemies, yes?"[392]

"I agree."

"And therefore we must distinguish such concepts as force and violence?"[393]

"Yes. Nonlethal punishment can be legitimate. Lethal punishment, including warfare, is illegitimate."

"And if lethal punishment is necessary to maintain a legitimate regime?"

"It should be firmly rejected. Thucydides' Athenian ambassadors were right to say that right in its worldly sense occurs only between equals, while the stronger do what they can and the weaker suffer what they must. They were also right to say that men rule wherever they can. They were wrong to say that this is a necessary law of nature. Or if it is, it is a law that Christians disobey on principle, and therefore transcend natural necessity through the power of the Holy Spirit.[394] 'Necessity' is but a mask for the vice of ambition; it is a reason of state, not a reason of God. It renders evil for evil, not good for evil. Those who render good for evil are never truly conquered; warriors remove evils they imagine someone else will commit with real evil acts of their own. But nothing is so necessary as conformity to the will of God. That is the true 'self-preservation.' The natural instinct of self-preservation is legitimate so long as it does not lead us to destroy the persons of others. Jesus Himself did not do that."[395]

"Then the question is whether or not killing human beings is intrinsically wrong for human beings? As distinguished from killing human beings in order to do evil, which everyone agrees is wrong? And as distinguished from God's killing of human beings.[396]

"Yes. We are commanded not to do so."

220

"But never explicitly and universally, given the qualifications to the Sixth Commandment provided by the Torah itself?"

"No."

"And in terms of justice alone, then, war could be justified. Although not itself just, it can aim at justice and provide a necessary though not sufficient condition of justice? And justice, political life itself, conduces to such greater ends-in-themselves as self-sufficiency, leisureliness, rest, happiness?"[397]

"But the country that goes to war judges its own case, and no justice will arise from that."

"It might or it might not. Judgments concerning international relations must be made in any event.[398] Your argument would preclude all decisions except mutual agreements. Not-to-decide is still to decide, yes?"

"Granted."

"And even agreements may need to be enforced? As when Xenophon describes the Persians' precautions with respect to the peace treaty they established with the Armenians and the Chaldeans?[399] And so do non-agreements, so to speak? That is, just and desirable conditions that exist without mutual agreement may need protection."[400]

"But who doesn't think his own cause is just? What impartial tribunal will judge? The only 'equality' that exists among nations is and always has been accidental; strong powers who happen to be in balance may reach some uneasy truce, violated as soon as either sees its chance.[401] Only measures directed and inspired by a spiritual world community could lead to genuine peace."[402]

"This is of course an important practical objection to the doctrine of just war. Is it really a theoretical objection?"

"The theoretical objection is that killing is a crime when done individually, but by some magic it becomes a praiseworthy act of heroism when it's done wholesale, at the behest of the state.[403] What is more, war is simply an unstable basis for justice and peace. Because it's the very height of competition, it ruins every balance of power. No balance, no equality. No equality, no justice. No justice, no peace."[404]

"Only the Nazis praised Nazi soldiers except insofar as those soldiers exhibited virtues transcending Nazism. Public endorsement by rulers is nothing more than that. It asserts but does not establish justice, yes?"

"Such assertions lead to wars."

"All the more reason to establish criteria for the justifying of some wars. Such concepts as 'just cause,' that is, a just reason for punitive action, and 'right intention,' that is, to promote the good and prevent evil, at least require some framework for public debate, do they not?"[405]

"Yes, but only if we assume that war *can* be just, or somehow justified.[406] But even these criteria for evaluating the justice of a particular war call the legitimacy of war itself into question. This is especially true of modern war, and the criteria of proportionality and noncombatant immunity. Take proportionality. Just-war theorists say that the good to be saved by war must be equal to or greater than any goods sacrificed; that there's no other way to salvage this good; and that its protection here and now won't undermine it in the long run.[407] Yet modern war is so costly in human terms, that its supposed benefits are outweighed by the evils it unleashes."[408]

"This would depend upon the war itself, would it not? Such matters are hard to calculate, but it is difficult to assume that, say, Poland would have been worse off, materially or morally, had it possessed the strength to defend itself against Nazi Germany in 1939, yes?"[409]

"Doing evil is always evil, proportions or no proportions."

"Perhaps we must distinguish between doing evil and inflicting evils, or pains. There are moral differences, are there not, among actions taken for an evil purpose, actions that have an evil result, actions that inflict pain for a good purpose, and actions that inflict pain with good effect."[410]

"But that kind of 'lesser evil' reasoning assumes that God's word is morally self-contradictory, obliging us to commit morally evil acts."[411]

"It isn't a matter of the degree of evil, I think, but rather of what is *morally* wrong."

"Proportionality alone doesn't give us the complete moral picture. There are moral judgments to be made that are independent of judgments related to ends-and-means calculations. Modern war involves killing innocent people – the very definition of murder. Means-and-ends casuistry ignores *rights*, and their complementary duties."[412]

"You refer to Exodus 23:7, that important qualification to the Sixth Commandment, prohibiting us from killing an innocent and just person?"[413]

"Yes."

"Then, in terms of the doctrine of the just war, would we be prohibited from punishing the guilty if innocents were killed?"

"No, just war theorists say that this can be done, so long as evils don't come out of the war that are greater than the evils the war would avert.[414] So it ties back into proportionality. What I'm saying is that if we do something that we know will involve our doing evil, such as murder or even mass murder, we are morally responsible for those consequences, even if they are supposedly 'incidental' to our purposes.[415] If we bomb innocents to punish their guilty rulers, we are doing evil in order to do good. That is wrong."

"There is a distinction, surely, between an intended effect of a voluntary action and a foreseen effect of a voluntary action? A doctor who aborts an unborn life in order to save the mother's life foresees the death, but does not intend it in the sense of desiring it.[416]

"Your analogy is inexact. The unborn child innocently threatens the life of the mother. The innocent civilian in war threatens no one, innocently or deliberately.[417] Modern weapons are often specifically designed for mass, indiscriminate destruction. War has become potentially totalitarian, and the preparation for such war will contribute to an ethos of moral callousness, even moral paralysis. This in turn risks the kind of war that will destroy political life itself."[418]

"Is not the very destructiveness of these weapons more conducive to peace between rival countries than any other thing, except the end of the rivalry itself?"

"That remains to be seen. I don't see how one country, a so-called 'superpower,' can seriously threaten another country with nuclear retaliation, if its leaders know that such retaliation will occur only after their own people have been destroyed. At that stage, retaliation is pointless, a mere act of vengeance, which properly belongs to God alone."[419]

"Perhaps the rulers of the other country will not take the chance that other rulers will restrain their vengefulness and wait for God."

"You're still not addressing the issue of killing innocents. God absolutely prohibits murder. He absolutely prohibits the intention to murder. So-called nuclear deterrence involves a conditional intention to murder. And don't say that a bluff would be acceptable, because it isn't. You'd still need people at some level of the government who sincerely intended to carry out the order to mass murder, whether or not the 'supreme commander' harbored that intention."[420]

"Is the death of innocents the aspect of massive retaliation that, say, Americans intend Soviet rulers to fear?"

"In my judgment, yes."[421]

"Is it not rather the destruction of the rival's military and political power that is likely the most serious threat, as perceived by the rulers themselves? That is, are not rulers more likely to fear loss of their power than loss of their people?"

"What a chilling thought!" Simon exclaimed. "You think like a Stalin!"

"To understand a Stalin, one must be able to think like him, without, if I may say in my own defense, agreeing with him. So: Am I right? Is that not the real deterrent?"

Simon was not ready to concede this, though not quite willing to deny it. I continued: "And, if so, then the resulting deaths of innocents *would* be *morally* unintended?"[422]

"All right. But look: We don't let the police take a would-be criminal's children as hostages in order to deter him from crime, do we?"[423]

"No. But I am not speaking of hostages. I am speaking of retaliation intended to defeat, and military forces designed thus to deter, rulers who would attack a more-or-less just regime. If men were always reasonable they would settle their quarrels differently; sometimes, force must be used to bring them to reason.[424] In this the just ruler aims not to satisfy the passion of revenge but to correct an injustice."[425]

"Most war deaths, especially in the modern world, don't touch the guilty at all."[426]

"That might be hard to measure. They do touch some of the guilty, as many tyrants and tyrants' sycophants have learned to their displeasure. Disagreements about justice yield wars.[s427] While no one imagines that war necessarily will bring a just outcome, we should no more suppose that the struggle between good and evil in the human soul will always issue in goodness. But I suppose that war and preparation for war can conduce to peace and some justice, both in self-defense and in conquest, but more often in self-defense than in conquest."[428]

"The right to self-defense, which is undeniable to the innocent, does not justify *any* means of self-defense. We must never become guilty in defending ourselves from the guilty. That's why Scripture refers to Christians as sheep, lambs, and doves — creatures made for flight, not fighting.[429] Reason must be used not after a war but before it to prevent war, because war breeds war, fostering the moral corruption that blinds reason, even after the most just of wars.[430] I have no faith in the propagation of free institutions out of the barrel of a gun. Freedom must come from freedom, religion from religion."[431]

"While it would be unwise to have faith in war, history shows that a just and lasting peace can follow a war, if the peace is justly founded, does it not? We see this when a neighbor arms himself; depending upon his character and the character of his institutions, we may be alarmed or we may not care at all. And if we also see this in a peace treaty that is oppressive; such treaties do not conduce to peace at all, whereas a just treaty stands a better chance.[432] Some treaties might actually reconstitute the regime of the conquered nation.[433] But in so doing, the use of force will normally be prudently restricted to ensuring conformity to natural justice, not so much to spiritual doctrines. Otherwise, endless persecutions, tyrannies, and wars will result, yes?"[434]

"Yes, of course. But the covenant between ruler and ruled, or among people governing themselves, cannot require the citizen to commit an evil act of any kind.[435] Yet the just war doctrines usually require blind obedience to governments, even when it's clear that citizens can't know the real causes of any war, nine times out of ten. This deifies the magistrate and denigrates the Christian."

"Given the Scripturally-acknowledged authority of magistrates to punish evildoers, thereby representing not the humanly-erring people but God, would it not seem that the distinctions between rulers and God, and also between rulers and people, are preserved? And even if ruler and people are the same, will they not have one relationship to God as persons, so to speak, another as rulers?"[436]

"I doubt it. But be that as it may, this doesn't touch the problem of not knowing whether you are acting justly or not in endorsing a war."

"A good citizen will learn as much as possible. But he could hardly be blamed for an honest error, if important evidence is withheld from him.[437]

"But if all are admittedly ignorant, does this not allow any war at all?"[438]

"Now you're the one thinking like a tyrant."

"I try to learn."

"No: because the ruler must answer any questions that do arise, and, if his reasons contradict each other or contradict the evidence, the citizen should avail himself of the proper legal recourses."

"And what of the disuse not so much of reason but of conscience? This problem is especially acute in modern times, when, as one just-war theorist admits, 'the sharp edge of right is blurred.'"[439]

"I doubt that reason or conscience is less well-informed today – only, perhaps, less well-educated, a circumstance for which we cannot blame war. Although Augustine teaches that a soldier may obey an unjust command because 'his position makes obedience a duty'...."[440]

"What an excuse!"

"...I should rather say that a soldier should not contravene the right. But he should incline to give his ruler the benefit of the doubt, given the need to sustain a good regime."[441]

"And a bad regime?"

"Is by its nature seditious – not the citizens who oppose it. So too with an unjust war, although a generally good regime fighting an unjust war must not be destroyed on that account. Theologians today are therefore in a sense correct to say that just war doctrines and pacifism both have truth in them.[442] But the reasons have more to do with circumstances, and their changeableness than with some polite pluralism. But tell me, do you suppose that justice is enough?"

"What do you mean?"

"Well, you wouldn't say that aristocracy is the only political regime."

"No, obviously."

"There are other regimes, with other desires animating them?"

"Many."

"We've already described the aristocratic virtue, justice, so we should consider another. War calls men to courage, and honor-loving men hear that call, do they not? And yet honor-loving men are not quite as admirable as justice-loving men?"

"Not at all."

"Yet they are superior to those who love money, and to those who freely love whatever they happen to love — fall in love with their own passion, I suppose, and love license itself?"

"Absolutely."

"If men who love justice really love God, then they are in a sense honor-loving men? Therefore, courageous, spirited, honor-loving men seek from other men, and also from women, what our aristocrats seek from God?"

"Yes, and that's the problem with them. Pericles tells his Athenians to seek immortality in human honor, which comes from seeking the dangers of war. He says this will bring them freedom and happiness; it really brings down worldly empire and eternal damnation."[443]

"True courage, then, does not seek the approval of men, no matter how powerful, but is rather founded upon real virtue?"[444]

"Yes."

"The spiritedness of true courage generates political life itself, does it not? Politics comes from our willingness to defend lives, lands, liberty, and our way of life from the love of dominance we see in others?"[445]

"Yes, but this courage, whether you call it political or natural, isn't real courage. It's not the courage of Christ in the soldier of Christ."[446]

"Would you not say that war can serve as a kind of touchstone of the soul, whereby false courage is exposed for cowardice?"[447]

"Yes, it can. But it is in the very act of fighting, not only in the act of running away, that the soldier reveals his fearfulness. He fears loss; he fears wrong. So he fights. He appears brave, but he's only flushed and frantic.[448] True courage finds its expression not in warlike vaunting but in patience, the calm willingness to accept martyrdom before committing any evil act."[449]

Andrew Docksman could not forbear to speak any longer. "There are limits to patience, just as there are limits to all human dispositions. We find the limit when our patience is about to play into the hands of evil. The courage of patience is no more to be allowed to impinge upon other goods, such as justice, than the courage of the soldier is to be allowed to tyrannize.[450]

"That's the way of the Old Testament — an eye for an eye, a tooth for a tooth," Simon replied. "Since the advent of Jesus, human beings are to overcome their spiritedness, to leave just retaliation to God. Human spiritedness is to be transferred to God, except for our righteous indignation that never may be allowed to issue in lethal or injurious action."[451]

"Andrew," I asked, "would you say that the life of unshakeable patience requires a certain moderation to guide it?"

"Yes, exactly."

"And that the most extreme, unmoderated patience would cause the loss of life, at least in this world?"

"Undoubtedly."

"A country animated by such patience, ruled by the poor, would end in famine or conquest?"

"Yes. And God would have no more worshippers. It would be almost self-defeating, for man and for God."

"Moderation is necessary both for the life of the country and the individual, including the individual's self-knowledge?"[452]

"Yes, peacemakers are first of all those who put themselves in order, subduing their own passions.[453] And peace among men occurs when moderation binds them together, like a harmony of musical scales. Moderated desires can be satisfied without blocking the moderated desires of others. Justice removes the obstacles to true peace; charity then achieves it."[454]

"And this moderation can bring peace among nations, as well, when they dispute over regimes, yes? Any decent regime should be respected by the rulers of other nations, as Comenius taught so long ago.[455] Doctrinaire claims about rights and regimes too often conceal passionate injustice, as for example greed, or am I mistaken?"[456]

"Not at all."

"At the same time, there is a false moderation or excess cautiousness that procrastinates with injustice, enabling it to grow huge and formidable, instead of moving swiftly to defeat it?[457] And would it be fair to say, then, that moderation itself needs a guide, namely, prudence?"

Andrew eagerly agreed. "This has been understood throughout our tradition. Prudence is first among the virtues, in peace and in war, as all men tacitly acknowledge, in preferring to obey those statesmen and generals whom they believe to be the best, the most knowledgeable.[458] Our Lord Himself tells His apostles, 'Behold I send you forth as sheep in the midst of wolves; be ye therefore prudent [*phronimoi*] as serpents and harmless [*akeraioi*] as doves.'[459] The need for prudence in peacemaking has been reaffirmed repeatedly in our tradition."[460]

"Philosophy itself depends upon prudence for its continued existence, does it not? There are times when political science must maintain a politic silence, for if conscience were an entirely effective force in human life, there would have been no need for Jesus of Nazareth to come the first time, let alone a second, yes?"[461]

"Conscience does not speak to us unequivocally and powerfully, because it speaks through our own flawed nature, and because our nature is reasonable, open to thought and not mere dictation, whether of sense or of conscience. Prudence learns from past and present in order to foresee the future; motivated by love, it compares experiences in order to discover how and through what we may strike, here and now in the circumstances given to us, the virtuous mean between vicious extremes. It then commands the right. Nature requires us to shape ourselves from within *and* to resist destructive forces outside ourselves; political prudence promotes the former in civil society, while military prudence attends to the latter.[462] Conscience itself is thoroughly bound up with prudence, with the application of knowledge to circumstances. In political terms, conscience is an amalgam of deliberation and consent, issuing in an authoritative action. The self-evident character of some conscientious decisions inheres in this God-given rational intuition, not in some irrational soul-force.[463] Conscience can be altered by argument, by new evidence, and thus cannot be called an autonomous 'sense.'[464]

"If memory serves, Erasmus begins his book on the education of a Christian ruler with the word, 'prudence.' He associates the ruler's wisdom with Aristotle, Xenophon, Solomon, David, Plato, Apollo (who arms Odysseus with the herb *moly*, the account of which is perhaps the first time the word 'nature' is used in our literature), Plutarch, and Alexander the Great after he spoke with Diogenes.[465] And in his pages describing those arts of peace a ruler must exercise so that 'the devices of war may never be needed,' he observes, 'they love long whose love was well judged to begin with.'[466] It may be that prudence governs Erasmus' careful way of writing, too, particularly in his refusal explicitly to rule out the use of military force.[467] Then again, perhaps he sees that no prince has the moral right 'to make his nation the Christ among nations,' that 'he who attempts to play the angel plays the beast.'"[468]

"We should distinguish, also, between prudence in the good sense and prudence in the bad sense, in the sense of Jesus when, he says, 'the sons of this age are more prudent than the sons of light.'"[469]

"I agree, Andrew, but a serious objection remains," I said.

"What is that?"

"You know what many people say about prudence, particularly with respect to the statesman who chooses to go to war. Prudence is too vague, too conjectural, too narrowly utilitarian, and too susceptible to self-serving rationalization."[470]

"Yes, I have heard that said."

"Of course, some of those who say this are individuals who prudently sense that they themselves are not too prudent, and so mistrust prudence as such, yes?"[471]

"Many, I would say."

"So the real issue is probably the balance we must strike between the intrinsic character of our actions and our prudential judgment of their probable consequences.[472] For example, some people say that what they call 'consequentialist' arguments are nothing more than attempts to compare incommensurable goods. They say 'How can you begin to compare the evils involved in the deterrence of war through war preparation with the evils of surrender?'[473]

"How do you?"

"I notice that we all do this all the time, in freely preferring to live with the evils of deterrence, rather than submit to tyranny. Throughout human history, human beings who have had the choice freely risked their own lives to maintain their freedom. This is because military preparedness may circumscribe our freedom, but does not crush it. It does not take a learned theologian to see this, though there are times I think that it takes a thick veneer of learning *not* to see it. What is more, have you not noticed something else about anti-consequentialists, Andrew?"

"What?"

"That they eventually have recourse to some larger consequentialism."

"Of course. They want to become citizens of the Kingdom of God.[474] So do we all, but I doubt that pacifism will take us there."

"Pacifists often claim, if not to be initiating the coming of the Kingdom, at least to be more effective than warriors are. They say that war fails more often than do peaceful means...."[475]

"The mistake of the modern Quaker is to claim that peaceful means usually work in *this* world, and then to generalize this, saying that such means should *always* be used. But if helplessness were almost always a credible defense, women would not be raped and children would seldom be abused. The blood of *those* martyrs is not necessarily the seed of any Church, but only an encouragement to greater depravity. A simplistic moralism will only serve as an invitation to viciousness.[476] A wise Christian has written, "Kingdoms and commonwealths acknowledging no superior, except God alone, can reasonably hope to be protected by him only; and by him, if with industry and courage they make use of the means he has given them for their own defense. God helps those who help themselves" instead of tempting God by expecting His miraculous intervention. What is more, history teaches us that the prudential Christian just war doctrine did succeed in limited conflicts, at least within Christendom.[477] This is not surprising, because God's Providence itself is so closely associated with prudence.[478] Much of the debate among nonresistant and just-war Christians turns on the issue of absolute dependence upon Providence by nonresistants, and limited dependence by the orthodox."[479]

"So, then, prudence is *morally* obligatory, not merely utilitarian, as is so often supposed in democracies?"[480]

"Exactly."

"And the prudential question is first and foremost a judgment concerning probabilities of effects measured against ultimate laws, principles, and goals?"[481]

"And the radical unpredictability of the future does not blind us to the *nature* of the tyrant, for example, who acts much the same throughout human experience?"[482]

"The cure of a living tyrant, I suppose, is his own discovery of the truest happiness, which will not occur in his passionate soul by the exercise of prudence, the practical wisdom he does not possess, but by theoretical wisdom, as it were – *sophia* as distinguished from *phronesis*?"

"Yes. There can be no complete and final happiness for any of us except in the vision of God. The tyrant needs this, too, more desperately than anyone."[483]

"But for the tyrant, mastered by the most loathesome passions, will wisdom be possible, except by God's grace?"

"Of course not."

"Therefore, the tyrannic – really tyrannized – soul at war with itself will only come to philosophy by a sort of divine intervention?"

"Undoubtedly."

"But a potentially tyrannic soul, one not yet hardened in its vices, might be directed in the right way by education?"

"Yes."

"And this is far preferable to waiting for divine intervention?"

"Far preferable."

"The tyrant's soul never tastes freedom or true friendship?"

"Never."

"And his life is a waking nightmare, worsening the longer it lasts?"

Simon spoke up. "Necessarily so. Absolutely. He is the slave of his own passions, imprisoned by his own people, who would gladly kill him. While the coercive power of the state is indispensable, tyrannical use of that power, might without right, locks ruler and ruled into a prison of mutual viciousness.[484] Only the church can unlock that prison."[485]

"At the same time, the Church cannot bring unity to civil society as a whole?"[486]

"Not so long as the Parousia is delayed," Simon admitted.

"And the sword is ordained by God outside the perfection of Jesus?"[487]

"Yes, and war makes this obvious more than anything else. Although one side may be less reprehensible than the other, both choose a *way* of life that cultivates war."[488]

"Christianity, then, in times before the Parousia, does not so much transfer political life as it moderates it — as Origen teaches."[489]

"You are probably right."

"This accounts for Jesus of Nazareth's firm refusal of *political* messianism during the time of His ministry?"[490]

"Yes, although in another sense Jesus is, as we said before, the Founder of a new regime, the only one that is truly workable."[491]

"It is a regime within souls, and among like-souled persons, but one so different from the ordinary political regime that one great Christian nonresistant could argue that patient Christian suffering would be well served by the most immoderate, tyrannical behavior of rulers."[492]

"I wouldn't go so far. But perhaps we should be less passionately concerned than we have been about politics in the worldly sense."[493]

"You want Christians to be Christians, not mixed Christians?"[494]

"It's all too easy to be seduced by worldly ambitions, in the name of social utility or justice.[495] But if government before the Parousia rule cannot maintain itself without lethal force, maybe Christian people should stay out of it altogether."[496]

"Perhaps one might formulate a nonresistant Christian realism? One that no longer expects nations generally to adopt nonresistance, and can recognize the just war as second best?"[497]

"I suppose there's *essentially* no alternative, although in any given situation a Christian may exercise his ordinary citizenship to a degree. But never to the ruin of civil society itself.[498] In fact, by our prayers, our example, and our educational activities, I believe Christians do more good for our countries than conventional patriots.[499] The small number of nonresistant Christians hardly threatens the civil order by tempting aggressor nations."[500]

"This is usually the case. But would not Christians refuse simple political indifference or apathy, given the tendency of some governments to persecute Christians, to declare war on their own citizens?"

"Yes, and this understanding is the origin of Quaker politics — which, however, can go too far in the direction of optimism and activism, I am beginning to suspect."[501]

"Still, do I recall we've acknowledged that the New Testament teaches that God grants the possibility of salvation through repentance to nations as well as individuals?"[502]

"You're right, although some Christians deny this.[503] The point is, we don't need Christians secretly ambitious for secular power.[504] We should intercede politically — if by doing so we do not violate our principles — first and foremost in order to protect our right to evangelize.[505] But we must never sacrifice the critical distance that exists between the Church and secular governments. Jesus chose us out of the world, and the commands to lay down our lives for one another and to distribute possessions equally are commandments to Christians, not to the world — although of course men of the world are commanded to become Christians."[506]

"And in a war between a country that permitted evangelism and one that does not?"

"We pray for the country that permits the right, and refuse, to the extent that humaneness permits us to refuse, to cooperate with the country that violates that right.[507] This is no crusade to save the world. It's not really much in terms of political involvement.[508]   Nor does it run to the other extreme of so-called Christian anarchism, which denies any legitimate role to secular government."[509]

"Christians shall not rule on earth, after all?"

"Not at this time. If it were possible to hold political office without violating the commands of Jesus, then a Christian might rule.[510] We are instead the leaven of the coming kingdom, not the rulers of the present one.[511] Non-Christians will make the most effective rulers; let just pagans fight it out with unjust pagans, nominal Christians with other nominal Christians.[512] Our mission is not to rule and not to ruin, but to cure.[513] For its part, government protects all of us, including Christians, from our own unrighteousness; while never *fully* moral, secular government has moral foundations and limited moral responsibilities and purposes."[514]

"Limitation implies regularity, which may be described as law?"

"Yes."

"And there is a distinction to be made between the law of cities and the ultimate law of nature, as Origen tells Celsus?"[515]

"I think so."

"And we distinguish bees from human beings in that we are genuinely political, endowed with speech and reason enabling us to deliberate about our actions, in public? And this reflects God's own image?"[516]

"Yes."

"And yet I see a problem."

"What is it?"

"The words 'regime' and, of course, the modern word 'state' are nowhere to be found in the Bible."[517]

"Yes, but 'law' is very prominent, there."

"Indeed. And so, after Lucretia was raped, preliminary to the founding of the Roman republic, she was in one sense too political, too humanly political, when she committed the crime of suicide to avoid a bad reputation. But a genuine politics will care for a good reputation with God, the supreme witness.[518] God's laws, as revealed and as seen in His creation, constitute the heavenly city within the human soul during its time on earth, ending or at least alleviating the *psychomachia* or war within the human soul. Can His laws also help to constitute a reasonably just regime on earth?"

"Yes, because even those who do not heed the revealed law may still perceive and obey the law of nature. Nature's laws *are* God's laws, though not God's *revealed* laws. Such men and such regimes can partake of some part of virtue, even if they concern themselves too much with all-too-human reputation."[519]

"And they do Christians the favor of leaving them alone, more or less?"

"Yes, as nonresistant Christians found when they left Europe for America."[520]

"So you are not so troubled by the critique of commercial republicanism advanced by the New England Non-Resistance Society in 1838, that there is 'a bullet in every ballot'?"[521]

"They were right, but there's more than a bullet in a ballot, and some of it is fairly good, provided that we don't absolutize that good, or forget about the bullet."[522]

X

"Now in reflecting upon the Christian Bible with respect to war, and many other things," I said, "would it be reasonable to say that there are at least three responses to it: using it, making something of it, and imitating it?"

"Explain to me more of what you mean."

"Consider the early Christians, for example. Even the worst atheist might wonder at their lasting effect on human history."[523]

"They did more for the peace of the world in which they lived than has ever been done before or since.[524] They sincerely tried to apply the mind of Christ to their own lives, and this led them to reject military service."[525]

"The question of whether and to what extent early Christians participated in military service, and the significance of that service, remains a vexed one, yes?"

"Yes, very much so. I believe that the handful of early Christians who were in the Roman army performed police functions, not as warriors. Christians who mix pagan just war doctrines with those of Scripture try to explain the antipathy of the early Church toward the military as a reaction to the systematic pagan idolatry of Roman army ceremonies or as a reaction to mistaken eschatological expectations. Once Christians saw that the end was not nigh, the argument goes, they started thinking about how to defend themselves in this world."[526]

"And indeed the Apostles had no families, homes, or property to defend.[527] This may have augmented the zeal that made them effective in the early years, I suppose, although zeal alone may bring war not peace."[528]

"True enough."

"And zeal is by nature unreflective?"

"Of course."

"And the unreflective part of mankind will be the majority, more often than not?"

Simon accepted this, reluctantly.

"Then perhaps much of the controversy concerning the relation of early Christians to war arises from a mildly embarrassing fact: modern pacifists, who often embrace egalitarian and democratic principles, see nonresistance upheld most vigorously by early Church elites, but much less so by the ordinary Christians of that time. Nonpacifist Christians, many of them not so egalitarian, find themselves defining the Church broadly and inclusively on this one issue, while preferring to look to the teachings of the Church Fathers in every other area."[529]

"You may have a point, there. But in the firm statements of such early Christian writers as Tatian the Assyrian and Athenagoras, war is explicitly condemned as an activity for Christians."[530]

"Some ambiguities may remain, encouraging those who would make something of Christianity, I suppose. Now, as Origen taught, the existence of the Roman Empire at that time hastened the spread of Christian doctrine, precisely because it provided peace, defended Christian proselytes, neither extirpating them nor tempting them to defend themselves with carnal weapons?"[531]

"Yes."

"And this also happened during the growth of the British Empire?"

"Yes, although by then Christians had taken the sword."

"And in both instances, there was a tendency eventually to ascribe *Biblical* righteousness to those emperors who defended the Faith?"[532]

"Yes."

"Now," I said, turning to Andrew, "am I mistaken in thinking that the Roman Emperor Constantine, the first to say he had converted to Christianity, is the statesman to consider in this regard?"

"Not at all mistaken," Andrew said. "Constantine combined authoritatively the Christians who prayed with the Christians who fought, and brought victories in spiritual and physical war to Rome. The *imitatio Christi* was enlarged to become the *imitatio Dei* of the Christian Roman Emperor; victorious over his passions and his enemies, he became the first true philosopher-king — the first king who was truly wise — and brought peace to his realm by representing God's sovereign power on earth. As such, he availed himself of the authority to wage war, as his God does. And, like God, he governed humanely, opposing tyranny. He understood that clemency alone will never suffice in human governance, that pity for an evil man will not change him, but will only prolong his opportunities to deprive decent, potentially Christian citizens of any chance for salvation."[533]

"And does not one of his historians remark on the extraordinary character of Constantine's conversion — Constantine's report of a miraculous vision of the Cross, accompanied by the words 'Conquer By This' — as an account that 'might have been hard to believe had it been related by any other person'?"[534]

"Yes and, we might add, if there had been some great objection to Christians serving in the army, it surely would have been voiced at this point. In fact there was none."[535]

"And so, gradually, men of great abilities began to gravitate toward the Church, an increasingly attractive alternative to established political life?"[536]

"It was not so innocent as all that," Simon interjected. "Political power endowed the priests with worldly goods, goods they then sought to defend; the priests made the wrong kind of peace with the world, twisting Scripture to fit their newfound political role. The sanctification of carnal war was the inevitable result."[537]

"Would it be accurate to say that the most subtle temptation came from the fact that, after Constantine, the world's favor came too close to the core of faith, which had hitherto rejected the world's favor?"[538]

Andrew spoke up. "Still, we have to live in the world. In certain places, we can come close to fulfilling all of the Gospel precepts; for the most part, we cannot come so close. We must adapt, and adapt such unChristian institutions as the pagan armies, or perish — today as before. It is the richness of our tradition that allows us to do so, a tradition that affords scope for our own conscientious prudence."[539]

"And although the blood of the martyrs can be the seed of the Church, there are times when the prudent advancement of Gospel truth may better be served by peace on earth? Even as, in a different way, the sufferings brought on by modern tyrants make survivors, even some partisans of the tyrants, welcome the unheroic life of regimes that are not so extraordinary?"

"Yes. Those who have no fear of death often admire martyrdom. Those who must *live* with the possibility of martyrdom often tire of that life."

"There is then a paradox of sorts, yes? Men who promise to remake the world, criticizing 'abstract' thought as do-nothing escapism, end by fraying the human will, pulling it beyond the limits of nature."

"Yes, yes: *They* are the 'abstract' ones; *they* are the ideologues."

"On the other hand, the self-identification of the Emperor with God had its own despotic consequences, did it not? Government by consent of God supersedes government by consent of citizens.[540] And this in turn makes the most fanatical kinds of war more likely, yes?"[541] Andrew conceded that it was so.

"Of course," I continued, "there is an equally great danger from the imitators of Christian belief, the heretics."

"Perhaps even a greater danger," Andrew was quick to say. "These groups often claim that human nature itself is not merely formed in God's image, but has creative divinity within it, a divinity that needs only the right sort of regimen to elicit. They make utopian claims to sinlessness, often ascribing diabolism to all those who do not share their illusions.[542] There is a close association of these groups with pacifism."[543]

"And utopian claims water and cultivate passions that ought to be severely pruned, do they not, Simon?"

Evidently foregoing a response to Andrew's last remark, Simon agreed.

"It's an old quarrel, of course, this struggle between the love of truth and the love of illusion, and I don't suppose we'll resolve it tonight," I said. "But I suppose we can continue to seek out those who can distinguish truth from illusion, to try to order our souls so that we too can make that distinction, practicing a way of life that will conduce to peace."

CHAPTER FIVE

Christianity and Nonviolent Resistance

The Christian nonresistant Simon Liteson does not avail himself of the characteristic argument made by pacifists in his own century. In contradistinction to nonresistants, nonviolent resisters claim that certain techniques of economic, political, and social conflict, known collectively as 'civil disobedience,' if employed by well-organized and disciplined groups, can prevent rulers from ruling. Deprived of authority – that is, deprived of both recognized moral legitimacy and effective physical force – rulers must compromise, capitulate, or even cede office.

Nonviolent resisters understand that political authority finally requires consent. Even regimes founded upon force and fraud actually depend upon consent because "people do not always do what they are told to do, and sometimes do things that have been forbidden."[1] The harshest engines of coercion cannot bend the human will. Citizens and subjects, even guardians selected by rulers to enforce unjust laws or edicts, enjoy free will and may exercise it. Despotic rulers' attempts to override and conceal the fact of free will can be exposed and successfully fought by sufficiently courageous, prudent, and just opponents who avail themselves of no violent means. Machiavelli is no realist. He is an illusionist. He must be unmasked and exiled from public life.

As this book is being written, optimism prevails among proponents of nonviolent resistance. Nonviolent resistants have overthrown rightist tyranny in the Philippines and despotic leftist oligarchies in Poland and

Czechoslovakia. "Gone are the days when sophisticated scholars and policymakers could dismiss the phenomenon of nonviolent action as being able to work only in India against 'gentlemanly' British, or as too weak to challenge powerful dictatorships, especially Communist ones."[2] This notwithstanding, some caution may well prevail among those not carried away with enthusiasms of this moment. It remains true that nonviolent resistance has worked only in countries where a civil society has persisted, even flourished, under despotisms more 'totalitarian' in aspiration than in fact. Where tyrants succeed in destroying civil society, then vigilantly prevent its reemergence to any considerable degree — retaining their willingness to kill in order to perpetuate their tyranny — nonviolent resistance fails (as in communist China) or barely gets started in the first place (as in Romania).

Unlike 'civil' war, civil disobedience inextricably depends upon civility. Without a core of civility in those who disobey, and without more than a suggestion of civility in those who are disobeyed, civil disobedience cannot prevail. The term 'nonviolent resistance' obscures the civil character of a project whose proponents often dramatically imagine themselves as warriors not civilians. Civil resistants disobey the laws or even seek to overthrow an existing system of laws and the regime that established it. But disobeying particular laws may reaffirm the system of law; overthrowing an existing law may bring a regime back to its original principles; and revolutionizing a regime may strengthen civility.[3] Genuinely uncivil resistants could gain at most a false victory, substituting one tyranny for another, if they could discipline themselves to gain victory at all.

Strong-willed persons who carry, as it were, a civil society within themselves might suppose no external civil society to be necessary, at least for adults. They would be right, were it not true that a strong, free will may direct itself in any number of directions — toward tyrannical ambitions as well as civil peace. The extreme voluntarism some nonviolent resisters espouse equally requires public safeguards against extreme voluntarists who seek 'the triumph of the will.'

If nonviolent resistance or civil disobedience promises much, delivers some of what it promises, yet also potentially endangers the very civility it seeks to affirm, then the confrontation between *the* nonviolent resister,

Mohandas K. Gandhi, and a principal embodiment of the modern civil and civilizing order, the British constitutional empire,[4] will remain perennially relevant to any serious consideration of the theoretical and practical consequences of civil disobedience. Additionally, it is convenient for our purposes here that British constitutionalists were often Christians. Gandhi was of course no Christian. His methods of nonviolent resistance were not necessarily consistent with Christianity. British constitutionalists had to ask themselves not only whether nonviolent resistance was good for Indian civil society and their own, but whether it was good for Christian civilization. In particular, Gandhi forced British Christian nonresistants into a conscientious internecine debate.

Gandhi's Challenge to British Constitutional Imperialism

Contemporary Indian scholars look back at British rule with some ambivalence. One writer describes colonial Indians as "bewitched by British moral and imperial values" inculcated by pedantic conquerors who "were not masters but headmasters." The headmasters made their own customs and institutions into "values for others, an illicit logical move lying at the heart of every ideology." But the same writer also admits that Indian civilization had degenerated in the decades before the British arrived. Eighteenth and nineteenth-century Indians too often lacked courage and justice.[5] Another writer, while observing that a "habit of self-congratulation was part of the ethos of the British rulers of India," contends that Indians "had outgrown" British imperialism by the twentieth century – an indirect way of conceding that that imperialism had its benefits in the nineteenth.[6] While patriotic pride may be said to preclude any but a grudging acknowledgment of imperialism's benefits, honesty brings to light the "lack of nationalism" in India before the British came, which enabled the British "to conquer the country by swallowing it piecemeal" and, more, to make their conquest "acceptable" to the Indians themselves, at least initially.[7] By the nineteenth century the British Empire had become the modern, bourgeois Rome. Christians saw opportunities for evangelization in the modern empire similar to those afforded to their spiritual ancestors by the ancient one. As before, traditionalists objected. Banning such practices as infanticide and suttee (the immolation of widows on their husbands' funeral pyres) and suppressing the murderous cult of Kali offended devout Hindus, as did energetic Christian evangelizing. In 1857 a violent rebellion failed, but persuaded the British that "[a]ny attempt to convert Indians to Christianity promised to subvert the very foundations of civil peace."[8] By reasserting their authority while limiting interference with local customs and seeking the cooperation of 'native' elites, the British imperialists restored civic order for decades.

Gandhi contended that this order was not genuinely peaceful or civil. British imperialists disagreed, not only from self-interest and ambition. Winston Churchill made the principled defense of British rule in India.[9]

Churchill understood that Gandhi, "the supreme figure in Indian political life," intended no compromise with British rule in the long run. As such, Gandhi's enterprise would have to be "grappled with and crushed."[10] "The rescue of India from ages of barbarism, tyranny, and intestine war, and its slow but ceaseless forward march to civilization constitute upon the whole the finest achievement of [English] history". Indian self-rule at any time soon would result in "the immediate resumption of mediaeval wars" or, alternatively, "Hindu despotism" exercised over Moslems and the lower castes of Hindus themselves."[11] "Already," Churchill warned, "Mr. Gandhi moves about surrounded by a circle of wealthy men, who see at their finger-tips the acquisition of the resources of an Empire on cheaper terms than were ever offered in the history of the world."[12] These "Brahmins" who "mouth and patter the principles of Western Liberalism," hold 60 million 'Untouchables' in "sub-human bondage" and would build an "India for a very few Indians." Ceding rule to this "highly artificial and restricted oligarchy" would be "altogether wrong" in moral, political, and (one might add) religious terms alike.[13]

In Churchill's view Gandhi undermined government by consent in India and in the Empire as a whole. "The British way of doing things has always meant and implied close and effectual cooperation with the people of the country." British "parliamentary institutions," already "in a state of decay," further degenerated whenever Gandhi flouted the rule of law, however nonviolently, and substituted for it his own "fanaticism," however sincere (Churchill rather doubted that it was).[14] Indian self-rule would emerge justifiably, at a pace dependent "upon the self-discipline and self-regeneration of the Indian people themselves," as reckoned by the British.[15]

This prudential reckoning could easily succumb to either of two extremes: the extreme of false 'idealism' (the "misguided benevolence" of the Viceroy, Lord Irwin, all too eager to compromise with Gandhi, or the "Utopian dreams" of Socialist parliamentarians);[16] and the extreme of narrow self-interest, the smug mediocrity of 'ugly Englishmen' who would never relinquish their petty privileges. Churchill himself appealed to British self-interest, although he did not conceive it narrowly. "The loss of India would mark and consummate the downfall of the British Empire." The Empire's downfall "would reduce us to the scale of a minor power" perhaps unable to support a domestic population of some 45 millions.[17]

Absent the unifying "technical and administrative apparatus" of British rule, India – "no more a political personality," no more "a united nation," than was Europe – "will fall back quite rapidly through the centuries into the barbarism and deprivations of the Middle Ages."[18] A "firm and coherent policy of the simple maintenance of law and order" would prevent calamity for both India and Empire.[19]

With more than half a century's advantage in hindsight, one may fairly assess these imperialist concerns. Churchill was right to suppose that Indian independence would effectually end the British Empire; he was wrong to imagine that this would ruin Britain economically, as free trade turned out to be more beneficial than heavily regulated imperial trade. Thus Britain neither remained a major 'power' nor became a minor one. As for the optimists' hopes, there too realities proved mixed. After independence in 1947, at least one million Indians died in violent religio-ethnic struggles leading to the partition of the country.[20] Such struggles, threatening additional partitions or outright secessions, continue to threaten the Indian political union. The union has so far been maintained by the same forceful – that is, nonpacifist – means that other governments have employed throughout history – including the British Raj. Nor has political or social-economic justice much advanced since the British departed.[21] The Hindu elites remain firmly in control of most institutions, somewhat as Churchill predicted. Still, India maintains a commercial republic of sorts – resembling

Mexico's regime more than those of Europe or the United States — and has not lapsed (for long) into the despotism seen in neighboring China and Southeast Asia. Barbarism has not recurred. British imperialism was indispensably helpful but not permanently so. It is difficult to see how self-government could be secured without the actual practice of self-government, including those memorable lessons learned by reflecting upon errors and injustices committed by oneself, not by 'oppressors.'

Gandhi understood the imperial concerns. As a young man he shared them. In 1896 he wrote that in England unlike India, "a man's worth, not his birth, is taken into account in judging him" — a practice that must have appealed to an ambitious young lawyer unsuccessful in his homeland.[22] During the Boer War of 1899, the Zulu Rebellion of 1906, and the First World War, Gandhi supported the Empire and participated in medical assistance work, although of course he "never wielded a weapon."[23]

> I felt that, if I demanded rights as a British citizen, it was also my duty, as such, to participate in the defence of the British Empire. I held then that India could achieve her complete emancipation only within and through the British Empire.[24]

"[A]t the root of this loyalty," he wrote, was "my love of truth"; the British Constitution served not only the British but human beings as such, with institutional safeguards of racial equality and religious freedom.[25] When the Rowlatt bills of 1919, proposed and adopted to meet the threat of violent subversion, abrogated certain Indian civil rights, Gandhi "lost faith in the British Administration in India" without rejecting British constitutionalism altogether.[26] He did reject key parts of the British Constitution, particularly those he associated with modernity.[27] In 1930 Gandhi vented decades of frustrations.

> Pax Britannica is not a beneficial operation. It has as much value to India as the slave dwellers have in an estate whose owner keeps the slaves from fighting with one another, protects the estate from foreign inroads and makes the slaves work with a regularity that is just enough to keep the estate going in his, the owner's interest. The slaves of this imaginary estate when they grow to consciousness of their position, prefer anarchy to slavery if there is no other choice. Even so should I prefer

anarchy to the existing rule and its much-vaunted peace if I can have no other choice. Surely no-rule is better than misrule.[28]

Thus Gandhi unintentionally confirmed Churchill's suspicion that the logic of nonviolent resistance must lead to anarchy and war. Some seventeen years later, Gandhi would see what "no-rule" entails, how much worse it can be than relatively mild rule, even mild misrule, by a civilized if mediocre class of foreigners. Gandhi's over-passionate aversion to British Constitutionalism, reminiscent of a disillusioned lover's bitterness, overbalanced his prudence.

Lacking Gandhi's resentments, English pacifists initially experienced even more serious ambivalences than he did with respect both to Indian independence and to nonviolence resistance. Neither pacifistic nor (once established) bellecist and tyrannical, British imperial rule had its defenders among pacifists; neither anti-Christian nor Christian, nonviolent resistance also evoked mixed sentiments. Between the two Government of India Acts 1919-1935, the major pacifist periodicals in England published numerous articles and letters on Gandhi, airing the concerns of sincere pacifists sympathetic to Indian aspirations yet esteeming British Constitutionalism.[29] The most extensive information and debate on 'the Indian question' in a pacifist forum appeared in *The Friend*, a weekly published by English Quakers. Although the infrequent editorials on Gandhi supported British rule, most articles defended him. *Reconciliation*, published by the British chapter of the Fellowship of Reconciliation, featured a higher percentage of critical articles than *The Friend*, and took the same editorial line.

In 1920, longtime Quaker missionary Joseph Taylor recounted his thirty years of work in India.[30] He did not mention Gandhi, who had returned only recently after many years in England and South Africa. In discussing Quaker educational, medical, agricultural, and evangelical activities Taylor emphasized the spiritual goods introduced thereby. He made no mention of imperialism. The following year Taylor reported that "a very great change has come over the people of India generally during recent years," owing to English education in "freedom and national patriotism," technical and business knowledge, and recent trends toward anarchism and socialism. In addition the Great War "caused a great outburst of 'national' spirit in all the countries concerned."[31] Taylor first mentioned Gandhi in an article published in January 1922; while admiring Gandhi's personal virtues Taylor deplored "a variety of men of quite different temperament who only use [Gandhi's] reputation as a cover to their own quite different actions."[32] These probably were not the rich Hindus Churchill would warn against, but non-pacifist revolutionaries. In 1919 and in 1921, Gandhi had initiated campaigns of nonviolent resistance that turned violent; *The Friend* editorialized in support of the Viceroy, Lord Reading, who cited the "indirect responsibility of agitators who, among ignorant people, suggest a course of lawlessness." In such circumstances the people soon disregarded nonviolence as passions flared.[33] At this time 'civil disobedience' looked like a contradiction in terms.

A much more optimistic view came to light in February 1922, when *The Friend* published John S. Hoyland's first article on Gandhi. From then until 1930, when the London Yearly Meeting of Quakers officially and fully addressed the question of Indian independence, Hoyland wrote sixteen of *The Friend*'s twenty-seven articles on India. Hoyland conceded that violence had occurred as an indirect result of Gandhi's activities but, "on the whole, the discipline of the movement is phenomenal." While Gandhi often lacked "political insight," took a too-critical view of the British government, and shortsightedly led boycotts of schools and colleges, his was "by far the most extensive effort that has ever been made to apply the original principles of Christianity to the problems of practical life." Gandhi had "chosen Christ's way of fighting" and enjoyed "extraordinary success" overall.[34]

After Gandhi's arrest, a trial, and conviction, for sedition in 1922, Hoyland praised Indians' obedience to Gandhi's commands of nonviolence as "a most extraordinary act of discipline and self-control...and a real triumph of the Kingdom of God."[35] Gandhi's greatness

> ...lies, not in political foresight (in which he is indeed disastrously lacking) but in his uncompromising loyalty to lofty ideals and in his extraordinary power of enforcing the allegiance of others to those same ideals.... One has the feeling that a nation has never been greater than India during the past ten days.[36]

India's greatness, actual and potential, inhered in its congruence, not yet an identity, with Quaker Christianity: "There is a willingness [among Indians] to believe in spiritual forces as superior to natural law in its ordinary manifestations," allowing "the direct influence of the supernatural on human affairs." Thus Gandhi was said to be an incarnation of the god Vishnu. "It is easy to see how close these conceptions lie to many of our Quaker convictions, and especially to the Quaker belief in the Inward Light."[37] Hoyland cautioned that Indians did not yet share the Quaker concern with the moral content of spirituality, the Biblical "fruits of the spirit." He recommended teaching them "the Inner Christ" and observed that Indians themselves already compared Gandhi to Christ in His nonviolence, dignity, simplicity, straightforwardness and, above all, His fearlessness.[38] Gandhi was "a prophet far more than a patriot, combining nationalism with aspirations to "a new Kingdom of Heaven," and waging "spiritual warfare" against what he regarded as "essentially and fundamentally immoral, anarchic and self-destructive Western civilization."[39]

By 1929 Hoyland openly called for Indian political independence and for "the permeation of Indian life and society by the ideals of Christ."[40]

> [T]he real enemy of progress and enlightment in India is not the Hindu system of ideas, which is rapidly reforming itself, but the secularism which is coming in like a flood from the West....[I]n the battle with materialism, which is the real foe of the Kingdom of God, both in East and West, the essential Hinduism is to be regarded as an ally rather than as an adversary.[41]

Hoyland acknowledged that "erotic elements" in some Hindu scriptures, as well as the social institutions of Untouchability and early marriage, contradicted the spirit of Christianity. He called for support of Gandhi's efforts to reform Hinduism "from within" and for continued Christian evangelizing that would build upon Gandhi's moral example.[42]

Careful not to denigrate British imperialism in articles for an English readership, Hoyland affirmed that "the British saved India from anarchy" and bestowed "the inestimable gift of peace." Systems of communication, irrigation, uniform standards of education, administration, and guarded frontiers all brought some unity to an extraordinarily diverse land. "On the whole the British record in India is the cleanest and most credible shown by any imperial race in ruling a subject people since the beginning of history."[43] He acknowledged the difficulties in governing the country – its racial and linguistic heterogeneity, religious and political tensions.[44] But he reported without demurral Hindu complaints against the British: that the states ruled by Indian princes saw none of the Hindu-Moslem clashes prevalent in states governed by the British, who were suspected of divide-and-rule tactics; that the Indian economy was locked into perpetual inferiority to that of England; that industrialism was evil; that, despite the value of British institutions, "the careless boorishness of the individual Englishman" repelled a people who esteemed personal courtesy as indispensable to legitimate rule.[45] The modern university system had propagated nationalist sentiments throughout the educated classes, sentiments encouraged by the 1905 defeat of Russia by Japan, the first war-victory for an Eastern over a Western country. Finally, if the Great War was fought for democracy, Indians would not forego the fruits of victory. Unworkable and wrong, alien domination should be replaced by an Indian government operating under a federal constitution.[46]

> The argument that India should not be given freedom because she might abuse it, is one that is all too familiar.... A people, like an individual, can only become 'fit for freedom' by using it in practice.[47]

Other writers for *The Friend* shared Hoyland's sympathy for Gandhi's means and ends.[48] Still others expressed sympathy with reservations.[49] An Indian Christian warned, "We are not one people: we are a continent" in need of a common language (he recommended English) and more extensive Christian missionary work; "absolute freedom at once" would not benefit Indians.[50]

John W. Graham argued against independence. He agreed with Hoyland and others that "the central message of Quakerism fits India." Without "the Western system of the religious Establishment" and its doctrines (including, as Graham's lists them, stories of the Creation, Adam and Eve, and the Flood, Old Testament wars, miracles, and prophecies, Jesus of Nazareth's divinity and Atonement, Heaven and Hell, and the Second Coming), both India and modern Quakerism were open to the moral teachings of Christianity. Nor would Hinduism offer much resistance to evangelism. A "decaying, slowly dying faith," Hinduism has made "so many people miserable" that it possessed "neither strength nor charm...to withstand Christianity."[51] But independence might strengthen Hinduism, bringing a restoration of the Brahmins and subjecting the majority of Indians to "demoralizing servitude to a class of worldly priests" — a prospect not at all palatable to Quakers.[52]

Worse, the Indian character itself lacked self-government. Indians had "little backbone"; prone to "shirk responsibility" and "subject to mass suggestion," they lied and took bribes as a matter of course, then hypocritically complained of greedy, overly competitive Westerners. They lacked public spirit and remained sunk in the caste system and religious begging.[53] In a debate at the London Yearly Meeting of 1930, before the first of the three Round-Table Conferences held by British and Indian representatives preliminary to the framing of the Government of India Act of 1935, Graham denied that the British exploited this people; Gandhi lead a "movement of rebellion." Hoyland called for independence and requested Quakers to write to the Labour Party in its support. There being no coherent 'sense of the Meeting,' as is required by Quaker custom, no message was formulated.[54]

Editorially *The Friend* reaffirmed its imperialist stance in 1930, after the Yearly Meeting. Since 1958, when authority over India was transferred from the East India Company to the British Crown, "'the trend of policy of the British Government of India has been directed steadily towards the introduction of the representative institutions of the West, appropriately adapted to the complex conditions of India." Given the extraordinary diversity of the Indian peoples, such concepts as representation and liberty eluded easy practical embodiment. Gandhi was a nationalist without a nation. Without stronger social and political bonds, India would fall into "chaos" if reform proceeded too rapidly.[55]

The Friend's editorialist reminded readers of the threefold Quaker witness with respect to the relation of Christianity to citizenship. First, Quakers shall tolerate no governmental invasion of the individual conscience; the Quaker response to such policies is forthright refusal to obey coupled with physical *non*resistance up to and including the point of martyrdom. Second,

Quakers are conscientiously law-abiding; that is, they regard obedience to the law, except in the cases of governmental intrusion previously remarked, as morally required. Third, the Christian Church has a prophetic mission "to exhort and empower right-doing." This "prophetic claim," seen in the lives of Robert Barclay, William Penn, and Steven Crisp, "was not in favor of a particular form of Government, but of provision *for liberty of conscience and opportunity of right living*" under whatever form of government existed.[56] Since the time of the early Quakers, "the instruments of governance have come into the hands of the people," raising questions for Christians' relations with a democratic government – particularly, the government that arose as the British Constitution had evolved. While sympathizing with the oppressed, "we cannot support revolution or sedition," which would mean "disaster for [Gandhi's] cause as well as for India."[57] Correspondence to *The Friend* continued to be published for the balance of the year, with no major new arguments adduced by either side.

In *Reconciliation*, C.H. Watkins and the editorialist writing in the "Special Indian Number" of 1930 criticized both imperialism and nationalism. These "two rival partialities" have "no place in the kingdom of God." They distinguished Gandhian nonviolent resistance from "pacifism in the Christian sense." Nonviolent resistance "tries to make government impossible, and this *must* tend to violent means" despite the intentions of the resisters. Gandhi's way was "highly provocative" and "not the way of Christ as we see it." The burden of proof or justification must be on the one who resists, "cooperation being the normal channel of the kindly Christian will."[58] John S. Hoyland defended Gandhi by calling nonviolent resistance "the greatest asset on the side of law and order," the practical alternative to a violent nationalism that would make British rule impossible.[59] John W. Graham again took the opposite view, arguing that nonviolent lawlessness would encourage not discourage violent lawlessness.[60] F.E. Pollard concurred, describing Gandhi's intention as revolutionary and "consistent only with the belief that government is essentially bad." He called upon pacifists to work with both sides for conciliation, without suggesting what the content of a just settlement would be.[61]

Absent from the English pacifist debate over Gandhian nonviolent resistance was Churchill's concern for the reduction of England's political authority and economic well-being. But many pacifists shared Churchill's fear of religious war, his warnings against Hindu oligarchs, priests, and violent revolutionaries. They also agreed that nonviolent resistance undermines government by consent along parliamentary lines and the rule of law, that it weakens self-discipline and replaces it with a sort of zealotry. Pacifist imperialists doubted that Indians possessed the moral, civic, and intellectual virtues needed for self-government. As a result, they argued India's riotous diversity of peoples, religions, languages, and customs would never generate peaceful union.

The anti-imperial pacifist argument faulted modern Western civilization as immoral, anarchistic, secularist (that is, 'bourgeois' or selfish and materialistic), and ultimately self-destructive.[62] Although flawed, India's Hinduism could act as a counterbalance to the modern West; Indians by no means lacked the self-discipline nonviolent resistance requires.

Anti-imperial pacifists compared Gandhi to Jesus of Nazareth as an exponent of spiritual warfare. They felt that Gandhi resembled a modern Quaker. Imperialist pacifists denied that a movement of active political resistance, however nonviolent, amounted to a new form of Christian nonresistance. Political, social, and economic activity would provoke resentment not reconciliation, unlike the spiritual warfare of *non*resistance.

These opposing religious assessments of Gandhi complemented the opposing political assessments. Consciously or not, anti-imperialist pacifists sought a new form of political rule, a new foundation of political unity. Gandhi's nonviolent resistance appeared to point the way toward a radically new means not only of resisting government but of self-government, a means that would actually work in this world. Imperialist pacifists supposed no such new politics possible, only new variations of political arrangements already well known in human history. Only the rulers themselves might change. For imperialists the political question remained, 'Who rules?' They asked themselves, 'Which among the would-be rulers of India will rule best?' and doubted that Gandhi and his followers were those men. Imperialist pacifists lacked the anti-imperial pacifists' supreme ambition for a new empire on earth.

What of Christian pacifists generally, outside of England? And what of Christians generally? Without any personal stake in the British Empire or independent India, they could be expected to take a less partisan yet perhaps also a more 'abstract' or doctrinaire view of Gandhi and his movement of nonviolent resistance.

Gandhi's Challenge to Pacifist Christianity

It is a sign of ethnocentrism, or perhaps of political prudence, that Western writers on Gandhi so often search for Christian and other 'influences' on Gandhi's thought, and so seldom try to measure Gandhi's influence on Christian pacifism. Their accounts of Gandhi rarely fail to cite his study of the Gospels, Thoreau, Tolstoy, Ruskin, Garrison; Gandhi himself took pains to mention these in his interviews with Europeans and Americans. Gandhi and Western pacifists alike sought to make nonviolent resistance resemble the traditions of the West. But the reverse flow — from East to West, from Gandhi to Christians in Europe, North America, and elsewhere — scarcely wins more than passing attention, despite two clear possibilities: that Gandhian nonviolent resistance, as a coherent and comprehensive doctrine and practice, had forerunners but no real predecessor in the West;[63] and that Gandhi influenced the West at least as much as he was influenced by it. Gandhi's early writings, his 1927 *Autobiography*, and recent biographical research confirm that the Christian and quasi-Christian 'influences' Gandhi encountered as a young man in England and South Africa had themselves been influenced by Eastern religions, modern rationalism, or both, and that these encounters caused Gandhi not so much to change his mind as to develop and focus it.[64] "Gandhi's whole approach differed radically from Western pacifism, and the pacifists clearly recognized this."[65]

Before Gandhi, Christian nonresistant pacifism had resolutely pursued the kinds of policies that provoke Nietzsche's derision as he comments on Jesus of Nazareth's last words, *"Comsummatum est"*:

> It is plain *what* was finished with the death on the cross: a new, an entirely original basis for a Buddhistic peace movement, for

an actual, *not* merely promised, *happiness on earth.* For this...remains the fundamental difference between the two religions of decadence: Buddhism does not promise but fulfills: Christianity promises everything but fulfills nothing.[66]

Christian belief in *personal* immortality devalues this life, Nietzsche charged, debasing the "noble, *male* instincts" and sinking Europe into a swamp of effeminate egalitarianism.[67] "Our politics is sick from this lack of courage."[68] As Quaker historian Charles Chatfield has observed, "the transformation of pacifism" — that is, traditional Christian pacifism — "into a movement for social justice without violence required the assertion that there was power in nonviolence"[69] — not only spiritual power but this-worldly political, even physical power. While it is true that Quakerism and other nonconforming Christian sects potentially would seize control of social and political institutions,[70] Gandhi presented nonviolent resistance as a practical way to do this, one that does not require unusual activities by an approving Providence — for example, an apocalypse.[71]

The potential physical and political power of nonviolent Christians was understood by at least one early Christian. Tertullian asked, rhetorically:

> For what wars should we not be fit, not eager, even with unequal forces, we who so willingly yield ourselves to the sword, if in our religion it were not counted better to be slain than to slay? Without arms even, and raising no insurrectionary banner, but simply in enmity to you, we could carry on the contest with you by an ill-willed severance alone.[72]

Tertullian does not consider the possibility of good-willed severance or loving civil disobedience, perhaps because disobedience to magistrates is so rarely loving, or perhaps because he regards disobedience to authorities as inherently unloving — rather as Lear does 'ingratitude.' The Christian licitness of civil disobedience or nonviolent resistance may depend upon its adaptability to an innocent, loving heart and a mind of serpentine prudence.

Gandhi has had admirers who did not hesitate to compare him to Jesus of Nazareth in both love and prudence. Gandhi "combine[d] the wisdom of the serpent with the gentleness of the dove"; he was "patently good but also extremely astute, a combination that is normally believed to be impossible."[73] Romain Rolland — who, as a Frenchman, had no hesitation in comparing the

British Empire with Rome — also compared Gandhi to Jesus and called Gandhi's disciples "a sacred legion of apostles who, like those of Christ, will be as the salt of the earth"; "the only thing lacking is the cross."[74] While admitting that "Christ never set Himself to break the Roman rule," another Christian pacifist explained this as a difference in circumstances only: "To [Jesus] the sins of His own people and their leaders loomed larger than the evils of foreign domination." Gandhi "has shown the world a type of pacifism which can truly take the place of war," to say nothing of Western pacifism hitherto, which "too easily degenerates into passivity."[75]

Gandhi's example and personality renewed the faith of many Christians in the increasingly secularized West. The American missionary W.E. Sikes met him and found "a deeper and purer view of Christianity than I had ever known."[76] The Unitarian minister John Haynes Holmes read some of Gandhi's writings in the aftermath of the First World War:

> Instantly I seemed to be alive — my vision clear, my mind at peace, my heart reassured. Here was the perfect answer to all my problems.... [Gandhi] was living in the faith that I had sought. He was making it work and proving it right. He was everything I believed but hardly dared to hope. He was a dream come true.[77]

In 1921 Holmes delivered a sermon titled "Who Is The Greatest Man in the World Today?" telling his listeners,

> When I think of Gandhi, I think of Jesus. He lives his life; he speaks his word; he suffers, strives, and will some day nobly die, for his Kingdom on earth.[78]

He added, "If Lenin falls short anywhere, and I am sure he does, it is in the field of moral idealism"; Gandhi, the "universal man," both "dreamer and doer," puts forward "a program of statesmanship to the great end of political and social liberation."[79]

A Christian missionary in India named E. Stanley Jones testified that Gandhi "taught me more of the spirit of Christ than perhaps any other man in East or West"; Gandhi's assassination was "the greatest tragedy since the Son of God died on the Cross."[80] Gandhi's advice to Christians in India was to "live more like Jesus Christ," and Jones described Gandhi as "a natural

Christian rather than an orthodox one" – a view the unorthodoxy of which did not escape Jones.[81] Natural Christianity would seem to overcome the need for grace – that is, the one thing needful. And indeed Gandhi "never seemed to get to Christ as a person," and therefore lacked the "certainty and joy and release from past and present sin" that makes the Christian "bubble with gratitude, and which make him want to share Christ with everybody." Gandhi's suspicions of Christian evangelism derived from his lack of experience of grace; "he could not understand why Christians would want to share their faith," and suspected unconscious pridefulness in their zeal. Gandhi's understanding of salvation, fundamentally erotic, striving, emphasized *at*tainment and works, "strict, disciplined efforts, a rigid self-mastery," not "*ob*tainment and grace." Consciousness of salvation obtained not attained brings humility even as it inspires zeal. "This the Mahatma never understood."[82] Jones shrewdly supposed that Gandhi had a political purpose in his opposition to Christian evangelism. Gandhi wanted to 'save' the Untouchables for Hinduism, and for India – and, not incidentally, for Gandhism as the instrument of Indian independence. When Jones threatened civil disobedience if Christians were not permitted to evangelize, Gandhi reacted sourly.[83] Christians, it seems, commit acts of civil disobedience primarily in order to win the right to practice their religion; Gandhi committed acts of civil disobedience in order to revolutionize a government *as part of* his religious practice. Jones nonetheless insisted that God "used Mahatma Gandhi to help Christianize unchristian Christianity" to "turn our resolutions into revolutions" and build "a Kingdom of God society."[84] Nonviolent resistance would be the practical, moral equivalent of the revolutionary war needed to do this.[85]

In 1938 a group of men described as "Christian statesmen" met with Gandhi in Madras, India. The Christians sought "to gain from him advice as to how they might learn to follow Christ better." This extraordinary attempt by Christians to improve themselves as Christians by consulting a Hindu arose from a sense that Christianity had "gone wrong" in compromising with industrialism and imperialism, and that Gandhi had "come nearer to the discovery of the mind of Christ and to the practicing of the way of Christ" than had contemporary professing Christians.[86] Nor was the problem so recent as industrialism and modern imperialism. "Western civilization," one participant wrote, had "never been able to enforce or implement" the "message" of Jesus: the West was "therefore breaking down before our eyes." Gandhi told the Christians that if "a people make up their mind that they will never do the tyrant's will, nor retaliate with the tyrants own methods, the tyrant will not find it worth his while to go on with his terrorism." Tyrants can be redeemed because "human nature in its essence is one, and therefore unfailingly responds to the advance of love," the nonviolence of which is "the central teaching of the Bible."[87] This makes the central teaching of the Bible an act of graceful morality not overcoming a fallen or sinful human nature but rather appealing to a fundamentally good human nature. This approach dovetailed with much of contemporary Protestantism, which had silently abandoned the doctrine of original sin.

Quakers remained the Christians closest to Gandhian practice, dedicated as they were "to the proposition that men can and must be effective and compassionate, tough-minded and tender-hearted in matters of social change," and committed to "nonviolence as a *way of life*, and not just as a temporary tactic in a particular historical situation."[88] The example of Gandhi changed Quaker practice nonetheless. Quakers ventured beyond 'social work' and conscientious objection to war, even beyond institutional politics.[89] After Gandhi's influence pervaded the Society, it became less likely that Americans – or Quakers of any nation – would declare, with the American Friends Service Committee in 1917, that

> We are united in expressing our love for our country and our desire to serve her loyally. We offer ourselves to the Government of the United States in any constructive work in which we can conscientiously serve humanity.[90]

With an increasingly critical view of the West generally and of commercial republicanism in particular, and with perhaps more confidence in the non-Christian world, post-Gandhian Quakers would become more committed to 'direct action' but less well-focused politically. Whereas in 1918 William E. Wilson thought he knew exactly what the League of Nations needed – disarmament, democracy, and Christianity[91] – Robert O. Byrd, writing in 1960, was much less sure, or perhaps more diffident, with respect to the needs of the United Nations. Wilson wrote of democratization; Byrd wrote more vaguely of "change as a matter of principle," of "a gradual, continual realization of the moral order." Byrd called, merely, for "clearer organizational expression" of "the essential unity of all mankind" – not "a centralized world government" (he hastened to add) but some sort of "federalism" rooted in localities. Quakers had no well-defined political agenda that they cared to elaborate publicly. They wanted simply to establish "a sense of community with other peoples" in order to pioneer the international community. These meetings sought to resolve conflicts "by projecting [two parties to a conflict situation] to a higher level where both may meet in an apex." Byrd confessed that "a principle of indirection is at work here...making it appear at times that Friends are less than candid and are reluctant to recognize problems" – such as opposing political opinions with respect to the character of the just regime – "when they are obvious to others."[92]

Quakers at times acted forthrightly on the basis of perceived regime distinctions, as when they refused famine relief to the Soviet Union in the 1930's. They saw that "famine conditions existing at that time were created consciously by public policy and that Friends could not be expected to do useful work under such conditions."[93] Just as often Quakers blurred such distinctions, as when Mary Hoxie Jones imagined that, "while the Bolshevik Government may be terrible, it's less so than the Czarist regime," and, "after all, this revolution wasn't so different from the French Revolution."[94] C.H. Mike Yarrow called the construction of the Berlin Wall "a tragic but necessary event for the building of peace in Europe," giving credence to the longstanding lie that Soviet rulers feared the potential military power of a reunited Germany. Roland Warren delivered speeches in republican and in communist Germany, claiming that "ideology" ("Western capitalism" and Marxism-Leninism) had prevented Germans and other nations from seeing "reality"; he put the word 'free' between inverted commas when speaking of the commercial republics and advocated socialism in the West. "In effect, [the Quakers] said, 'Tear down the psychological wall and the concrete Wall will lose its significance'" – a slogan that failed to remark the political causes of both walls.[95]

Clearly, Gandhi alone should not bear the blame for this. The advance of 'German' philosophy among Western intellectuals obviously contributed to the problem perhaps even more than Gandhi did. But Gandhian attacks on British imperialist constitutionalism were easily conflated with 'German' attacks on commercial republicanism, given the commercial-republican character of the contemporary British Constitution as it existed *within* England, and given that Constitution's commercial-republican *effects* in India and elsewhere in the Empire. Gandhi's preference for an entirely different kind of regime based on small communities not extended republics, also appealed to those aspects of 'German' ideology not in the thrall of large-scale industrialism. That the Jeffersonian commercial republicanism of agrarian 'ward republics' resembled Gandhiism more closely than did 'soviet' pseudo-republics, often escaped Quaker notice. Even had Quakers noticed this resemblance, they would have been compelled to observe that commerce and agrarian*ism* (farming as a way of life, not as a small if productive fraction of society) had turned out to be incompatible. Quakers were looking at the world around them and at 'what might be,' not 'what might have been,' and in this sense may be excused for insufficient consideration of Jeffersonianism. Some of them may not be excused for excessive sympathy for Marxist despotism, even when that sympathy was partly tactical or Gandhian. Perhaps Quakers were not Gandhian enough even here, for Gandhi himself never hesitated to condemn the injustices of his opponents, even as he negotiated with them. Unlike the Quakers, Gandhi usually *negotiated* on behalf of his nation's interests as he perceived them, instead of *conciliating* as a third party. Gandhi wanted to be (albeit indirectly) a ruler not a diplomat, and this forthright ambition brought responsibility with it. Quaker coyness (a *de facto* recognition that despotisms do differ from republics?) at best may have encouraged the growth of civil societies within despotic countries. This was accomplished at the price of no little obscurantism among Quakers themselves and among those in their commercial-republican homelands who listened to Quakers. For the nations they visited, the severe political realities served as inoculants against obscurantism.

A survey of Christian responses to Gandhi would fill a volume well worth writing. The preceding paragraphs and those that follow barely suggest the themes a full historical study would explore.

Non-Quaker Christians responded to Gandhi with varying degrees of caution. American Mennonite theologian Guy F. Hershberger rejected nonviolent resistance for Christian use. Among Hindus, he wrote, self-sacrifice is intended to appease the gods, who cannot resist the sight of human suffering. Gandhi applied this belief to politics, pacifying tyrants instead of gods. But nonviolent resistance goes beyond the mere pacification of tyrants. Nonviolent resistance, "a new form of [physical] warfare," obstructs rulers in various ways and may overthrow them. Christian nonresistants may disobey rulers, but "without the use of pressure methods to overthrow the government." Mennonites, for example, have in the past "disobeyed to do right, and perhaps to do justice." Doing justice is for God and neighbor; obtaining justice is for one's neighbor (at times) and for oneself, as well as (perhaps) for God. "This is a fundamental difference," and the coercive element in the Gandhian enterprise rules it out for Christians.[96] Hershberger rejected nonviolent resistance because, although nonviolent, it still resists, positing an illegitimate right to revolution and a concealed egoism.

Roman Catholic writers, having long asserted the right to revolution and the legitimacy of physical force including warfare, could not finally balk at nonviolent resistance. Jacques Maritain argued that Catholics, out of their very catholicity, should "lay hold of the element of good" in any practice. Nonviolent resistance deserves not rejection but "recasting" into a Catholic mold. Governments need force; Gandhi suffers from "angelism" in this respect and therefore "lacks the power to register in history broad political results or to remodel the temporal regime in an organic way."[97] More important, Maritain recommends that Catholics relate nonviolent resistance to the Thomistic doctrine of fortitude as primarily the act of "enduring, bearing, suffering with constancy," and only secondarily the act of attacking. "Two different keyboards... stretch along the two sides of our human nature, though the sounds they give are constantly intermingled": the courage of attacking and the force of coercion properly mix with the courage of enduring and the force of patience. The latter forms of courage and of force should predominate, and may be organized politically, particularly in three circumstances: the struggle of a nation for freedom from foreign domination; the struggle of a people to maintain or gain control over "the big anonymous machinery" of the modern state; and "the struggle of Christians to transform civilization by making it actually Christian." Given the excessive destructiveness of modern weapons, which "ensure success only through the agency of sin, nonviolent resistance will often remain the only just means of war in the modern world.[98]

More recent Catholic writers have displayed still more sympathy. P. Regamey called nonviolent resistance "a way of love" that "stands as a challenge which the Christian conscience cannot ignore." Violence "destroys [people] as persons" by "treat[ing] them as things." Although he endorsed the just war tradition, he called for an evolution away from war towards "the defense of right" by "peaceful methods" only.[99] Regamey partially associated Gandhi with Francis of Assisi, who did not share the Hindu's absolute reverence for all life as such (life is not God, but a created thing, and thus not to be worshipped), but profoundly respected and cared for all living things. Regamey appreciated "the Christian paradox" that peace at times "can only be achieved through some form of war," even physical war can find the Christian "loving the enemy in a real way while one resists him." But, whenever possible, nonviolent resistance may better put an end to "the fatal vicious cycle of ever-increasing violence." With Maritain, Regamey doubted that modern war would often be just, and affirmed that the moral decline of war made nonviolent resistance all the more needed.[100]

Protestant writers had long agreed with the Anglican churchman William Cunningham when he spoke of England: "civil obedience has been constantly, if not universally, recognized as a duty to be rendered from religious motives" as prescribed in Romans 13. Cunningham viewed moral crusades as tending toward an "unwholesome" state of mind in the crusaders, who engage in "habitual thought about the evil they deplore," leading to anger and uncharitable accusations.[101] Crusades against war were no better. Fortunately, in the early years of Gandhi's public career war seemed unlikely to require a moral crusade for its abolition. Writing in 1915, Cunningham observed that until "July of last year, there was a general belief in England and

America that war had become an anachronism; that, though it might survive among half-civilized and decadent people, it could no longer occur amongst the most highly developed nations." When it did, the problem of conscientious objection reappeared with it. But in Britain and elsewhere, political circumstances had changed since the previous major war a century earlier: the "obvious incompatibility" between obedience to the Crown and obedience to one's own conscience had disappeared with the decline of monarchy. In contemporary and more nearly democratic Britain, "the citizen has a voice in the government of the country and helps to decide what the law shall be, but he is also a subject who must obey the law." Conscientious choice ought to be limited to political participation; once the country as a whole has chosen, the conscientious citizen will consent to be ruled. Peacefully to resist democratically determined public choices amounts to "an insidious method for paralyzing civil authority and bringing it into contempt." The assertion of conscientious individualism, "constitut[ing] [one]self a supreme judge of what ought to be done in the community," only reproduces on the moral plane the Hobbesian atomism of laissez-faire economics. In each case, selfishness issues in "the inability to look at the community as an organic whole" and the replacement of personal responsibility with self-assertion. Universalized, this will lead to international war, with each nation acting as a knight-errant of collective egoism.[102]

Gandhi himself had responded to similar criticisms around the same time. A Transvaal legislator named Wygerd had accused Gandhi of "transferring the battle and the violence from the physical to the mental plane" but not yet to the spiritual plane. "You are still fighting to win, and fighting harder than ever, and in my opinion, all fighting in modern times is tending to become more and more a matter of intellectual and psychic force and less of physical." Its cruelty does not thereby decrease; it increases. True heroism and true spirituality inhere in suffering not political triumph. Gandhi replied that a nonviolent resistant's fighting-to-win is indeed spiritual. The hard-won political reforms issue from harder-won reforms in each individual's soul, reforms "obtained through self-suffering, self-purification."[103] Gandhian moral crusades therefore need not bring self-righteous or bitter accusations. The issue of democratic consent did not concern Gandhi in his immediate circumstance as a colonial subject, but clearly a democratic majority might tyrannize as cruelly as any tyrant, and Gandhi avoided or at least discouraged atomistic moral selfishness by insisting on individual moral reform achieved by suffering.

In the United States, Paul Ramsey recognized nonviolent resistance as war "under another name," although not therefore illicit.[104] Observance of the law remains "a Christian principle"; "public protest movements and direct action must, on the Christian understanding not only of justice remedying sin but of order restraining it, be kept compatible with maintaining the rule of law...which alone makes possible any life of sinful man with sinful man." By definition deliberate lawbreaking, civil disobedience can only uphold respect for lawfulness by accepting the legal punishments prescribed by law for the illegal actions taken by nonviolent resistants. Democracy increases but does not absolutize the obligation to obey laws. "Democracy itself," with its clashes of opinionated and interested citizens, "in a very real sense is nothing more than *justum bellum*," but democracy's everyday conflicts violate no law. Still, both participation in democratic politics and civil disobedience are forms of resistance, not nonresistance, and therefore are "in need of justification and limitation in Christian morality, like any other form of resistance."[105]

In continental Europe's harsher climate, both the charms of and the objections to nonviolent resistance appealed to moral necessities, not the comparative luxuries of empire and democracy. Karl Barth considered Gandhi "a hundred times nearer the truth" than the Lutheran doctrine of the Christian magistrate with a soul divided between public severity and private gentleness. Barth may have associated the Lutheran refusal better to integrate public and private as the opening to *Realpolitik* and finally to Hitler. He rejected exclusive reliance upon nonviolent resistance, because he did not believe nonviolent resistance could do God's will against a Hitler. A Hitler threatens the very existence of the God-endowed political community and the people it protects physically, morally, and spiritually. To abandon the political community to a Hitler is worse than war. Gandhi's prohibition of violence was too legalistic and not sufficiently flexible. Nonviolence should be "a direction for service" not a law, leaving "room for the living God to give man direct instructions as well, in the same sense and with the same intention as the direction, but not necessarily in the precise same verbal form." The spirit not the letter of divine law should rule human actions.[106] Barth could then formulate a highly qualified endorsement of just war doctrine.[107]

Christians, we may conclude from the above – admittedly a bare sketch, if not a caricature – readily saw that nonviolent resistance raised serious questions with respect to moral opposition to tyranny and support for lawful democracy. It would be hard to conceive of Gandhi and his mass 'movement' of nonviolent resistance abstracted from a democratic age. In a democratic age egalitarianism elicits the contempt of unchristian tyrants; democracies therefore need statesmen 'more equal than others' to defend democracy against those tyrants. Those statesmen's souls will find themselves pulled between Christian principles and the requirements of effective statesmanship.[108] No one understood these matters better than an African animated by both Christianity and political ambition, Kenneth Kaunda of Zambia.

In his youth Kaunda learned "Bible-centered" Christianity, which he continued to prefer to 'liberal' Christianity. "For all its sincerity and passion, it was not easily translated into political terms." To effect that translation, Kaunda turned to Gandhi, who seemed to answer the problem of how a Christian could become "an effective politician *without hurting anyone*." Kaunda recognized that *the* problem for pacifist politics is unity, especially after pacifists have formed a government: "When the marching stops," when national independence has been achieved, "where do they go from there?" What do pacifists do when "unity becomes shaky and political party loyalties revive"? Not only disunity issuing from the insolence weakness encourages, but the imposition of "an inflexible truth" by disappointed moralists will threaten the regime. "[T]he saint in power tends to create an authoritarian regime." Against these dangers, Gandhi's example cannot fully instruct the conscientious statesman. "Gandhi and I were equally fortunate in facing a colonial power which fell far short of being a ruthless tyranny"; moreover, Gandhi "was the holiest of men in a country which venerated holy men and gave them respect and authority," a country ruled by unsteady imperialists worried by decidedly nonpacifist forces next to whom Gandhi appeared less and less unattractive. And (Kaunda need not say this explicitly) Gandhi never ruled.[109]

For maintaining a just unity, persuasion alone will not suffice. Circumstances (geographic, historical, and other) will limit the statesman's possibilities for action.[110]

> Shangri-Las never last.... So far as I know, no state has managed to survive long without the use of compulsion, including if necessary, violence.[111]

Kaunda did not reject the possibility that future states might eschew violence. He believed in mankind's spiritual evolution, "the survival of the highest rather than the survival of the fittest." But in the meantime, something very like the Lutheran divided soul afflicts every Christian statesman. "The statesman and the believer are at odds not simply in the same state but in the one person."[112]

As he surveyed the ranks of pacifists worldwide, Kaunda saw them as religious and "politically innocent" members of the bourgeoisie.[113]

> Some pacifist literature boils down to saying that there is really nothing to choose between one side or the other in a conflict if force is used to resolve it. It is immaterial who wins, victory will be sterile because it was achieved by violence. This attitude makes the pacifist the dupe of totalitarianism because a strong despotic power very often does not need to use force to intimidate a weaker one whereas free nations mobilizing to resist such aggression have to marshall their military resources, and thus incur the pacifist's wrath.[114]

By contrast, statesmanship requires "knife-edge judgments that one course of action will be slightly less harmful than another"; consequences must matter to the statesman, not only intentions. "I shall have to bear with fortitude the understandable cries of outrage and merely reply to my critics – have *you* tried running a country on the pacifist principles without qualification or modification, and do you know anyone else who has?"[115]

Kaunda turns the dividedness of the Christian statesman's soul into an advantage, into the reconstruction of classical moderation on Christian terms. Inspired *and* guilt-ridden, the Christian statesman will act decisively but never unrestrainedly. "[T]hose who feel compelled to use violence even for noble ends must not have it made easier for them to deaden their consciences and get rid of their sense of guilt, otherwise they will end up killing for pleasure." Kaunda proposes the appropriate prayer for the Christian statesman. In keeping with the statesman's espousal of the active life, he makes it short: "Dear Lord! How does one run a country by sticking to the letter of Jesus' teaching?" The answer to this prayer seems to be silence. "As a political leader I cannot accept [the] Cross as the standard for my public life; as a penitent sinner I cannot evade it." The closest thing to an answer to "the riddle of violence" – the evil of violence and the moral necessity of the statesman to commit this evil at times – is divine forgiveness.[116]

Gandhi did not suppose that he needed divine forgiveness. To see the exact sources of the similarities and differences between Gandhi's teaching and Christianity, we turn to that teaching as presented by Gandhi himself.[117]

The Foundations of Nonviolent Resistance

Gandhi told one inquirer that his teaching was "not a subject for research – you must experience it, use it, live by it." Gandhi taught a practice, not a theory, even if that practice was 'idealistic.'[118] In this Gandhi's teaching resembles any religious morality, including Christianity and particularly Christianity as practiced by Quakers.[119] Because experience accumulates, Gandhi asked his students to view his later statements as more authoritative than early ones.[120] Gandhi's true student, then, experiences or tests Gandhi's teachings and reads his writing, with care. Today, many of us have tested Gandhi's teachings and seen them tested, but few have read his writings with care.

Gandhi was called "Mahatma," translated "Great Soul." Gandhi's greatness of soul evidently differs from the greatness of soul admired in the West, described by Aristotle.[121] Still, Gandhi addressed himself to each of the classical virtues cultivated by Aristotle's great-souled man: prudence, moderation, courage, and justice.

Human beings need prudence because they make choices. "Man has got a choice, but as much of it as a passenger on board a ship does," Gandhi wrote. He added, "It is just enough for him."[122] Gandhi's sense of prudence often matched, and was sometimes overmatched, by that of his countrymen.[123] While urging selflessness, Gandhi never urged thoughtless or fanatical self-sacrifice:

> Self-surrender does not mean giving up one's judgment. Sincere self-surrender is not inertia, it is energy; knowing that there is someone to whom to turn ultimately, the person undertakes, with due regard for his limitations, a thousand experiments one after another. But they are all undertaken with humility, knowledge and discrimination.[124]

"Life is made of compromises," and the very purity and unselfishness of nonviolent resistance imposes the strongest moral requirement for its governance by prudence, including a due regard for circumstances. The nonviolent resistant must never confuse himself with God, Who alone is perfect.[125] Gandhi sharply distinguished this view from utilitarianism, whose practitioners will never sacrifice themselves, and also from 'Satanism,' which denies not that man can be perfect but that he can even be virtuous. This latter denial he associated with atheism. Life according to Gandhi's teaching "presupposes the living presence and guidance of God," upon whom the statesman depends for "the Voice within [that] guides him" through the maze of politics. "Very often therefore what are practical politics so-called are unrealities to [the Gandhian statesman], though in the end his prove to be the most practical politics."[126]

Manifestations of Gandhi's prudent absolutism may be seen throughout his career. He once described an earthquake as "a visitation for the sin of untouchability," while cheerfully conceding that his opponents might blame the earthquake on "my crime of preaching against untouchability.[127] More important consequences followed from Gandhi's prudent absolutism with respect to the dangers nonviolent resistance posed to civil society in India. Warned of possible carnage if the British left, Gandhi cited purification by suffering, not self-preservation:

> [I]f the result there is chaos, that should not frighten us. We shall emerge from the ordeal all the stronger.[128]

In practicing "the Law of complete Love," non-violent resistants should expect failures. Gandhi did not imprudently expect "a whole mass of men and women to obey that law all at once." He did expect the Law to rule India in time, perhaps centuries hence.[129]

In place of moderation or temperance, Gandhi required asceticism – including strict dieting and fasting, celibacy, and abstinence from all intoxicants. Nothing more disturbs Gandhi's 'modern' admirers than this aspect of his teaching.[130] As it should: even in his earliest writings, Gandhi aimed his asceticism directly at the modern West. Western materialism claims to be realistic and claims to give man the key to 'creation,' i.e., the free manipulation of nature. But its "greatest achievements are the invention of the most terrible weapons of destruction," social anarchy, and the abuse of animals; materialism must issue in war, not peaceful hedonism. "[M]aterial progress is in inverse relation to moral progress," and even interferes with sound physical health.[131] Materialism begets vice begetting war, begetting more vice:

> It is yet too early [he wrote in 1926] to measure the effect on mankind of the collapse of sexual morality brought about by [the First World] War. Vice has usurped the throne of virtue. The brute in man has for the time being gained supremacy.[132]

The example of Berlin in the 1920's and the subsequent destruction of the Weimar Republic give at least some evidence of Gandhi's insight.

More than "mere physical self-control," Gandhian asceticism "means complete control over all the senses." Such control generates power:

> All power comes from the preservation and sublimation of the vitality that is responsible for creation of life. If the vitality is husbanded instead of being dissipated, it is transmuted into creative energy of the highest order.[133]

This control, "unattainable save by the grace of God," will redirect the soul away from all desire, all egoism, and toward God and neighbor.[134] Ascetic self-perfection brings greater real mastery of material reality than all the stratagems of modern technological materialism.[135] It also brings spiritual authority translated into political authority – both of these felt in Gandhi's case by admirers and opponents.[136] Asceticism will simultaneously strengthen national economic life and the nation's spiritual life by ending famine. "You cannot present the hungry and famished masses with God,"

Gandhi warned, because "their God is their food." Covetousness and exploitation cause extreme mass poverty, and asceticism destroys the root of covetousness, which is eros in the comprehensive sense of the word. If asceticism is impossible without God, and yet God is inaccessible to the starving, a program of asceticism for the poor seems problematic. However, not all Indians were poor and not all the poor were starving; asceticism among the non-starving would end exploitation and provide the starving first with food, then with God.[137]

Gandhian courage is not thumotic but agapic — founded upon lovingkindness not spiritedness.[138] Nor is it a mean between the extremes of cowardice and rashness. Gandhian courage is primarily fearlessness. "Fear and nonviolence are deadly enemies" because "love cannot act through fear."[139] "Man, to realize his full stature, has to become absolutely fearless." The fearless "consider it too troublesome even to summon up anger against one who is vainly trying to injure him.[140] Nonviolent resistance depends essentially upon fearlessness:

> Nonviolence cannot be taught to a person who fears to die and has no power of resistance. He harbors violence and hatred in his heart and would kill his enemy if he could without being hurt himself.... Before he can understand non-violence he has to be taught to stand his ground and even suffer death in the attempt to defend himself against the aggressor who bids fair to overwhelm him. To do otherwise would be to confirm his cowardice and take him further away from non-violence. Whilst I may not actually help anyone to retaliate, I must not let a coward seek shelter behind non-violence so-called.[141]

Nonviolent resistance — above all, nonmaterial and nonerotic — results from *satyagraha*, translated "soul-force" or "truth-force." "Superior to the force of arms," a physical force based upon fear and resultant anger, *satyagraha* or the Law of Love will animate the truly great nation, "which rests its head upon death as its pillow." By contrast, "people afraid of even a squirrel had much better think of improving their own condition than of getting independence."[142] Individual and national freedom requires fearlessness, one element of the genuinely civil society without which any attempt to gain political freedom, nonviolently or otherwise, will fail.[143]

Gandhi approved of soldiers' courage in those who had yet to achieve *satyagraha*. He praised the Bhayas, a people of India's northwestern provinces, as "the guardians of peace...largely employed in the native armies." Arms-bearing "is the least necessity of the brave," who learn the needlessness of arms by "faith and experience," not argument. As for arms-bearers, their work "is considered more honorable than that of the ordinary worker," their courage greater, because their real work is "not slaying, but being slain in defense of others."[144] Soldiers' courage consists in risk-taking, not in anger. Nonviolent resistance is soldiers' courage perfected.

Soldiers' courage serves justice. Full justice is nonviolent; violence is always unjust. "Once you admit the lawfulness of the use of physical force for purposes other than the benefit of the person against whom it is used, as in the case of a surgeon against his patient," Gandhi claimed, "you cannot draw an arbitrary line of distinction" between terrorism and legitimate force. Even in a just *cause*, violence undermines justice and perpetuates itself, that is, perpetuates injustice.[145] Gandhian *nonviolence* (ahimsa) extends to the whole of organic creation.[146] As such, it cannot not be perfectly attained in this life of *embodied* souls. "Life itself involves some kind of violence" – treading on insects, white blood cells destroying bacteria. Nonviolence "choose[s] the path of least violence." Violence cannot be eradicated; "the confrontation between violence and nonviolence has lasted from time immemorial and will last till eternity."[147]

Although Gandhi wrote an article on the Japanese form of self-defense, *jiu-jitsu* (which he described as the art of controlling an opponent's body by applying force to strategic points on his body, instead of using muscle-power) and applied this technique to politics ("the problem will now be to find something else after all the nations have learned *jiu-jitsu*"),[148] he did not regard nonviolence as a mere tactic. Nonviolence requires self-purification and moral strength; it eschews conquest and defeat alike, the conventional soldier's cry of 'victory or death,' because it concentrates on means not ends.[149] Ahimsa or non-violence is, however, insufficient to assure full justice; it is negative, a matter of restraint or prohibition.[150] Nonviolence is one aspect of satyagraha or truth-force.

The justice of satyagraha arises from the nonresistant's consciousness of his own strength, not from self-protective weakness. Satyagraha will win as its disciples the 'angry young men,' the natural warriors of a nation. "This is in the interest both of the rulers and the ruled." Gandhi declared, "I am not ashamed to stand erect before the heroic and self-sacrificing revolutionary because I am able to pit an equal measure of nonviolent men's heroism and sacrifice untarnished by the blood of the innocent." Satyagrahic self-sacrifice "is the most powerful retort to tyranny that has yet been conceived by God or man." To effect the transition between violently-enforced justice and full justice, Gandhi recommended the formation of "community peace brigades" to enforce the law and to learn from criminals what needs "the community is failing to supply."[151]

Satyagraha-justice will serve to unite the community because it is loving, agapic.[152] "Gandhi sees the modern malady as a malady of distances, the distance between government and governed, rich and poor, city and village, hills and plains, high castes and low." Satyagraha is more than tolerant or 'liberal'; it concentrates each soul on deepening its adherence to religion into which each individual is born, instead of trying to convert other souls to that religion. Conversion conquers; it too easily serves the selfishness of the missionary.[153] Unity founded upon satyagraha-justice will take time to develop; it cannot be achieved with 'violent' suddenness. "It must be recognized," Gandhi cautioned, "that there are evils to which Satyagraha cannot be applied" — as for example the disunity between Hindus and Moslems in India ("I have owned defeat on that score"). On the whole, the selflessness of nonviolence and satyagraha will tend to unite human beings with each other and with God.[154]

Action animated by satyaghraha is "the moral equivalent of war,"[155] and is a continuation of politics by other means.[156] To a British clergyman who objected that Jesus of Nazareth did not refuse cooperation with government, Gandhi replied in terms strikingly similar to Augustine's defense of conventional war: "Enlightened non-cooperation is the expression of anguished love," and is therefore compatible with Christianity.[157] Satyagraha — *satya* means truth, *agraha* means good-will insistence — thus comprehends agapic love or goodwill and lovingkindness.[158] Nonviolent resistance is just war with the justice 'built into' the action itself. Gandhiism melds means and ends, denying that good ends can be approached by any but good means; satyagraha "becomes both the means and the end, and the terms become convertible."[159] Gandhi understood the foundation of his teaching: "If love or nonviolence be not the law of our being, the whole of my argument falls to pieces, and there is no escape from a periodical recrudescence of war."[160]

For Gandhi justice is first individual, then political. Truth or *Sat* "is what the voice within tells one," even as it is for the Quaker.[161] This voice is not of the individual or the ego as conceived in the West. It is God's voice. Gandhi hopes to avoid the megalomania that seems implicit in this claim by submitting his body to suffering for the sake of the voice's instructions. Suffering tests those instructions in practice, pointing to the experiential and experimental results of Gandhi's way of life.[162] The ultimate or metaphysical unity the satyagrahic soul will find is not painful, however:

> Truth stated in a spirit of nonviolence may hurt at the moment, but its ultimate effect must be as sweet as *amrit*. This is an essential test of nonviolence.[163]

This is unity with God. The Hindu God is "bliss incarnate"; it sustains the cosmos but, unlike the God of the West, "neither does, nor causes to be done," and "does not govern" in a cosmos that is uncreated, eternal. Not fear and awe but love is inspired by the Hindu God, who is "above both good and evil." God and Truth are the same. Each 'individual' soul in reality manifests the flow of God through every living being, and this constitutes the essential unity of all living beings with each other as well as with God.[164] Gandhi concluded, in the words of one scholar, that soul-realization or goodness "is not possible without worldly involvement," without active justice-seeking among others. Gandhi "identified the *vita activa* and the *vita contemplativa*."[165]

Gandhi therefore laughed *and* cried.[166] He insisted, "We should try to become philosophers" and praised Socrates as "a soldier of truth." He saw that "when [Socrates] vindicates the City" – as in the *Crito* – "it is for his own reasons, not for reasons of state." Gandhi shared the philosopher's understanding that the old is not necessarily identical with the good, that the conventional need not serve as the highest authority. Still, he also cried. He wanted not so much to think as to do, to exercise moral virtues, to suffer fruitfully.[167]

Gandhi assigned priority to conviction over reason: "Argument has never convinced any man, but, on the contrary, conviction precedes argument."[168] What changes convictions, then? If experience does, what prevents a resolute man from 'interpreting' experience in order to retain his convictions?[169] If theory and practice, contemplation and action, are taken to be identical, how can either refute the other? To conceive of the world as "essentially a moral order"[170] is to raise the question of how to apprehend moral truth after rejecting conventions.

Gandhi agreed with the philosophers that "true friendship is an identity of souls rarely to be found in this world." Unlike the philosopher, he did not want simply to awaken the souls of his fellow-citizens who are not his friends, but to reform them. Because "a reformer cannot afford to have close intimacy with him whom he seeks to reform," and because "he who would be friends with God must remain alone, or make the whole world his friend," Gandhi entertained much vaster political ambitions than any of the old philosophers.[171] During the First World War Gandhi claimed that "India can conquer all by soul-force." He told his countrymen that if they "have your faith in your civilization and keep to it steadily," then "India will one day hold sway over the entire world." Although in light of his disappointment with Indian violence in the 1940's Gandhi entertained doubts that India would conquer, he never doubted that his ideas *would* conquer − if not in India then elsewhere.[172] Gandhi's teaching evidently appeals to a spiritualized version of the will to power.[173]

Gandhi teaches that satyagraha fails only when the resistants' love is not strong enough. Strength "comes from an indomitable will." He insisted that "nothing is impossible for those who are prepared to suffer"; when they seem to fail, it is only because nonresistant leaders "lack the purity or the faith or both."[174]

> [P]hysical force is nothing compared to the moral force, and...moral force never fails. It is my firm belief that this is the fundamental difference between the modern civilization and the ancient, of which India, fallen though it is, I venture to claim is a living representative.[175]

Nonviolence "can tame the wildest beast, certainly the most savage man."[176]

> It need not be assumed that such resistance is possible only against civilized rulers. Even a heart of flint will melt in the fire kindled by the power of the soul. Even a Nero becomes a lamb when he faces love. This is no exaggeration. It is as true as an algebraic equation.[177]

Lambs must allow the tyrant to feed on them, for "if sufficient food is given to the tyrant, a time will come when he will have had more than surfeit." Tyrants are human; human nature "unfailingly responds to the advances of love"; and "there is no limit to the capacity of nonviolence to generate heat" sufficient to melt even "the hardest heart."[178] Tyrannicide is therefore profoundly unjust. One ardent disciple of Gandhi went so far as to compare the Gandhian "law" governing "the release of spiritual energy" to Einstein's law governing the release of physical energy.[179] All previously downtrodden groups – including the poor, women, Jews – can empower themselves by discovering this law and living in accordance with it.[180]

To those who found his claims implausible, Gandhi replied that

> ...non-violence can be effectively taught only by living it. When there is an unmistakable demonstration of its power and efficacy the weak will shed their weakness and the mighty will quickly realize the valuelessness of might and becoming weak acknowledge the power of nonviolence."[181]

Critics both sympathetic and unsympathetic have regarded this claim as overstated. They find that no such "unmistakable demonstration" has occurred in a world of mixed motives and results. Some question the moral influence of countries whose only influence is moral.[182] Others cite "the teaching of experience" that loving resistance to tyranny, unrequited, eventually sours and yields to resentment and hatred.[183] Tyrants have in fact destroyed nonviolent resistant movements.[184] No thoroughgoingly tyrannical regime has been revolutionized by nonviolent resistants, although nonviolent resistants have assisted in such revolutions.[185] In India itself, "when the British resolved upon the unrestrained use of force, they mobilized India for war in spite of the decision of the Congress Party and a show of semi-active resistance"; nonviolent resisters seldom convert *enough* of their fellow citizens to the movement.[186] Nonviolent resistants fighting invaders in small, densely populated, industrialized countries have not in the past and could not in the future cause sufficient damage to the enemy to make a difference, provided the enemy's goals were short-term.[187] In the long term, "a population determined to resist cannot be conquered but can be exterminated, or enough people can be killed to make the rest submit."[188] The problem of unarmed defense of justice arises from the character of deep-seated conflicts. Deep-seated conflicts are by definition caused by opposing passions, opinions and interests for which opponents willingly kill and risk being killed. Nonviolent resistants must find ways to avoid triggering this 'kill or be killed' response, or at least to avoid its widespread application. Practitioners of Socratic nonviolence admit to themselves that the philosopher, even if he is a philosopher-king or a king who philosophizes "cannot protect those [he] loves."[189] Practitioners of Platonic nonviolence defend themselves by camouflage and by making the right friends. Practitioners of Christian nonviolence trust in God's protection, perhaps here and surely in Heaven. Practitioners of Gandhian nonviolence prefer not to admit that they can fail here, as they seek to inspire their fellows to action here. Gandhi's personal experiences reinforced his hopes: "Few can withstand the force of his personality," one early acquaintance observed.[190] Just as there are geniuses of the body — in the past, warriors, and now athletes who seem to sweep all opponents before them — and geniuses of the mind — a Socrates, a Mozart, respected or envied by their contemporaries — so there are geniuses of personality. Gandhi was perhaps the greatest genius of personality in his century. Such individuals succeed so often in their field of combat — Achilles on the battlefield at Troy, Socrates in the agora, Gandhi from his ashram to the rural villages to the palace of the Viceroy — that they may forget temporarily the limitations of their powers, overreach their own humanity, divinize themselves before falling back, reminded. Some poet may immortalize them — absent that, historians. Their virtues are always worthy of gratitude and even of emulation so long as we their imitators recall their limitations and our own more considerable ones.

In his quest for justice Gandhi often found limitations in his countrymen.

> The more I penetrate the villages, the greater is the shock delivered as I perceive the blank stare in the eyes of the villagers I meet. Having nothing to do but work as laborers side by side with their bullocks, they have become almost like them.[191]

He hoped to 'humanize' Indian villagers by introducing them to work that required a degree of foresight and dexterity. Hence the celebrated spinning wheel which, not incidentally, would also help to liberate villagers from dependence upon urban textile mills in England.[192] Justice and all the other virtues required choice; where men are bullocks they can be stampeded by rulers and would-be rulers.[193] Virtue is self-government or true independence. A political regime "is but a concrete expression" of the satyagraha, the soul-force, of the average person within the political unit.

> ...violence may destroy one or more bad rulers, but, like Ravana's heads, others will pop up in their places, for, the root lies elsewhere. It lies in us. If we will reform ourselves, the rulers will automatically do so.

More than most, Gandhi was entitled to say, "I believe that after all a people has the government [that] it deserves." A self-governing India would *encompass* independence from the British Empire, effected first and foremost by "a moral revolution in the governed." Imperial government could not be good government because it was not self-government, and therefore did not call up the virtues of each individual Indian.[194]

Gandhi could claim a "nationalism as broad as the universe" — including every living thing — while at the same time praising *swadeshi*, "that spirit in us [that] restricts us to the use and service of our most immediate surroundings to the exclusion of the more remote." If God-Truth flows through all that lives, the particular is to be cherished as sacred: the particular in religion, in politics, in economics. Gandhi avoided both modern nationalism based upon the assertion of national superiority or at least uniqueness (God is neither superior nor unique in its particular manifestations) and modern internationalism, with its weakness for bureaucracy and a humanitarianism that never gets down to earth.[195]

In economic life Gandhi returned to the classical understanding of economics as household management.[196] In Gandhian economics self-rule entails self-sufficiency. Trade is permissible for goods that are needed, but genuinely free trade is not "backed by the navy." Gandhi opposed machinery, holding the chimerical but popular belief that machines "create unemployment" and the more plausible but also untenable belief that they "concentrat[e] wealth and power in the hands of the few and for the exploitation of the many."[197] Although Gandhi's conception of technology was superficial and one-sided, he rightly associated machines with political power and (somewhat more questionably) with the ambitions of materialism – ambitions, he claimed, that generate wars.[198] Gandhi opposed modern state-socialism because the modern state embodies "violence in a concentrated and organized form"; as "a soulless machine," the modern state cannot be trusted with the additional power control of the means of production would give it. The individual, who has a soul, at least has the potential for the moral management of property, for "trusteeship." This, added to the obviously lesser power of the individual, means that "the violence of private ownership is less injurious than the violence of the State."[199]

Gandhi sought not to empower governmental institutions but "to restore the meaning of politics to its root," namely, "the science of citizenship," the knowledge and practice of right morals and manners. Not so much political as religious institutions form an indispensable part of this restoration.[200] In emphasizing the science of citizenship Gandhi again sought to minimize and eventually eliminate the claim that government as an agent of retribution, of doing evil in return for evil, constitutes the core of statecraft.[201] A politics of soul-force and self-rule internalizes political rule in each human soul, making governmental retribution unnecessary. Gandhi did not believe that internalization of justice could occur in many people without religious encouragement; he required a strong religious foundation for his political order. "Politics, divorced of religion, have absolutely no meaning"; religionless politics resembles "a corpse only fit to be buried." Far from denying this, Gandhi contended, Christianity points the way; "Jesus, in my humble opinion, was a prince among politicians," a man who "would not have hesitated to defy the might of emperors had he found it necessary." ('Necessity' in Gandhi occupies exactly the same place as it does in just-war theory; it is the moral trigger of conflict). Gandhi's Hinduism, "intensely practical," avoids theocracy because it does not involve a government religion any more than it involves a government-ruled economy.[202] If anything, religion and a truly economical economics should 'rule' the government, animate it with their characteristic spirit.

The characteristic spirit of Gandhian religion and economics is the recognition of human equality. Human inequalities are "temporary and superficial," but "the soul that is hidden beneath this earthly crust is one and the same for all men and women belonging to all climes."[203] Both violent and nonviolent conflict affirms this ineluctable fact — nonviolence affirming it more convincingly.[204] 'Externally,' the equality of human nature should issue in equality before the law and in economic equality.[205] Socially, the caste system properly understood conduces to equality as well. "In its origin caste was a wholesome custom and promoted national well-being"; the original quadripartite caste system prevented competition for social place and privilege, the egoistic striving characteristic of the modern West. Caste does not so much differentiate privileges as it differentiates duties, promoting social cohesion within castes and the dependence of each caste upon the others. Inter-caste dependency qualifies Gandhian swadeshi or self-rule; in needing each other, the castes remained differentiated yet linked together in each village and throughout India.[206] Self-rule applies to individuals, villages, nations, but not entirely to castes, although each caste does rule itself in the sense of minding its own proper business. In the case of the ruling caste, however, ruling others is its proper business.

The prototypical Gandhian community is the *ashram*, a commune or extended 'family.' Gandhi himself lived in an ashram he founded after returning to India in 1915. The ashram was constituted by agreement to a series of vows; these included truth-telling, nonviolent love, celibacy, "control of the palate," refusal to steal, self-rule, fearlessness, and opposition to Untouchability. The rulers or "Controllers" of the ashram "make an effort to learn and teach politics, economics, social reform, etc. in a religious spirit and work in these fields with all the zeal that they can command" 'Rule' or 'control' becomes something very much like education and persuasion. Gandhi envisioned an eventual world community consisting of an all-pervasive ashram spirit in each local community.[207]

Gandhi's vision of a new world order contrasts with that of the founders of commercial republicanism. Rival republicanisms animate the two great 'assimilating' countries of the world – India and the United States – even as contrasting imperialisms animated the two great 'conquering' countries of the West – Rome and Britain. Gandhi shared the commercial-republic desire for elective, representative government, but claimed that for Indians the "contents" of the terms 'representation' and 'election' "were far different from the European" before Europeans arrived in India. He did not offer a definition of those terms as understood by the ancient Indians.[208] He was even reluctant to define his own republicanism. In 1939 Lord Lothian wrote to Gandhi suggesting that nonviolence would succeed in "a liberal, democratic, and constitutional form of government"; however, "international peace" would not occur until the founding and securing of such governments throughout the world. Gandhi replied that he had "purposely refrained from dealing with the nature of government in a society based deliberately on nonviolence" because "I cannot say in advance what the government based wholly on nonviolence will be like."[209] Gandhi denied that existing commercial republics were truly constitutional or democratic. England, the United States, and France were "only so-called" democracies, "no less based on violence that Nazi Germany, Fascist Italy, or even Soviet Russia." The despotic regimes merely organized violence more efficiently. Genuine democratic constitutionalism founded upon "the recognition of nonviolence" was only "a distant dream".[210] Meanwhile, war by regimes of poorly organized violence against regimes of well organized violence, even if won by the "so-called democracies," would not need war, and would not end the use of coercive force domestically. "[T]he world will fare no better," as "more polite but no less ruthless" rulers (in the United States, "capitalist owners") will divide the spoils and continued the unjust ways of "diluted Nazism or Fascism," practicing a "superior Nazism."[211]

Leaving these caricatures aside, we do have some indications of what Gandhian republicanism would be. Gandhi agreed with Madison that direct or 'participatory' democracy would not be "possible for a single day." Representatives chosen by election (not, as in more democratic schemes, by lot) would govern.[212] Gandhi departed from Madison in endorsing representation as a bulwark of moral purity, as distinguished from mere virtue. "[A] man who wants to be good and do good in all circumstances must not hold power"; instead, he will send a representative, avoiding personal exposure "to the corrupting influence of power."[213]

> Political power means capacity to regulate national life through national representatives. If national life becomes so perfect as to become self-regulated, no representation is necessary. There is then a state of enlightened anarchy. In such a state everyone is his own ruler.... But the ideal is never fully realized in life.[214]

Morally inferior representatives will not tyrannize a superior citizenry because "legislation in advance of public opinion has often been demonstrated to be futile"; the morally superior would presumably, resist nonviolently and successfully any such attempts. Further, the political and economic division between ruler and ruled will progressively narrow as the satyagrahic ethos pervade the nation.[215]

Gandhi's putative solution to the political problem of coercive force must entail a solution to the problem of religious strife. His insistence on the religious character of sound politics makes this all the more urgent. Gandhi's conception of Hinduism is even more elusive than his conception of republicanism. He drew political strength among the villagers from his apparent traditionalism, a practice many commentators have admired.[216] Yet Gandhi also seemed to "use the traditional to promote the novel," even the "revolutionary."[217] Gandhi himself resolved the contradiction by claiming to defend the "old Hinduism...a pure faith, free from idolatry" from materialist corruption and the consequent political degradation of India. Gandhi represented himself as the vindicator of Hinduism and India from corruptions introduced first by Hindus themselves, then by foreigners.[218]

Gandhi needed a principle of selection, a means of choosing one element over another from a vast, diverse tradition. Reason and "moral sense" enabled Gandhi to select from authoritative texts.[219] Among the elements of Hindu tradition Gandhi did *not* select was of course physical warfare. Gandhi 'interpreted' the battles of the *Ramayana* and the *Mahabarata* as Origen 'interpreted' the battles of the Old Testament – as allegorial presentations of conflicts within the human soul.[220] In addition, to

Gandhi 'reason' means reasonableness much more than it does logic, the principle of non-contradiction. This enabled him to employ the intellect as a synthesizing force more freely than a non-historicist Christian would do.[221] Gandhi's 'interpretations' or selections also responded flexibly to circumstances. Whereas he understood that "Buddhism had failed precisely because it advocated forbearance," and even in his own time war remained an occasional, "necessary evil even as the body is," individual and even group perfectibility had become increasingly possible thanks to spiritual and cosmic evolution.[222] In the political realm this evolution acted a bit like history did according to the nineteenth-century Whigs — causing ever-increasing democratization. Although traditional Hinduism, like Christianity, had allowed rulers and warriors to employ violent resistance as a necessity entailed in their responsibility for community defense,[223] the democratic pervasion of responsibility throughout all social orders did not entail a moral necessity for violent self-defense by the people. On the contrary; Gandhi was convinced that the devolution of political authority, involving moral and political self-discipline, would convert into a practical means of community self-defense against conventional warriors.

All this notwithstanding, it was not synthesis or evolution that finally provided a foundation for peace in Gandhi's doctrine. The foundation of all religions is satyagraha. To a hostile Moslem questioner he replied, "Religions are meant to tame our savage nature, not to let it loose." "[A]ll the great religions are fundamentally equal," i.e. identical; this fundamental identity means that conversion, proselytization, and the conflicts they provoke are spiritually unnecessary.[224] Reason and moral sense uncover these fundamental elements in each tradition, distinguishing them from materialist heresies — e.g., warfare and tyranny (in India, 'Untouchability'). Nonviolent resistance by 'fundamentalists' against heretics brings on conflicts the 'fundamentalists' will finally win, because they adhere to God-Truth.

No religion challenged Gandhi's claims more sternly than Islam. The *Koran* is a book that tells readers how to read it. Readers should adhere to its verses that are precise in meaning; only those with hearts infected by disbelief follow the ambiguous verses, whose meaning only Allah knows. The *Koran* thus effectively disinvites Origenists.[225] With Gandhi, the *Koran* teaches that originally human beings followed on religion, and humanity was then one nation. 'Egoism' caused disunity not through the adoption of materialism, as in Gandhi, but through envy. Envy also causes "People of the Book" (Jews and Christians) to attempt to lead Moslems to their own doctrines. Although some Jews and Christians, are righteous most are evildoers; as peoples they should be treated with forbearance until Allah makes His will known with respect to their disposition, but they must not be friends of believers.[226] If unbelievers incline to peace, believers should make peace; if unbelievers are not so inclined, believers should make war.[227] Men should be killed for a just cause. Although individuals should requite evil with good, and he who does so will make the evildoer his best friend, and although forgiveness is better than vengeance, there are limits to forgiveness. Those who fight against believers on account of their belief, those who drive believers from their homes or abet those who do so, should be fought. Aggressors should be fought, killed wherever you find them. Idolatry is worse than bloodshed.[228] Warriors are superior to those who stay at home; action, therefore, is better than contemplation. Those who retreat from battle (except for tactical purposes or to join another band of believers) shall suffer the torments of Hell. Not the warrior himself but Allah through the warrior strikes down His enemies.[229]

To locate the root of evil in materialism and egoism, as Gandhi does, concentrates moral effort on the overcoming of greed. For Gandhi as for Christianity, agapic love replaces erotic love, but love remains central. Islam by contrast locates the root of evil in envy. Islam concentrates moral effort on the overcoming of nonmaterial vice; Islam is thumotic or spirited and active, albeit in a manner restrained by justice. Efforts to 'soften' this spiritedness typically come from sources extraneous to it, not from within its own scriptures, which are indeed clear to those who read them for purposes of moral instruction.[230] Gandhi claimed that "Islam did not attain its greatness by the power of the sword but *entirely* through the self-immolation of its fakirs."[231] While publicly proclaiming that "the true beauty of Hindu-Mohammedan unity lies in each remaining true to his own religion and yet being true to each other," and sincerely admiring Moslems' asceticism, their devotion to the poor, their faith, their combination of spirituality, and Mohammed's initial suffering, humility, and patience, Gandhi acknowledged

Hindu-Moslem antagonism as "one of the gravest difficulties to be overcome in India.[232] Some Muslims adopted the principles of nonviolent resistance, often tactically; most did not; some were "overtly hostile" to those principles.[233] Moslem hostility to non-Moslem Indians caused the partition of India after independence, and remains a source of disunity and of potential disunion within the current borders of India.

The most extreme form of modern spiritedness, totalitarianism, also troubled Gandhi. Marxist atheist materialism repelled him; he called two visitors to his ashram "arm-chair socialists" whose "ideal is to provide a motor-car and a bungalow to everybody in India."[234] The residents of his ashram, by contrast, lived socialism. Marxist exaltation of class warfare also repelled him:

> ...I do not like the assumption underlying many of its propositions which go to show that there is necessarily antagonism between the classes and the masses or between the laborers and the capitalists such that they can never work for mutual good. My own experience covering a fairly long period is to the contrary.[235]

Centralized state control of the means of production he judged "too sweeping to be admitted" (the poet Rabindranath Tagore "is an instrument of marvellous production" but "I do not know that he will submit to be nationalized"). State-controlled child care evidently "absolved the parent from the duty of caring for the maintenance of his children."[236] Not only the family structure but the agrarian character of India contradicted Marxist dogma; "I have come to depend more and more on the peasants," whereas Stalin (and later Mao Zedong) killed them more and more. Communists offended Gandhian nationalism by taking orders from Moscow. They traduced morality by refusing "to make any distinction between fair and foul, truth and falsehood." In government they sanctioned violence and everywhere they generated hatred. Oddly, he venerated Lenin as a "master spirit" whose unspecified "sacrifices" had "sanctified" the "ideal" of the abolition of private property.[237] In a sense Gandhi opposed Marxism with no more success than he opposed Moslem-Hindu antagonism. Jawaharlal Nehru, who admired Lenin more than Gandhi as a political leader, ruled India for some two decades after Gandhi's assassination and made Lenin the "unofficial father" of independent India.[238]   There is no likelihood that Gandhi could have opposed rightist 'totalitarianism' any more effectively.[239]

'Totalitarianism' represented only the most extreme form of the European civilization that Gandhi deemed "Satanic." Western imperialism in particular is "the great Satan of our time" [240]   Western civilization has corrupted the moral wisdom of the East, where moral wisdom originated.[241]

> I do not deny that India had armies, warfare, etc., before she came in contact with Europe. But I do say that it never was the normal course of Indian life. The masses, unlike those of Europe, were untouched by the warlike spirits.[242]

Europeans "appear to be half mad" from their irreligion, "lack[ing] real physical strength or courage," they "keep up their energy by intoxication." The imperialistic West "does ungodly acts in the name of God"; its "worship [of] the war-god" gives it a merely apparent strength, a strength concealing the weakness of all irreligion. The West's vaunted "political economy" conceals the same egoistic weakness and bestiality.[243]

By "Western civilization" Gandhi meant the modern West, even the late modern West (roughly since Britain had taken direct control of India).[244] "Ancient ideals" had "lost their hold" on England, and now served as the "best exponent" of modernity's "mad desire to destroy distance and time, to increase animal appetites and go to the ends of the earth in search of their satisfaction."[245]   As the false strength and real weakness of the modern West became more apparent, not only would an independent India face no lasting danger from "foreign powers,"[246] but India would finally conquer the West:

> What I want you to understand is the message of Asia. It is not to be learnt through the Western spectacles or by imitating the atom bomb. If you want to give a message to the West, it must be the message of love and the message of truth. I want you to go away with the thought that Asia has to conquer the West through love and truth.... This conquest will be loved by the West itself.[247]

While Gandhi never doubted "that eastern civilization will become predominant," he saw a serious problem among the Asians. "[S]unk in their contemplative mood," they had grown "lazy"; they needed to be "quickened with Western spirit."[248]

> If anyone thinks that the people in the West are innocent of humanity, he is sadly mistaken. The ideal of humanity in the West is perhaps lower, but their practice of it is very much more thorough than ours. We rest content with a lofty ideal and are slow or lazy in its practice. We are wrapped in deep darkness, as is evident from our paupers, cattle and other animals.[249]

If, indeed, the modern West were altogether bad, and peace is good, why would commercial republicanism, modern in so many respects, foster peace so much more successfully than Islam (from the beginning) or even Hinduism (when not 'Origenized')? Why could a Christian sympathetic to Gandhi, hoping that Gandhi's principles might restore Christianity to health, nonetheless write, "It is the glory of the Western world that Gandhi came to no harm in our hands"?[250]

Gandhi enjoyed more success against modernity as (incompletely) embodied in the British Raj than he enjoyed in his confrontations with Islam and the ideologies of modern tyranny. The success was limited. One historian disenchantingly argues that the Japanese invasion, the English people, and the weariness caused by the Second World War brought down the Rah, not Gandhi, and that "Hindu society remain[ed] ugly and repressive" throughout the years since the British got out[251] — still in the thrall of what Gandhi detested as modernist corruptions. Gandhi in many ways benefitted from the West — from its constitutional protections, its principles of equality and liberty — without being able to conquer it in its 'decadence.' It is fitting that Gandhi never came to the United States — not so much because "America is not ready to receive me," to receive "my message" — but because he was not ready to receive America's message. America became ready to receive his message in time. Indeed Gandhi predicted the means: "[I]t may be through the Negroes that the unadulterated message of nonviolence will be delivered to the world," he told a delegation of American blacks in 1936.[252] But Gandhi never fully apprehended the American combination of 'ancient' and 'modern' principles. While understanding some aspects of modernity very well, he did not understand modernity with sufficient rigor or subtlety, and thus could not successfully conquer or even tame it. The thought of modern writers on peace deserves more careful study than Gandhi afforded it.

What a Gandhian Christianity Might Resemble: Liberation Theology

Christian nonresistance effectively moderates Christian zeal. While Christians may condemn particular laws – laws permitting gladiatorial spectacles, abortion, brothels – they will undermine only the worst regimes. They will not usually undermine the rule of law itself. Nonviolence resistance, being a kind of nonlethal physical warfare, inclines more to civil disorder, except in those instances when a lethal civil war may be imminent and nonviolence channels passions away from savagery.

Christian nonresistants proselytize and help, but exclude from their communities, those unreached by proselytization. Gandhi proselytized for nonviolent resistance but not for Hinduism, and included in his movement, though not in his *ashram*, those unreached by his proselytization and by Hinduism. As a result disunity often prevailed in his movement if not in his *ashram*. Gandhi could adopt this policy because he did not accept the Christian doctrine of original sin. To Gandhi, the only 'Fall' was 'cultural' – the vast moral and intellectual error that is modern civilization. As for the origin of sin, Gandhi located it in the body, not in flesh-dwelling evil spirits exorcised only by the Holy Spirit. While Christian nonresistants often judge rule employing injurious force to be necessary, given the existence of evil spirits in men, Gandhi saw no permanent need either for exorcism or for severe physical punishments.

Gandhian nonviolent resistance formed one part of his political enterprise. Important parts of that enterprise translate poorly into the modern regimes of European and American Christendom. Agrarianism, communalism, celibacy, and vegetarianism have had little appeal in the modern West, except in certain religious orders. To see what Christian nonviolent resistance might become, one must develop in a social and political context closer to that of Gandhi's India. The first (or at least the most prominent) Christian movement developed in a 'Gandhian' context is Latin American 'liberation theology.'[253]

Gandhi's nonviolent resistance unintendedly strengthened Christian faith in some Christians; liberation theology deliberately seeks to restore the Gospel's "credibility" while offering "an alternative to capitalism *and* socialism." With the formulation and practice of liberation theology,

"Christianity can no longer be dismissed as the opium of the people." Liberation theologians raise "a question concerning *the very meaning of Christianity*," namely, the comprehensively political character of Jesus as humanity's Christ and *archegos* of the Kingdom of God.[254] Liberation theologians thus follow Gandhi's demand that each people explore their own traditions, religious and political; liberation theology speaks of and for Latin American Christians (mostly Catholics). While therefore relative to its 'time' and place, it nevertheless "raises the permanent, universal problem of the real meaning of the social contents of the Christian message" in "the continent [sic] among the exploited and oppressed peoples where Christians are in the majority."[255]

Liberation theologians occasionally describe Latin America as "semifeudal."[256] More often they describe it (rather too broadly) as 'capitalistic.' Catholic Christianity entered Latin America with the Spanish conquests of the sixteenth century; Protestant Christianity and republican anti-clericalism arrived with the modernizing "neocolonialism" of the nineteenth century. "Especially after the First World War, United States commerce and capital has established the third colonization of Latin America in the name of democracy and free enterprise"; unfortunately, "democratic institutions could hardly function in countries where there was almost no middle class" and where illiteracy prevailed among the many who were poor. These masses preferred the paternalistic rule of the *caudillo* to the "herodian" oligarchs. Although for centuries "the Catholic church remained firmly allied with elites opposed to change," changes in Church teaching set forth by the Second Vatican Council in 1962 legitimized democratic sentiments among lay Catholics and urged Catholics to act in accordance with those sentiments. In Latin America, democratization first appeared as the attempt to stimulate economic development with foreign investment. Investors mistakenly − or, as liberation theologians would have it, maliciously − restricted funds to "the modern sector of the economy," to those more accurately described as semifeudal oligarchs. As a result, oligarchs grew richer, the poor poorer, in an imitation of Marxian 'dialectial' impoverishment. "Development and underdevelopment are two sides of the same coin." A 1968 conference of Christian churchmen convened in Medellin, Columbia, under the auspices of the Consejo Episcopal Latinoamericano (CELAM) resulted in the issuance of a report denouncing these injustices and calling for a new social, economic, and political order.[257]

Liberation theologians advance a Gandhi-like critique of modern civilization and its imperialism. "A movement against idolatry," liberation theology sets "the faith in the God of Life versus the antilife idols" of modernity, the "system of death."[258] Other theologies "remain silent about the major problem of our time: the domination of the whole world by a small minority, which submits to the false god of economic expansion, with the complicity of Western culture and the Western churches themselves," including much of the Roman Catholic Church. With the transformation of the old, overtly political and military colonialism to contemporary, economic "neocolonialism," Latin American "servitude" continues "under different signs and other lords." The imperialist countries themselves suffer "a wild atomization of existence and a general anonymity of persons lost in the cogs of the mechanisms of the macro-organizations and bureaucracies."[259] The apparent religious toleration of the new imperial societies is in fact "profoundly atheistic," the result not of agapic love and mutual respect but indifference to religion as such. "Consumer majorities...artificaly bound to Christianity," adhering to Church institutions "out of insecurity" not "personal conviction," retard the formation of "meaningful community." Although commercial republics acknowledge "the rights and dignity of the human person," they conceive of and live those rights "individualistically, without adequate regard for social responsibility." As a result, such rights as freedom of speech, of religion, of the press, and of private property take precedence over rights to education and a minimal level of economic sustenance. And as a result of these false priorities, "the capitalist social mould...up to now has not succeeded, in any country in the world, in resolving the basic problems of the people in terms of work, shelter, health and education." This impoverishes people spiritually as well as physically. One liberation theologian tells the story of an American priest who moved from a poor parish in a Puerto Rican neighborhood, where he was "needed for everything," to a middle class parish where congregants came to him only on Sundays. A priest not needed for everyday economic needs finds himself as 'marginalized' in a commercial republic as are the poor in a Latin American oligarchy. This may account for the sympathetic chord liberation theology strikes among Western clergy, as well as its cautionary power among Latin American clergy. They too, after all, have 'class interests' to defend.[260]

Unlike Gandhi, liberation theologians defend their 'class interests' as clergymen, expending much energy upon such specifically theological concerns as hermeneutics and epistemology. The results are nonetheless fairly Gandhian, albeit with a heavy 'German' accent. Liberation theologians share the universal concern of modern moralists to avoid 'abstractions' and 'dogmas,' to be 'concrete' and 'practical,' to associate reasoning with bloodless scientism and sympathy with vitality, 'life.' "Let us start with the reality of everyday life," interpreting the Bible in accordance with "the continuing changes in our present-day reality, both individual and societal," forming a "hermeneutical circle" from life to Bible to changed life to reinterpreted Bible, "and so on."[261] Morality is prior to science because "life is more important than reflection" — a formulation that neglects to notice that reflection is part of human life, and that thinking human beings often reflect upon life. Although "faith does not exclude nor does it dispense with reason," love "sees a lot further and with greater depth than cold reason." Moral *norms* depend not on "abstract, univocal, and immutable principle" but on "an intricate web of conditions"; liberation theologians avoid historical relativism, *mere* positing of 'norms' or conventions, by insisting upon the existence of God and His "Truth." Unlike Gandhi and the Greeks however, liberation theologians conceive of historical reality not as cyclical but as dialectical, moving towards God and Truth. Although historicist progressivism is well known to issue often in the severest totalitarianisms, liberation theologians tends to associate stable 'natural law' teachings alone with hierarchy, "authoritarianism," and "patriarchal culture."[262] Even worse than natural law is modern "analytic-instrumental reason" aiming at "its own defined irrationality and power." Modernity however derives from "the great turn from the pre-Socratics to the Socratics, when Logos took its own path, overtaking Mythos, when the concept gained dominion over the symbol." Reason must be re-eroticized, as seen even today in the 'daimonic' "mysticism that consumes the scientist."[263] There is no human *nature*, only "creatureliness," the fact of human creation, which can either accept or reject God. The rest is history, specifically "the history of salvation and perdition," a history authored principally by God but also by those of his creatures who enjoy free will, their activity "penetrated, sustained, animated, adapted and sublimated by the divine activity."[264]

Liberation theologians prefer "orthopraxis" to orthodoxy, as indeed did Gandhi. "Worthy" theology "stems from a pretheological commitment to change and improve the world," even as does modern historicism, 'left' and 'right,' Marxian and Nietzschean. One senses a certain excitement here: "No longer is the theologian a mere professor.... Now he or she is a militant," writes Leonardo Boff. "Organic intellectuals" and "militant theologians" live with the people, reflecting upon their "life and progress" toward liberation – that is, toward "whatever oppression [is] not," toward God. Jesus of Nazareth, "the Word...made flesh," is "the new humanity." We are to follow, "defining ourselves" in Him through faithful study in the Christian community. In this, if we are successful, we shall become saints: "neither ancient nor modern" but "simply true, always true." Liberation is salvation.[265]

Various forms of 'German' ideology or historicism inspirit and vex liberation theology. Educated in 'Western' universities, liberation theologians obviously owe much to "the general cultural climate of the West," perhaps even more than Gandhi owed to his education by the English and in England.[266] It should not be surprising that, like Gandhi, they seized upon those elements of 'Western' culture that seem most critical of the West. The educator Paulo Freire, unanimously praised by liberation theologians, well exemplifies this tendency. Freire titled his book *Pedagogy of the Oppressed*, the 'of' meaning *for* and also *by* the villagers he worked with in Brazil. Citing Hegel's analysis of the master-slave relationship, he calls upon the oppressed and educators to collaborate in risking their lives to obtain freedom by way of "*conscientizacao*" or "critical consciousness" that will liberate the people from their "fear of freedom." Teachers must stop lecturing at students and instead fit words together with action, giving them "transforming power" over "paternalistic social action apparatus." Because "the essence of consciousness is intentionality" or will, Freire seeks, with Marx, not to know the world but to change it. Freire urges the use of words for denunciation, that is, as an expression of *thumos* not *eros*. Without consciousness there would be no world, 'because' there would be no one to say 'This is a world.' Although this claim as it stands could be theistic, in Freire it is not; the world, not God, "brings consciousness into existence." The world is "process"; all is 'becoming' — "revolutionary," "prophetic," and "hopeful." Human beings are "historical beings" whose words are deeds and deeds thoughtful.[267]

Thoughtfulness may dilute strong-willed denunciation, which has so regularly issued in moralistic despotisms 'right' and, more often, 'left.' Freire hopes to avoid the despotic tendency in Marxism by criticizing the polemical use of words and by praising dialogue. "No one can say a true word alone — nor can he say it *for* another." Dialogue requires a "profound love for the world and for men;" revolutionary praxis (words and deeds) is "an act of love." "The naming of the world, which is an act of creation and re-creation, is not possible if it is not infused with love." This sounds very nearly Christian unless the reader overlooks the men of praxis cited by Freire in affirmation of it: Fidel Castro, Mao Zedong, and Che Guevara.[268]   This astonishing sentimentalizing of Marxist revolutionaries and tyrants calls Freire's common sense into question, if not his sincerity, and is unfortunately taken over by many liberation theologians. Similarly, Freire's pedagogy itself cannot resolve the tension between teachers/leaders and their students/followers. If the problem "of our epoch" is "domination," and the solution is "liberation," and if the world (particularly the social-political world) constitutes consciousness, then a "dominated consciousness" such as that of a Latin American villager will see only epiphenomena.   How to avoid a "methodology of *conscientizacao*" that does not dictate or impose? How to democratize Marxist 'science' and thus avoid psychic and even physical violence?[269]

Freire recommends that educators arrive at villages first as "investigators" to study "the people's thinking." Teachers will first of all learn from the people. They will engage the people in this enterprise; both shall "act as *co-investigators*." However, problems arise: Freire recommends "problem-solving" as the means to engage the people. It is the "investigators" who determine "the area in which they will work," the problem to be solved; they 'set the agenda.' After observing, listening, and 'dialoguing' to uncover "the structure of [the people's] thought," the teachers discuss their findings among themselves and with a small number of volunteers from the village.

They identify "contradictions" in popular opinions; they then develop "codifications" (in words or in pictures) of recognizable and familiar situations that will serve to illustrate those "contradictions." These "codifications" should be "neither overly explicit [i.e. propagandistic] nor overly enigmatic," Freire recommends, without a trace of irony. Finally, teachers and students review these materials in an effort to correct their contradictory opinions. "Individuals who were *submerged* in reality, merely *feeling* their needs, *emerge* from reality and perceive the *causes* of their needs." The people "come to feel like masters of their thinking;" after "several days of dialogue" they too may suggest themes for discussion.[270] Clearly, a well-trained educator working with villagers could, with a reasonable degree of sensitivity and cleverness, insinuate a highly ideological construction of 'reality' with Freire's techniques. This is Marxism 'democratized,' persuading instead of dictating. But it is still Marxism – dubious as an account of morality, economics, and politics.[271]

In 1970, as liberation theology gestated, a polemical defense of contemporary commercial republicanism appeared in France under the provocative title, *Ni Marx, Ni Jésus*.[272] Liberation theology has attempted to proceed most emphatically '*with* Marx *and* Jesus.' To be sure, liberation theologians do not confuse Marx with Jesus. As one of them observes, the Latin American Marxist group "Christians for Socialism," founded in 1971, was "completely independent" from liberation theology and should not be associated with it; the Argentinian liberation theologians Lucio Gara and Juan Luis Scannone are "openly anti-Marxist."[273] Gustavo Gutierrez, who first systematized liberation theology, views Marxism with some ambivalence. He praises the Castro revolution in Cuba while calling Marxist determinism "completely alien to the kind of social analysis that supplies a framework for the theology of liberation." Yet he finds liberation theology's "confrontation with Marxism" to be "direct and fruitful," and cites with approval the 'soft' (and thus popular) Marxists Antonio Gramsci and Herbert Marcuse. He applauds Marxist dialectic, the "transformation of the world through work," and calls for "a permanent cultural revolution,"[274] which is nothing other than a Gramscian twist on a doctrine shared by Trotsky and Stalin. The brothers Boff insist that liberation theology submits Marxism "to the judgment of the poor and their cause, not the other way around"; their pedagogy is Freirean, however, and thus suspect. They share Marxism's interest in economics and class struggle, and its interest in demystifying ideologies; they reject Marxism's atheism and materialism. God's word is sovereign, even over the poor.[275] Liberation theologists generally reject Marx's atheism;[276] one prefers to deny that atheism is the core of Marxism, anyway.[277] They emphasize instead the notion of "building up a new humanity," a "new man,: found both in the New Testament and in Marx.[278] A voluntaristic and providential dialectic that acts like Marx's dialectical materialism replaces dialectical materialism.

At the same time, liberation theologians want to preserve Marx's "class-based analysis" of the existing world sociopolitical order. "Class struggle is a fact" that makes Marxism "indispensable" even with its flaws,[279] although Juan Luis Segundo concedes that 'class analysis' itself is not uniquely Marxist but may be seen in a variety of places beginning with the Bible.[280] This raises the question of the exact character of Marxism 'class analysis.' Aristotle and James Madison, for example, both analyze class struggles; they differ from Marx, and from the Bible as interpreted by liberation theologians, in their disinclination to believe that one social class so far exceeds another in its justice as to require the conscientious observer to commit himself to its side of the struggle. In 'preferring' the Indian villagers but refusing to attack the caste system, insisting that each of the four major castes has a legitimate social function, Gandhi came closer to Aristotle than to liberation theologians. Christianity, which predicts the triumph of one 'class' (Christians and God's angels) over another (pagans and Satan's demons), distinguishes the liberation theologians from Gandhi on this point; Marxism confirms the difference.

Liberation theologians depart from Marx in viewing him as inadequate in confronting death. "All humanist-inspired attempts at liberation are sooner or later bound to ask themselves what sense there is in the finally radical act of dying for others." Death is "the final alienation to which Marxism can find no satisfactory answer." Only Christianity, with its doctrines of the Cross and of Resurrection, holds out hope after death, a genuine reason for self-sacrifice.[281] The promise of resurrection frees the human soul for a life on earth of universal love; this agapic love, they claim, "is partisan and committed," indignant at evils and insistent on their transformation. One must love one's enemy, "but this does not mean he or she ceases to be a class enemy – just as those who rejected the good news of the kingdom of God did not cease to be enemies of Christ."[282]

Still, the wishful impulse to 'save' Marxism not only intellectually but spiritually remains strong, almost compulsive, among liberation theologians. Materialism, one writes, has not "much at all to do with Marx." This tendency to extract Marxian dialectic from Marxian materialism often leads liberation theologians back to Hegel. This does not quite solve the problem, as some of them see.[283]   In their practical assessments of revolutions liberation theologians strain to believe even more ardently than in their theoretical musings. The Sandinista seizure of power in Nicaragua after the 1979 popular-front overthrow of the tyrant Somoza brought on a disgraceful stream of apologetics. Orbis Books, owned by the Maryknoll Order of the Roman Catholic Church, published a book of statements by Sandinista Minister of the Interior Tomas Borge titled *Christianity and Revolution: Tomas Borge's Theology of Life.*   Purporting to eschew revenge on former Somozist National Guardsman, proclaiming a future of "political pluralism and a mixed economy" in a society whose "essence is love," Borge proclaimed, "We intend to convert Nicaragua into a showcase, an example of human rights" including "the right to life" defended by a people who have learned "to love our enemies." "Christ was a revolutionary," and Nicaraguans enjoy "full freedom to worship God" and "not freedom to worship the golden calf"; Saint Francis of Assisi "created a world of *campaneros*, of brothers and sisters; a world that has ceased to be utopian in Nicaragua."   An army "created to defend peace" will "never be able to carry out aggression against the Nicaraguan people, because our army *is* the Nicaraguan people." This popular army would defend Nicaragua against the dark forces commanded by United States President Ronald Reagan, whom Borge compared to Holy Roman Emperor Frederick Barbarossa. At the end of the book Borge admitted that he was not a Christian.   The churches animated by liberation theology nonetheless believed this was a christian if not a Christian regime.[284] "Nicaragua may be seen as a test case for collaboration between Christians and Marxist revolutionaries," one sympathetic North American theologian wrote.[285]   After a decade of state terrorism, including but not limited to attacks on churchmen by Sandinista mobs, seizure of property for the private use of the proletarian vanguard, the destruction of agriculture, kidnappings and beatings of Christians, censorship of sermons and newspapers, the exile of 500,000 people from a nation of 3 million, military regimentation, and the systematic self-deception of the Sandinistas themselves, the revolution derailed in an internationally supervised national election. The same god that failed Europe failed Central America.

Sandinistas persisted, retaining control of the army, national universities, labor unions, and many churches.[286] And if the revolution proved impermanent, the illusions of liberation theologians appear quite permanent. Cuba's Castro, after decades of praise by the principal liberation theologians, continued to be the object of the most pious hopes:

> It is worth noting that Fidel Castro is devoting considerable attention to the political and ethical significance of Latin American liberation theology, regarding its arguments as far more persuasive as those of Marxism itself. He is known to be personally studying and discussing the works of its principal authors.[287]

There may come a point when liberation theologians conclude, with one of their critics within the Catholic Church, that Marxist historicism "is not really a historical perspective at all, because it is continuously contradicted by actual history."[288]

That day has not yet come, with one notable exception. José Comblin has addressed liberation theology's self-contradictory attempt to attack 'German' ideology with another variant of 'German' ideology. Comblin shares the consensus view that Latin America lives under "the postwar American Empire" and "its farthest-reaching import — the national security state." After the Second World War, the establishment in the American government of such institutions as the National Security Council, the Central Intelligence Agency, and the National War College "caused a radical change in the [government's] balance of power," which became overweighted in the Executive Branch. This imbalanced government adopted an ideology of German not American origin, namely, "the theory of the state as a geographical organism," including state totalism. The ideology combines

Herder's organicism, Hegel's idealism, Fichte's statism, and List's economic nationalism; "the nation takes the place of God," exercising, when and where it can, Godlike power. Latin Americans have imitated this new state; given the relative instability of Latin American societies and the weakness of their republican traditions, the "national security state" appears in much purer form there than in the United States.[289] "Most liberation movements are ambiguous" because they employ both Christian and 'German' notions of liberty. "The future of liberation movements, and the future of the Christian share in such movements, and especially the future of any liberation theology depends upon the church's ability to make the distinction between Christian and [German] idealist liberation and act on it." Christian liberty, a gift that changes individual wills and thereby establishes new social ties, opposes "pantheistic totalitarianism" seen in the Marxist regimes that end in a "national security system...permanently mobilized for permanent war."[290] Some of those sympathetic to liberation theology have ignored Comblin's critique; others write as if they have not ignored it, albeit without citing it.[291]

Liberation theologians share Gandhi's opinion that all aspects of human life are political although for liberation theologians this may be a circumstance only of the contemporary world. "Every human act, even the most private, possesses not only a social content (because it transcends the individual), but a political content (because transcending of the individual is always related to change *or* stability in society)." Politics, "the organized seeking of the common good," traditionally has defined the common good according to a political theology that seeks to "legitimize the status quo." For elitists "democracy and wisdom are mutually exclusive," but "third-world revolution" and the theologians who commit themselves to it are "anti-imperialistic and anti-technocratic." As revolutionists including theologians struggle for economic equality and civil liberty, they encounter "the mystery of God working in history" along with them. They learn that "sacred power lies within the entire community, and not only in the hands of the few"; "power in itself is not rejected, only its monopolization and expropriation" − its desacralization and perversion − "by the 'elite.'" Among Latin American Christians this learning came from studying the Bible and Christian tradition "from a perspective which would promote liberation and would denounce the alliance of Christianity with the forces of domination and the maintenance of the present status quo." Christ's rule thus "is concretized historically."[292]

Christian rule in Latin America, like Gandhian rule in India, would be the rule of Christ through the poor. Because "the great Latin American masses are made up of the poor" this rule would be democratic or majoritarian. As in Western antiquity, the many in Latin America are poor; yet their movement toward liberation has resulted from the introduction of modern principles into the Catholic Church.[293] This can lead to tensions between modern historicist ideology and Christianity; liberation theologians want it to lead back to Jesus of Nazareth. "Theologically speaking, the shepherds [in Bethlehem] are the representatives of the poor, to whom the good news was announced and to whom Jesus was sent." Moses was the first liberator of an oppressed people; Jesus was the final liberator of all oppressed peoples. His Kingdom "implies an absolute revolution which must first begin with the poor, as they will be the first to receive the Kingdom (Luke 6:20)." The people of Latin America, Christian communities "feel that they are a continuation of the Biblical people." Jesus' mother, Mary, also bespeaks this liberation, this transformation of the world in her prayer called the Magnificat.[294]

Gandhi considered extreme poverty a block to religious devotion. Liberation theologians concur, decrying the "violence" of poverty and observing that, while the poor are blessed, poverty is not. Extreme poverty leads to the denial of God. Extreme poverty means death of body and soul; it is "the most painful and bloody wound in the history of humanity," aggravated by unjust socio-political structures. Fortunately, an all-powerful God reaches out to the poor. Liberation theology gives priority to the poor not because the poor have some inherent virtue "in themselves" but because "God's agapeic love" extends to them first and foremost. "We are in a *Kairos*, a propitious and demanding time in which the Lord challenges us and we are called upon to bear a very specific witness" to "the irruption of the poor" after "centuries of their absence "from our history." "Liberation theology was born when faith confronted the injustice done to the poor" and began "to recover the practical dimension in biblical faith" *for* the oppressed, against "the pharaohs."[295] This involvement of God's love with the poor protects their liberation from perversion toward mere interests "understood in the bourgeois, individualistic sense." The rights of life, including the rights to food, health, housing, employment, education – prior to the rights of freedom of conscience and opinion, and of religious practice – are "the rights of God." The story of Job proves that human beings can have a disinterested faith in God, "without looking for rewards and fearing punishments." Liberation theologians identify the poor with Job, without sufficiently observing that Job is uniquely excellent and faithful among the human beings of his time. A previous sort of collective 'Job-ness' may be found in the Franciscans, who practiced voluntary disappropriation of their property. The Franciscans gradually declined, liberation theologians admit, but perhaps the modern church can reverse this.[296] In general liberation theologians tend to criticize the poor far less than Gandhi did, and to minimize the significance of Jesus' appeal to the poor *in spirit*, who may or may not be economically poor.[297]

Liberation theologians compare the struggle to found a new Christian order to the Jews' exodus from Egypt, "the central event in Israel's life," the event "that constitutes Israel as a people."[298] The first step in this constitution was liberation from Pharaoh, "a basic requisite for worship": "Let my people go, so that they may serve Me" (compare Exodus 5:1). Jesus "graft[s]" the political "into the eternal" even more firmly than Moses did, and liberation theology, and modernity itself speed this process, as "people are crossing centuries in a matter of weeks" thanks to "conscientization" by Christian educators and the proliferation of radio, television, and films. 'Closed' societies no longer exist, and their opening can enable their 'filling' by the Holy Spirit.[299] Human effort alone will not suffice; reliance upon our own strength discourages us when we are weak and inflates us with pride when we are strong. Liberation by and with the Holy Spirit will be progressive but remain partial within history; only Jesus' Second Coming, ending history, will bring full liberation of His people.[300]

Liberation theologians divide on the issue of violence,[301] but there is a strong Gandhian side to many of them. The "Medellin Document on Peace" issued at the 1968 conference of the Latin American Episcopal Council reflected this ambivalence. Peace, "a work of justice," must be "built" not simply found; peace is "a fruit of love." Following traditional Catholic just war doctrine, the Document says that the Christian "can fight, but he prefers peace to war" and recognizes the "institutionalized violence" that is tyranny. "Revolutionary insurrection," while it can be legitimate, can also yield new injustices.[302] The Document concluded, "If we consider, then, the totality of the circumstances of our countries and if we take into account the Christian preference for peace, the enormous difficulty of a civil war, the logic of violence, the atrocities it engenders, the risk of provoking foreign intervention, illegitimate as it may be, the difficulty of building a regime of justice and freedom while participating in a process of violence, we earnestly desire that the dynamism of the awakened and organized community be put to the service of justice and peace."[303]

Juan Luis Segundo chooses to emphasize the just-war argument:

> ...will not Latin America be in a context closer to that of the Old Testament than of the New? It is tremendously frightening to imagine that what may be imperative in Latin America is sinful in Europe.[304]

While frightening, this is nevertheless true, reflecting the Bible's 'duality' on the subject of violence. Oddly, Segundo associates this 'duality' with changed historical circumstances and not with the advent of Jesus as Christ. Segundo, unlike Gandhi, does not regard violence as "the main problem" in the modern world; he concerns himself more with manipulativeness, using human beings as means not treating them as ends. Violence is inevitable because human beings need a system of laws; laws are impersonal and distancing not intimate. But intimacy requires these impersonal structures in order to survive. Jesus Himself "had to put some people at arm's length in order to let other people get close to him as a real human being"; He insults people even after telling his disciples not to. "Jesus is urging us to use the least amount of violence compatible with truly effective love"; in this formulation Segundo begins to resemble Gandhi.[305]

The historicist aspect of liberation theology makes some writers reluctant to endorse nonviolence or just war doctrines. Jose Míguez Bonino, citing Marx, Engels, and Lenin on the 'necessity' of violence in the class struggle, calls this 'necessity' "open to correction." But nonviolent revolution is equally open to correction. It "is still too early to draw clear consequences one way or another"; therefore, "we must resist all hypostatization of *la violencia*, either to defend it or to attack it." This said, Bonino prefers nonviolence both for Christian and for revolutionary reasons, even as he acknowledges the "human cost" of pacifism.[306] In still sharper contrast to Segundo, other liberation theologians – in particular Segundo Galilea, José Comblin, and Elsa Tamez – find violence a profoundly damaging part of the Latin American ethos and decisively oppose it.[307] Gustavo Gutierrez, often called the father of liberation theology, carefully avoids committing himself on the issue of violent vs. nonviolent revolution in his seminal book *Theology of Liberation*.[308] But he obviously prefers nonviolence. He describes the suffering Job as a peacemaker and a just man. He rejects the culture of *"machismo"* and describes liberation theology praxis as "forging *shalom*," peacemaking, "transform[ing] history in the light of the reign of God." God is the *gö'ël*, an "avenger of blood" (2 Samuel 14:11). God defends and revenges His adopted family, the people, who may then turn their attention "to eliminat[ing] [the] deepest root" of conflict, "which is the absence of love."[309]

Dominique Barbé calls for the use of the "active nonviolence" of Gandhi and Martin Luther King in the "Battle of Jesus" against "the demonic forces of destruction." This kind is indigenous to Latin America, whose oppressed and disarmed peoples "have spontaneously been living" in accordance with the principles of active nonviolence for centuries.[310] One of the most consistent advocates on nonviolent resistance has been Leonardo Boff. While conceding that "Jesus employs physical violence against those who profane the Temple (John 2:15-17)"; he deplores the human tendency to "make war to achieve peace" and "prepare for war in order to avoid war." He observes that Jesus rejects "messianism grounded on the use of force and power" for a messianism grounded on "martyrdom and sacrifice." Jesus the Christ "is the crisis of the world: Either one transcends oneself and thereby is saved or one falls back on oneself, eliminating Jesus from one's milieu, and is lost." Jesus' command to love not kill our enemies precisely requires self-transcendence not self-reliance. "All oppression and subjection constitutes acts of violence and goes against the intimate meaning of human life" whose "excellence" is "basically defined by freedom." Vengeance is wrong for Christians. Before the Emperor Constantine, the Catholic Church "was more of a movement than an institution"; it should become so again, relying on "the power to love" that "differ[s] in nature from the power of domination" typical of the "pagan tyrant," "It is in weakness that the love of God and the God of love are revealed (I Corinthians 1:25; II Corinthians 13:4; Philippians 2:7);" today "a new Church is being born" among the poor, the powerless. Without property to defend, Saint Francis needed no carnal weapons. He made peace with a Moslem sultan and with heretics; he attempted to make peace in many cities in Italy. Peace should be Christians' goal and their method. Class struggle can remain lovingly nonviolent. Genuine Christians do not fear physical death, nor do they achieve mere Stoic indifference. Saint Francis died singing, having joyfully reached the root of life, nature, and the people: God.[311]

The new or renewed church in its political aspect will be democratic and communal; Gandhi's *ashram* was communal though not democratic so long as he lived there. 'Participatory democracy' survived the universities of the 1960s, associating itself with the preexisting movement to establish "ecclesial base communities." Communalism institutionalizes the 'Sixties-left contention that "the personal is the political"; communes are, and are perceived to be, an extended family: in this instance "the 'kin-dom of God." Liberation theologians cites New Testament passages on communalism and call Marxism "a mere episode in the history of the communist project," a project "defended in the Bible as proper and characteristic of Christianity." They insist that communism is not utopian – no-place – but 'eutopian' – the best place. "The *eutopia* of the individual [Christian] becomes by contagion a *eutopia* for a group or religious community."[312].

Like Gandhi, Leonardo Boff envisions a "participatory democracy" that "must transcend the limits of bourgeois representative democracy which in Latin America functions in an elitist and anti-popular way." Also like Gandhi he endorses representative government, but one "controlled by the popular organizations themselves." He shares Gandhi's hope for a combination of equality, pluralism, and communion – principles perhaps as incompatible in Latin America as they proved to be in eighteenth-century France. This political democracy would form part of a "cosmic democracy," a Franciscan "universal fraternity" with the worm on the road, treating all with respect and devotion, gentleness and compassion – all under the Fatherhood of God.[313]

The base ecclesial communities consist of fifteen to twenty families instructed in the Gospel by organizers using Freirean pedagogic techniques. Theoretically at least, decisions are to be made by a two-thirds majority; "otherwise [the communes] would not be able to live" but "would break into factions." Regular general assemblies "institutionalize this search for consensus." Dominique Barbé sets down ten "commandments of active nonviolence" whereby commune members should live. These resemble Gandhi's *ashram* vows respecting nonviolent love, self-rule, fearlessness, and opposition to oppression; they omit the requirement of celibacy, emphasize struggle much more, and replace the prohibition against stealing with a prohibition against hiding things.[314] Even, without "alienating structures" and "rigid rules," the communes still tend toward stratification, standing in "constant need of revitalization. "Leading" people to "commitment to our fellow human beings" remains necessary," and, perhaps most alarmingly, Boff recalls that the modern bourgeoisie arose from Christian communes of Saint Francis' time – though not, *Deus gratia*, from Saint Francis' communes themselves. Predictably, a variety of communes have arisen in Latin America; 'leadership' in their founding and preservation brings a certain *de facto* hierarchy, and reportedly this tendency increases over time. Is "the dream of equality" "necessarily coercive"? In this respect one notices that Gutierrez, unlike Gandhi, would eliminate private property.[315]

"Religion is the memory of a lost unity and the nostalgia for a future reconciliation." Unity and "open dialogue," particularly "with those, be they Christians or not...are committed to the historical liberation that should serve as the basis for the 'service of reconciliation' in and through justice," has proven as elusive for liberation theologians as it did for Gandhi. Divine grace "alone can conquer egotism at the root," liberationists and Gandhi agree, but "what comes from God is difficult to determine" and the unity depending upon it only intermittant.[316]

Some writers in the West, perhaps reacting to the intermittant character of divine grace in establishing human communities, take refuge in imagination. "The work of futuring – that imaginative opening to better historical possibilities even in the face of enemies, cynics, scoffers, and even liars – is the minimal requirement of peacemaking," one admirer of liberation theology claims.[317] Another calls "all theology...primarily a work of the imagination."[318] Thus 'eutopia' begins to return to utopia, despite the desire to make imagination real. Still others, impatient with God's timing and with the slow establishment of small communes, look to a world organization to implement Gandhian principles. Secretary of the United Nations Economic and Social Council Robert Muller works for "a true global, God-abiding political, moral and spiritual renaissance to make this planet at long last what it was always meant to be: the Planet of God," a "world spiritual democracy" wherein "the world of the heart" overcomes "the imperialism of reason." The "most sacred law of humanity" should be "Thou shalt not kill, not even in the name of a nation." Muller contends that "Everyone has a different perception of the Christ"; 'his' Christ preaches love, peace, progress, and a belief in 'resurrection' – that is, the recycling of atoms in the eternity of matter and historical contributions to human progress. With Gandhi, he regards Christianity as an authoritative but not uniquely or unqualifiedly authoritative source of "global education" for this new order. He promotes a religious syncretism including "atheistic" Buddhism.[319]

The 'global' vision of world federalism can also inform liberation theologists' communalism. Perhaps recalling the Buddhism Nietzsche claimed to see at the heart of Christianity,[320] Rubem Alves warns against "fundamentalist" Christianity, which, he claims, "Nietzsche rightly described...as the enemy of the future," with its "negation of the world" and "absolutization of eternity" in "conspiracy against life." With Nietzsche, Alves asserts that the body, not the soul, is "Great Reason." "Religion reveals the logic of the heart."[321] Boff initially calls "adherence to Christ" "the indispensable condition of participation in the new order to be introduced by God (Luke 12:8-9)."[322] However,

> Jesus' present existence is our future. He is the first of many brothers (Rom. 8-29; Col. 1:18). In this sense Christ is *an* absolute within history. He does not thus diminish his predecessors or followers such as Buddha, Confucius, Socrates, Gandhi, Martin Luther King, and others, but rather gives full and radical form to what they lived and carried forward.[323]

Jesus the Christ "*can* play *a* determining role" in "forming a planetary, ecumenical, and communal consciousness among people in search of a new humanism." This new humanism aims at "the vocation of the human being": "divinization." With liberation "all is possible." Boff 'Nietzsche-izes' the Platonist Justin Martyr, who taught that all who live according to the Logos are Christians, including those who do not know of Christianity. A "truly catholic" church will learn much from Hinduism and Buddhism, even as the world has learned "the idea of revolution from Christianity." ("Even Gandhi confessed that he thought up the idea of a pacifist revolution while reading the Sermon on the Mount," Boff claims, not quite accurately). Boff calls for a 'Christian' form of pantheism supported by religious syncretism. In this way would Gandhiism complete its conquest of Christianity in the name of Christianity.[324] Or, as a feminist liberation theologian contends, Jesus was the Christ for Christians but not for others.[325]

An Indian Jesuit has proposed a "Gandhian theology of liberation."[326] Gandhi was an *alter Christus*, but one who denied that Jesus was the only Christ. "Gandhi challenges Christians to the Christology of Jesus as servant rather than the Christology of the church about Jesus as Lord"; Gandhi preached "equality of religions," all of them equally liberating.[327] Many of these teachings resemble those associated with the 'New Age' movement popularized in North America during and after the 1960's.[328] In this respect it is prudent to recall a project uncannily anticipatory of Gandhi's:

> And perhaps there will come a great day on which a nation distinguished for wars and victories and for the highest development of military discipline and thinking, and accustomed to making the heaviest sacrifices on behalf of these things, will cry of its own free will: 'we shall shatter the sword' – and demolish its entire military machine down to its last foundations. To *disarm while being the best armed* out of an *elevation* of sensibility – that is the means to *real* peace, what must always rest on a disposition for peace: whereas the so-called armed peace such as now parades about in every country is a disposition to fractiousness which trusts neither itself nor its neighbour and fails to lay down its arms half out of hatred, half out of fear. Better to perish than to hate and fear, and *two-fold better to perish than to make oneself hated and feared* – this must one day become the supreme maxim of every individual state! - As is well known, our liberal representatives of the people lack the time to reflect on the nature of man: otherwise they would

know that they labour in vain when they work for a 'gradual reduction of the military burden'. On the contrary, it is only when this kind of distress is at its greatest that the only kind of god that can help here will be closest at hand. The tree of glory of war can be destroyed only at a single stroke, by a lightning-bolt: lightning, however, as you well know, comes out of a cloud and from on high.[329]

Dominique Barbé observes, "To try to transform the world without grace leads one into the will to power."[330]

THIRD PART

SECULAR PACIFICISM

Such is the miserable condition of men, that it is necessary for them to search in society for consolations for the evils of Nature, and in Nature for consolations for the evils of society.

−Chamfort

Who will then decide this great issue? Will it be reason? But each sect claims to have reason on its side. It must then be force that will judge, until reason penetrates enough heads to disarm force.

−Voltaire

CHAPTER SIX

Man's City: On the Justice of Peace

1. *Why No Philosopher Is a Pacifist*

Just after Rome fell to the Allied armies in the spring of 1944, Albert Einstein wrote to Benedetto Croce − as philosopher to philosopher, so to speak. Recalling Plato's philosopher-kings, Einstein noted "it does not appear very probable that reason and philosophy will become the guides of men in the very near future." The few philosophers constitute a genus "which neither oppresses men nor arouses their envy." Yet "any person who belongs" to this genus "may be destroyed by other people."[1] Perhaps the differences between philosophers and other kinds of men − and the fear and anger that the stranger's difference can provoke − endanger the philosophers, even as their powerlessness *qua* philosophers leaves them particularly vulnerable to assault. Philosophers must take a lively interest in peace. Surely they incline to pacifism?

They do not. Alberico Gentili scarcely exaggerates in writing that "all our jurists and all our philosophers of every time" reject pacifism.[2] Philosophers since Gentili's time seldom if ever deviate from the judgment of their predecessors, perhaps agreeing with the Marxist John Lewis's warning: "Unless the noblest of human beings can either defend himself successfully or be defended by someone else, he will certainly lose his valuable life, if he meets a gangster who is determined to kill him."[3] While pacifism "is in the last resort a faith in the ultimate reasonableness of mankind," C.E.M. Joad "doubt[s] whether evil can ever be eradicated from human nature so long as it remains human."[4] And even if "reason never will and never can justify war," and if "all attempts of *modern* men to justify it have failed miserably," G.F. Nicolai concedes that a genuinely defensive war would be rational.[5]

The philosophers' personal defensive war mostly entails camouflage, as philosophers from Grotius to Russell affirm.[6] However, if in modern times philosophy, or something called philosophy, becomes a public doctrine, disdaining all protective coloration, this would seem to end the philosophers' dilemma. "Philosophy, so far from deserving contempt," has become "the glory of human nature," "dart[ing] her eagle eye over all the busy world, detect[ing] error and mischief, and point[ing] out modes of improvement." "Truth and good are eternal and immutable; and therefore philosophy, which is solely attached to these, is still one and the same, whether ancient or modern, in England or in France." Only antiphilosophic men who "refuse to submit to reason" will "govern by violence," their swords "cut[ting] away all the opposition." Yet the people as a whole can be enlightened, making common cause with philosophers against the martial spirit of despotism.[7] Enlightenment is a philosophic necessity, i.e., a project necessary for philosophers' self-protection. By contrast, the Platonic attempt of reasoning men and women to regulate others' dangerous passions by the means of 'noble lies' would allow passion in the form of rhetoric to rule the reasonable. Similarly, an appeal to tradition *à la* Burke also deifies unreason. Socrates brought philosophy into the city, even if only to small cliques within it; whatever its masks, philosophy's rational passion to know inevitably leads to a more general enlightenment. Only a poor-spirited pessimism would attempt to repeal this progress.[8] Perhaps even nothing less than warrior spirits − not holy warriors but philosophic warriors − must conquer the world to make it safe for philosophy.[9] Still, this only means that an untraditional set of doctrines and practices replaces the traditional sets, unless reasoning itself can be 'built into' the new traditions, as for example John Dewey supposes.[10] And while the governing of some passion by rhetoric may appear to subordinate reason to passion, this depends upon whether or not the reasonable choose their rhetoric wisely. In the interstices of conflicting passions one may be crushed − or thrive. Need reason directly rule in order to thrive? Can public veneration of reason encourage reason, or is veneration (and its inevitable deflation by opposing forces) inherently unlikely to be reasonable? One is tempted to think that only a reason that discovered an object of veneration, such as God, could remain venerable. Can reason discover the true God, or only construct false ones? Reason helps to discover the articulations of nature, but nature may more properly be described as impressive, not awesome or venerable.

Public philosophy, whatever its feasibility or worth, at a minimum requires a kind of war-for-peace, not pacifism. Nor do Enlightenment thinkers eschew physical wars, however they may deplore them. The principal character in one of Voltaire's dialogues describes war as a disease to be remedied by fear and pity, and denies that there can be justice in war. But he quickly justifies defensive war as "nothing but resistance to armed robbers": "Let a prince disband his troops, let him allow his fortifications to fall in ruins, and let him spend his time reading Grotius, and you will see if he has not lost his kingdom in a year or two."[11] Jailed for conscientious objection to the First World War, Bertrand Russell refused to succumb to dogmatism: "No one who holds that human conduct ought to be such as to promote certain ends — no matter what ends may be selected — will expect any hard-and-fast rules of conduct to which no possible exception will be found." His 'pacifism' was not a rule, "to be deduced from Christ's teaching or from the categorical imperative," but "a course of action recommended in certain circumstances, by consideration of practical common sense." Russell found the use of force "justifiable when it is ordered in accordance with law by a neutral authority, in the general interest and not primarily in the interest of one of the parties to the quarrel"; this committed him to approving wars undertaken for the general good by a disinterested country. Even an interested party may go to war "if some principle is at stake which we honestly believe to be of great importance to the human race, and if there is reason to think that that principle will survive by our victory but not otherwise." War "is justifiable if it promotes happiness or civilization" — as for example the American Revolution or Caesar's conquest of Gaul. In the mid-1930s Russell described himself as an advocate of an "absolute pacifism...limited to the present time," a time of potentially devastating air warfare. He argued that "it would be less disastrous to permit German domination than to destroy Germany, France and England in a really scientific war." He imagined that "there would...almost certainly be a complete change in the character of the German Government, if the fear of foreign enemies were removed," in which case "bullying would soon lose its charm, and a liberal outlook would become common." When these prudential claims began to look imprudent, Russell reversed himself.[12] C.E.M. Joad took a more stubbornly pacifistic stance based on a hedonic calculus ("I consider physical pain to be the greatest of all evils"). But he too restricted the 'absolute' charge of injustice to modern wars, on the Russellian grounds that "they are likely to prove more destructive of happiness, to engender more misery and suffering and to engender them in more human beings than any alternative course which it was open to the war-making nation to pursue."[13] This clearly admits, first, that war can be just and, second, that a given modern defensive war might be just, depending upon the degree and amount of misery and suffering to be caused by the would be conqueror. Probabilities constitute the realm of prudence, not absolute principles. Nor are such prudential calculations the province of hedonists alone. Albert Einstein seemed an absolute pacifist before 1933, but the election of Hitler changed his mind, or perhaps brought out a different side of his mind:

> Until quite recently we in Europe could assume that personal war resistance constituted an effective attack on militarism. Today we face an altogether different civilization.... Indeed, I will go so far as to assert that if [the nations of Western Europe] are prudent, they will not wait, unarmed, to be attacked.... [I]n my heart I loathe violence and militarism as much as ever; but I cannot shut my eyes to realities.[14]

By 1937 Einstein praised "the true pacifist," who "works for international law and order" precisely by avoiding "neutrality and isolation."[15] And during the Second World War he wrote:

> Organized power can be opposed only by organized power. Much as I regret this, there is no other way.... There are two kinds of pacifism: sound and unsound. Sound pacifism tries to prevent wars through a world order based on power, not a passive approach toward international problems. Unsound, irresponsible pacifism contributed in large measure to the defeat of France.[16]

Einstein measured his "pacifism" according to circumstances, primary among which was the intention of his enemy. Enemies who would compromise should be met with compromise. But "in the face of an enemy unconditionally bent on destroying me and my people" Einstein considered force justifiable.[17] The measured use of force confirms rather than denies the reasoning nature of human beings, recognizing that tyranny or absolute power can deny all measure in a way just was does not.[18]

Measure presupposes a standard. War being the extreme case of a circumstance in which people disagree on the application of a standard, or even disagree on the standard itself, the reconciliation of war and measure must remain problematic.[19] War is technology with a vengeance. War has followed from human nature in the weak sense that "human beings are moved not only by immediate pressures but by distant goals that are contemplated by the imagination," and that these goals, as well as the means adopted to attain them, often contradict one another.[20] The ends discovered by teleology traditionally devolve from God, from nature, or from both. For some two hundred years philosophers have attempted to dilute the human proclivity for conflict by discouraging appeals to God and nature. Typically, they appeal instead to 'tradition,' 'history,' 'culture' — to concepts and practices sufficiently baggy (that is, both capacious and flexible) to hold almost anything — including contradictories.[21] Historicism in hand, the philosopher may then attempt to reconcile any remaining conflicts by referring to laws and other practical restraints or limits rather than to dangerous and perhaps irremediably contradictory ends or goals. Aside from the obvious problems — laws and systems of law may also contradict each other; interpretations of laws often contradict each other — historicist pacifism (its own relativism usually bars its proponents from outright pacifism) does not really settle the question of ends. As a matter of historical fact human beings do question the ends served by laws and customs, both their own and those of other countries. The very judgment to try to deflect such questions must answer the question, 'What for?'[22] Something very much like the natural human capacity for practical judgment or prudence eventually must rule if there is to be any non-contradictory (and therefore unwarlike) settlement of historical conflicts.[23]

Prudence tends to doubt that any absolute prohibition can be morally sustained. Because philosophy or love of wisdom must cultivate practical wisdom in politics, the philosopher, when he understands himself, will eschew pacifism, though not pacificism. (This is true *also* because "serene agitation" is the "artist's and philosopher's version of happiness.")[24] Philosophers today might invent a philosophic pacifism if they wanted radically to depreciate the world. Some sort of neo-Stoicism or (what is much more likely) a neo-Epicureanism commending retired cultivation of one's garden could claim that nothing is worth fighting for.[25] An endowed chair at a major university beckons some ingenious soul who will reformulate the Epicurean argument, whose critics will riposte, 'Without armed protection, how shall your garden grow?' Perhaps, then, neo-Stoicism would be the only lane to travel. It would have the merit of untimeliness, if nothing else; it would do nothing for one's career, but, fortunately, would want no career.

The reluctance of philosophers to commit themselves to pacifism has not discouraged secular writers who are not philosophers. Nor has it stopped religious writers from essaying what they take to be philosophic arguments against war. Absent God, some secularists proclaim the sanctity of life; coupled with the doctrine that each life is unique, and therefore uniquely sacred, this becomes the foundation of pacifism.[26] (The 'sanctity-of-life' claim by itself cannot establish pacifism because, as Douglas P. Lackey notes, "if a person can save more lives by killing than by refusing to kill, arguments about the sacredness of life would not show that killing in these circumstances is wrong"; further, one could not always permit oneself to be martyred).[27] But the uniqueness of an individual example of a sacred class does not itself entail sanctity. If life is sacred and I am alive, and I am unique, this means that I am sacred in a unique way, but my uniqueness is in no way a measure of my sanctity. My uniqueness may rather involve unusual viciousness or baseness, a unique degradation of sacred life. Therefore the addition of the concept of individuality or uniqueness to the concept of the sanctity of life does not lead to a moral requirement for pacifism.[28] Finally, secularism cannot establish the *sanctity* of anything.

Others claim that war "inevitably tends to lead on to further war, and to worse war," as violence begets resentment, begetting more violence.[29]

History reveals this as moralism, because war may also lead to a lasting peace, depending upon the political settlement reached after the war is over.[30] The cry, "Suppress war, and the unity of the human race is instantly realized," smacks of optimism.[31] To assert that war "causes many more good men to perish [than evildoers] and greatly increases the number of evildoers" is to make an empirical-sounding claim without empirical evidence.[32] Far from necessarily involving "the evil of murder on a larger scale,"[33] war can restrain destructive violence.[34] War would be irrational if "prospective belligerents must do all they can to arouse and intensify their feelings of antagonism,"[35] but war can and has been waged to control and channel feelings of antagonism as part of an overall policy of peacemaking. If war left "no room for such refinements as the distinction between persons and things," violating the categorical imperative by treating persons as mere objects,[36] then Kant could not have justified war under any circumstances without involving himself in contradiction; more important, one could not reasonably think it better to kill an evil man − better *for* the evil man − than to allow him to persist in evildoing. While it may be true that "only if means and ends are totally separate can good consequences emerge from evil actions,"[37] it is not rationally demonstrable that killing an evildoer is always an evil action. And if "the end cannot justify the means, for the simple and obvious reason that the means employed determine the nature of the ends produced,"[38] it must be replied that there are different kinds of ends. There are ends that are humanly *produced* − artifacts, projects, or sometimes artificially enhanced products of nature − and there are ends humanly discovered, humanly striven for, but 'produced' only by nature, such as well-being or happiness. In secular terms, if these ends do not justify means, then nothing does. This does not mean that a given end justifies *any* means, but those means themselves will be justified by their actual ends or results. If indeed good cannot come out of evil, then those means can be reasonably judged by their results, known by their fruits. Fruits are embodied ends, and as such require physical preservation:

> Those who insist on the distinction between might and right and accuse the warrior of practicing might in the name of right, are likely on their part to forget that the work of civilization is to

> make the right also *mighty*, so that it may obtain among men and prevail. This end is not to be obtained by any philosophy of abstinence and contemplation, but only by a use of the physical forces by which things are brought to exist and by which alone they are made secure against violence and decay.[39]

War sometimes actually preserves such embodied goods and sometimes destroys them – usually it does both at the same time. Judging the balance of goods preserved and destroyed will not yield unequivocal results, and therefore will not yield pacifism. A secular pacifist might argue that war is punishment and punishment is irrational. Rewards work better, including the reward of kindness returned for injury. Aside from the objection that war may be justified as self-defense, not as punishment, and self-defense is not irrational,[40] there is no evidence that rewards always work better than punishment and that absolute pacifism therefore obtains. Although vengeance is unreasonable because "reason forbids a man to do anything whereby another may be harmed, unless this action has some good end in view," punishment can serve good ends: correct a wrong-doer, assert power of the wronged over the wrongful, and perhaps deter potential wrongdoers, thereby serving the public good.[41] "Pity for the wicked is a very great cruelty to men."[42] Pacifists are right to warn against the tendency of war "to enthrone force and defy justice," to replace justice with the "hot passions of the battlefield" and with the "cold indifference to human miseries and human wrongs" war may instill in noncombatants.[43] If justice requires impartiality but war makes citizens on both sides *partial* spectators, then fanaticism threatens.[44] There is little reason to suppose, however, that refraining from a just war would strengthen justice or the impartiality upon which justice depends. Restraint would only ensure the victory of your enemy's particular form of partiality.[45] Punishment is irrational because it is coercive, and "all coercion sours the mind" – failing, in William Godwin's words, to "place an intrepid confidence in the single energy of intellect." But intrepid confidence need not itself be reasonable. Godwin offers the story of the Roman, Marius, who frightened off a would-be assassin by fixing him with a stern gaze and intoning, "Wretch, have you the temerity to kill Marius!" Two things may be said in reply: First, as Godwin admits elsewhere, when "a dagger is pointed to my own breast or that of another" there may not be "time for expostulation";

second, time for expostulation or not, this gambit wouldn't work in a lot of neighborhoods in south Philadelphia. Godwin concedes that reason does not now rule; during this period of the transition to rationalism, "I ought to take up arms against the despot by whom my country is invaded, because my capacity does not enable me by arguments to prevail on him to desist, and because my countrymen will not preserve their intellectual independence in the midst of oppression." He adds that homegrown despots are no better.[46]

If natural reason were to rule, and if human nature were the most rational force in nature, and finally if justice is fully rational, then Proudhon is right to claim that "justice is immanent in the human soul," constituting the soul's "highest power and its supreme dignity," the true "right of force." The rational use of physical force then would be "one of the thousand faces of justice." The radical separation of justice and force leads to the embarrassing result that justice has no foundation except in dreams. To exert force against irrational force can be to require "the recognition of human dignity in all its faculties, attributes and prerogatives." Without such counterforce, reasonable human beings will be destroyed.[47]

There is a better way, some pacifists insist. They deny that "the unique destructiveness of violence makes it specially effective as a means of deflecting the enemy's will."[48] Some even claim, sophistically, that military preparedness degrades security because the countries devoting large portions of their national budgets to the military are most often at war.[49] Others more generously concede that while military weakness does not "guarantee a country against foreign invasion," some countries do "function successfully" without formidable military defenses.[50] If we can learn "how to struggle [successfully] against injustice without using violence," the claim that war is a *necessary* evil dissolves. Civilians' nonviolent defense can make a country "far less likely to be feared by other countries as a potential invader, and thus far less likely to be targeted by them."[51] As this would be no guard against an enemy motivated by ambition or greed, this calculation requires some demonstration that the removal of the fear that provokes some wars – wars of preemptive attack – would not commensurately inflame the ambition inspiring other wars – wars of aggression. Advocates of civilian defense can reply that whatever the war's cause, nonviolent defense can win it. They begin with an insight well formulated by David Hume:

> Nothing appears more surprising to those, who consider human affairs with a philosophical eye, than the easiness with which the many are governed by the few; and the implicit submission, with which men resign their own sentiments and passions to those of their rulers. When we inquire by what means this wonder is effected, we shall find, that, as FORCE is always on the side of the governed, the governors have nothing to support them but opinion. It is therefore, on opinion only that government is founded; and this maxim extends to the most despotic and most military governments, as well as to the most free and popular.[52]

Kenneth E. Boulding concurs: "Authority in some sense is always granted from below"; what he calls "soft power" or "integrative power" is "often much more powerful and successful than hard power" or "threat power." Hitler rose to authority through the exercise of soft power − perhaps the softest, parliamentarism − and destroyed himself in exercising hard power.[53] Concerning this last assertion one should note that Hitler rose by combining "soft" and "hard" power; as did the Communists, the Nazis had their own partisan army in Weimar Germany. Further, Hitler did not destroy his regime by exercising "hard" power; his regime was destroyed by having "hard" power exercised against it. Faced with the concentrated power of weapons, nonviolent resisters need either overwhelming mass or an unusual degree of organization. One may doubt that one or both of these manifestations of political unity could occur reliably.[54] Certain 'civilian defense' tactics date back at least as far as the third century B.C. in China, where the military writer Sun Tzu taught that "to subdue the enemy without fighting is the acme of skill." But this was to be accomplished with none of the well-burnished moralism of modern advocates of civilian defense.[55] Studies of the 1923 German Ruhrkampf and of the Norwegian resistance to the Nazis during World War II show that civilian defense has enjoyed strictly limited effectiveness, limitations stemming precisely to the problems posed by unity and coordination.[56] Such considerations compel sympathetic critics to recommend civilian defense as part of an overall defensive strategy including military forces.[57] It would be mistaken to argue that civilian defense must always and everywhere prove practically superior to military defense in order to confirm the pacifists' assertion that war is unnecessary. However, pacifists do need to show that the world overall would be a more just place if their country unilaterally adapted civilian defense. This would not be easy to do in all countries.[58]

2.   *Is War Natural to Human Beings?*

Hume speculates that one-man rule began in war:

> It is probable, that the first ascendant of one man over multitudes began during a state of war; where the superiority of courage and of genius discovers itself most visibly, where unanimity and concert are most requisite, and where the pernicious effects of disorder are most sensibly felt. The long continuance of that state, an incident common among savage tribes, enured the people to submission; and if the chieftain possessed as much equity as prudence and valor, he became, even during peace, the arbiter of all differences, and could gradually, by a mixture of force and consent, establish his authority.[59]

By contrast, Georg Simmel claims that "the absolute absence of all warlike instincts and the equally absolute absence of all political centralization correspond with each other."[60] The anthropologists Robert Briffault and Pierre Clastres side with Hume, arguing that war precedes political centralization.[61] Is war natural to human beings?

One of Voltaire's characters playfully claims that war once was natural – when undertaken for cannibalism.[62] The moralistic Mumford calls war unnatural, the product of "a series of aberrations" including "an organized effort to obtain captives for a magical blood sacrifice."[63] But if primitivism is natural then magic is quite 'natural' indeed; primitives often do not distinguish between what we, following the philosophers, call natural and what we call magical or mystical. To the primitive human being, imagination seems real, *is* real in its effects on his chosen actions. This confusion may have led to tensions between elders who ruled by magic and the young warriors who sought honor by pillage.[64] Rites of initiation, including deliberate scarring of skin, may have served to imprint subordination upon the young warriors; controlled violence helped to prevent uncontrolled violence. Prepolitical tribalism does not prevent war in the form of piracy or other raids. It does prevent war on any grander scale; as indeed it prevents anything on a grander scale. Hence Thucydides' sneer at "the weakness of ancient times."[65]

Tribal societies are vulnerable in at least two ways. "Primitive society...is a society from which nothing escapes, which lets nothing get outside itself, for all the exits are blocked."[66] Left alone, they might endure forever. But they are not left alone. Foreign intercourse, made inevitable by the tribes' success, their increasing population, and perhaps also increasing wealth — the availability of revenues to ambitious men — undermines the simpler customs.[67]

The search for human nature in primitivism suffers from well-known practical difficulties: The oldest societies left few records; existing 'primitives' may not be primitive at all. The theoretical problem is even more serious: Why seek nature only in origins? Should we not see it in fully developed civilizations, in human nature empowered to do as it wants, unrestricted by distorting external necessities? Human nature cannot easily know its limits without testing them; war and the 'peace of war,' tyranny, test those limits. In modernity human nature has tested the limits of war and tyranny.

As late as the nineteenth century, intelligent men could glorify war as purifying, strengthening, or even evolutionary. Giving a thumotic twist to the thought of Adam Smith, Joseph de Maistre calls mankind "a tree which an invisible hand is continually pruning and which often profits from the operation"; "the real fruits of human nature — the arts, sciences, great enterprises, lofty conceptions, manly virtues — are due especially to the state of war." Whereas Thomas Jefferson described the blood of patriots as the natural manure of the tree of liberty, de Maistre writes that "blood is the manure of the plant we call *genius*."[68] Jefferson thinks of just war as subservient to a mediate good; de Maistre believes any war subservient to an ultimate good. He conflates the natural and the divine:

> Man, seized suddenly by a divine fury foreign to both hatred and anger, goes to the battlefield without knowing what he intends or even what he is doing.... Thus is worked out, from maggots up to man, the universal law of the violent destruction of living beings. The whole earth, continually steeped in blood, is nothing but an immense altar in which every living thing must be sacrificed without end, without restraint, without respite until the consummation of the world, the extinction of evil, the

death of death.... War is thus divine in itself, since it is a law of the world.[69]

A century later, before the First World War, the German military writer Bernhardi still called war "a biological necessity of the first importance," because "those intellectual and moral factors which insure superiority in war are also those which render possible a general progressive development." "Without war, inferior or dying races would easily choke the growth of healthy budding elements, and a universal decadence would follow." War tests might, "the supreme right," the arbiter that "gives a biologically just decision," a decision weighing not only material strength but the intellectual and moral powers of statesmen and soldiers.[70] Writers after the First World War occasionally have made naturalistic arguments resembling these, but usually as part of an argument whose utopian element may be seen in a vision of eventual peace, not of perpetual or recurring war.[71] Refutations of evolutionary bellecism usually stop at noticing that war cannot select the fittest because in war large groups of the fittest kill each other.[72] If any are to be 'selected' by modern warfare, it will be that "rabbit-like race" most adept at digging in.[73] This ignores the possibility that those among the fittest who do survive battle may well reproduce at a higher rate than those who stay behind the lines, given opportunities afforded both by the conqueror's welcome abroad and the hero's welcome at home. No one seems to have any useful statistics to support any of these probabilistic arguments. The statistics on violent and nonviolent death show that wars generally have accounted for a small fraction of deaths in modernity, apparently too small to make any evolutionary difference for the species as a whole.[74] As a result, scientists 'hard' and 'soft' consider war an expression of human nature, not a mere convention, without supposing that it does the human race much good, and without denying that the nature underlying the behavior can be rechanneled into other forms of struggle.[75]

Near-pacifists sometimes argue that human beings and other species are by nature peaceable because they depend for their survival upon mutual aid.[76] But this at most shows that mutual aid should be the human practice at most times. As a result, political pacificists anticipate the scientific pacificists, recognizing human bellicosity as natural but not necessarily to be expressed in war.[77] Perhaps in reaction to the mixed results of naturalistic investigations, pacifists often hope for the conquest of human nature, or (what is sometimes a strategy in that attempted conquest) they deny that human nature exists at all. They commit themselves to the thesis of the radical malleability of what is called human nature.[78] "The malleability of human nature is such that there is no reason why," Aldous Huxley writes, "if we so desire and set to work in the right way, we should not rid ourselves of war...."[79] Barthelmy de Ligt calls war "a historical, not a biological, phenomenon: it is not a consequence of human nature as such but of certain social, economic, and political conditions which at a certain time have come into being, and which are bound later to disappear." As a "new type of man" develops, war becomes anachronistic.[80] Anthropologists are especially inclined to adopt historicist beliefs, often presenting them with a polemical edge that undercuts any claim to scientific disinterestedness.[81] Some writers use the discipline of psychology to the same effect, claiming that war results from correctable mental disorders, that is, merely subjective passions that, if removed, will end all reason for war. This approach might well be described as the method of selective solipsism; war itself actually exists 'out there' but the causes of war are all in our minds, which can be changed. Thus we hear that "the degree of danger" we face from a perceived threat "is largely a psychological question"; that the human being's "sense of rectitude" is "in fact and manifestly a product of mere belligerency"; that "war is more about words than about things," and words are mere manipulable symbols of manipulable "cultural and personality problems"; that war is provoked by an almost subjective 'perception' expressing an underlying "death instinct," a "masochosadistic fanaticism" resulting from frustrated love or perhaps "social irresponsibility, hysteria, masculinity, and paranoia."[82]

Such shrill and dubious assertions, resembling an odd academic form of war propaganda, should remind us that historicism requires historical proofs − if only the 'proof' afforded by the prevalence of its own claims in the struggle for ideological survival. Absent such proofs, historicism needs some natural human capacities, notably prudence and moderation, to foresee the likely practical limits of *technë* when applied to human beings. But in availing itself of natural capacities it might no longer be historicism.

A political regime is an invention of prudence – the invention may take generations to perfect – for the sake of genuine civic peace or practical justice. The Hobbesian *bellum omnium contra omnes* will occur whenever the hearts of ordinary citizens no longer seek "inward contentment" and civil society no longer seeks "the public good."[83] Aristotle points to the importance of consent to the survival of any political regime; [84] civic and international peace will require the combination of justice and consent. Here is where the concerns of pacificism require a consideration of the political regimes.

In modern secular thought the concept of rule includes the rule or attempted rule over life itself – most modestly in terms of comfortable self-preservation. Inasmuch as "the ultimate object of Magic in all ages was, and is, to obtain control over the sources of life,"[85] modern science, including modern political science, may be said to carry on the same project primitives undertook with their sorcery. Francis Bacon writes that knowledge should "not be as a courtesan, for pleasure and vanity only, or as a bond-woman, to acquire and gain to her master's use; but as a spouse, for generation, fruit, and comfort."[86]

The immediate natural source of human life being mothers and fathers,[87] modern science would replace the patriarchy that replaced matriarchy. Modern science claims that it can finally generate and protect human life better than natural families and those among the ancient political regimes that amounted to families writ large.

3. *Patriarchy, Matriarchy, and Peace*

Patriarchy rejects the individualism, equalitarianism, and secularism of modernity. In criticizing 'patriarchal society,' some feminists confuse androcracy, the rule of men, with patriarchy, the rule of fathers; no predominantly modern society is or can be patriarchal.[88] Patriarchalism persists today in certain Middle Eastern, Asian, and other countries that have not fully adopted modern 'method.' These societies are never pacifist; they are seldom even pacificist internationally. But they can conduce to civil peace. Patriarchists usually argue that social and political unity requires a king, a father of fathers. In Plato's *Critias*, for example, the speaker tells of

Atlantis, a city founded by Poseidon, consisting of ten divisions, each ruled by a king exercising absolute power over his subjects. These kings could not make war against each other or against the royal palace, whose resident, *primus inter pares*, descended from Atlas, the first king of Atlantis.[89] Patriarchists argue that the practical alternative to monarchic patriarchalism is stratocracy or military government, which leads as in Sparta and Rome to constant external war to keep internal peace, followed by the unjust conquest of all rivals, followed by civil war and the self-destruction of the so-called republic, ending in the return of kings. In modern times, the Dutch Republic fought wars through ninety percent of its history: "Two things they say they first fought about, religion and taxes, and they have prevailed it seems in both, for they have gotten all the religions in Christendom, and pay the highest taxes in the world." 'Republican' governments eventually disintegrate "into the atoms of monarchy."[90]

Further, the republican doctrines of natural liberty and equality contradict Scripture, the natural law, and long experience. In practice, who shall judge when the alleged right to revolution shall be exercised? "Most of us," Robert Filmer warns, will "censure and mistake those things for great and certain dangers which in truth many times are no dangers at all, or at most very small ones" – a criticism a student of Filmer might level at the American Declaration of Independence. Although "tyrant kings" admittedly are cruel, their cruelty "extends ordinarily no further than to some particular men that offend him, and not to the whole kingdom" because his people are "the strength and glory of every prince," and their preservation is his own preservation. Popular rule leads only to each citizen judging public affairs by private, selfish criteria; the people, unfettered by fears of personal safety (there is safety in numbers) will persecute their enemies with impunity. "There is no tyranny to be compared to the tyranny of the multitude." No compromise such as limited monarchy or mixed government can solve this problem; such regimes yield only incoherence, disorder, war.[91]

The natural duties of a father and a king are identical, differing only in "latitude or extent." They include preserving, feeding, clothing, instructing, and defending his people. This "moral law" of God subsumes both the law of nature and the law of nations. At creation God made Adam and succeeding patriarchs the sole ruling authority; the "subordination of children is the foundation of all regal authority," which includes the "power of life and death" — that is, the right to enforce laws capitally at home and to wage defensive war with other countries.[92] Filmer conceives of human nature not as a set of virtues to be freed for full action but as a lineage to be maintained unbroken:

> It is a truth undeniable, that there cannot be any multitude of men whatsoever, either great, or small, though gathered together from the several corners and remotest regions of the world, but that in the same multitude, considered by itself, there is one man among them that in nature hath a right to be the king of all the rest, as being the next heir of Adam, and all others subject unto him: every man *by nature* is a king, or a subject....[93]

Therefore, "the integrity of excellency of the subjects does not take away from the order of eminency of the governor." If usurpation does occur, it is "sinful and damnable" although also providential, as God works by means of evil men as well as good, thus demonstrating the ultimate powerlessness of all men. Subjects must obey the new father; Filmer goes so far as to fabricate a statement whereby God gave Cain sovereignty over Abel.[94] "There is not in Scripture mention and approbation of any other form of government"; even at the time the Israelites begged Samuel for a king "they were governed by kingly power already," namely, by God Himself.[95] "There never was any such thing as an independent multitude, who at first had a natural right to a community: this is but a fiction, or fancy of too many in these days, who please themselves in running after the opinions of philosophers and poets, to find out such an original of government, as might promise them some title to liberty, to the great scandal of Christianity, and bringing in of Atheism, since a natural freedom of mankind cannot be supposed without a denial of the creation of Adam."[96] Since the popularization of the doctrine of popular sovereignty, "monarchy hath been crucified (as it were) between two thieves, the Pope and the people; for what principles the papists make use of for the power of the Pope above kings; the very same, by blotting out the word Pope, and putting in the word People, the plebists take up to use against their sovereigns."[97] Monarchy saves the people from "the inexorable rigor of the law, which without [the royal prerogative] is no better than a tyrant."[98] The king properly writes, corrects, enforces the law; the people obey, and may also petition and give counsel through their representatives. This is only practical and necessary, as "the last appeal in all government, must be to an arbitrary power, or else appeals will be in infinitum." Popular sovereignty, with every man a kinglet, resembles nothing so much as polytheism, and leads to it; the people will choose their own gods as well as their governors, thus "imagining aristocracy and democracy in heaven, as on earth."[99]

Patriarchists cannot quite bring themselves to claim unqualifiedly that a king's word must be obeyed in all cases. Just as consent cannot legitimate government because "then all customs, even evil customs, would be lawful," just as conquest without a "precedent title" to the territory is unjust, so even kings cannot be obeyed blindly. "[I]f men command things evil, obedience is due only by tolerating what they inflict: not by performing what they require." Passive disobedience will make wars less frequent and reinforce the religious requirement to do God's will instead of one's own will.[100]

Although its origins are presented in the form of stories, patriarchy's theory and practice are well known. We can see patriarchies. We can read the defenses of their partisans. Matriarchy occurred in prehistoric times. It remains almost as much a matter of myth as of archeology and anthropology. Perhaps more important, no contemporary defense of matriarchy has come down to us. This frees its modern partisans to write their own defenses.[101]

Matriarchy, like patriarchy, enlarges the family to the size of the country — "familial society writ large." Its partisans claim that it would end the politics based upon fear of and anger at the stranger, the foreigner, believing that mother-love resembles Christian agape in its unconditionality. A politics of mother-love eventually would eliminate war.[102] The patriarch preserves, feeds, clothes, instructs, and defends his people; the matriarch, according to her modern admirers, preserves, nurtures, and instructs her people.[103] Paternal defense and material support constitute a claim to authority "not earned by care" and therefore amounts to a "cruel" myth, or at best an outmoded one.[104]

Matriarchalists do not explain why the authority constituted by the necessity for child care should supersede the authority constituted by the necessity for defense and material support. If the universalization of mother-love would make defense and material support unnecessary, and if mother-love could be universalized, the matriarchalist claim would deserve enactment. But mother-love is not likely to be universalized, at least by the means available to secularists, because mother-love's unconditionality has strict limits. Mothers love *their own* children.[105] They need not love anyone else's, and often do not, describing them as bad influences, social undesirables, and the like. Some Universal Mother or Mothers, God-Mothers, could love all the children; God-Mothers cannot be posited by secularists, except as salutary myths. But how does one evaluate a myth? What gives it its legitimacy, its title to rule?

The distinction between motherhood that nurtures whom it loves and fatherhood that defends and acquires for whom it loves has some natural roots. Women often do not fight because their deaths in large numbers would prevent population recovery after a war.[106] As the early feminist Mary Wollstonecraft argues, society and its preservation must be natural (*pace* Rousseau) because human infancy and childhood are long.[107] Matriarchalists argue with some plausibility that the earliest human groups, like primate and other animal groups, were matriarchal because only mothers visibly produced young, the young need nurturing, and therefore women are the ones who insist upon a social order. As Briffault puts it, men are free but women are permanent. Mothers can materially support their children as well as men can, not by hunting but by gathering and weaving. To divide labor between the sexes hunting had to be invented.[108] Matriarchalists do not consider that this invention may have been natural, given men's freedom or spirited independence. Masculine (though not always patriarchal) spiritedness leads to war.

These matriarchal and masculine tendencies alike inspire feminist pacifism and pacificism. Olive Schreiner may have been among the first to maintain that motherhood itself implies pacifism. "Men have made boomerangs, bows, swords, or guns with which to destroy one another; we have made the men who destroyed and were destroyed!" "[O]n this point almost alone, the knowledge of woman, simply as woman, is superior to that of man; she knows the history of human flesh; she knows its cost; he does not." While "to the male, the giving of life is a laugh" to the mother it is "blood, anguish, and sometimes death." This 'labor' theory of value entails pacificism; it does not (for Schreiner at least) entail pacifism: "It is true that the woman will sacrifice as mercilessly, as cruelly, the life of the hated rival or an enemy, as any male; but she *always knows what she is doing, and the value of the life she takes!*"[109] As with the modern economic labor theory of value, the matriarchal 'labor' theory of value expresses an important part of the truth. Masculine fecklessness is one manifestation of masculine freedom; disrespect for life can be its result, a disrespect diluted considerably by the lively interest in self-preservation men share with women. But it is also true that no labor theory of value alone can express a full ethical understanding. After creating the cosmos out of chaos (to take the ultimate act of 'labor' as our standard) God "saw that it was good." The goodness of any created thing inheres in its own nature, owing its origin to some powerful goodness but now separated from it. The value of human life is not only or even primarily a reflection of a mother's suffering during childbirth; it inheres in the child's potential for good, and in the extent to which the child fulfills that potential, independent of parents. For this reason, and because the potential for good goes together with potential for evil, the choice to go to war will depend not only on an appreciation of mothers' suffering, and the endangerment of the body that war entails, but on an assessment of goods and evils beyond physical suffering.

The original matriarchies surely did not attempt to justify themselves on these naturalistic-ethical grounds, there being no evidence that human beings had yet discovered the concept of nature. It is more likely that their claim to authority rested on magic; "religious ideas arose from the desire to acquire magical powers and not from an intellectual desire to interpret nature."[110] Contemporary matriarchalists posit an association of magical or godlike power and childbirth. Robert Graves proposes that "Woman worships the male infant, not the grown man: it is evidence of her deity, of man's dependence on her for life."[111] This power accounts both for the matriarch's claim to rule, to legitimacy — as seen most obviously in matrilinear descent — and men's ambivalence toward that claim.[112] It is conceivable that men's suffering in war provided a foundation for an analogous legitimacy claim; men suffered in order to preserve the lives women had generated.[113]

How peaceful were the matriarchies? Modern matriarchalists concede that the old priestesses were not pacifists. There are too many reports of ritual sacrifices, Amazons and other female warriors, declarations of war, and the capture of women in war to deny the warlike capabilities of the ancient matriarchs.[114] Finally the matriarchs may have fought, but not well enough. Riane Eisler finds "the violent end of Crete...particularly haunting – and instructive." Located on an island, the city survived longer than most other matriarchies thanks to its isolation from marauders and its "defensive fleet." After a final "guerrilla war" it succumbed to male-dominated invaders, surviving only in "the garbled folk memory" of Atlantis.[115] Matriarchalists deplore the invasion of Indo-Europeans from the north who conquered the more peaceful goddess-worshippers between the fifth and third millennia B.C.E.[116] The Jews come in for especially bitter denunciations by matriarchalists associated with 'New Age' beliefs.[117]

"The simple biological fact of *adult male grouchiness*, common to many beasts and man, has exercised a tremendous influence on the course of history."[118] Feminists, some of them matriarchalists, deplore this combativeness, which reflects the masculine will to power, to domination. They seek to wed feminism to pacifism.[119] Androcracy and the wars fought by androcracies originate in "primitive fear of the other" including misogyny, the hatred of women arising from male fear of women; the military is androcracy's "distilled embodiment." Androcracy reaches its logical conclusion in late modernity, when technology has so overpowered nature that it threatens the existence of those it claims to protect.[120] Modern scientific method has lost its charm if not its magic, to be replaced by a new magic of creativity or transformational 'imaging.'[121] Paradoxically, this stoking of world-remaking ambition can accompany a denigration of mind and an exaltation of something that is by definition limited, namely, the body.[122] Some feminists are uneasy with the term 'matriarchy,' which implies the rule of women over men as distinguished from the rule of the womanly or matronly spirit over the masculine spirit. These writers prefer the term 'matrilineal' in order to convey the supposed egalitarianism of pre-androcratic societies.[123] One may be excused for suspecting that this egalitarianism expresses more a hope for the future than an assessment of the past. Be that as it may, radical feminists associate themselves with such "modern humanist ideologies" as pacifism, anarchism, anticolonialism, and environmentalism — with two constants, communitarianism and egalitarianism. Feminists contend that the other ideologies attack the many heads of the "androcratic monster," but only feminism pierces its heart.[124]

Pacifist and pacificist feminists aim to end or limit wars by taming the most dangerous shrews, who are almost invariably male. Although they admire the ancient matriarchies, few if any believe the old time religion; without exception, these writers are strict materialists, some even social determinists. Generally they do not propose a new or old religious system with which to tame men, although some of them might use religious symbols and ceremonies to advance and reinforce their political goals. Rather they intend to use rhetoric and customs, with perhaps a few institutions, to bring forth communal and egalitarian societies. The same passions that animated socialism animate this feminism. Whether feminism is a mask of socialism or socialism a discarded mask of feminism need not concern us here. What should concern anyone is the sanitizing of ideologues' motives that attends the rhetoric. Observation of socialists and of feminists in action suggests that they are at least as ambitious as they are egalitarian. Riane Eisler's distinction between "domination hierarchies" based on threat of force, and "actualization hierarchies" based on progress and leadership[125] begs the question of what happens when people don't want to progress, don't want to be led in a 'progressive' direction. If nothing happens, then something happens: the return to hierarchy forced by those among the people who do not scruple to organize force, including physical force, and use it. To what extent shall men tolerate being scolded and cajoled into line?[126]   What exactly will "actualization hierarchies" actualize?[127] And can they be actualized? Mary Wollstonecraft set an optimistic tone at the beginning of modern feminism: "Rousseau exerts himself to prove that all *was* right originally [in the state of nature]; a crowd of authors that all *is* now right: and I, that all will *be* right."[128] It is hard to resist commenting that all of them were mistaken. It is even harder to resist skepticism when told that the ancient matriarchies offer us "amazing vistas of possibilities for a better life," that human sociopolitical evolution will produce a sudden, revolutionary shift to a "pragmatopia" wherein we will "live free of the fear of war."[129] Building on the Barthesian claim that 'images' transform history into nature ('imaging' is used as a verb, as in "new ways of imaging reality"), pacifist and pacificist feminists overlook the fact that those who make the effort to 're-image' reality by saying 'struggle' instead of 'fight,' 'tools' instead of 'weapons,' and by engaging in "global thinking" already have converted to pacific intentions.[130] When describing the actions they intend to take in self-defense, these writers without exception cite Gandhian non-violent resistance.[131] Some supplement Gandhiism with recourse to war as a last resort.[132] As Jean Bethke Elshtain argues,

> The hard truth for feminists seeking to construct a theory of women and war is this: despite the paeans to the day when the Beautiful Souls all get together to curb and defeat the primitive beasts and usher in the reign of harmony and peace, no sane person really believes this outcome. It does seem rather late in the day for facile romanticism.[133]

Beautiful Souls and beasts, matrilinealists/gylanists and androcrats, "by definition cannot speak to one another." The speechless action and propagandistic anti-speech of warfare will remain a principal means of communication.[134]

4. *The Conquering Prince*

Grotius defines a people as a human group with a single spirit or character, a "union of civic life." A people can be destroyed physically or politically — "either by the destruction of the body, or by the destruction of [its] form or spirit."[135] A sovereign people loses its sovereignty while the individuals comprising it preserve their lives only by consent. Consent may well occur under such severe duress that it approaches no-consent or necessity.[136] Such conquests evidently occurred when matriarchalism disappeared. While conquest "can destroy harmful prejudices" and "put a nation under a better presiding genius" or spirit, it can also destroy salutary prejudices and impose a worse regime.[137] If, as writers ancient and modern affirm, the welfare of the people is the supreme law on earth, then military conquest must be resisted, but only within the limits imposed by that welfare.

For secular writers it therefore matters whether, in considering peace and war, the public welfare entails bodily self-preservation as an end or as a means to some other good. This in turn implies a distinction between kings and tyrants.[138] Victory is indeed "the main object in war," but it is not the only object.[139]

What today's feminists call androcracy is in its undiluted form more accurately called by its familiar name, Machiavellianism. Machiavellianism denies the existence of human rights and sneers at justice.[140] Not government by consent but government by necessity, physical necessity, will endure. All means must accordingly submit to this necessity, whose aspects are titled 'reasons of state.'[141] The Machiavellian prince rules by means of the strongest passions or necessities − particularly, fear rather than love. Wars are usually won by princes and officers most feared not only by their enemies but by their own subjects, their own troops.[142] Efforts to combine Machiavellianism with 'idealism' tend toward the destruction of both elements.[143]

Machiavellian 'realism' nonetheless distorts reality. In reality, rival soldiers often admire and respect one another, recognize each other's virtues and common humanity.[144] Not necessity alone but choice sets war aims and strategy.[145] War aims in turn limit strategic and tactical choices. One of those aims in reality may be the public good or welfare.[146] Although Proudhon asserts that "between State and State, the only recognized right is the right of force," that "among the masses, all liberty and all right come from the same sources," that force underlies both despotism and democracy,[147] the same Proudhon denies that any and all use of force is right or creates right. Conquest can be just or unjust, depending upon whether it is undertaken for just ends with just means.[148]

Machiavellian 'necessity' exalts the human will to power, predicts the triumph of that will. Machiavellianism seeks to make conquests a moral and philosophic imperative; Spengler calls "Faustian" culture the "Will-Culture."[149] This project requires human beings to *realize* "absolute truth" by "unlimited self-determination"; "the human and the divine are essentially one" in creative power, conquering the given, ('nature' or chaos) and replacing it with a willed order.[150] Hence Machiavellians emphasize government as legislation not government as deliberation. They prefer method to contemplation, changing the world to understanding it. If nature is not orderly or beautiful, then philosophy is not pleasurable and the classical gentleman's love of the noble is groundless.[151] "When one has no character one *has* to apply a method," lamented a man of classical tastes adrift in a Machiavellian age.[152] The doctrine of a 'state of nature' real or imagined, with its chaos, its endangerment of human beings, always becomes, in Machiavellian hands, not a *state* at all, but a threat to stability, a deadly threat to the human being who wills his own preservation, immediate or eternal.[153]

Man the creator and re-former self-legislates. This is how the Machiavellian prince can so easily metamorphose into a governor by consent of the governed. In its republican form, Machiavellianism leads to questioning the right of military conquest, and thus to pacificism if not to outright pacifism.[154] For a justification of pacifism in secular terms, writers need only take the familiar, though patently false, step of pretending that conquest never succeeds because it can never win more than the temporary acquiescence of the conquered.[155] It is closer to the truth to say that conquest followed by tyranny (particularly an ineffective tyranny) will provoke resentment and rebellion at the first opportunity.[156] For this reason non-Machiavellian philosophers seek to minimize the tyrannical potential of force, including forceful conquest.[157]

As for tyranny itself as an instrument of peace, it has had its modern defenders. Since antiquity tyrants have differed from kings in not deriving their authority from the gods.[158] This is why Robert Filmer, monarchist and patriarchalist, read Hobbes' *De Cive* and commented, "I consent with him about the rights of exercising government, but I cannot agree with his means of acquiring it" — namely, by the actions of men not divine right. Hobbes presents "a commonwealth by conquest"; Hobbes wrongly ascribes to man a natural right derived from the liberty to preserve oneself instead of subjection to the authority of Adam's lineage, and thus to God's creation. The doctrine of the social contract is a blasphemy. Real human beings require families in order to survive; they could not have originated as solitary individuals in nature.[159]

Hobbes rejects the family as the foundation of civil society because the family cannot defend itself adequately.[160] Self-defense is a corollary to the individual's absolute right to self-preservation; the Christian doctrine of nonresistance violates that right.[161] All men are naturally equal and, because nature is entropic, they are naturally at war, competing for gain, safety, and reputation. This intermittent but persistent war of all against all, among individuals in nature and among civil societies under no international authority, tends toward lives that are "solitary, poor, nasty, brutish, and short." To avert these pains and to acquire the means to a commodious life, individuals and civil societies seek peace.[162] Both war and peace arise from self-defense. The celebrated social contract among individuals who desire self-preservation — supposedly an exercise in liberty, in consent, whereby individuals give up their natural 'right' or power to use their own power as they wish in exchange for the artificial but more effective security of civil society — in fact rests on necessity. War and peace derive from the same necessity or 'right.'[163] The 'consenting' multitude becomes one artificial person, the "mortal god" or Leviathan. For those who worry that this man-made god might destroy the very subjects who comprise him, Hobbes answers tersely, "Sovereign power is not so hurtful as the want of it."[164] Civil society not only originates in necessity, it is preserved by it. This means that conquest is merely another means of inducing consent. In either case men fear one another, ruling and 'consenting' to be ruled in accordance with their passion for commodious self-preservation. Fear or necessity in no way contradicts consent or liberty, Hobbes insists straight-facedly, "as when a man throweth his goods into the sea for fear the ship should sink, he doth it nevertheless very willingly." The human will can be 'free' in the sense that it is unimpeded in pursuit of its goods; it is not at all free in the sense that it is self-caused. Passions drive it.[165]

Popular 'consent' immediately or at least quickly ends in monarchy or one-man rule. This original contract or covenant supersedes any subsequent ones — say, for establishing a democracy — because the right to change one's mind would lead to the very anarchy that civil society was founded to prevent.[166] If this line of reasoning proves too remote for popular comprehension, Hobbes does not despair: "I believe it is the desire of most men to bear rule; but few of them know what title one has to it more than another, besides the right of the sword."[167] In most circumstances swordly instruction will suffice when needed. In extreme circumstances, as when the subject prefers not to risk his life in war, Hobbes allows a right to refuse military service if the subject finds a replacement; Hobbes equally allows the sovereign the right to punish his subject's refusal with death.[168] And may the better man win. The same rule obtains with respect to the treatment of innocents in war. In war, including civil war, "all infliction of evil is lawful." If "it be for the benefit of the commonwealth and a violation of no covenant," innocents may be harmed in accordance with the "original right of nature" — i.e., necessity. "The law of nations, and the law of nature, is the same thing."[169]

The power of nature needs the counteraction of an even more powerful artifice. The Leviathan must be mighty; his artificial soul, sovereignty, giving life to his body, must be absolute and undivided.[170] Therefore justice means obedience to the commands, including the laws, of the sovereign legislator; "no law can be unjust."[171] The best legislator is one man; one man rule provides political unity, eliminating the Babel of many voices, contention, and indecision, of representative government, giving subjects an understandable, visible power to fear so as to dissuade them from lapsing into the misery of war. The monarch will provide the stability of an "artificial eternity," that is, hereditary royal succession, which avoids the uncertainties of elective monarchy.[172]

Hobbes' new science of politics, being scientific, tolerates no political error. He denounces "the toleration of a professed hatred of tyranny" as "a toleration of hatred to commonwealth generally," there being "nothing that the sovereign representative can do to a subject, on what pretense soever, [that] can properly be called injustice or injury." The sovereign's only obligation to his subjects is to retain the power "by which he is able to protect them" if he so chooses.[173] Hobbes argues that the sovereign in pursuing his own interests will protect his subjects: maintaining peace at home; resisting foreign enemies; exhibiting a fortitude unnecessary and undesirable in non-soldiers; exercising both frugality and liberality as utility dictates.[174] Utility cannot be so well served in any regime wherein sovereignty is divided; Hobbes fulminates against "seditious blockheads" in and out of Parliament who were "more fond of change than either of their peace or profit." The classical mixed regime, which Hobbes calls "mixarchy," is "nothing else but pure anarchy." "There could be no peace" under "divided power."[175] Today's egalitarians would find in Hobbes a sympathetic anticipation of their claim that peace requires equality. Hobbes would only add (much to their alarm) that to maximize equality in the real world one needs strong one-man rule.[176]

The new science of politics is methodical, modelled on geometry, allowing statesmen to replace prudence with sapience. Unlike Plato's *Republic*, Hobbes' *Leviathan* is written to be applied. Its "science of natural justice is the only science necessary for sovereigns and their principal ministers." Hobbes hopes that a sovereign will read his book and proceed to "convert this truth of speculation, into the utility of practice."[177] The clarity and precision of geometric method comports well with the unified sovereign Hobbes favors.[178] As exercised by the sovereign, scientific method will settle the religious question in politics, eliminating the religious warfare that has wracked Christendom.

Machiavelli professes admiration for the religions of antiquity, which "greatly contributed to making [soldiers] do their duty." Christianity, by contrast dispirits men while enspiriting a woman (and martyr), Joan of Arc.[179] Christianity effeminates men and makes women ineffectually masculine. Hobbes takes a different view. Deriving spiritness or courage from fear (even as he derives deliberation and will from the passions), he calls all religion the "fear of things invisible," and can therefore regard Christianity as a spur to fanatical courage. "A part of human politics," religion serves the will to power of ambitious and contentious rulers and would-be rulers. Peace or civil obedience can also stem from fear, but more reliably from "love of ease," love of arts, and the desire for knowledge — all of which require leisure. Peaceful economic and scientific pursuits will rechannel the "general inclination of all mankind," the "perpetual and restless desire of power after power, that ceaseth only in death," away from war.[180] Commercial and scientific conquests will replace military conquests if Hobbesian political science successfully advises princes of the most powerful necessities.

Religious dissent is really political dissent and for that reason should not be tolerated. Religious dissent causes civil war as surely as religious disputes cause international war − by serving as vehicles for the will to power of the ambitious. (The common people will take "either side for pay or plunder"). In seventeenth century England, Presbyterians, Catholics, Independents, Anabaptists, Fifth-Monarchy men, Quakers, and other sects all put forward "private interpretations of the Scripture," interpretations at variance with those of the established Church. "This doctrine" of religious freedom "divides a Kingdom within itself"; allied with certain business interests, the poor, people "ignorant of their duty" and, centrally, liberally educated Parliamentarians who admired classical republicanism, religious dissenters destroyed the authority of the King. "The power of the mighty hath no foundation but in the opinion and belief of the people"; religio-political heterodoxy poisons civil peace.[181] For the sake of civil peace, religion "ought to be a law," an "indisputable" command, in every country, even if the law differs from one country to another. "[I]n every Christian commonwealth, the civil sovereign is," and should be recognized as, "the supreme pastor."[182] Hobbes of course knew that obtaining this recognition was problematic:

> A state can constrain obedience, but convince no error, nor alter the minds of them that believe they have the better reason. Suppression of doctrine does but unite and exasperate, that is, increase both the malice and power of them that have already believed them.[183]

For this reason Hobbes advanced a minimalist Christianity for the sake of civil peace, a Christianity restricted to those teachings necessary for the salvation of the individual soul. A "quiet waiting for the coming again of our blessed Savior, and in the mean time a resolution to obey the King's laws" will prove the only way to "lasting peace" among the English.[184] For rhetorical purposes, within Christendom, Hobbes melds his prince of peace with the Prince of Peace.

Hobbesian monocracy has had its defenders, the greatest being Hegel.[185] In practical politics Hobbes' arguments still appeal in parts of the world where factional violence deranges public order and private lives. Generally, however, the institution of secular monocracy has not conduced to civil and international peace to the degree and extent the Hobbesian science of politics predicts. But the spirit of the Hobbesian prince has conquered much of the world in the form of the modern religious settlement. In this respect, Hobbes' quest for peace has succeeded in many countries.

Edward Gibbon shares with the nonresistant Protestant sects the opinion that early Christians' participation first in church politics then in secular politics corrupted the innocence of the dove even as it refined the wisdom of the serpent.[186] A more recent historian describes Christendom as "a warrior society," and a Quaker scholar laments, "To anyone brought up, as I was, in the belief that Christians worship the Prince of Peace, it must be startling to notice the predominant occurrence of wars involving Christians, and especially of those in which Christians fought each other."[187] Grotius deplores the "lack of restraint in relation to war, such as even barbarous races would be ashamed of," that he observed "throughout the *Christian* world."[188] Burckhardt agrees:

> Of all struggles, the most appalling are the *wars of religion*, more especially those between religions in which the thought of a future life predominates, or in which morality is in other ways bound up with the existing form of religion, or in which a religion has taken on a strong national coloring and a people is defending itself in its religion. Among civilized peoples they are the most terrible of all. The means of offense and defense are unlimited, ordinary morality is suspended in the name of the 'higher purpose,' negotiation and mediation are abhorrent — people want all or nothing.... To its believers, Christianity lent a frightful strength.[189]

To counter the fanatic misuse of Christianity, theologians and philosophers of Christendom had elaborated the just war doctrine found in Roman law, Cicero, and Aristotle. The philosophic response to religiously-channeled passions had not been 'enlightenment' but the moderation of those passions with the help of reasoning and laughter.[190] The more public version of the just war doctrine replaced laughter with lawfulness. By the seventeenth Christian century, the restraints provided by the just war doctrine seemed insufficiently effective. 'Enlightenment' combines the Scripture's caring or shepherding love and the passion for universal proselytism with a new, methodical form of rationalism. "The only remedy for [the] epidemic malady" of religious war and persecution is "the philosophical spirit which, spread gradually, at last tames men's habits and prevents the disease from starting."[191] Unlike classical philosophy, which depended upon prudence and friendship to sustain itself, 'Enlightenment' commands real power in the form of methodical science. Bertrand Russell could look back to the events of his own long life as well as those of the two preceding centuries and proclaim that the political regimes sponsored by "empiricist liberalism" had won "every important war."[192]

The 'Enlightenment' program calls first for religious toleration — i.e., the toleration of a variety of Christian sects and often of Judaism within a regime characterized by an established church — then for freedom of religion and disestablishment, perhaps followed by outright religious indifference based upon moral relativism.[193] The more minimalist the religion the more multiplicitous the sects; 'Enlightenment' wants a thousand small religions to compete peacefully, none able to muster the power to oppress the others.[194] Religious passions will also weaken if the religious must engage in practical, economic pursuits — pursuits that themselves incline toward numerous social and political divisions that compete peacefully with each other.[195] The attempt to conquer the desire for material things gives way to the regulated (to some extent self-regulated) liberty of that desire.

The crucial institutional move is disestablishment. John Locke sets down the foundation of disestablishment by judging it "necessary above all to distinguish between the business of civil government and that of religion, and to mark the true bounds between the church and the commonwealth." Absent this settlement, civil and religious goods, "the just possession of these things that belong to this life," will coexist in tension, often in conflict, with the goods of the soul. While "the magistrate is not obliged to put off his Christianity" in the Lockean settlement, he must not enforce Christianity by laws and arms. "[L]ight can by no means accrue from corporal suffering." Force wielded for religious ends tempts rulers and ruled alike to fanaticism; persecutors "hardly ever exhibit this zeal of theirs for God, with which they are so heated and inflamed, except when they have the civil magistrate on their side." Moreover, various rulers hold different and even contradictory opinions on questions of religion. "[N]one but a mad-man, I had almost said none but an atheist, would dare to assert to any honest man, who worshipped the true God, could obey their religious decrees without offending against his conscience and his reverence for God." For these reasons, and because no magistrate can peer into the conscience of a citizen in any case, Locke restricts government to legislating for the utility of the commonwealth and for natural rights; morality most emphatically can be legislated, but only in its outward manifestations, and only insofar as it prejudices the rights of others or disturbs the public peace. As in Hobbes, the civil magistrate will make the final determination in cases where the commonwealth's good and church doctrine conflict. If the religious citizen disagrees with the magistrates he must "undergo the punishment which it is not unlawful for him to bear." Public atheism is "not to be tolerated at all" not because atheism is mistaken but because promises, covenants, and oaths, "the bonds of human society," are not respected without religious convictions to support them.[196]

Aside from Machiavellians who clearly want to use religion, though not necessarily Christianity, for frankly political purposes,[197] critics of the Lockean settlement have raised concerns about its consequences, some of which may have been unintended. Perhaps the most thoughtful critic is Edmund Burke. In his *Reflections on the Revolution in France* Burke at first appeals to Hobbesian suspicions of clerical politicking, deploring the liberal clergy in England who had sermonized in favor of the French republicans. ("Wholly unacquainted with the world in which they are so fond of meddling, and inexperienced in all its affairs, on which they pronounce with so much confidence, they have nothing of politics but the passions they excite.") He doubts that the multiplication of dissenting sects advocated by the liberals will yield "rational and manly" results. Indeed he fears a majority tyranny whereby popular passions will animate a thousand self-sanctified interests. A Lockean settlement insofar as it may entail disestablishment will fail to inculcate habits of responsibility, moderation and respect, including self-respect, in the citizenry. By contrast, the English church establishment stands against "all the impurities of fraud, and violence, and injustice, and tyranny." Not a state religion but "a religion connected with the state" will secure citizen liberty by delimiting citizen power, satisfy the nature of the "religious animal," man, and help to ensure the cooperation of human will and human reason for the benefit of the commonwealth. The church establishment prevents the fanaticism and selfishness of dissenters by educating the ruling class to habits of sincere piety and public service; the gentlemen for their part "liberalize the church," preventing it from falling prey to momentary passions inflamed by demagogues. The independent but allied establishments of church, nobility, and monarchy can prevent a new fanaticism of "Atheistical fathers [who] have a bigotry of their own," who "have learnt to talk against monks with the spirit of a monk." To such *philosophes* as Voltaire, it is "indifferent whether [political and economic] changes were to be accomplished by the thunderbolt of despotism or by the earthquake of popular commotion." Only a sound church establishment can inculcate "the true spirit of toleration" that governs men who "would reverently and affectionately protect all religions, because they love and venerate the great principle upon which they all agree, and the great object to which they are all directed," namely, justice. Justice cannot be maintained by fostering habits of "enlightened self-interest." Money and the scramble for it, however, well-balanced by the workings of the invisible hand, cannot replace institutions promoting reverence for the law, public spirit, and charity. Unstable gases eventually will ignite, despite all efforts to keep them in steady-state. There is no substitute for the permanent things in public life or private.[198] Burke is surely right to suggest that toleration can only stand out, so to speak, against a background of intolerance, that pluralism survives only within some stable monism that justifies it in principle and protects it in practice. It is not enough to say, 'We will tolerate everything except intolerance' without accounting for the good or goods such tolerance serves. The competent secularists understand this, too.[199] The problem for the Burkean settlement inheres in the nature of toleration itself, specifically when toleration meets the nature of religion, when the religious animal resolves to be tolerant. "Doubtless, the world is more dangerous when it flatters than when it afflicts us, and we must be more on our guard when it entices us to love it, than when it warns us to despise it."[200] Augustine's warning came near the beginning of the rapprochement between the Church and 'the world' or 'Rome,' but it remains perennially relevant because religious spiritedness, which seeks to include the like-minded but rigorously to exclude the heterodox, must remain profoundly ambivalent towards worldly peace. A devoted Christian pacifist captures this ambivalence well if inadvertently:

> The Christian must expect persecution. This is the promise of the gospels, and it is a sign of our ineffectiveness that most of us have not experienced it. Not that we should provoke martyrdom....[201]

The author of these lines lived in a commercial republic, where Christian failure to experience martyrdom measures not so much the ineffectiveness of Christians as the effectiveness of the regime in keeping peace.

5. *The Republic of Peace*

Surveying the early years of the American republic, Henry Adams describes a new phenomenon:

> For the first time in history, great bodies of men turned away from their old religion, giving no better reason than that it required them to believe in a cruel Deity, and rejected necessary conclusions of theology because they were inconsistent with human self-esteem.[202]

In turning away from their old religion Americans did not turn toward irreligion. They turned toward a milder and simpler form of Christianity, one that reinforced the political foundation of a stable religious settlement. The American Founders argued that only commercial republicanism can provide that foundation. Since their time, defenders of secular monocracy have grown increasingly discouraged. One of the last pacifist monarchists, Alfred H. Fried, wrote a panegyric to the German "Peace Emperor" William II. Published in 1912, its timing was unfortunate. ("The spring time of pacifism is leaving its traces upon the German Emperor.... It may be assumed with certainty that he will not disappoint mankind.")[203] Although Montesquieu exaggerates when he asserts that "the spirit of monarchy is war and expansion" whereas "the spirit of republics is peace and moderation," even Nietzsche concedes that the tendency of commercial republicanism promotes peace: "Democratic institutions are quarantine arrangements to combat that ancient pestilence, lust for tyranny: as such they are very useful and very boring."[204]

Commercial republicans criticize secular monocracy first on moral grounds. It degrades citizen virtue by ruining prominent men and women of character, by employing servile and often vicious accomplices, by preventing freedom of thought, by severing the social bonds that make friendship possible, and by restricting the decent activities of the ruled and encouraging the base.[205] "They who are enemies of virtue, and fear not God, are afraid of men, and dare not offer such things as the world will not bear, lest by that means they should overthrow their own designs"; despotism thus requires fraud.[206] Despotism is "the art of conquering at home" conducted by the excitation of war in order to raise taxefi and thereby further to restrict citizens' liberties.[207]

Politically, despotism abrogates the rule of law and destroys politics itself, that is, the condition of both ruling and being ruled.[208] Ruling without being ruled and being ruled without ruling are unnatural because they threaten or risk life itself. Although Grotius subordinates political liberty to life because life "affords the basis for all temporal and the occasion for eternal blessings,"[209] republicans reply, with Locke, that

> ...he who attempts to get another Man into his Absolute Power, does thereby *puts himself into a State of War* with him; It being to be understood as a Declaration of a Design upon his Life....I have no reason to suppose, that he, who would *take away my Liberty*, would not when he had me in his Power, take away everything else. And therefore it is Lawful for me to treat him, as one who has put himself into a State of War with me, i.e., kill him if I can....[210]

In saying 'Your liberty or your life,' the tyrant acts as a highwayman who never rides away.

International war and external conquest feed the tyrant, giving him a pretext for maintaining large, standing armies that (he believes) will help preserve his domestic rule by reinforcing the sentiment that might makes right, the slogan of terror.[211] Such foundations seem strong but are weak. Because "those institutions which act as barriers against power simultaneously support it" by moderating its excesses both of energy and of complacency, by aligning the interests of various citizen groups with it, and by promoting citizens of character and ability to positions of power, the tyrannical destruction of independent institution undermines power even while appearing to extend it.[212] This weakness invites still more civil and international war, this time with the tyrant as the victim not the aggressor. Commercial republicans would replace government by fraud and force with government by reasonable consent. The 'social contract theory' may invoke dubious anthropology but it is politically indispensable to republicanism. Any good contract rests on and in its turn supports several kinds of just equality: including equal knowledge of the facts; equal freedom to choose the terms of the contract; and equal obligation to 'make good' on the contract, including compensation for any unforeseen defects.[213] Contracts or pacts lead to peace; 'pact' and 'peace' are even etymologically associated.[214] Violations of the social contract can lead to a well-known problem of just war theory: if the violations are so serious that the aggrieved party no longer trusts the enforcement provisions of the contract, and no third party enforcer may exist, the aggrieved party will take the law into its own hands at the risk of destroying the peace for reasons that appear in retrospect rash and ill-judged; at the same time, failure to enforce one's own rights unilaterally may leave a real injustice unrepaired and unpunished. Even Grotius, who recommends the endurance of injustice instead of forceful resistance in order to maintain a framework of public order, will not renounce the right to revolution "in case of extreme and imminent peril."[215] The citizens must finally judge, if only because the alternative, that a tyrant judges, is worse.[216]

Commercial republicanism will reduce the number of international wars in the long run if it becomes prevalent in large portions of the world. Republicanism places the authority to declare war in the elected representatives of the people, removing many of the fiscal and personal temptations to war seen in other forms of government.[217] Representative government secures justice better than other regimes, thereby reducing the causes of civil and international strife.[218] Commerce also discourages war, giving people everywhere a lively interest in the continued survival of their trading partners. Commerce weakens national prejudices by encouraging social intercourse and mutual understanding for the sake of trade. Commerce liberates small ambitions while making the grandiose ambitions of the conqueror difficult to achieve and somehow less desirable. In a commercial society personal power attracts less than personal independence, ensured not by conquest but by temporizing and compromising. The thirst for public esteem gives way to private satisfactions; even the thirst for public esteem can be slaked by personal fame or notoriety instead of political and military power. A middle class, neither impoverished nor luxurious, neither servile nor arrogant, rules and is ruled by itself.[219] "If...a state of society can ever be founded in which every man shall have something to keep and a little to take from others, much will have been done for the peace of the world."[220] As Tocqueville sees, the dangers in that world would be the excessive peace of stagnation or perhaps the seductive peace of some benevolent despotism.[221] Commercial souls will misread noncommercial souls in naively ascribing commercial appetites, and only commercial appetites, to uncommercial men. [222]

This means that the spirit of republicanism must supplement, finally govern but not overbear, the spirit of commerce. While the spirit of commerce strengthens the individual's desire to defend and enhance his own life, and perhaps the life of his family and his business enterprise, the spirit of republicanism strengthens the individual's desire to defend and enhance the life of his family, community, and country. *Res publica*, the public thing or "property of a people," belongs to "an assemblage of people in large numbers associated in agreement with respect to justice and a partnership for the common good," bound by law.[223] Republicanism strengthens the country by attaching private to public interest, by widening the scope of self-interest to include the welfare of fellow-citizens.[224] Republicanism additionally energizes the minds of the citizens, inducing them to 'think for themselves.'[225] Moral and intellectual strength will deter war and win wars for peace. Such strength will be needed because wealthy nations are "of all nations the most likely to be attacked; and unless the state takes some new measures for the public defense, the natural habits of the people render them altogether incapable of defending themselves."[226] Some of the sharpest debates among republicans concern the search for a way to defend the republican regime in a manner consistent with commercial republicanism. Some, from Adam Smith to Charles de Gaulle, argue that a professional army using the highly-developed technology that commercial regimes best generate must replace or supplement citizen-soldiers. If civilians command it, a standing army will not endanger republican liberty; the spirit of commerce will not bear for long the mass regimentation of universal conscription and militia, nor will it produce sufficient unpaid or low-paid volunteers for a large army.[227] Others, perhaps most notably Algernon Sidney, insist on retaining the classical republican tradition of the citizen-soldier, on the grounds that ultimately a citizenry must defend itself.[228] A volunteer citizen-soldiery would blunt if not remove the argument that any army at all threatens republicanism, government by consent, because soldiers must obey, not deliberate and discuss.[229] However, a volunteer professional army might blunt that arrangement still more.

The degree to which the ancient or classical military spirit must remain in any commercial republic need not entail a citizen-soldiery. But the ancient republican spirit must manifest itself in citizens' support for good soldiers. This support will endure so long as commercial republicans remember the alternative to soldiers commanded by themselves, namely, defeat by soldiers commanded by others. "'Tis ill that men should kill one another in seditions, tumults, and wars; but 'tis worse to bring nations to such misery, weakness, and baseness, as to have neither strength nor courage to contend for anything; to have nothing left worth defending, and to give the name of peace to desolation."[230] Or, more succinctly, "ballots are convincing only so long as bullets are remembered."[231]

The commercial republican insistence on liberty as the most effective means of securing life can lead to rebellion against government as such. In pacificist thought, this often involves the claim that commerce alone, unaided by republicanism, can eliminate war. Starting with Montesquieu's assertion that "the natural effect of commerce is to lead to peace" because commerce fosters both mutual dependency and a certain exact if modest form of justice, commercial pacificists admire the egalitarianism of economic life, wherein all must work in order to eat and the feudalities collapse.[232] Add to this an economic determinism that credits commerce and manufacturing for good government, not good government for increased commerce and manufacturing, a determinism that blames statesmen not businessmen for wars over markets; add also the observation that modern economics invents a new kind of property in money circulation and credit — a property that cannot easily be seized by a conqueror: in all this politics and soldiering begin to appear anachronistic.[233] Without irony, Richard Cobden calls commerce "the great panacea, which, like a beneficent medical discovery, will serve to inoculate with the healthy and saving taste for civilization all the nations of the world." "We do not advocate republican institutions" for Great Britain, he assured his readers, as "democracy forms no element in the materials of English character." But political regimes are irrelevant to peace, and military establishments signify, indeed cause, "real poverty and weakness in a people."[234] Warfare never makes commercial sense; with the spread of the spirit of commerce, universal enlightened self-interest will persuade men never to fight. Montesquieu writes:

> One has begun to be cured of Machiavellianism, and one will continue to be cured of it. There must be more moderation in counsels. What were formerly called *coups d'état* would at present, apart from their horror, be only imprudences.[235]

A moderate Machiavellianism will avoid all kinds of what has come to be called extremism.

Although "honor will not fill the belly, nor clothe the back" neither will man live by bread alone, as the history of modern warfare so amply attests.[236] Accordingly, commercial pacificists sometimes attempt to ennoble or at least defend the morality of commerce. Emeric Crucé sets the tone:

> Agriculture and trade are two necessary occupations that are no less honorable than anything else. It is wrong to think that these trades are uninventive or degrading to the nobility....The merchant has every right to increase his wealth in return for his work which is often done at the risk of his own life, but without injuring or offending anyone else. In this respect he deserves more credit than the soldier....[237]

Conversely, the political and martial spirit has become merely hubristic, in the opinion of commercial pacificists − vain and self-destructive.[238] Government not only interferes with commerce, it perverts peaceful economic competition into war; "where freedom prevails," however, "competition and cooperation are identical."[239] Conquest and its usual object, empire, impede commerce.[240]

Critics of commercial pacificism, whether they are pacifists, bellecists, or pacificists themselves, typically deplore the vices associated with commerce: greed, dispiritedness or moral indifference, a petty restlessness and narrowness of soul. Commerce's strength is its reliance on the low but solid ground of appetite; commerce's weakness is the variability, the inconstancy, of the appetites.[241] As a matter of historical fact, trade does not prevent wars and – just as damaging to the thesis of commercial pacificism – wars can and do prevent trade.[242] Commercial exchange requires the military defense of the means of exchange, such as shipping.[243] The prudence cultivated in the commercial man's soul will not make sound political or military judgments, leaving its country vulnerable to those who do.[244] Commerce may not entirely satisfy even commercial human beings, who may seek outlets for frustrated political ambitions while still appealing to commercial principles.[245]

A more radical attack on politics may be seen in anarchism. Anarchists appropriate one strand of Rousseauan thought – that "war originates not in human nature but in states," that natural man is a "shy, indolent being," quite harmless – and conclude that to eliminate war humanity need only eliminate governments and civil societies.[246] Governments everywhere are "presumptuously working to *unmake* man," with war as a principle instrument of destruction.[247] "[T]he Sword, glutted with foreign Slaughter, turned its edge upon the Bowels of the *Roman* Republic itself...." Under natural conditions no such organized carnage could occur, as there would be no nations to fight and no rulers to dupe and inflame them. All traditional political regimes are fundamentally similar. Democracy is but "a sort of complex Nero." All are tyrannies, garlanded over by laws and religions.[248] Anarchy or "holocracy" – government by all, equally sharing the power – alone can bring peace.[249]

In a sense the only real anarchist was Buridan's ass; it had no reason and none of its passions could rule. As for human beings, some disposition must rule even the solitary walker. Prince Kropotkin takes reason for his authority, "absolute sincerity" for his *moeur*.[250] Tolstoy for his part decries "the impotency of human reason" seen in war, and praises the law of love as the way of peace; nonetheless, Tolstoy elsewhere praises the "light of reason," leading his reader to suppose that he objects primarily to modern-scientific or 'Cartesian' rationalism.[251] Murray Rothbard appeals to a rational account of "human nature," which coercion or violence "cripple[s] by interfering with the full development of human faculties" by thought and action; "the central axiom of the libertarian creed is nonaggression against anyone's person and property," an axiom derived from reason.[252]

Anarchism as the nonviolent rule of reason invites the same questions with respect to its practicability as any other form of political rationalism or 'Enlightenment.'[253] One of these problems is that of getting from here to there. Anarchists often have recourse to progressivist historicism, as seen in Tolstoy's pleasant vision ("All human history from the earliest times to our own day may be considered as a movement of the consciousness both of individuals and of homogeneous groups from lower ideas to higher ones"; government "has long been useless and therefore superfluous and bad" and simply "will be abolished"),[254] in Benjamin Tucker's somewhat more violent urgings,[255] and in the historical determinism of Kropotkin.[256] This historicism convinces no more than any other; the longer it goes unfulfilled the less it convinces any but the most determined fanatics.

The secular alternative to rationalist anarchism is an anarchism of passion, of willfulness, the anarchism of Max Stirner. Not the rational discovery and articulation of nature but the willful assertion of oneself as God: Stirner's "[I] am my all, [I] am the only one," I am "the nothing out of which I myself as creator creates everything" obviously imitates the "I am that I am" of the Biblical God.[257] Stirner recognizes – or wills – that each thing and person also asserts power, making "the combat of self-assertion" "inevitable." Hegelian *Geist* becomes in Stirner's system not mind or spirit but courage and shrewdness. In back of each person's thoughts is the person thinking them; Stirner urges human beings to stop serving their 'ideals' and to make their 'ideals' serve the creator of the ideals: Not *the* ego, some Kantian transcendental ego, but *my* ego, the real ego of the individual thinking. Break "the tyranny of the mind" by listening to the ego through the body.[258] Mind-tyranny yields fanatical neglect or even rejection of the body. "Because the revolutionary priests or schoolmasters served *Man*, they cut off the heads of *men*."[259] The French revolutionaries humbled themselves before an external deity, 'Man,' just as much as the Catholic priests they detested, with identically Inquisitorial results. The anti-rationalistic critique of abstraction seen in Burke in Stirner serves the agenda of radical individualism, rejecting both God and nature, rejecting "the fancy that man was created to be a *zoon politikon.*"[260] 'Political liberty' means only "that the *polis*, the state, is Free":

> State, religion, conscience, these despots, make me a slave, and their liberty is *my* slavery. That in this they necessarily follow the principle, "the end hallows the means," is self-evident. If the welfare of the State is the end, war is a hallowed means; if justice is the State's end, homicide is a hallowed means, and is called by its sacred name, "execution," etc.; the sacred State *hallows* everything that is serviceable to it.[261]

Slavery to the law replaces slavery to persons. "The commonalty wants an *impersonal* ruler," and the principle of bourgeois rule is nothing but mediocrity confused with the Golden Mean — *in*tolerance of thieves, murderers, proletarians, gamblers, vagabonds. A change to socialism will only once again relocate the source of tyranny, of violence; we will become "*equal children* of our mother, the State," compelled to work in service of another empty 'ideal,' the dignity of labor, serving another abstract 'God,' Society. For Stirner's Egoist, *society* is the 'state of nature.'[262] "[T]he State can be really overcome only by impudent self-will."[263] Self-will extends only so far as that which the self 'owns,' namely, the individual body. Self-will over other bodies is tyrannical. "I am *my own* only when I am master of myself, instead of being mastered either by sensuality or by anything else." 'Mastery' requires no effort at *becoming*, as in previous moral philosophy; rather it means *being* what one is right now. "*I* am my species, am without norm, without law, without model."[264] Stirner thus asserts a radically individualized Spoonerism: "*your might, your* power gives you the right."[265] He rather optimistically predicts, "Defend yourself and no one will do anything to you!"[266] This could lead to peace, because each unique self will have nothing in common with any other, and therefore, perhaps nothing to fight over. "[O]pposition vanishes in complete — *severance* or singleness," a parity in disparity. But this is unlikely because, absent any concept of right, "what I can get by force I get by force, and what I do not get by force I have no right to."[267] Stirner deploys a rhetoric of 'empowerment':

> Take hold, and take what you require! With this the war of all
> against all is declared. *I* alone decide what I will have.[268]

This notwithstanding, Stirner insists that his would be a more peaceful world. The philanthropist can kill and torture, as thousands of 'well-intentioned' radicals have demonstrated. The egoist can kill but does not torture because torture serves none of the ego's needs. Torture is not useful to the individual. [269] The problem becomes clear at this point. *How* will the ego distinguish between its needs and its desires, between the useful and the exciting, the seductive, the satisfying? Why, for example, does Stirner *write*?

> Do I write out of love to men? No, I write because I was to procure for *my* thoughts an existence in the world; and, even if I foresaw that these thoughts would deprive you of your rest and your peace, even if I saw the bloodiest wars and the fall of many generations springing up from this seed of thought − I would nevertheless scatter it. Do with it what you will and can, that is your affair and does not trouble me. You will perhaps have only trouble, combat, and death from it; very few will draw joy from it.[270]

Why does Stirner want to procure an existence in the world for his thoughts? "I sing because − I am a singer. But I *use* you for it because I − need ears."[271] But why does he need the ears of others? Why not sing to oneself? Socrates, whom Stirner denounces as "a fool" for "conced[ing] to the Athenians a right to condemn him," actually made his 'concession' only in private to a mediocre man who in Socrates' judgment needed to be more firmly attached to the laws. Socrates engaged in dialogues, to be sure, but when Socrates danced he danced alone.[272] Stirner's egoism is far less perfect than that of Socrates, who left no writings and advocated no anarchism. Stirner's 'Egoist' claims "the power of life and death, because it *may* be exercised, give him satisfaction."[273] Socratic 'egoism' can avoid the embarrassment of disguising desires as 'needs' because it *knows* itself, it discovers nature instead of willing its own idiosyncrasies. Willful anarchism or nihilism cannot know because finally it does not dare to know − this despite its exaltation of courage.

It also dares not to live. Evidence indicates that extreme individualism destroys the social bonds that prevent suicide, that suicide varies inversely with the degree of social cohesion.[274] The self-isolated 'self' does not liberate but destroys itself. The denial of the social and political character of human nature can neither empower nor pacify people, except insofar as it undermines the authorities that prevent ambitious persons from seizing power.[275]

Anarchism rightly denies that political life can 'create' the principles by which human beings should live. It fails to establish that individuals 'create' such principles. More important, it fails to establish in theory or in practice that individuals acting alone or in purely voluntary groups can protect a way of life founded on such principles. While setting extraordinarily high standards of voluntary conduct for extraordinarily large numbers of people, anarchist pacifism simultaneously praises nonviolence as a practical necessity because some people are very bad. If such persons are only bad because they are in a government, how did governments arise all over the world?[276]

The pacificism of commercial republican liberty radicalizes into commercial pacificism or anarchistic pacifism. The commercial republican principle of equality radicalizes into secular Christianity or socialist egalitarianism, which can be pacifist or pacificist. On the central page of *The Law of War and Peace* Grotius distinguishes between "true legal right" and "the rule of love." Violations of the Christian rule of love should not be punished by secular authorities, who should restrict their punitive actions to violations of legal right.[277] This prudent restraint weakens in Rousseauian or 'Continental' liberalism, as Kant understands. In emphasizing love instead of command, Kant writes, Christianity anticipated "the *liberal* way of thinking," in which "the feeling of freedom in the choice of their ultimate purpose is what makes the legislation worthy of [citizens'] love."[278] The difficulty of enforcing the law of love disappears, at least conceptually, if one waxes sufficiently optimistic about the universality and intensity of love in a well-ordered country. Thus Michelet:

> Aristotle says very well in opposition to Plato, "The City is not made of similar but rather dissimilar men." To which I add, "Dissimilar, but harmonized by love and made more and more alike." Democracy is love in the City and common bonds.[279]

And the resolutely unbelieving Shelley can still praise the "invincible gentleness and benignity" of Jesus of Nazareth, whose counsels of nonresistance Shelley endorses as a remedy for the "malice and evil" that the practice of retaliation only exacerbates.[280] The British Labour Party's "attempt to translate the Sermon on the Mount into political terms" proved an unstable mixture of pacifism in peacetime and crusading militarism in wartime,[281] rightly called by one of its apologists – entirely without irony – "the politics of the unpolitical," a "politics of those who desire to be pure at heart," of "men without personal ambition."[282]

The unpolitical politics of love and compassion cannot be sustained because it cannot address either the extraordinary or the ordinary in politics. A pacifist wisely remarks that "triviality is the ritual that protects us against the abyss of love";[283] much decent politics is indeed trivial and ritualistic, and necessarily so. A Gandhi or a Dorothy Day will infuse small acts with spiritual significance, but most of us cannot. Secularists cannot do so in principle. As for 'great politics,' the politics of the tribe of the lion and the eagle, love rarely penetrates. "Because love does not honor, ambitious men are, secretly or openly, recalcitrant towards being loved."[284] Good or bad, statesmen or tyrants, extraordinary political actors tend not to cultivate love or to respond with melted heart to manifestations of it. Christian love can claim divine power; secular love cannot claim much power of any kind in public life except among those too sentimental to succeed in public life. A country might be made safe for love, but such love cannot make a country safe, prosperous, or even just.[285] If a government attempted to arm love and to make the spirit of lovingkindness pervade a civil society, this would end liberty, the freedom love itself requires.[286] Universal like-mindedness, unenforced, requires a divine intervention in human affairs. Secularism by definition cannot depend upon that intervention.

6. *Historicist Tyranny: The Dialectic of War in Quest of Permanent Peace*

Pericles told the Athenians that individual liberty, leisure, and prosperity are not at war with discipline, energy, deliberation, and courage. "All this ease in our private relations does not make us lawless as citizens," nor need it weaken Athenians' sense of honor and even of magnanimity.[287] Still, Pericles does *tell* the Athenians these edifying things; the facts somehow need the articulation and perhaps the enhancement of speech. The Athenians need inspiring; they need encouragement in harsh times. At other times, such as the occasion of the Sicilian expedition, they might have benefited from moderating speech.

What was true of Athenian democracy remains true of commercial republics, where comfortable private life enjoys far sounder institutional protection. If as a general rule in politics the people become revolutionary when the distribution of property is unequal whereas men and women of superior education become revolutionary when the distribution of office is equal,[288] then commercial republicanism moderates the most intense revolutionary ardor while perpetuating revolutionary irritations. In commercial republics property is far more equal than elsewhere but far from equal; offices are distributed unequally with a strong bias towards the educated but not without considerable opportunities for individuals of less than the finest education. If these regimes effect a "domestication of pride"[289] and thus make themselves hard to revolutionize, they still generate revolutionaries, often for export. A democratic socialist describes the twentieth as "a century of counterrevolution, one in which the liberal conquests of the nineteenth century, inadequate as these may have been, have been systematically destroyed by left-and-right authoritarian dictatorships."[290] Taking a longer view, one might describe the last two centuries as a struggle for hearts and minds of the middle class, in which monarchy, at least two republicanisms, and several despotisms contended for adherents, sometimes in the name of other classes and of anti-'bourgeois' sentiments.

The middle class wants peace but it does not always want boredom. Its youth in particular does not want boredom. The first thoroughgoing philosophic attack on commercial republicanism (and commercial monocracy) rejects the 'interesting' Periclean attempt to combine prosperity and citizen virtue (shared to some extent by Sidney) while firmly opposing the humdrum life of factory and shop. The statesmen of antiquity spoke of virtues; "ours speak of nothing but commerce and money," Rousseau complains. "Good neither for himself nor for others," "always floating between his inclinations and his duties," neither a natural man nor a citizen, concealing his own inadequacies beneath veiled chains forged by the arts and sciences, bourgeois man stands in desperate need of a radical reforming.[291]

Nature being malleable, bourgeois man can indeed be radically reformed, even as he originated as a reformation of a previous human type. "Bad men spring from bad things; hence, let us correct the things."[292] Among the things corrected will be representative government. Sovereignty belongs to the *general* will, which cannot be represented.

> As soon as public service ceases to be the chief business of the citizens and they would rather serve with their money than with their persons, the State is not far from its fall. When it is necessary to march out to war, they pay troops and stay at home; when it is necessary to meet in council, they name deputies and stay at home. By reason of idleness and money, they end by having soldiers enslave their country and representatives to sell it.[293]

Only by personal thought and action – a noncommercial, money-less economy of personal services and small-scale, non-representative, 'participatory' democracy – can popular sovereignty find its true expression, defended militarily by federation with other small states. The arts and sciences, commerce, the direct or nearly direct rule by *philosophes* for the public good: the Enlightenment project is unworkable and illegitimate.[294]

The denigration of all privacy for the average person in the name of full citizenship, coupled with the notion of human malleability and therefore 'historicity,' yielded in practice terror at home and wars of conquest abroad, as Constant sees in retrospect, Burke in prospect.[295] The attempt to bring ancient, republican virtue to rule, even abrogate, the 'bourgeois virtues' "suppl[ies] weapons and pretexts to all kinds of tyranny" by demanding that individuals alienate their rights "without reservation" to the political community. Met with the resistance of 'their' people, rulers animated by "philosophy as prejudice and democracy as fanaticism" scrupled not to destroy the recalcitrants in whose 'sovereignty' they putatively acted. Rulers soon "declared that despotism was indispensable as the foundation of liberty." "Liberty, they argued, had to be postponed until factions died down; but factions only die down when liberty is no longer postponed," a "vicious circle" and a violent one, as "anger is fed by anger" and "laws are forged like weapons."[296]

The danger of this enterprise conceded, its seductiveness must not be overlooked. Hardly a rabid anti-bourgeois, even John Stuart Mill laments the rule of "collective mediocrity," the paucity of outstanding individuals, the "despotism of mind" that makes public education in commercial regimes "a mere contrivance for molding people to be exactly like one another."[297] John Ruskin claims that "no great art ever yet rose on earth, but among a nation of soldiers," whereas while commerce "is barely consistent with fine art, [it] cannot produce it."[298] Georges Sorel wants intellectuals to "help to ruin the prestige of middle class culture" – far from an utopian aspiration – while proletarians and their leaders frighten the "timorous humanitarian[s]" of the bourgeoisie. A "great foreign war" or "a great extension of proletarian violence" might reinspirit the bourgeoisie, wipe out the "middle class desire to die in peace." But whether the bourgeoisie surrenders or fights back, it must not be allowed to compromise its way to survival, to "correct the abuses of economics" with mild reforms; if this occurs, "the future of the world becomes completely indeterminate," and the bourgeois "degradation of the sentiment of honor" could continue *ad infinitum*.[299] Sorel's rhetoric equates class war within a country with international war, then appeals both to Realpolitik and to aristocratic contempt for cowardice and aristocratic love of honor in order to encourage the class war that will end bourgeois complacency or pacificism.

The dangers and attractions of conflict as a means of remedying the humdrum character of bourgeois life induce some secular writers to invent new kinds of war, inspiriting but not too vicious – *moral* equivalents of war. Nietzsche surveys the offerings that had surfaced by the end of the nineteenth century – navigation, mountain-climbing, 'adventure' generally, usually practiced by restless Englishmen – concluding that these amount to "vain reverie and beautiful-soulism," insufficiently stern or dangerous to toughen the "feeble humanity" of "the present-day European."[300] William James' later proposal, a conscript army of youth "enlisted against *Nature*" engaged in socially useful, hard physical work – "painful work done cheerily because the duty is temporary" – aims at a polity of "martial virtues" without Mars. As such, it cannot serve as more than a diluted version of real military activity.[301] The attempt to fit the war-spirit to the works of peace ends in socialism, vulnerable either to the same 'decadence' as commercial republicanism or to a militant statism that threatens civic and international peace.

If war is the most extreme human movement or activity, then many of the most radical reformers of human conventions and of human nature will seek it.[302] Thought itself will become militant, not only or even primarily in the sense that it will advocate physical wars. Thought will mimic the spiritual warfare of the religions, producing "the age of the intellectual organization of political hatreds" whereby "everyone...claims that his movement is in love with 'the development of evolution' and 'the profound meaning of history.'" History, *movement* even of ideas, replaces nature and God.[303] Although Voltaire replaces the classical 'chain of being' with an historical-physical "chain of events," although Rousseau and Kant clearly anticipate many historicist themes, Hegel deserves to be considered the author of the first fully articulated historicism.[304] Insofar as writers conceive of history as leading to a *telos* their doctrine will resemble the theological doctrine of providence, whereby the worst vicissitudes are justified by the wisdom of the God Who directs them and by the goodness of the End He has in mind.[305] Wars are among the principal means by which perpetual peace will finally obtain.

Hegel calls the nation-state "the absolute power on earth." International law, such as it is, "depends on different wills each of which is sovereign." The relations among these sovereign wills or minds constitute the dialectic of the finitude of these minds, and out of it arises the universal mind or universal history, the self-differentiating, self-conquering Absolute Spirit. The self-differentiation and self-conquest introduce novelty to the world; by contrast, nature is merely cyclical. The "essence of Matter is Gravity," Hegel claims (following Newton), whereas the essence of the Spirit is freedom. Given this capacity for novelty, ordinary or conventional morality becomes irrelevant in assessing "world-historical figures," embodied Absolute Ideas on horseback. Beyond good and evil as currently conceived, these figures are uniquely interesting. They contrast with the boredom of ever-cycling nature, with its "eternally dead masses."[306] Because he finds no energy in nature Hegel cannot explain the generation of natural things; because he believes nature fundamentally lifeless, he sees no life in form.[307] These preconceptions lead to the historicist attack on the 'social contract,' the 'state of nature,' and to the rejection of political science's emphasis on governmental forms, in particular separation and balance of governmental powers. All of this prepares an assault on commercial republicanism – first and foremost an assault on the concept of prepolitically-held natural rights of individual human beings. [308] The 'dialectical' or historicist view 'relativizes' the justice of war to certain epochs. It finds difficulty in condemning any war at all in certain epochs, or in justifying any war at all in others. It must claim knowledge of providence in retrospect and, what is more daunting, prophetic knowledge in prospect. Hegel believes the 'dialectic' of war to be elevating to the consciousness, particularly in the bourgeois epoch, with its unmanly and antipolitical biases. Other historicists demur, claiming that modern war must be overcome immediately – dialectically of course.[309]

Two major theoretical and practical consequences of historicism are Marxism and Fascism (particularly in its radical or Hitlerite form), with their doctrines of class and race war, respectively. Although these materialist forms of historicism appear similar to many traditional just war theories – equally commending just wars for the sake of an eventual peace – they are actually quite different. Because they imagine the course of events as dialectical, as a war of opposites in which one 'side' overcomes the other, these historicisms encourage the most stubborn assertions of the most extreme claims at the expense of the moderation they call mediocrity. And because they aim not merely to carry on history in a more just and prudent way, but to end history, often in a manner that imitates the apocalypses anticipated by religious prophets, extreme claims and warlike practices seem only righteous. These historicisms, then, *systematically* exalt spiritedness.

As is well known, Marx in a sense naturalizes Hegel, makes Hegelian dialectic a material process. Nature, conceived as matter, moves dialectically; human nature, equally material and 'dialectical,' produces social relations "in conformity with...economic productivity," relations that themselves generate principles, ideas, and categories. Because the material conditions of human life change, social relations and the mental structures they produce are "historical and transitory products."[310] In rejecting Hegel's "mysticism" with respect to 'the State,' in rejecting the notion that the State amounts to the march of 'God' or the Absolute Spirit on earth, Marx insists that "only the people is a concrete fact."[311] Concretely, the people have divided themselves into social and economic classes, rather as Hegel's Absolute Spirit differentiates itself into contradictions. "[T]he whole history of mankind (since the dissolution of primitive tribal society, holding land in common ownership) has been a history of class struggles"; "the ruling ideas of each age have ever been the ideas of its ruling class."[312]

The actual history of mankind since Marx's death saw the emergence of his disciple, V.I. Lenin, who dismissed "all doctrines of *non*-class socialism and *non*-class politics" as "sheer nonsense." The very existence of the State "proves that the class antagonisms are irreconcilable"; the State exists in order to subordinate weaker classes to the strongest class. The dialectic of history requires not reconciliation but retaliation, even as logical dialectic requires not compromise but refutation. "Communist ethics" requires belief and action "entirely subordinated to the interests of the proletariat's class struggle." There is no "eternal morality," nor any souls to save. "Morality serves the purpose of helping human society rise to a higher level and rid itself of the exploitation of labor." What is true of morality is equally true of reason. "[T]here can be no 'impartial' social science in a society based on class struggle," only social sciences committed to the advancement of class interests, be they those of the retreating bourgeoisie or those of the advancing proletariat.[313]

Many critics see that the historicist use of logical terms ('dialectic,' 'contradictions') to describe economic, social, and political life must lead to serious distortions of reality. Conflicts are not exactly contradictions; one social class does not 'refute' another as one argument may refute another.[314] Committing oneself as a scholar, a philosopher, or even as a politician to a particular class interest will likely coarsen the mind, fetter it instead of freeing it, incapacitating it both for science and politics.[315] The mind reduces itself to a weapon of war, calculating strategy, tactics, and not much else.[316] Because all of this takes the form of an attack on 'reactionary, bourgeois morality' it feels very much like liberation; because it is in principle irrefutable, claiming a supposed scientific certainty without much bothering with scientific gathering of evidence or experimentation, it affords some of the most exquisite satisfactions of dogma at the very same time."[317] The dialectical dogmatist has a ready war-propaganda assault or counter-assault against any independent or impartial thought: such thinkers exhibit "seraphim tendencies," attempting to stand above the world-historical struggle.[318] Under Marxism 'realism' soon becomes the imagining of the desired future as if it had already existed — a dreamworld appealing to great madmen like Stalin and little ones like the poor soul Richard Wright describes, an escapee from a mental hospital who quickly ascended to leadership in the Detroit John Reed Club.[319] Under Marxism sanity finally seeks refuge in a bureaucracy even less attractive to free spirits than the banal life of the bourgeoisie.

Historicism of the 'Right' displays a similar structure and tendencies. Nietzsche complains that "lack of historical sense is the family failing of all philosophers." He contrasts "metaphysical" philosophy, which teaches that the object exists independently of the knower, with "historical" philosophy" — "no longer [to] be separated from natural science" — which "has discovered that there are no opposites," that "there exists, strictly speaking, neither unegoistic action nor completely disinterested contemplation." If all is ego, self-assertion, will to power, then "there exists neither a natural right nor a natural wrong," and "in reality every man is himself a piece of fate," warring by necessity against other pieces of the self-differentiating cosmic will-to-power. Violence is not death; pity, compassion, benevolence — these are deadly, coddlers of sickness. Violence signifies life.[320]

Politically, rightist historicism predicts worldwide wars among the existing political life-units, the nations. Barrès, though merely derivative of Nietzsche, differs in one respect: Barrès takes nationalism seriously 'in itself.' "I have redirected my piety from the heavens to the earth," he intones, "the earth that contains my dead," the dead who physiologically transmitted his own thinking and the shape of his thoughts. "Nationalism is the acceptance of a particular kind of determinism," not of class-consciousness and class-warfare but of national instincts and national wars.[321] Nietzsche of course spurns the suggestion of piety. (But with how much justice, given his propensity for prophecy? Perhaps *his* piety is only redirected toward the will-to-power?) He also predicts that a new, world-historical, therefore super-national, 'overman' will arise out of these national wars.[322] But even the overman will not be the end; he will face over-dragons.[323]

Fascism is Nietzsche narrowed, Nietzsche without manifoldness, Nietzsche *brought down*. Mussolini called Fascism "both practice and thought" in the service of creation, of life-struggle. "Outside history man is nothing," and history will not end. But unlike Nietzsche, for whom the State is the coldest of cold monsters, Mussolini "reaffirm[ed] the State as the true reality of the individual." This is nationalism but it is statist nationalism; "the nation is created by the State," which is "the universal ethical will...the creator of right," "not only the giver of laws and the founder of institutions, but the educator and promoter of spiritual life." The state's will to power promotes physical and spiritual wars for physical and spiritual empire.[324]

Hitler shared Mussolini's historicism, appealing frequently to 'nature' as natural *history* – nature as evolutionary struggle. He called not for the conquest of nature (a Jewish concept, he complained, based upon the first book of *Genesis*) but for the recognition that nature is conquest.[325] Human evolution depends upon great men who combine in themselves the theoretician and the politician. These are "the Marathon runners of history" who die crowned with the laurel wreath. They are partisans; their party "philosophy" is "the formulation of a declaration of war against the existing order." "Every philosophy of life, even if it is a thousand times correct and of highest benefit to humanity, will remain without significance for the practical reshaping of a people's life, as long as its principles have not become the banner of a fighting movement which for its part in turn will be a party so long as its activity has not found completion in the victory of its ideas and its party dogmas have not become the new state principles of a people's community." "Party principles" or "philosophy" serve exactly the same function as dogma does in religion. The wars the Party undertakes therefore will be both physical and 'philosophic' or 'spiritual.' Only physical wars with a 'spiritual' dimension succeed; only 'spiritual' wars with a physical, violent dimension succeed. 'Philosophy' or dogma inspirits politics. Ordinary political parties "are inclined to compromises; philosophies never." 'Philosophies' "proclaim their infallibility."[326] The 'infallible' and uncompromising 'philosophic' party leader Hitler proclaims a typically historicist dialectic: "[T]here can be no compromise — there are only two possibilities: either the victory of the Aryan or annihilation of the Aryan and the victory of the Jew."[327] As with Marxism, we enter a dreamworld of madness, wherein "facts do not exist, only interpretations."[328]

Philosophers tend to decline the mantle of the prophet. Loving wisdom without expecting to become all-wise, they recognize the unpredictability of future contingencies, which at best will be met with prudence by citizens at liberty to act at the right time.[329] Historicists, however, say with Comte: *"Voir, c'est savoir; savoir, c'est prévoir; prévoir, c'est pouvoir."*[330] *Fore*knowledge especially is power. It is power not only because the knower can position himself to 'catch a trend,' as shrewd politicians do, but because the knower also *wills* the trend, participates in the shaping of an emerging "consciousness."[331] If this shaping includes propaganda, even outright lies, this is only historically — dialectically — necessary, as in any war.[332] Because this war aims at total conquest and annihilation of the enemy class or race there is no room even for soldierly respect for a valiant foe, who is instead demonized as a Beast of a secular Apocalypse.

The question to ask concerning a Lenin, a Hitler, or of any among the crowd of their epigoni is not 'Is he cynical?' The politicians of historicist tyranny are no more or less cynical than politicians anywhere. The question is, 'What form does their cynicism take?' Corruption and other petty injustices, conceit, dog-and-pony shows and political kitsch of all sorts are universal. Historicism adds a uniquely self-delusory and aggressive form to the politics of secularism. When told in all seriousness that *The Communist Manifesto* is "the most prophetic book in the history of the world";[333] that in the 1930s the "capitalist system" had reached "its incurable crisis" and that "bourgeois democracy" would soon follow Germany into fascism in a "last, desperate form of defense of capitalism;[334] that "no power on earth can stop" the advance of communism and that Marx "is the prophet of fully conscious ethical passion"; [335] that while in the 1960s all of Europe "run[s] headlong into the abyss," the "Third World," adopting the wholesome Marxist elements of "European thought," will "try to set afoot a new man";[336] that, in 1939, "if the international Jewish financiers in and outside Europe should succeed in plunging the nations once more into a world war, then the result will be the bolshevization of the earth, and thus the victory of Jewry, but the annihilation of the Jewish race in Europe";[337] when told all that and more, any reader still in possession of common sense unhampered by cowardice or ideology will recognize the unmistakable accents of paranoiac fear and wish-fulfillment gone fanatic.[338] The call for militant action to ensure the fulfillment of 'ideal' and therefore absolutely valuable wishes, which are at the same time self-serving or 'empowering,' guarantees a warfare whose only limit will be exhaustion.[339] "The truly characteristic development of our time is the *exaltation* of violence,"[340] the endowing of violence with cognitive and even apocalyptic significance.

Historicist tyranny attacks both commerce and republicanism. Following the Hobbesian complaint against merchants — "their only glory being to grow excessively rich by the wisdom of buying and selling," who "mak[e] poor people sell their labor to them at their own [i.e., the merchants'] prices"[341] — Marx calls capital "dead labor, that vampire-like, only lives by sucking living labor, and lives the more, the more labor it sucks."[342] Capital is — to complete the image of Victorian horror — none other than the ghost of the ancient world's slavery and warfare, haunting the modern world in a new form, money. The money-economy of capitalism enslaves with wages, and wars against the proletariat with the weapons of debt and poverty, causing despotism in the workshop, anarchy in society. Money is a kind of wandering Jew, an "alien entity," ruling and ruining wherever it goes.[343] Although Marx speaks ill of politics and the State, denying that human beings are naturally political — eliminating any possibility of a political remedy for inter-class conflict — Lenin expanded and centralized the state in order to root out bourgeois practices and habits.[344] These habits are the result of pernicious illusions or 'abstractions,' including 'country' and 'democracy' that conceal tyranny and its unjust warfare beneath fine-sounding phrases and fine-seeming institutions.[345]

Mussolini too despised "middle-class mediocrity" with its policies of apparent economic drift in the service of "Occidental plutocratic nations." Capital was not to be "exiled, as in the Russian communist dream" but cast in a well-directed role "in the drama of production."[346] This attempt to dramatize life was shared by Hitler, who complained that the "economic life" lived by "the German bourgeoisie had very little heroic about it." Drama is a popularized form of dialectic: Hitler's drama pitted the villains of gold, capitalism, and reaction against the heroes of work, peoples, and progress.[347] Above all it pitted the 'the Jew," a compendium of all villainies, an unproductive, uncreative internationalist without a home, parasitically ruling the nations after winning the Great War on the backs of English, French, and American soldier-dupes, against the noble and heroic Aryans who synthesize the nationalism of the non-Jewish bourgeoisie with the fraternal socialism of Marxists.[348]

Hitler claimed that races or nations, not classes, determine the course of history. Out of such commercial cities as Vienna — the "Babylon of races" that repelled Hitler as a young man — arise bourgeois and proletarians — liberals with their "Jewish tendency," as spokesmen for the first, "the Jew, Karl Marx," as spokesman for the second. Both stand for majority-rule. Both propagandize for "equality of the races." Both are products of "the bourgeois world" with its commercial cosmopolitanism (the proletariat in the Marxist scheme is international), its no-work technology and capital, its easy egalitarianism and license mis-called liberty, its complacent toleration of the chronically and hereditarily diseased, cripples, and cretins: all a poisonous recipe for racial degeneration, for "a unified mash" of mongrelized humanity. If this regime were to succeed, "the mission of humanity could then be looked upon as finished."[349] The "folkish philosophy" of National Socialism will prevent this by bringing humanity to consciousness of "its basic racial elements," elements arrayed in an evolving or dynamic hierarchy in accordance with "the basic aristocratic principle of Nature." This will lead to "an idealization of humanity, in which [folkish philosophy] alone sees the premise for the [continued] existence of humanity."[350] For this task economic life alone can never suffice.

> Never yet has a state been founded by peaceful economic means, but always and exclusively by the instincts of preservation of the species regardless whether these are found in the province of heroic virtue or of cunning craftiness; the one results in Aryan states based on work and culture, the other in Jewish colonies of parasites. As soon as economics as such begins to choke out these instincts in a people or in a state, it becomes the seductive cause of subjugation and oppression.

> The belief of prewar days that the world could be peacefully opened up to, let alone conquered for, the German people by a commercial and colonial policy was a classic sign of the loss of real state-forming and state-preserving virtues and of all the insight, will power, and active determination which follow from them; the penalty for this, inevitable as the law of nature, was the World War with its consequences.[351]

This state, as in Leninist theory, will not enslave the history-bearing elements, but will serve as "a means," as "the premise for the formation of a higher culture" to be created by the Aryan race.[352]

Marxist and national-socialist historicism attack commerce and private property with the state for the sake of humanity, which will be prevented from self-destruction and led to a regime of justice by a salvific element within itself. In both cases historicist practice intentionally or unintentionally reduplicates the results of Hegelian statism. The attack on economic liberty empowers the state and weakens social resistance to the state. Private property is diffused power; diffused power means resistible power; resistible power cannot accomplish much directly, frustrating all radical reformers — including tyrants first of all.[353]

Historicist tyranny attacks representative government with equal fervor. Hitler scorned "democracy" as "the culture in which [Marxist] germs can spread." A "fluctuating majority of people" cannot be "responsible" because it lacks intelligence and courage, "sin[ning] against the basic aristocratic principle of Nature." Hucksterism and haggling replace "creative work"; there is none of the leadership that the people crave and need to defend themselves against "the attack of Marxism." "[D]emocracy is fundamentally not German: it is Jewish," reinforcing the racial egalitarianism of commerce, further weakening the Aryan virtues.[354]

Marx applauds "democracy" as the first regime in which the constitution rests "on its actual Foundation," the people, "not only *implicitly* and in its essence, but in its *existence* and actuality." Democracy is "the final form" of human emancipation "within the existing order of things." However, the proletarian revolution will destroy the existing order, including democracy; it will first establish not democracy but "*the revolutionary dictatorship the proletariat.*"[355] Lenin followed these teachings faithfully. He applauded "bourgeois revolution" and its "democratism" because parliamentary government would sharpen class antagonisms and assist the Bolshevik party in its organization of the proletariat. "[W]ith the aid of democratism [the proletariat] has the whole world to win." Because democracy cannot solve the economic problem it will instruct the proletariat, more effectively than any propaganda, that "the root of evil is capitalism, not lack of rights." Lenin believed for many years that democracy was indispensable to the advance of communism; the pressures of the First World War hastened the dialectic, but even then his regime followed a short-lived democracy. His regime was indeed a dictatorship of the proletariat or, more precisely, of the "proletarian vanguard," the Bolshevik Party. This dictatorship, he had predicted, "must inevitably rely on military force, on the arming of the masses, not on institutions of one kind or another established in a 'lawful' or 'peaceful' way."[356]

Commercial republicanism or 'the bourgeois state' does not go far enough for international or for national socialists. Marx objects to the State as such because 'state' separated from 'society' implies a private life not to be violated by political rule.[357] In communism politics will be internalized. Marxists utterly despise the "formal" character of commercial republicanism even as they attempt to use it. Lenin riposted:

> From the vulgar bourgeois standpoint the terms dictatorship and democracy are mutually exclusive. Failing to understand the class struggle and accustomed to seeing in the political arena the petty squabbling of the various bourgeois circles and coteries, the bourgeois understands by dictatorship the annulment of all liberties and guarantees of democracy, arbitrariness of every kind, and every sort of abuse of power in a dictator's personal interests.[358]

Taking the Machiavellian line that all "major questions in the life of nations are settled only by force," Lenin accused commercial republicans of delusion or of fraud.[359] Trotsky concurred and probed deeper:

> The doctrine of formal democracy is not constituted by scientific socialism, but by the theory of so-called natural right. The essence of natural right resides in the recognition of eternal and invariable juridical norms found in different epochs and

among different peoples in expressions more or less constricted and deformed.[360]

Such "ideal norms" merely express "class interest." "The mystical equality of Christianity has descended from the heavens in the form of the natural equality of democracy," which cannot be made real by commercial republicanism. Proletarian dictatorship must replace commercial republicanism; dialectical materialism must replace natural right.[361] Hitler offered essentially the same critique of representative government — that it is really ruled by "capital," that its "liberty" is only an "uncontrolled economy" serving the rich, that its free press is bought and paid for by the rich, and so on. And with the Marxists he claimed to be the people's only true "representative."[362] He differed from the Marxists only in denying that political rule can ever be internalized equally by the people. There will always be natural leaders, natural followers.

International and national socialists also charge that commercial republicanism brings not liberty but imperialism to the world, although Marxists necessarily analyzed this phenomenon much more elaborately, given their egalitarian rhetoric. Hitler berated international commerce as a vehicle of imperialism involving the French on land, the British by sea, and the Jews (so to speak) in the invisible air of finance.[363] Lenin denied that France waged war in 1914 for political freedom; "she is fighting to retain her colonies," only, and so was England. So was Germany. "[E]veryone knows that this war is not due to the conflict between republican and monarchist principles, but is a war between two imperialist coalitions for the division of colonies....." In order to avoid "a turn from imperialist war to imperialist peace," a *status quo* peace, Lenin's Party rejected pacifism, "declaring that socialists must seek to transform the present war into a civil war of the proletariat against the bourgeoisie, for socialism."[364]

Commercial imperialism transforms whole countries into oligarchs. "The world has become divided into a handful of usurer states and a vast majority of debtor states." Even the workers in the usurer states become bourgeois, if only petty-bourgeois. But the same class rules everywhere, regardless of the local political regime: "A comparison of, say, the republican American bourgeoisie with the monarchic Japanese or German bourgeoisie shows that the most pronounced political distinction diminishes to an extreme degree in the epoch of imperialism." When beset by exacerbated class conflicts, these bourgeois rulers start a war to bind their local workers more closely to them, all the while awaiting war's end to pick up business as usual more or less where they left off, plus or minus some colonies. End capitalism, end imperialism; end imperialism, end war.[365]

The commercial imperialism thesis ignores or rather explains away such political motives as the ambition for fame and sway, and the genuine hostility between republics and other regimes because its proponents assume the core claim that the thesis supposedly proves: that economics drives modern political life.[366] By contrast, the traditional republican claim that the political centralization of tyranny will likely produce a larger military establishment than seen in commercial republicanism has held firm.[367] Even on the purely economic level the argument fails, as 'underdeveloped' (including state-socialist) countries need the financial investments by commercial republicans far more than the 'capitalists' need them.[368]

The falsehood of the tyranno-historicist critique of commercial republicanism glares so obviously that one must search for an explanation of it not in reason but in political psychology. Commercial republicanism comes to light as a quest to answer the problem of human spiritedness. With Plato and most political philosophers since Plato, commercial republicans find in spiritedness or *thumos* the distinctively political part of the human soul. Commercial republicanism was deliberately designed to give scope and regulation to *thumos*, and most urgently to frustrate those souls so spirited that they will tyrannize. Souls of tyrannic inclination are in fact frustrated by life in commercial republics, and so are other souls, spirited and generous, with a passion for justice, who will chafe against the blandness, the low-grade selfishness, of so much public life in these regimes.

Historicist politics appeals both to the tyrannical and the passionately just, to warrior-spirits had and good. It is nothing more than a sustained appeal to *thumos*. Hitler's appeal was first of all to masculinity and femininity, to the manliness of "the great world" of public life and to the "small world," the domestic world, of womanliness. This strict demarcation of masculine from feminine honor will end the conflict between the sexes.[369] A similar tendency has been observed among Marxists, although often in more convoluted or shall we say dialectical form, owing to their official egalitarianism.[370]

Hitler told his nation, "I am one of the hardest men Germany has had for decades, perhaps for centuries." Not only Hitler but "every one of us...should be a fighter − brave, forth-right, daring and true − true to his last breath." Against the "generally unheroic" but dangerous Jew, Hitler was "defending myself" and "fighting for the work of the Lord." The rule of law may − must − be rightfully swept aside when a nation's very existence is threatened: "The world is not for cowardly peoples." The national socialist state would "devote the highest attention to the training of the will and the force of decision" against "the unclear will" of bourgeois-democracy. "A people of scholars, if they are physically degenerate, weak-willed and cowardly pacifists, will not storm the heavens, indeed they will not even be able to safeguard their own existence on earth." Pacifism and legalism conspire "to unman the people," to denature humanity; "bolshevist Judaism" seeks "to make the nation defenseless in arms and to make the people defenseless in spirit." These forces must be opposed with "holy hatred."[371] The people will respond instinctively to the leader's rage, share it, multiply its force.[372] Even as Nietzsche insists that the struggle for mere existence or comfortable self-preservation is only an exception, that the real struggle "always revolves around superiority, around growth and expansion, around power," so Hitler claimed that "a stronger race will drive out the weak, for the vital urge in its ultimate form will, time and again, burst all the absurd fetters of the so-called humanity of individuals, in order to replace it by the humanity of Nature which destroys the weak in order to give his place to the strong."[373] Politically this struggle will eventuate in peace, "a peace, supported not by the palm branches of tearful, pacifist female mourners, but based on the victorious sword of a master people, putting the sword into the service of a higher culture."[374]

The thumotic character of leftist historicism is perhaps less notorious than Hitler's. It is no less pronounced. Marx praises human sociality, deplores politics because its "principle" is "will" − "one-sided," inclined to believe itself omnipotent, incapable of "discovering the source of social ills."[375] Perhaps his very denial of freedom of the will stems from his distaste for the political.[376] The intention behind the proletarian dictatorship might then be to enact a supreme act of will to end all willfulness. If so, in practice the supreme will only seeks to perpetuate its supremacy. The Leninist proletariat functions exactly as Hitler's Aryan race; "the only class...capable of manifesting courage and decisiveness," in contraposition to the fearful bourgeoisie,[377] the proletarian vanguard knows "that Might is the mother of Right," that not only politics but economics, labor, must be militarized in order to destroy petty individualism and trivial liberties of bourgeois life.[378] The Leninist warrior is by his fighting a "social reformer," the "true priest of the reform to which he aspires."[379] The colonial world especially lays bare the violence of bourgeois rule; there, the violence is literal, not camouflaged with legalities as in "the so-called free world." The imperial forces attempt to make "the native" into a passive beast. The native's retaliatory violence is "a cleansing force" because it "restores his self-respect," his very humanity, by "this mad fury, this bitterness and spleen, by [the] ever-present desire to kill [the imperialists]." "[O]ur historic mission is to sanction all revolts, all desperate actions, all those abortive attempts drowned in rivers of blood," as stages in a dialectic that will bring "liberation" and the creation of a "new humanity."[380] This humanity will be at peace because the proletarian violence-to-end-all-violence differs from all other kinds. Proletarians and natives, the erstwhile victims of the first international or universal economy, 'capitalism,' alone retain the consciousness of the tortures of alienation. A universality of suffering that is lived and not merely imagined or conceived, as in the various humanitarianisms, will yield a world-society of "authentic intersubjectivity," the first "coexistence at once of fact and value, in which the logic of history joins the forces of labor and the authentic experience of human life."[381] The attempt to enact utopia exalts thumos.[382]

Historicist tyranny is the political exaltation of *thumos*. Because the most spirited individuals will not stand to be ruled by conventional procedure or persons, and may not stand being ruled at all, these tyrants acknowledge, insist on, the right to revolution and somehow to combine this with absolute state power for themselves. Hitler derided those who would respect state authority for its own sake, never opposing even "a bad, ruinous regime," and deprecated the "principle-mongers" who would accept a parliamentary majority of inferiors when a Frederick the Great is available. "Men do not exist for the State, the State exists for men," "the living organism" of the nation, with which Hitler "replace[d] the liberalistic conception of the individual by the conception of a people bound by their blood to the soil," ruled by one Party, itself ruled by one will. "I am the only representative of my people." This is true democracy. "[P]olitics is nothing else and can be nothing else than the safeguarding a people's vital interests and the practical waging of its life-battle with every means," defending the "holy rights of the eternal racial life." National socialist politics would institutionalize heroism in the office of the Fuehrer, elected by national plebiscite to absolute power and, therefore, entirely responsible for his actions.[383]

Lenin too required "democracy without parliamentarianism" after his Party seized state power. The dictatorship of the proletariat, more precisely the proletarian vanguard, will abolish the need for the state by abolishing the class warfare the state exists in order to manage. Even the administrative function as a specialized activity of a particular segment of society, a bureaucracy, will disappear, as "the functions of control and accounting, becoming more and more simple, will be performed by each in turn, will then become a habit." No subordination, no rule; no rule, no coercion, except in rare cases of individual excesses to be halted "by the armed people themselves." Immediately after the revolutionary overthrow of the bourgeois state, the new, proletarian state will violently attack the bourgeoisie.[384] Lenin assured his readers that this state will scarcely be a state at all:

> It is no longer a state in the proper sense of the word; for the suppressing of the minority of exploiters by the majority of the wage slaves of *yesterday* is comparatively so easy, simple and natural a task that it will entail far less bloodshed than the suppression of the risings of slaves, serfs or wage-labourers, that it will cost mankind far less. And it is compatible with the extension of democracy to such an overwhelming majority of the population that the need for a *special machine* of suppression will begin to disappear.[385]

"Democracy means equality." Communism is the condition of equal social life amongst persons so well habituated to "the elementary rules of social intercourse" that no state apparatus will exist or be needed. Communism will not be vulnerable to outside attackers or internal enemies; "the armed workers are practical men and not sentimental intellectuals, and they will scarcely allow anyone to trifle with them." The transitional or "socialist" government of proletarian dictatorship must be "really firm and ruthless in crushing both exploiters and hooligans," and in exacting "unquestioning obedience" to the one-man decisions of Soviet directors" appointed or elected by the Party. By March 1919 Lenin was telling his fellow Bolsheviks, "Nobody will deny that in the matter of true, not paper, democracy, in the matter on enlisting the workers and peasants, we have done more than has been done or could be done by the best of the democratic republics in hundreds of years."[386] In fact, as Bertrand Russell saw at about the same time, and continued to report five years later, there was no "degree whatever of political justice" (by which he meant democracy) in the Soviet Union, and there was none foreseeable.[387]

What was foreseeable, because predicted and desired by the founders, was war against the external and internal enemies of the tyranno-historicist regimes. Commercial republicans had charged monocracy with the perpetuation and intensification of war instead of the peace Hobbes promised. The new tyrants agreed, only adding that the war would be historically necessary and good. "What dictatorship implies and means," Lenin wrote, "is a state of simmering war, a state of military measures of struggle against the enemies of proletarian power."[388] Mussolini explained that "in certain contingencies violence has a deep moral significance," so long as it is "surgical, intelligent, and chivalrous"; "the poesy of battle, the voices of an awakening race were multiplying" in the days of the Fascist revolution, "the energies of our nation."[389] Although the national socialists of Germany "want[ed] nothing else than the peace of the world," this must be peace "neither owing to weakness nor to cowardice," argued Hitler. Genuine peace will require "equality for the German people," including more territory so that Germans will have a sufficiency of fertile soil and colonies — both needed if commercial internationalism is to be abandoned for national self-sufficiency.[390] Commercial and proletarian internationalism are artificial. The true internationalism is nature:

> Nature knows no political boundaries. First, she puts
> living creatures on this globe and watches the free play of
> forces. She then confers the master's right on her favorite child,
> the strongest in courage and industry.[391]

Success in natural history requires imperialism. "[U]nfortunately, the best nations, or even more correctly, the only truly cultured races, the standard-bearers of all human progress, all too frequently resolve in their pacifistic blindness to renounce new acquisitions of soil and content themselves with 'internal' colonization" – i.e., the improvement of their own territory – "while the inferior races [e.g. the English and the French] know how to secure immense living areas in the world for themselves." Because "it is always primarily the Jew who tries and succeeds in planting such mortally dangerous modes of thought in our people," the "Jewish question" must be "cleared up," the "Jewish wedge among peoples" must be removed.[392] Lenin called the end of socialism the integration of all nations in a "free union," not by imperialism.[393] The socialist means to this apolitical end would be not only political but military, so as not to reinforce existing patterns of rule, of violence, by premature nonviolence.

> Pacification is impossible in politics, and only out of unbounded
> simplicity (and sly and unctuous simplicity) can the time-
> honored police methods of – *divide et impera*, divide and rule,
> yield the unimportant, in order to preserve the essential; give
> back with one hand, and take back with the other – be taken
> for pacification.... [394]

The Great War (according to Lenin the first imperialist, non-nationalist war in modern times) would advance proletarian revolution if it did not end too soon in a pacificist muddle. The proletariat, seizing political power in one country as a result of the war, would inspire the only non-imperialist *internationale*, the proletariat of the bourgeois countries and "the oppressed classes of all countries," to overthrow the exploiting classes and their states, "in case of need using even armed force." "[N]otwithstanding all the horrors, cruelties, miseries, and tortures, inevitably connected with every war," some wars have "a progressive character." The proletariat's revolutionary vanguard should act decisively, "to *fight* for a speedy end to the war" and then, by "crushing the resistance of the bourgeoisie" worldwide, to establish the social and economic conditions that will end war as such. "Marxism is not pacifism."[395]

> Marxists have never forgotten that violence must inevitably accompany the collapse of capitalism and the birth of socialist society. That violence will constitute a period of world history, a whole era of various kinds of wars, imperialist wars, civil wars inside countries, the intermingling of the two, national wars liberating the nationalities oppressed by the imperialists and by various combinations of imperialist powers that will inevitably enter into various alliances in the epoch of tremendous state-capitalist and military trusts and syndicates. This epoch, an epoch of gigantic cataclysms, of mass decisions forcibly imposed by war, of crises, has begun and it is only beginning.[396]

At certain junctures in this apocalypse, the proletarian vanguard will make appeal to pacifist sentiments. "You and I have both fought against pacifism as a program for the revolutionary proletarian party," Lenin wrote to his colleague G.V. Chicherin. "But who has ever denied the use of pacifists by that party to soften up the enemy, the bourgeoisie?" Trade agreements and temporary alliances with bourgeois parties and governments will form part of this strategy, serving much the same function as propaganda in wartime.[397] Domestically, a war policy means terror as an instrument not merely of solidifying tyrannic rule but of remaking human nature, radically redirecting the course of human natural history. In this the historicist tyrannies have followed a hint from Rousseau. "Most peoples, like most men, are docile only in youth; as they grow old they become incorrigible." Only violence and revolution cause the "horror of the past" that "takes the place of forgetfulness." "[T]he State, set on fire by civil wars, is born again, so to speak, from the ashes."[398] Although national socialists and other rightists tended to be as reticent in discussing the use of terror as they were assiduous in practicing it,[399] the Leninists are much more open. Although "terror can never be a regular military operation," Lenin wrote in 1901, it can "serve as one of the methods employed by a decisive assault." After the revolution "the state will be an instrument of violence exercised by the proletariat against the bourgeoisie." Whereas during the French Revolution, "the guillotine *only* terrorized, *only* broke active resistance, for us, *this is not enough*." The "forcible suppression of the exploiters" by the proletarian vanguard, of the minority by the leaders of the majority, must be "legalize[d]...as a principle, plainly, without any make-believe or embellishment." Not only active but passive resistance must be broken. Not only resistance must be broken, but the active cooperation by those surviving bourgeois elements that are 'corrigible' must be compelled.[400] The exact numbers of those destroyed and those who would survive remained an open question to Lenin's partner, Trotsky:

> History works with titanic relentlessness. What is the Rheims Cathedral to History? And what a few hundred or thousand political reputations? And what the life or death of hundreds of thousands or of millions?[401]

The attack on the bourgeois order thus results in anti-individualism quite literally with a vengeance. The Russian Marxist Karl Kautsky objected to the "bloody terrorism practiced by Socialist Governments" that "justif[ied] their slaughter on the grounds of the rights of the Revolution." He argued that the Paris Commune of 1848 described by Marx in his articles "The Class Struggles in France, 1848 to 1850," was "far removed...from any form of terrorism" and, despite "violent" factional infighting, the socialists were "inspired throughout with a spirit of humanity" not seen in Lenin's regime.[402] Trotsky replied not by "trying to defend 'terrorism' in itself" but by "defend[ing] the historical laws of the proletarian revolution": "History has not yet found other means to advance humanity than opposing every time to conservative violence of the condemned classes the revolutionary violence of the progressive class." 'Democracy' or commercial republicanism is obsolete, unable to "resist the pressure of contemporary [class] antagonisms." Terror, violence by the revolutionary state, is therefore a necessary means to the most just end, as none but a "Quaker hypocrite" will deny. The only bad terror is terror by the reactionary classes against revolutionaries. "Revolution is revolution only because it reduces all contradictions to the alternative of life or death"; good lives and good deaths advance the historical dialectic. "Whether this method is good or bad from the point of view of normative philosophy, I do not know, and I must confess I am not interested in knowing."[403]

Hindsight allows anyone now to conclude that 'history' has judged tyranno-historicism and condemned it. Bertrand Russell's foresight was rarer. "Believ[ing] that Communism is necessary to the world," he still denied that the dictatorship of the proletarian vanguard could result in "a stable or desirable form of Communism." The regime of spiritedness provokes spirited resistance, which will lead to Bolshevism's defeat by 'capitalism,' or Bolshevism's victory "accompanied by a complete loss of their ideals and a regime of Napoleonic imperialism," or a "prolonged world-war" ending in the destruction of civilization.[404] Political minorities other than Bolshevists might also turn to violence in the struggle for power.

> Bolsheviks tacitly assume that every other party will preserve [respect for the law and the constitution] while they themselves, unhindered, prepare the revolution. But if their philosophy of violence becomes popular, there is not the slightest reason to suppose that they will be its beneficiaries....
> The civilized nations have accepted democratic government as a method of settling internal disputes without violence. Democratic government may have all the faults attributed to it, but it has the one great merit that people are, on the whole, willing to accept it as a substitute for civil war in political disputes. Whoever sets to work to weaken this acceptance, whether in Ulster or in Moscow, is taking a fearful responsibility. Civilization is not so stable that it cannot be broken up; and a condition of lawless violence is not one out of which any good thing is likely to emerge.[405]

Russell published those words two years before Mussolini took power in Rome, thirteen years before Hitler won power by election. This should have been the common sense of the matter, at least in the established commercial republics. Historicists want certain principles deemed philosophic to saturate the 'consciousness' of all the people. This requires not merely the subjects' silence but their enthusiastic public consent, the emptying out of private thoughts and their replacement with correct beliefs, as was foreseen near the beginning of the historicist project.[406] Add to this doctrine the seizure of political power and the results should have been predictable and were in fact noticed quickly. These included state-sponsored terror, compulsory or slave-labor, economic egalitarianism as a figleaf for a corrupt oligarchy (one that, unlike other oligarchies, cannot even generate much wealth), a parasite-class of spies, the ruin of agriculture.[407] What Russell calls "the habits of despotism"[408] intensify the very problem of human 'alienation' from government that both Marxism and national socialism claim to be able to solve.[409] This must lead ultimately not to union, commune-ism, but to disunity, to war against the warriors who claim to war in order to end wars.[410] Maritain writes that the new tyranny brings "not a revolution which finally gives control to the people, but an ultimate disintegration by a slow rotting of human conscience within it.[411] Constant insists that this disintegration will betoken health as much as decadence.

> No matter how debased a nation might appear from the outside, generous affections will always find refuge inside a few isolated spirits, and there, outraged, they will slowly ferment. The vault of the assemblies can resound with furious declamations, the walls of the palaces with expressions of contempt for the human race; the flatterers of tyrants denounce courage to them. But no century will ever be so disinherited by heaven as to present the whole of mankind as despotism would need to have it. The hatred of oppression, either in the name of a single individual or in the name of all, is transmitted from age to age. The future will not betray this good cause.[412]

7. *The Advance of Republicanism and the Perpetuation of Peace*

The defeat or exhaustion of tyranno-historicist regimes has renewed intellectuals' interest in the commercial republics, which generate more wealth and even win more wars than the new tyrannies. In the 1930s Einstein complained that "of late pacifists have harmed rather than helped the cause of democracy" by ill-judged calls for the appeasement of tyrants.[413] Later pacifists and pacificists have found it increasingly difficult to slight the regimes that protect even as they frustrate peace-minded citizens, regimes that actually do make peace among others of their own kind.

If commercial republics establish the civil and international peace their first partisans expected from them, and if this peace is good or at least better than other practicable options, then the question of how to increase the numbers of commercial republics remains urgent. This is Kant's question, and altogether a more pointed one than his other practical political question, 'Is the human race constantly progressing?' An historian of just-war theories calls the question of the advance of commercial republicanism and 'perpetual peace' "circular." In order to establish peacemaking political institutions citizens must desire peace, but if citizens already desire peace they will enjoy it without needing any unusual institutions.[414] This argument has some merit, but not enough. Even if everyone *now* desires peace, will everyone desire it *later*? Will it not be prudent to establish peacemaking institutions while the consensual iron is hot? Further, everyone now does not desire peace; 'everyone' has never desired peace, and may never.[415] But does international peace need the consent of everyone?

Civil peace does not. Civil peace needs the consent of most, not all — often for reasons having little to do with the desire for peace. If citizens' warlike passions can be rechanneled in peaceful directions despite themselves, the ambitions of countries might be similarly rechanneled.

Kant shares Hobbes' belief that nature breeds war among human beings. The natural conditions of pain and death thwart the natural human desire for happiness; the disjunction between the natural conditions imposed upon the species and the natural end of each individual causes man's restlessness and dissatisfaction — *in extremis*, his wars. 'Culture' or "the production in a rational being of an aptitude for any ends whatever of his own choosing" alone leads reliably to human satisfaction. Culture liberates the human will from "the despotism of desires," desires "provided us" by nature merely to prevent us from neglecting "the animal part of our nature." We should not cut these "leading strings" but we can tighten or slacken them. The principal 'cultural' means of achieving regulated liberty from desires is the formation of a "civil community." War spurs human beings to found such communities and then to work to found "a *cosmopolitan* whale," a "system of all states that are in danger of acting injuriously to one another." "[T]he evils visited upon us, now by nature, now by the truculent egoism of man, evoke the energies of the soul, and give it strength and courage" to resist unlawful force and to "quicken in us a sense that in the depths of our nature there is some aptitude for higher ends"; human beings are "but a means to an undetermined final end." The final end of the human species is an as yet unknown act of self-legislation bring peace, constituting new, republican Leviathans. This legislation will be consistent with the two highest individual goods, the physical good of happiness and the moral good of the moral law or categorical imperative, that is "the earnest will" (achieved or not) to treat others as ends not as means.[416]

In forecasting this history, Kant avoids political sentimentalisms of all kinds. Dramatic mass uprisings of 'the people' play no part; revolutions proceed "from top to bottom" through education.[417] Republican government owes its superiority to other regimes not to any improvement of citizens' moral character but from its intelligent exploitation of their selfishness, arraying individual egoists against each other so "that one moderates or destroys the ruinous effects" — not the evil motives or vices — "of the other," thus "forc[ing]" men to be "good citizen[s] even if not...morally good person[s]." Nor does the act of founding a republic require moral virtue on the part of statesmen. Kant goes so far as to say that "the problem of organizing a state, however hard it may seem, can be solved even for a race of devils, if only they are intelligent." Under these circumstances international wars serve the same salutary function; they avoid the "soulless despotism" of some Chinese-like "universal monarchy" by strengthening men's bodies and wills, spurring them to independence, to resistance to any central authority. Meanwhile, "the spirit of commerce, which is incompatible with war, sooner or later gains the upper hand in every state." While not by any means a moral substitute for war, commerce does serve the good of the species by exploiting human selfishness while strengthening the competition that permits free will, morality's indispensable foundation, to flourish. Commerce enables the regulated antagonism of free society, "the social unsociability of men," to extend worldwide. Sheep-like or despotic peace would ruin the human species; without "vainglory, lust for power, and avarice," "all the excellent natural capacities of mankind would forever sleep, undeveloped." Sound regimes and a lawful international system are interrelated, but not so tightly interrelated as to prevent incremental progress towards both.[418]

> Through war, through the taxing and never-ending accumulation of armament, through the want which any state, even in peacetime, must suffer internally, Nature forces them to make at first adequate and tentative attempts; finally, after devastations, revolutions, and even complete exhaustion, she brings them to that which reason could have told them at the

beginning and with far less sad experience, to wit, to step from the lawless condition of savages into a league of nations.[419]

There is no predictable, inevitable course of events forecast here. Kant admits three possible courses of events: states will fall into a peaceable relationship randomly, as atoms form molecules; there will be a regular or lawful, if rough, progress to fully-realized universal human morality; humanity will fail to progress, resulting in "barbarous devastation."[420] In his desire to actualize the second possibility, Kant finally does not quite dismiss the practical effectiveness of morality, of philosophy, or of statesmanship. Although "it would be absurd to demand that every defect [in a regime] be immediately and impetuously changed, since the disruption of the bonds of civil society or a union of world citizens before a better constitution is ready to take its place is against all politics agreeing with morality," statesmen should prepare citizens' minds for political reforms. For example, a despot may rule by law in order to accustom the people to "the influence of the idea of the rule of law" and republicanism. Similarly, because "a state cannot be expected to renounce its constitution even though it is a despotic one (which has the advantage of being stronger in relation to foreign enemies) so long as it is exposed to the danger of being swallowed up by other states," Kant urges that statesmen adopt the morality of the categorical imperative to replace ends-oriented moralities. Not your country's welfare or happiness but "the pure concept of duty of right" should guide statesmen's actions. If it does, the end of perpetual peace will follow ever more surely, as evil states destroy themselves and dutiful states enjoy the fruits of their just conduct. "Decency" being the "real basis of all true sociability" because it "inspire[s] others to respect," the fruits of just conduct include peace with other dutiful states. A morality of rules and duties serves human beings better than a morality of ends because we cannot sufficiently foresee the effects of our actions and are perhaps too inclined to favor ourselves in our pursuit of happiness.[421] It should be noted that Kant's eschewal of a morality of ends is itself justified by Kant's claim to foresee the good effects of that eschewal. Rule ends out of ethics and the invention of 'metaethics' soon follows.

The categorical imperative, the rule that human beings shall be treated as ends not as means, clearly makes aggressive war morally dubious. It may

make war itself morally dubious.[422]   The emphasis on legalism in
international politics as conducted by some republicans who replace the
doctrine of just and unjust war with 'aggressive war' and 'defensive war'
clearly stems from Kantian morality. Legalism tends to conflate the real with
the 'ideal' because laws, unlike a Platonic idea or even an Aristotelian *telos*,
are made to be fulfilled not broken. In this sense a scholar is right to argue
that Kant anticipates the characteristic aspirations of historicism.[423]
Inasmuch as several of the more radical historicists expect the end of political
life as such in a sort of internalized politics or 'anarchism,' Aron well observes
that "acceptance of the principle that each person must be considered as a
finality in himself would require not a modification of but an end to
statecraft."[424] Kant himself retains too much prudence to push his doctrines
to such absurd lengths. He wittily publicizes a "Secret Article for Perpetual
Peace" stipulating that "the opinions of philosophers on the conditions of the
possibility of public peace shall be consulted by those states armed for war."
Philosopher-kings and royal philosophers are "not to be expected" or even
desired, "since the possession of power inevitably corrupts the untrammeled
judgment of reason."[425] But philosophers, first and foremost Kant himself,
will exercise power without literally possessing it by advancing a non-utopian
philosophic "millenarianism." "[T]he Idea can help, though only from afar, to
bring the millenium to pass" as Enlightenment "step by step ascend[s] to the
throne and influence[s] the principles of government." Philosophers should
"work out a universal history according to a natural plan directed to achieving
the civic union of the human race," specifically a series of histories showing
"what the various nations and governments have contributed to the goal of
world citizenship, and what they have done to damage it." This requires the
creation of an 'Idea' in the Kantian sense of the word – an a *priori* creation of
the human mind corresponding to nothing that physically exists but guiding its
creator and his disciples until they devise a realistic means of realizing it.[426]
For the present Kant not only does not condemn war, he praises it as morally
and politically necessary:

> Even now, the danger of war is the only factor which mitigates
> despotism. For a state cannot be powerful unless it is wealthy,
> but without liberty, wealth-producing activities cannot flourish.

> This is why a poor nation requires the broad support of a citizenry intensely committed to its survival, to take the place of its lack of wealth. But such support, again, is possible only in a free nation.[427]

The histories of the Soviet Union and Communist China qualify but do not disprove this argument, and Kant is on even firmer ground in endorsing the commercial republican contention that only regimes protecting unalienable human rights, and founded upon popular consent, representative government, and the separation of the legislative from the executive power will conduce to lasting peace.[428] Kant sees that the relations between citizens and their own government will influence that government's relations with foreign governments and peoples; Kant's republicanism of duty may be a compromise between the commercial republicanism of Locke and the more spirited republicanism of Rousseau.[429] This compromise, which results (as seen above) in legalism, may confuse some of Kant's readers with respect to regime issues, although some two centuries of historicism also have contributed to the confusion.[430] Nonetheless, Kant clearly espouses commercial republicanism of some sort, and this enables him to dismiss certain 'international law' theorists as "irritating comforters" who fail to appreciate the importance of the "internal juridical constitution" of countries, constitutions that need to be republican if an effective "league of peace" is to be established.[431]

Would confederated sovereign states keeping peace among themselves lose their civic and military courage and "lie at the mercy of the first comer?" Rousseau asks. No: If others attack, the martial virtues will persist; if no attack occurs martial virtues will be unnecessary.[432] The argument is sophistical, ignoring the possibility that a gradual softening of temper could yield a ripe and defenseless cluster of countries fit for plucking.[433] The agent plucking them might be the federal government itself grown despotic, as Kant himself acknowledges.[434] The persistence of such problems shows that liberalism cannot "elude the political." The 'us versus them' of politics "cannot be exterminated" by somehow combining morality and economics.[435] Consequently, as Kant sees, "even where civilization has reached a high pitch there remains [a] special reverence for the soldier," whose "mind is above the threats of danger" to life and comfort.[436]

> War itself, provided it is conducted with order and a sacred respect for the rights of civilians, has something sublime about it, and gives nations that carry it on in such a manner a stamp of mind only the more sublime the more numerous the dangers to which they are exposed, and which they are able to meet with fortitude. On the other hand, a prolonged peace favors the predominance of a mere commercial spirit, and with it a debasing self-interest, cowardice, and effeminacy, and tends to degrade the character of the nation.[437]

Kant writes these words – not Hegel, not Proudhon, not Marx, not Nietzsche, all of whom in various ways repeated them. The warrior gives and risks the most extreme physical harm; a 'moral substitute' for war that tried to distill the warrior's risk-taking from his harm-giving would fail to put the enemy at risk, leading to peace of one sort or another and therefore risking the perpetuation of the stern quest for right. The virtues and vices of warriors bind together inextricably.[438]

The opposite danger is almost as severe. "If war ennobles, then the most warlike nations should be the most moral, the peaceful nations the most corrupt."[439] A glance at history should suffice to show that this is not true. Yet insofar as republicanism inclines toward democracy it risks spasms of warrior-spirit. "The true Christ," Proudhon writes, with some Gallic exaggeration, "for the masses, is Alexander, Caesar, Charlemagne, Napoleon."[440] War-factions can be held as fatal to republican virtue as peace-factions, destroying the spirit of civilian rule.[441] "In one word, is there no hope of keeping a democracy *moral* except by keeping it weak?"[442] And no way of keeping it strong without erasing every vestige of democracy? In searching for answers to these questions Kant's 'idealist' philosophers will be of little assistance. It is rather the study of statesmanship and political history – not the 'History' of historicists – that brings forward the needed examples of courage, prudence, moderation, and justice, and their opposites. No 'theory,' no vision of history unfolding, can substitute for the practice of the kind of thinking that enables statesmen and other citizens of commercial republics to balance the spirited passions for justice and also for conflict with the low-but-solid appetites for comfort and gain.[443] For pacifists and for many pacificists this means recalling the argument of C.S. Lewis:

> Only liberal societies tolerate Pacifists. In the liberal society, the number of Pacifists will either be large enough to cripple the state as a belligerent, or not. If not, you have done nothing. If it is large enough, then you have handed over the state which does tolerate Pacifists to its totalitarian neighbor who does not. Pacifism of this sort is taking the straight road to a world in which there will be no Pacifists.[444]

Pacifists will help their own cause best by never allowing the liberty they enjoy in the commercial republics to become habitual but to remind themselves of its conditions.[445] Commercial republicans generally will perpetuate their preferred regimes by recognizing the tensions between commerce and republicanism as well as their congruence. It may be that this very tension helps to prevent both from declining.

8. *International Law: In What Senses It May Be Said to Exist*

A world full of stable commercial republics has never existed. If it did it might decline. The prospect of massive difficulties in establishing and maintaining these regimes throughout the world, and so to advance peace, can impel cautious persons to hope for some more orderly framework than the concatenation of so-called nation-states. International law is one such framework. What is international law? And is it actual? Is it really law? The proffered answers to the last question have "depended mainly on the definition of law chosen as a starting-point," Lauterpacht accurately remarks.[446] Herodotus describes Xerxes' refusal "to act like the Lacedaemonians, who, by killing the heralds, had broken the laws which all men held in common."[447] Here 'international law' would mean simply the alleged similarities among all the different law codes, each given authority by the political regime that generated it. No over-arching standard need exist — only undergirding ones, and perhaps not even these, as different regimes may enact the same law for different reasons. Montesquieu offers a quasi-Newtonian definition of international law as "the political law of the nations considered in their relation with each other."[448] In this definition the nations might as well be planets orbiting a common sun, governed, to be sure, by the same force or forces but only by forces; international law is as nations do to one another, a law in the way physical 'laws' are laws. Also, and not trivially, there are effective 'international' laws within most individual countries, which after all consist of more than one ethnic groups or nations. Obviously, these three conceptions of international law do not serve as examples of international law as it has come to be defined in ordinary usage. Grotius writes that good faith sustains individual countries and "that greater society of states" in which countries find themselves.[449] International law is law among countries, not only among nations, law that presupposes (at least 'ideally') the existence of a worldwide political order that is trust-worthy.[450] Thus Lauterpacht:

> International law is the body of rules of conduct, enforceable by external sanction, which confer rights and impose obligations primarily, though not exclusively, upon sovereign States and which owe their validity both to the consent of States as expressed in custom and treaties and to the fact of an international community of states and individuals.[451]

Because laws must bind but countries seldom recognize any authority over them, international 'law' frequently fails to act fully *as* law. Its violation can become almost routine.[452]

Enforcement of international laws at times requires military force, risking a "perpetual war for perpetual peace."[453] Yet to refrain from wars would be to abandon the enforcement of last resort that alone may prevail when other sanctions do not. These sanctions include military intervention in civil wars, as Kant and John Stuart Mill understand, and as the American Founders were grateful to acknowledge.[454] Vattel outlines this dilemma well by first denying the justice of military intervention in other countries' disputes, and then asserting it. Law is contract, and if a person or a country does not violate its contract with us, we have no justification for requiring justice toward others. To intervene internationally would be to "destroy the foundations" of the "natural society" of all countries, imperiling all, in much the same way as busybodies and prigs roil domestic waters. But if "a detestable tyrant" or "an unjust and rebellious people" violate the natural law and provoke civil war, "every man of courage may justly purge [them] from the earth."[455] And so may every nation of courage.

Absent a supreme international authority, is international law not, in Senator Moynihan's words, "an idea espoused in about equal proportion by people who would believe anything and those who believe nothing"? It can be little more than that – perhaps only a series of (at best) useful written agreements – if it has nothing but a conventional foundation.[456] Grotius observes that "in our day, as in former times, there is no lack of men who view this branch of the law with contempt as having no reality outside of an empty name," men who believe that "might makes right," that Mars rules all controversies between nations and that war is "irreconcilable with all law." Against this view Grotius urges the existence of natural justice and the natural human desire for peaceful, prudently organized social life that laws maintain:[457]

> ....it is meet for the nature of man, within the limitations of human intelligence, to follow the direction of a well-tempered judgment, being neither led astray by fear or the allurement of immediate pleasure, nor carried away by rash impulse. Whatever is clearly at variance with such judgment is understood to be contrary also to the law of nature, that is, to the nature of man.[458]

Conventional law cannot itself do this; it can help statesmen do it. International law, established among all states, or a great many states by mutual consent for common advantage, will help statesmen defend and express human sociability by regulating trade and providing agreements for just military defense. War undertaken "for the enforcement of rights" and "carried on only within the bounds of law and good faith" is sanctioned by natural justice. Central to Grotius' Prolegomena is the distinction between changeable conventional law and the natural law, which is the rule of moderation and of practical reason. The natural law underlies international law; it is the absolute standard from which contracts (including treaties) receive their legitimacy. International law is consent among countries to contracts in accordance with natural law. It may be enforced in a war by a country that metes out punishment to violators "in a degree proportionate to the injustice that lies in their action."[459]

Writers who follow Machiavelli also identify international law with the natural law, but it is an entirely different natural law. "[F]ishes enjoy the water, and the greater devour the lesser by natural right" – nature's 'right' being "coextensive with her power." "[T]he right of the supreme authorities is nothing else than simple natural right" or power.[460] Vattel recognizes that Hobbes "give[s] us a distinct though imperfect idea" of international law as natural law but calls Hobbes' principles "detestable" because they exclude the mutual assistance or sociality implied by the human capacities for speech and reason.[461] Subsequent writers who have wanted to avoid criticism from the Machiavellian or 'realist' school while rejecting Machiavelli's crabbed misconceptions of human nature ransack human experience for ways of expressing Vattel's thought without having recourse to natural law and the controversies it brings in its train. Lauterpacht appeals to "the ultimate solidarity of interests" of the "international community of states," to the "unity of moral sentiment inherent in the very nature of man," and to basic principles of all "civilized nations." He prefers not "to embark upon the uncertain path of enquiring as to the meaning" of 'civilized,' nor does he explain the common interests of states or the supposed unity of moral sentiment. He does warn against "embarrassment" about the "many ways" in which the principles of international law resemble natural law, whose influence he judges to be "more enduring and more beneficent" than that of positivism.[462] It is hard to resist concluding that Lauterpacht adheres to natural law without daring openly to associate himself with the name. Brierly lists six sources of modern international law: treaties, custom, consensual rules, judicial precedents, text-writers, and, finally, reason. Of these he calls custom primary. He explicitly rejects the doctrine of natural rights, denies that natural law should overrule positive law, and calls the law of nature "variable." But he concedes that "the ultimate explanation of the binding force of all law is that man, whether he is a single individual or whether he is associated with other men in a state, is constrained, in so far as he is a *reasonable being*, to believe that *order a not chaos is the governing principle of the world* in which he has to live."[463] The roots of natural right remain even after its branches have been hacked away.

Still, to exist in practice international law will need, in Kant's phrase, "a juridical condition." Kant strictly insists on federations of commercial republics.[464] Vattel more optimistically contends that federations are not necessary. Although governments exist in a 'state of nature' with one another, governments would not exist at all if the nations they represent had not left the 'state of nature.' Individuals in the 'state of nature' (and, too often, in civil society) act out of "blind rashness" and "whim." Governments do so much less often, precisely because they reflect civil society. Governments can be brought to cooperate with one another and "can be sufficiently regulated by the natural law" without any super-government to oversee them. A super-government would also abrogate the independence 'national' governments need to govern their peoples. "The Law of Nations is the law of sovereigns."[465]

More optimistic still are more recent writers who believe that a juridical condition can exist without any enforcement by war at all, particularly enforcement by a party to the dispute. Such warfare cannot be a sanction in a legal sense, although a disinterested third party presumably could launch a war of sanction.[466] Domestic courts, in this view, serve as more reliable enforcers of international law via the doctrine of incorporation, whereby treaties and international laws become part of each country's 'law of the land.'[467] The courts in their turn judge accordance with acts of the legislatures, as seen for example in Article III, Section 8 of the United States Constitution, which empowers Congress "to define and punish piracies and felonies committed on the high seas, and offenses against the law of nations." But clearly this does not solve the problem of impartiality, given the ingenuity with which definitions may be manipulated by legislatures and courts.

This fact does not faze the optimists, who observe that domestic law in most civil societies at most times had no system of enforcement. Enforcement, third-party judges, even legislation itself are not required for law to exist and for it to be obeyed. Custom can be powerful, and international law, lacking any centralized system of enforcement, can appeal to the power of custom.[468] The obvious riposte – that custom simply is not as powerful as it used to be – has been stated in a scholarly manner by Stanley Hoffmann, who recognizes that custom-bound societies are "highly integrated" societies, whereas international 'society' is not. The analogies drawn between tribal villages without formal laws or strong executives (but often *with* impartial judges) and the equally unenforced (but often legally formalized) international 'society' of recent centuries simply cannot be sustained.[469]

An honest writer will admit that international law in the conventional sense is much of it rhetoric. Its institutional foundations are weak. Quincy Wright more or less admits this, on the way toward urging the gradual establishment of a world government that would give teeth to the conventions.[470] Calls for third-party arbitration of international disputes amount to similar exercises in jawboning.[471] Although jaw-jaw is usually better than war-war, Vattel reminds his readers of those times when it is not:

> But if any one should seek to rob a Nation of an essential right, of a right without which it can not hope to maintain its existence, if an ambitious neighbor should threaten the liberty of a Republic or attempt to subject and enslave it, the Nation will take counsel only of its courage. A settlement by conference will not even be attempted with respect to so repulsive a pretension.[472]

Without enforcement, self-enforcement if need be, "the word of law would degenerate to a moral recommendation to be ignored at will."[473]

9. *World Government*

"Too many public men, blinded by too high an opinion of themselves, have not yet realized the profound problems of a lasting peace," wrote Georges Clemenceau, who had endured Woodrow Wilson at the Versailles Conference. "[F]or a lasting peace it is necessary for both sides to have the same fundamental ideas of right and the same quality of good faith."[474] The history of 'peace plans,' littered with wreckage caused by principled disagreements,[475] induces some to dream of international law enforced by a worldwide government. Because "God and nature make nothing in vain," there must be a purpose for human civilization worldwide. The distinctively human natural end or purpose is intellectual development, theoretical and practical, for which peace is the indispensable condition. Although God is "the true ground of unity," Dante writes, on earth human beings need an effective ruler to prevent the divisions that lead to wars. A secular world-ruler will have everything he desires — quite literally the whole world — and therefore will not act unjustly.[476] Unfortunately for this argument, there are different kinds of possession. The world ruler would 'have' his neighbor's wife in the sense that he rules over her juridically, but this might not be the kind of having he desires. Injustices remain likely. The same problems would occur if the world ruler were plural, a world-parliament, although it is difficult to say if a plurality of governors would dilute the problems or multiply them.[477]

Many writers therefore prefer to approach world government 'from below,' through economic and social reforms. Montesquieu writes that "movable effects, such as silver, notes, letters of exchange, shares in companies, ships, and all commodities, belong to the whole world, which, in this regard comprises but a single state of which all societies are members."[478] Commerce and 'Enlightenment' combine to destroy "the moral basis of national defense" while, their proponents hope, making national defense increasingly unnecessary. Although this recommendation occurs first in Hobbes it reappears in numerous writers considered rather more 'idealistic' than Hobbes.[479] Boulding envisions "the world as a total system," in terms of its nonliving physical features, its biology, its social, economic, political, communications, and moral systems, all of them evolving toward a "world 'superculture,'" although not necessarily toward a world government, which in any event might be rent by civil wars. The 'Enlightenment' model extends so far as biology; Boulding conceives of evolution as "a process in information [i.e., DNA transmission and alteration] rather than in just matter and energy." The constant movement typical of commerce thus becomes a comprehensive metaphor for every aspect of life on earth, rather at the expense (as in Hegel) of stable structures.[480]

In this not yet entirely enlightened world, 'globalism' has resulted in the most radical instability, global warfare, at least five times in the last 500 years.[481] This fact gives credence to the warning of Rousseau when he discussed a plan for a European government published by his contemporary the Abbe St. Pierre: "[W]hile we admire so fair a scheme, let us console ourselves for the fact that it was not carried into execution, by the reflection that it could only have been done by violent means which would have staggered humanity."[482] Many pacificists blame modern wars not on the existence of the wrong kinds of regimes but on the existence of plural regimes, upon the "international anarchy" that results from multiple sovereignties. Armed anarchy countervails against interdependence.[483] Paraphrasing Madison, Mortimer J. Adler claims that "only angels can live together in peace without living under the coercive force of government." The nations need a world government to enforce peace, and a world government needs a founder or legislator (to use Rousseau's word) of "the most sublime virtue" who can make law bringing the particular national wills into conformity with the general will to the good.[484] "Arm the law, not the litigants"; "if there is to be peace among nations there must be universal law" enforced by a universal government.[485]

There being some dispute concerning the character of the best regime, world-government pacificists must address the question of what kind of government they would institute, and how the rival countries could be brought to accept its authority. Few share the sunniness of John Middleton Murry, writing in the aftermath of the Second World War, who believed the "Capitalist and Communist societies have merely to resolve not to go to war with one another, and the thing is done," after which happy agreement "they must agree to the establishment of an authority which has the power to decide their disputes."[486] C.E.M. Joad's prewar optimism with regard to Hitler, if no less silly, took a more elaborate form. "[R]eplacing the policy of intimidation with the policy of appeasement" will make the example of political liberty "contagious." Therefore, allow the Nazi "triumphs which are not extorted from your weakness, but are conceded by your strength" (and hope he will know the difference). Call an international conference to deal with his "economic grievances." Redress them. Form an international commission with members from the major manufacturing countries to administer the equitable distribution of world territories and raw materials. The British Empire should disarm, declare its intention not to defend its empire by force, introduce free trade, and use monies saved in administrative and military costs for goodwill missions to foreign countries, public works, and other worthy projects.[487]

> It may, of course, be said, and on the basis of *Mein Kampf* it is said, that Hitler is incorrigibly aggressive and will be content with nothing short of war. It may be so, but if it is so, why, I

should like to know, has not Hitler gone to war with us already?[488]

The year was 1939. Unlike Joad, Hitler understood that adequate war preparation can take time.

More sensible observers have understood that radical political differences will not yield to wishes, however fervent and sincere.[489] Some have urged a confederation of commercial republics, pending salutary changes in the tyrannized nations.[490] This recourse discloses the fallaciousness of Adler's argument. Multiple sovereignties cannot be the cause of war because all *peoples* do live under government's coercive force — namely, their own government's coercive force. The relevant indicator of international peacefulness is the regime, not the mere existence of any regime. This is why Rousseau's notion of a confederation among the heterogeneous European regimes of the eighteenth century had no chance to succeed, and subsequent urgings of this sort, all animated by a call to supposedly shared self-interest, invariably fail.[491] Commercial republican world-federationists can be equally jejune, of course, following Paine, who believed that "it is at the present time [1790] pretty certain that the peoples of France, England, and America, who are at once enlightened and enlightening, will be able in the future to serve as models of good government to the universe and will also have sufficient influence to compel the practical enforcement of it everywhere."[492]

A more subtle approach to internationalism may be seen in advocates of a bureaucratic world government. In 1959 one such group issued a report stating that "We note with satisfaction the progress that has been achieved, particularly in some of the specialized agencies [of the United Nations Organization], in developing what might be called quasi legislation: procedures for the establishment of rules which bind member states, or create some limited type of obligation for them, even without their expressed consent or ratification." The authors quickly added that they did not want to eliminate government by consent. "But it is clear that statesmen whose eyes are fixed less on the dogma of sovereignty than upon the need for promoting the interests of their people in an interdependent world can and should identify many areas where the quasi-legislative process may be used to advantage." Under these circumstances the United Nations "serves as a kind of continuous constitutional convention."[493] It may be that bureaucracy attracts many pacificists because bureaucracy is already international in one sense: all modern regimes today have a bureaucracy. Bureaucracy can be imagined as a sort of universal regime — a bourgeois aristocracy, to speak paradoxically. This is clearly how Hegel supposed things to be at the 'end of history.'[494] Bureaucracy or 'management' appears to be a profoundly unwarlike means of conquest through social science and carefully directed technology — Machiavellianism in horn-rimmed glasses. Bureaucratic life seems to soften the bourgeois passion for liberty, the one passion that leads it to 'stand up for itself' even to the point of war. Bureaucratic life also dilutes the egalitarianism of the bourgeoisie, accustoming it to a stable hierarchy.[495]

Objections to a worldwide bureaucracy range from doubts concerning its practicability[496] to moral and political criticisms vindicating the place of 'nation-states' in human life. 'Nation-states' guard human beings from a universal despotism from which there could be no escape except through civil war and a return to 'nation-states.' Bureaucracy will not prevent despotism; it will abet it, crushing all beneath a blank uniformity imposed by technique.[497] Bureaucracy represents the attempt to combine the universal or transpolitical character of the human mind with the concrete realities of politics. Both the human mind and politics are natural, but not in the same way; the attempt to treat them in the same way leads to "sham universalism" — imperialism traditionally, bureaucracy in recent times.[498]

Would a worldwide commercial republic — or even a confederation of commercial republics — avoid the pretensions and dangers of other world governments?[499] No more and no less, probably, than commercial republics now avoid the drawbacks of other regimes in existing 'nation-states.' This government could only be built by statesmen who rejected historicist organicism, the contemporary underpinning of despotism:

> The way that takes the nation as the sovereign unit treats it as if it were itself a person, with the government its head and the citizens mere cells in its body. To start on this basis is to end by giving each nation, regardless of the size of its population, one vote, to be cast by its government — the citizen having little

more to say about it than a cell in his toe has to say about his own decisions.[500]

Not nations but individuals would be the units of a commercial-republican international order, a federal union that would "admit other peoples to the advantages of union with it when they rid themselves of dictators."[501] Even with proper institutional precautions, however, a world government should remain an object of suspicion. A world of many commercial republics would risk war, remotely, but would also defend liberty. A world of one commercial republic would, if the government were subverted, risk worldwide tyranny.[502]

10. Peace and 'The Other'

The Cretan lawgiver is said to have held that "what humans call peace [is] only a name; in fact, for everyone there always exists an undeclared war among all cities." Hatred for the foreigner, the other, animates much of political life throughout history.[503] This fact is often deplored by secular writers, but not often coherently. Bertrand Russell professes surprised distaste at wartime appeals "to atavistic moral notions which, in times of peace, civilized men would...repudiat[e] with contempt." He concludes that "moral reprobation is nothing but an embodiment of hatred, and hatred is a mechanical product of biological instinct," particularly fear. This does not explain how Russell himself eluded biology, nor, given Russell's insistence that "in all ethical questions" the "fundamental facts" are "feelings," why some other feeling – say, love – is privileged, superior to fear and hatred.[504]

The Hegelian claim that 'the other' embodies will – "thinking reason resolving itself into finitude" – which is to be respected and to be sharply distinguished from physical force, coercion – the action of blind nature, sheer causation or unfreedom – underlies the argument that coercion is usually wrong except when exercised in the conquest of nature. The use of force by human beings is wrong except when counteracting unintelligent force. Thus Hegel admits coercion against 'the other' only when 'the other' uses coercion first. Otherwise, coercion is evil, a denial of sociality, which Hegel associates with human freedom. It is true that coercion reminds each individual that others exist, and this reminder has been needed in history. But the end of history will bring the peace of common respect and, in the belief of left-

Hegelians, egalitarianism.[505] Except for the dubious promise of an end of history, this argument does not much differ from Kant's doctrine of defensive war. As in Kant, it is not clear how the 'us-them' passions of politics will be overcome permanently in practice.

The political soul, ruled by *thumos*, says, with de Maistre's Senator, "Ever since I began to think, war has been on my mind."[506] At its extreme it claims that "the good war hallows any cause."[507] But extremism is not ordinary, even in war, which extends rather than disjoins the citizens' enduring and everyday interests and whose participants, the warriors, are not "disproportionately drawn from the deviant or the isolated" in the community.[508] If morality requires choice, if choice pre-supposes liberty, if political liberty defends private liberty, if war is sometimes necessary to defend political liberty because tyrannical souls often can be stopped in no other way but by opposing your physical strength to their physical strength, then 'the other' in some form would only be exorcised from human life if tyrannical passions were permanently removed or at least permanently ruled. A certain caution with respect to concrete manifestations of 'otherness' such as foreigners and outlaws makes sense. This caution may be seen historically in the similarity in Latin between *hospes* or stranger and *hostis* or enemy. Such linguistic evidence reflects the inescapable need to make distinctions in the presence of real good and evil.[509]

The fact that good and evil in reality do not always coincide with political friend and enemy, respectively, should not lead us to commit the error of de Maistre and Schmitt, who radically dissociate ethics from politics. This claim leads to the inept remoralization of *Realpolitik* seen in Fascism. Because choice and therefore ethics are inseparable from political life, Fascism takes the 'realist' distinction of friend and enemy, countryman and foreigner, and makes it into a moral category, indeed a moral absolute.[510] Some pacifists and pacificists make the opposite error of disembodying morality, speaking of the thumotic passion, honor, as a purely inner or self-regarding phenomenon untouched by physical victory or defeat.[511] But it is historically true that "the shared sacrifice of war" can strengthen the political bonds of a people for good or for evil even more powerfully than shared labor does.[512]

There is an eminently practical limitation, properly a self-limitation, to political life and its ambitions. Nietzsche is right: "He who lives for the sake of combating an enemy has an interest in seeing that his enemy stays alive."[513] Even if the political soul cannot bring itself to admit that war is for the sake of peace, it must admit (if it reflects) that war cannot be perpetuated without an admixture of peace. To judge the right ratio of war to peace and to work toward its establishment distinguishes the work of statesmen from mere warriors, or makes warriors into citizens and statesmen.[514] The converse limitation needs to be recognized by pacifists, warriors-for-peace, as Ellen Key understands: "Only when there is a real wish for peace in the idea of national defense, and a real wish for defense in the peace-movement, only when the pacifists are actuated, not by a sense of opposition, but by real love for their country, will they gain all hearts."[515] Patriotism instead of a desire for a world government will correspond more closely to the natural powers of human perception and the natural limits of human feeling. Philosophy must rule any secular world government if it is to avoid despotism, but philosophy alone cannot rule most human beings, cannot sustain the institutions needed to govern them justly.[516] Those who believe otherwise succumb to mythology, albeit intellectualist mythology. The secular alternative to cosmopolitan mythology is patriotism. Patriotism is not to be confused with nationalism, a product of 'German' ideology no less prone to mythology than secular cosmopolitanism. Genuine patriots love their country because they love the land, their family, their civil society. Through the concepts of liberty, equality rightly understood, and responsibility, one pacificist observes, the United States regime has developed a patriotism that includes instead of excluding nationalities, a patriotism that does not begrudge other countries their peace.[517]

CHAPTER SEVEN

Philosophy and Modern War

1.   *The Weapons: Applications and Implications of Technique*

> Machines that are ends in themselves — is that the *umana commedia*?
>
>   Nietzsche[1]

The invention or at least the perfection of weapons of mass destruction was anticipated by the first commercial republicans. Montesquieu's Usbek slights the dilemma:

> You fear, you say, that some crueler method of destruction than that now used will be invented. No. If a fatal invention were to be made, it would soon be outlawed by international law, and unanimous agreement among nations would bury the discovery. Princes have no interest in conquering by such means. They have to be on the lookout for additional subjects, not territory.[2]

This prediction has proved true (so far) only in the tantalizingly weak yet saving sense that fear effectively 'outlaws' the use of such weapons as soon as *two* enemies have them. Still, Kant's even more optimistic contention — "Decline into wickedness cannot be incessant in the human race, for at a certain stage of disintegration it would destroy itself"[3] — must tax the credulity of our contemporaries, who have seen enormous crimes perpetrated by men of ordinary wickedness or even thoughtfulness, albeit instigated by men and ideologies of extraordinary evil. Technological progress is not the only cause of modern war's destructiveness. In an age of limited monarchies and the first stirrings of commercial republicanism Hume could regard modern wars as less destructive of life and property than the wars of antiquity, when the distribution of plunder, including slaves, made troops undisciplined, when the concentration of troops yielded more slaughter, when greater factionalism and stricter laws fomented an inhumane severity, when still-primitive commerce and manufacturing forged no strong ties among polities.[4] But increasing democratization failed to revive the measured spiritedness of aristocracy that the spirit of commerce had superseded. "In the somber wars of modern democracy chivalry finds no place. Dull butcheries on a gigantic scale and mass efforts overwhelm all detached sentiments."[5] With conscription "raising armies from the whole manhood of the nation," with modern financial and commercial systems making "the credit of the whole country...available for the purposes of war," war "became unfettered."[6] As a result the "Century of the Common Man," the twentieth century, has seen not only a "larger and more varied life" for almost all democrats, but also "more common men killing each other with greater facility than any other five centuries in the history of the world." The human "brain got no bigger, but it buzzed the more."[7] More than a decade before the invention of nuclear weapons, Guglielmo Ferrero saw an "obsession with war" in the contemporary West, an obsession "which unnerves us from within and feeds upon itself."[8]

> People have never thought so much of war and its future horrors, real or imaginary, with millions of men, women and children killed at a stroke. It would seem that our age has a foreboding that some day or other it is sure to be wiped out in some nightmare outburst of violence.[9]

Ferrero argues that Bismarck's Germany had revived the nationalist "military romanticism" of the French Revolution — the methods of democracy bent to the purposes of despotism — and brought on "the war of fantastic proportions, the 'super' war." "For the first time, Death was armed with an electric scythe."[10] The reality of war for both soldier and civilian became increasingly grim even as the dream of war took on a spurious glamor for the intellectual and political elites.[11] War became the rule of chance for those who experienced it,[12] "a chaos of human abasement,"[13] even as the new methods enabled rulers to suppose they commanded the more. While modern war generally and nuclear war especially tend to disappoint Hegel's hopes for war as an heroic antidote to bourgeois malaise,[14] war continues to inflame the ambitions of rulers, who then seek ever grander justifications for the sacrifices they impose.

While the pacifist deplores the "abstract hatred" of modern war,[15] the bellecist derides the abstract humanitarianism of the would-be ruler, the pacifist.[16] Neither sees himself as a mirror-image of the other, constructing "a world of self-confirming theorems invit[ing] fantasies of control over events that we do not have" – "thinkers of the abstracted unthinkable."[17] While 'German' bellecists refuse to distinguish between soldiers and civilians, dragooning all into the 'war effort' and attacking all of 'the enemy's' population, 'German' pacifists refuse on principle to distinguish friends from enemies. Both act under the sway of a misconceived universal.

Under the circumstances the rejection of modern war as an instrument of justice is understandable. Even if the end can justify the means, it does not therefore justify any means. As war becomes increasingly destructive and 'tyrannical,' "it becomes less and less well suited to the ends of justice." As there can be no real winner in modern war, political liberty will be subverted, and morality will be abandoned.[18] This condition was anticipated by Jean de Bloch prior to the First World War[19] and became a commonplace of political rhetoric in the decades after it.[20] It is, however, not exactly true. Limited wars have persisted, even multiplied.[21] Even major wars, before the invention of nuclear weapons, proved winnable and ultimately preservative of justice, although at a devastatingly high cost. Modern war, as Proudhon recognizes, is "as brutal among the civilized as it is among the barbarians";[22] it is not clear that it must be so, or that even a barbaric war subverts justice in the long run.[23] Some writers describe modern war as being usually more humane than the wars of antiquity. Colmar von der Goltz writes that "the more startling and intense the effects of the weapons, the sooner do they produce a deterrent effect, and thus it comes to pass that battles generally are less bloody in proportion as the engines of destruction have attained greater perfection."[24] The German's confidence must have been deeply embarrassed by the First World War. It also would have been embarrassed by consideration of the American Civil War, where intense battles indeed did not last long, but were repeated over and over for years until one army was destroyed.[25] Still, there is evidence and argument to suggest that it was not only advanced technology or mass mobilization that made these wars so bloody but mistaken strategy and, in the case of the World War, an ideologically-based attachment to offensive war.[26] Also, it is clear that recent technological refinements increasing the accuracy of modern weapons can largely obviate their hitherto indiscriminate character.

Most kinds of nuclear weapons remain indiscriminate, destroying soldiers and civilians alike in an inferno of explosion, heat, and radiation. When two enemies possess these weapons in sufficient number and kind to destroy each other, one must question, with Henry Kissinger, the significance of superiority in nuclear arms.[27] But even in this extreme circumstance the old virtues of courage and prudence remain indispensable. The very scientific method that invented the weapons that make any major war politically implausible could generate new weapons that make nuclear weapons themselves obsolete. Even without such inventions, a fearful or complacent country could so neglect its nuclear arsenal for so long that a tenacious enemy, assiduously enhancing his own arsenal, could fight and win a nuclear war by launching an unanswerably devastating first strike.[28] The likelihood of this is small. The likelihood will remain small as long as certain virtues steel the resolution and govern the actions of citizens in the commercial republics. If the perhaps temporary obsolescence of all-out war between major countries makes the war-virtues less necessary, the closely related civic virtues become all the more pertinent. "[N]uclear power makes it possible, for the first time in history, to shift the balance of power solely through developments *within* the territory of another sovereign state."[29] The internal structure of each country and the virtues that animate and sustain that structure can make the difference between peace preserved and peace lost.

Among the 'developed' countries the trend has been toward peace. Except for the 1956 Soviet invasion of Hungary, one writer declares, there have been no wars among the 44 wealthiest nations since 1945.[30] War is a form of predation, and predators by nature prefer to select the most vulnerable prey. Modern war generally and nuclear war especially impose a sort of invulnerability through vulnerability. Raymond Aron describes the defenses of the 'great powers' as "completely permeable," completely open to air attacks with nuclear weapons, but only at the highest risk to the attacker, who is similarly threatened. The result is "a new kind of impermeability,"[31] a psychological 'defense' based upon physical power unimpeded by reliable physical barriers. This combination of brute power with *mentality* (in the form of technique, in the form of character, and even in the form of principles) instances the *concrete abstractedness* of modern warfare, where underlying physical realities often play themselves out on nothing more dangerous than a computer screen.[32]

The abstracted or 'mental' character of nuclear war makes it and the weapons that would be used in it fair game for moralists, veterans of wars psychological and spiritual. Moralists have spilled much bromide over the supposedly idolatrous character of nuclear weapons, on The Bomb as a "technological deity" who demands blood sacrifices, and (in an adaptation of a familiar pacifist argument) on the supposed action-reaction dynamic of 'arms races,' whereby one side imitates the worst characteristics of the other and each thus makes war inevitable.[33] This is so manifestly nonsensical – Great Britain and France could destroy each other in minutes, but no one cares, and no one imagines that this 'makes' them enemies – that most writers prefer to ascribe the danger primarily to the immoral motives that have been so empowered: power-lust, the greed of the 'military-industrial complex,' paranoia, even blasphemous intellectual curiosity gone amok.[34] Inasmuch as these and cognate vices animate so much human activity everywhere, such explanations explain too little by explaining too much.

Arms races do not cause wars; that much has been established by historical research.[35] Wars, whether preceded by arms races or not, usually derive from concrete political interests as determined by statesmen's calculations on the spot[36] – hence the futility of any general theory purporting to predict a war. Given these calculations of political advantage, which are incessant, attempts at controlling an arms race between enemy countries will tend at best to redirect the competition from mutually disadvantageous activities (e.g., open-air testing of nuclear devices) toward those that can be conceived by each side as advantageous for himself (e.g., below-ground testing, with its superior secrecy). Even the outright abolition of mass-destruction weapons would only rechannel the competition in armaments into less spectacularly threatening but also more practically deadly (because more usable) weapons systems. "It is not weapons that create war: it is war that creates weapons."[37] And it is politics that 'creates' war. The failure of moralists to think politically − often because they misconceive politics as an Hobbesian play of amoral 'powers' − has confused public discourse in the commercial republics and quite likely impeded arms control efforts.[38] Fortunately, it is unlikely that any arms control treaty would be nontrivial absent a political settlement making such treaties unnecessary.

Herodotus reports that "in boldness and warlike spirit the Persians were not a whit inferior to the Greeks; but they were without bucklers, untrained, and far below the enemy in respect of skill in arms."[39] In a sense human history has seen the slow, not always steady triumph of 'the Greeks,' i.e., those peoples who have put technique at the service of victory. It has become a commonplace warning to say that technique may destroy the technicians, that a "lopsided development" of technique results in knowledge to the knower, whose "only means in sight for getting rid of the knowledge of how to destroy ourselves would be to do just that − in effect, to remove the knowledge by removing the knower."[40]

Machiavellian science directs knowledge toward conquest of nature, makes reason an instrument of *thumos*. Human beings being part of nature, this eventuates in self-conflict, even self-murder. It is easy for Christians to deplore this: "The greatest failure of modern science," one writes, has been in "putting itself at the service of vengeance and hatred"; "modern man is mad indeed if he thinks he can build a civilized world while maintaining his light-hearted attitude to the sixth commandment," writes another; "technological titanism" has been "facilitated in the modern age by the philosophical conditions of late idealism and by the technical powers (corresponding to the philosophical conditions, not anticipating them) which have permitted us to build a kind of shadow-infinity into our actions in the form of world-encompassing damage."[41] It is less easy for secular thinkers, very often enthusiasts of one portion or another of the Machiavellian project, to deplore the spirit of Machiavellianism. It is therefore more impressive when they do:

Bertrand Russell laments the First World War and its weaponry, observing that "Man's greater command over Nature has only magnified the disaster, because it has not been accomplished by greater command over his passions"; the military strategist Bernard Brodie recalls Milton's war of angels, writing, "Their superlative intelligence was reflected in the application of new techniques of warfare, but the origin of the war itself was marked by the absence or lapse of wisdom."[42] The kinds of machines employed for the conquest of nature for much of the 'modern' period tended toward egalitarianism, whether democratic or despotic.[43] Nuclear weapons were the consummation of this tendency, the supreme expression of leveling or egalitarianism in the military realm, equivalent to the new tyrannies or 'totalitarianisms' in politics.[44] Politically, the new alchemy of Machiavellian science produces 'the last man' — a being named and described decades before Nietzsche made him famous.[45] There is actually a variety of last men, if a survey of recent writings on nuclear weapons gives any fair indication. Their utterances range from the technostrategic calculations of military planners to the hysteromoralist exclamations of Helen Caldicott and Carol Cohn — last women worthy of last men — to the Heideggerian conjurations of literary critics.[46] But whatever their shadings, they bear the unmistakable profile of historicist ideology, with its peculiar combination of brute realism and utopian dreams of peace.[47]

Recovery from historicism will require no further 'inventiveness' or 'creativity.' The cure for the replacement of prudence with making cannot be cured by some new making, however imaginative (or imaginary).[48] Recovery will require, first, the recognition that the technologists who have invented and developed weapons of mass destruction and the military strategists who have planned for their use (if only as deterrents to attack) have not in fact acted as amoral wizards fascinated by technology 'for its own sake' or even for the acquisition of power. In the commercial republics these weapons were developed in response to serious political and military threats from regimes animated by the most virulent forms of historicist ideology: Hitler's Germany and Stalin's Soviet Union.[49] Raymond Aron is right: After the first use of nuclear weapons at Hiroshima and Nagasaki, optimists supposed that "peace would reign at last, thanks to the progress of technology, not a universal change of heart"; pessimists "heralded the approach of the apocalypse" of the "Faustian West"; but realists saw that "no single weapon – however revolutionary – changes history" to such extremes, that wars would continue to occur, that the old forces of deterrence, persuasion, and subversion would continue to find their places in a world of continuing political designs.[50] Impressive as they are, the instruments of industrial technology do not finally change human nature, although they can shake and destroy some human traditions.[51] Even if nuclear war really were to be Wilsonianism in nightmare form, "the war to end all wars"[52] – and it likely would be so for the participants and perhaps for their immediate neighbors, at worst – overemphasis on the machine-character of nuclear weapons only exacerbates the inner contradictions of historicism: the weakness for fatalism on the one hand (if the destructive power of the machines themselves is the sole focus of attention) and for a facile voluntarism on the other, a belief that all human makings can be unmade, that all noxious artifacts be unmade at once. C.P. Snow's 1961 prediction that it was a "certainty" that "some of these bombs are going off" in the next ten years is perhaps the most egregious example of this mind-set,[53] although Helen Caldicott's prophecies of an apocalypse within three years of the introduction of cruise missiles in Europe was much more colorfully expressed.[54] At the same time, these predictions probably formed part of a rhetorical strategy intended to manipulate public opinion into unmaking nuclear weapons, a strategy open to the objection that loose talk of inevitable mass destruction may as well contribute to apathy as energy, making destruction somewhat more likely.[55] But because "nothing is sure but the *threat* of nuclear destruction,"[56] there has always been the opportunity for reasoned choice arrived at by political discourse. It is therefore not surprising that the statesman Churchill proved wiser than his scientific and philosophic contemporaries when he addressed them at the Massachusetts Institute of Technology in 1949:

> Scientists should never underrate the deep-seated qualities of human nature and how, repressed in one direction, they will certainly break out in another. Laws just or unjust may govern men's actions. Tyrannies may restrain or regulate their words. The machinery of propaganda may pack their minds with falsehood and deny them truth for many generations of time.

> But the soul of man thus held in trance or frozen in a long night can be awakened by a spark coming from God knows where and in a moment the whole structure of lies and oppression is on trial for its life. Peoples in bondage need never despair. Let them hope and trust in the genius of mankind. Science no doubt could if sufficiently perverted exterminate us all, but it is not in the power of material forces in any period which the youngest here tonight need take into practical account, to alter the main elements in human nature or restrict the infinite variety of forms in which the soul and genius of the human race can and will express itself.[57]

It should be noted that Churchill did not preclude the possibility of a radical, scientifically engineered change of human nature and therefore of politics. But he sees that nuclear weapons cannot be the instrument of that change.

2. *The Political Reform of Science?*

> The more unified the planet becomes, the less does diplomacy seem to obey the ordinary calculations of force and the more military technique differs from continent to continent and conflict to conflict. It is as though some artistic genius were trying to reunite in a grand finale every method of warfare practiced by men for thousands of years, on the eve of the day when the progress of science condemns the human race to choose between wisdom and death.
>
> $\qquad\qquad\qquad\qquad$ —Raymond Aron[58]

If not nuclear weapons themselves, then perhaps the scientific project that produced them, that may produce more sophisticated and dangerous future weapons, must be radically transformed. The Machiavellian science that aims at the conquest of nature works all too well, threatening life itself without being able to create new life.[59] This destructive or as it were 'analytical' power poses an additional problem: the experimentalism of Machiavellian science, surely its least questionable aspect, fails most noticeably when human life itself is risked, because human life is unique as far as human beings know. There is obviously no way to experiment with the destruction of all humanity because there is no 'control group' and because the experiment would destroy the experimenters.[60] Aside from ever-dubious computer simulations, the controversy over 'the fate of the earth' in the event of a major nuclear war quickly descends into an agony of rhetorical assertions.[61]

There is then a disjunction between Machiavellian science, eminently successful on its own terms, and Machiavellian politics, far less successful even on its own terms, which are the preservation of the lives of its practitioners and the enhancement of their power. Science as an instrument of this politics evidently risks the destruction of scientists and all they study. Those who want to relinquish neither the ends of Machiavellian science nor the more modest of Machiavelli's political ends often seek to formulate a politics of survival. Bertrand Russell claims that our opinions on "political and economic systems" are "not relevant in discussions of the dangers of nuclear warfare," that under the circumstances one should be "solely concerned with the welfare" — most particularly the continued survival — "of the human species as a whole and not with any special advantages of this or that group." Survival "has become a *common* interest owing to the nature of nuclear weapons."[62] Jonathan Schell calls survival "the principal obligation of politics" today, but, more ambitiously than Russell, claims that all moral worth derives from the continued existence of human beings, the inventors of morality itself. This means in effect that mankind is God, albeit a mortal god. To threaten the life of this god is a kind of sacrilege. Schell sees the danger here, adding hastily that "it does not follow that any action is permitted as long as it serves the end of preventing extinction." But this is Victorian drapery, a failure of Schell's intellectual courage if not a polite concealment, because *the* god must always be saved, no matter what, unless he is evil. And how could he be evil, as the only source of all 'value'? If one replies that the ground of mankind (in secular terms) is nature, that the extinction of mankind would not extinguish the nature that could generate another mankind, Schell can only argue that we have no right to take the risk of destroying this god because nature *might* not produce another.[63] But once admit that a god was created or produced, and you must 'value' his creator even more highly as the more powerful god, although its wisdom in creating the self-destructive mortal god might be questioned.[64] Schell's humanism fails equally from the standpoint of those committed to the existence of a non-human Creator-God and from the standpoint of those who decry "human chauvinism" or anthropocentricity — in the name of the nature that supports human beings.[65] Schell's humanism even fails in its own terms. Although human life provides the foundation of all human thoughts and actions, it does not follow that a necessary condition takes moral precedence over the goods it serves. Even if one could not conceive of any reason to destroy mankind, this does not mean that no good is sufficient to justify the risk of destruction, particularly if the risk is extremely small.[66] Secular thought fails to produce any *absolute* moral rule, even the rule of species survival, unless that rule would be the prohibition of the destruction of nature itself, an act well and permanently beyond the reach of humanity, which can only do local damage.

The reality of local damage and the prospect of more of it suffices to impel some writers to call for the defense of the earth by a counter-attack on Machiavellian science. Machiavellian efforts to conquer nature and fortune, to call such conquest 'progress' or even, with deplorably misplaced organicism, 'growth,' must be thwarted with a new society and a new science.[67] Generally speaking, such writers retrace more or less arduously the arguments of Rousseau's second *Discourse*, with its search for the "natural man" and its claim that "civil society" and its ills originated in property.[68] The most striking example is Paul Shepard, who condemns the development of agriculture as the thin end of the modern wedge, and locates the only true home for humanity in the hunter-gatherer societies of the Pleistocene. Politics and war arose from the first property, agricultural lands. "The swords of war are hammered from plowshares"; therefore, to beat swords back into plowshares will only renew the cycle of violence. Because "to be few is to be wealthy" — to enjoy all of the earth and its fruits freely — a neo-Pleistocene age will see the earth happily depopulated.[69]

There is of course an odd congruence between the slogan 'Back to the Pleistocene!' and the policy recommendation of United States Air Force General Curtis E. LeMay, who reportedly urged that the Communist Vietnamese be bombed back to the Stone Age. The notions of "global ecopolitics," the "living planet" or "Gaia hypothesis," need not animate any especially humane or peaceful programme.[70] Although ecopolitical writers uniformly speak of conflict resolution and gradual world population reduction resulting from a transformed socioeconomic order, all leading to "not simply *Pax Romana* or *Pax Humana*, but *Pax Gaia*, the Peace of Earth,"[71] there is no denying that the same effect might be achieved much more rapidly by a programme of ecologically sensitive mass murder. Indeed, the ecopolitical distaste for 'speciesism' or anthropocentricity might very well inspire some ecologically-minded tyrant to war against the ecologically unfit. It is one thing to say that, left alone, the ecological balance between predator and prey will obtain in the long run. But given the ongoing, swift march to extinction of so many animal species − all of them no less morally valuable than mankind, according to the Gaians − would not some such forceful intervention make sense in Gaian terms? Gaianism cannot eschew tyranny and war in the short and intermediate terms on the basis of Gaian principles. The Gaians cannot tell how to resolve conflicts in nature, including human conflicts, precisely because their egalitarianism prevents them from judging, except in 'global' terms that in some respects are and will remain imponderable.[72] As ecopolitical writers struggle to think their version of the unthinkable, they emit such terms as "globalism," "new level of consciousness," "species consciousness," "Earth wisdom," and even "ecosophy."[73] The lack of theoretical precision bothers none of them because they have scant interest in theory. Heirs of historicism (albeit most emphatically *not* its 'progressivist' wing) they cultivate thought solely for the purpose of practice; "all 'sophical' thought should be directly *relevant* for *action*," one writer emphasizes.[74] Hence the stated affinities with Taoism, some forms of Buddhism, Western utopianism, Heideggerianism and, among Christians, Francis of Assisi.[75] As with Gandhi, the project is far from being free of a certain kind of will-to-conquer.

It is this ethos, rather than any rigorous logic, that issues in ecopolitical calls for nonviolence and in an admiration for Gandhi. This is particularly noticeable in the ecopolitical ambition to construct a socioeconomic model imitating the diversity-in-unity of nature. The differences among peoples, their plurality need not entail moral or cultural relativism because the differences are analogous to colors on a spectrum − that is, they contribute to a unitary phenomenon.[76] That the rainbow is no analogue of nature as a whole, where conflict not continuity so often occurs, is acknowledged by the Norwegian 'ecosophist' Arne Naess: "The ecological viewpoint presupposes acceptance of the fact that big fish eat small [Naess is an enthusiast of Spinoza], but not necessarily that large men throttle small."[77] To the obvious question, 'Why not?' Naess replies that Gandhian *satyagraha* works. It and it alone converts the conflict of difference in nature to the harmony of difference in the rainbow. If *satyagraha* cannot do this, then Gandhi and Naess are mistaken, Naess concedes.[78]

The difficulty, then, arises in *human* nature:

> Mankind during the last nine thousand years has conducted itself like a *pioneer invading species*. These species are individualistic, aggressive, and hustling. They attempt to exterminate or suppress other species. They discover new ways to live under unfavorable external conditions − admirable! − but they are ultimately self-destructive. They are replaced by other species which are better suited to restabilize and mature the ecosystem. If mankind is to avoid being replaced then the struggle *against* nature must cease.[79]

To stop the humans' struggle against nature, it appears, human nature must be struggled against. The statistic "nine thousand years" gives away the solution: as does Shepard, Naess regards civilization as we know it as unnatural; the human struggle against nature is unnatural. Naess claims that the relinquishment of nature-conquest will betoken humanity's "self-realization" or "maturity." The language is that of historicism. Life, Naess writes, is "a vast historical process." In maturity it respects the equal right of all "fellow beings" to "unfold [their own] potentials" in a comprehensively "class-free" society. That is, Naess' egalitarianism extends beyond the anthropocentric rights of communism or socialism, throughout nature. It is a democracy of mutually enriching life forms.[80]

It is tempting to dismiss all of this as Norwegian, all too Norwegian. If each fellow being has an equal right to fulfill its own potential, on what basis can any irreconcilable conflict be resolved? Naess argues that a hunter may kill a bear for food if the hunter is mindful that he too will die someday and nourish the vegetation eaten by future bears.[81] Substitute "HIV virus" for "hunter" and "human body" for "bear," and shall we view the ecological balance of predator and prey with such equanimity? Indeed, reverse the role of bear and human being, and are we satisfied (if *we* are the human being devoured, that is)? Naess surely would not involve himself in these absurdities, but he offers no criterion by which he can avoid them. Radical egalitarianism is radically absurd, as may also be seen in Naess' arbitrary biocentrism. Why democracy of *life* forms? What can privilege life over non-life in Gaian terms? Indeed, what privileges Gaia over, say, the planet Pluto? If the comet Kahoutek had been about to strike the planet earth, for 'whom' should we have mourned? Conflicts are strictly speaking undecidable on radically egalitarian terms. This as easily brings not the peace of 'live and let live' anarchism but an intensified war of all against all. Egalitarian anarchism leads as easily to catch-as-catch-can as live-and-let-live.

Ecopolitical writers take some pains to avoid this consequence. Shepard argues that hunting leads to the life-giving activity of eating whereas war does not. The argument could as well lead to the revival of cannibalism as the abolition of war, which, even when it is not healthily cannibalistic, does aim at the expansion of territory and − this from a Gaian viewpoint − of gene pools. Shepard prefers exogamy among totemic clans, claiming that agrarian territoriality is what leads to inbreeding and the need for wars, in addition to the political hierarchies that violently aggrandize themselves at human expense. Shepard goes so far as to claim that the nutritional content of foods is lower today than in the Pleistocene, although he does not claim that life spans were longer then, as he urges us "forward to tribal society."[82] Naess does not push so hard, retaining Gandhi's agrarianism, which he calls ecologically balanced, and targeting for abolition only cities, representative government, bureaucracy, and large-scale 'growth'-oriented economies. He retains politics, but it is a direct-action, participatory-democratic politics on a 'local' level, guarded by "local defense patterns, non-violent groups."[83] Exactly what a locality is remains somewhat vague in ecopolitics. Several writers speak of "bioregions" such as New York State's Hudson Valley. Most ecopolitical writers leave procedures for peacefully determining the boundaries of "bioregions" happily unmentioned, as if boundary disputes might never result in serious conflict.[84]

Naess does address the problem indirectly and more generally by considering the potential conflict between specialized, scientific opinion and public opinion generally. His egalitarianism is not so dogmatic as to cause him to imagine that the people are always right. He complains that although technology appears to expand the range of human choices, one should not falsely suppose "that the population knows its possibilities for choice." He therefore calls for "life quality research" whereby social scientists will map the people's "normative systems," relating the resulting data to natural resources "as we see them and as the people see them." "We" refers to scientists; presumably, the scientists would then attempt to persuade their fellow-residents of the bioregion to pursue certain policies.[85] Naess would thwart any incipient authoritarianism by emphasizing the plurality of scientific opinion. Pointing not to any specific scientific research program but to the work of historians of science, Naess observes that historians' judgments of the truth of conflicting scientific opinions are themselves conflicting, radically plural. Although science attempts to establish 'truth' by experimentation, the 'truth' should always be regarded as provisional. Different theories require us to 'read' the results of experimental research differently; it is important to keep theoretical alternatives alive so as not to reduce the multiplicity of possible significations. The proliferation of crank notions will be avoided because in practice if not in theory these are easy to winnow out. Also, mere possibility "is not enough for action"; the theoretical possibility that the earth is flat will not in itself much concern rocket scientists. As for theoretical systems themselves, "two mutually inconsistent systems may both correspond to reality"; 'reality' is only a regulative idea, not a "definite structure or substructure." Naess is at bottom a Heraclitean, as are all those historicists who do not claim that history has ended or will end.[86]

Morally and politically, the same principles of pluralism and 'possibilism' or revisability apply, although Naess encourages clear, forthright statements of "value-priorities" while leading ecopoliticians away from rigid moralizing and vituperation. This will help to prevent a new scientific establishment from replacing the existing one. A science that seeks to rule must popularize itself, thereby rendering itself dogmatic, "authoritarian and monolithic," in the end unscientific.[87] Not only science but political life will benefit from the eschewal of populism:

> The relief from pressure towards conformity seems to me to offer great political advantages. Possibilism tends to diminish the uniforming effect of science upon society and upon the individual. It increases the personal freedom in choice of

philosophical principles by furnishing precise and elaborate alternatives.[88]

Although Naess deserves praise for at least recognizing the tensions between science and politics that Rousseau (but few of these Rousseauians) so clearly describe, it cannot be said that he appreciates the severity of them. It will not suffice to try to make both scientists and political society more easygoing and 'pluralistic.' Truth-claims arouse passions, both in themselves and in combination with the individual and group egoism that Naess deplores. Democratization through direct action or participation — a 'movement' politics corresponding to Heraclitean philosophy of movement — will strengthen passion and weaken deliberation. There is no reason to believe that a world of small, participatory democracies would be any more stable than was ancient Greece. Their very similarities would encourage faction. The denigration of structure (including institutional structures), far from liberating the ambitious from conflicts, will encourage conflict. Ecopolitical writers rightly associate violence with oppressive institutions; they wrongly fail to associate violence as well with the absence of structure or anarchy. Theirs is the reverse of the typical 'conservative' error, the overvaluation of any existing order.

3.   *The Political Reform of the World?*

> In sum, the task is nothing less than to reinvent politics: to reinvent the world.
>
> —Jonathan Schell[89]

The invention of nuclear weapons and their use by the United States against the Empire of Japan prompted calls for a world government to control the new technology. Churchill predicted that other countries would have nuclear weapons in three or four years and urged that the "relationships of all men" be remolded so that nations would no longer "wish or dare to fall upon each other" out of ambition or ideological passion. A "supreme authority" should be constituted to "give peace on earth and decree justice among men."

He hoped that the United Nations would not become "merely a cockpit in a Tower of Babel."[90]   Einstein recommended a world government with a constitution drafted jointly by the United States, Great Britain, and the Soviet Union — none of which would have been required to change its own regime.[91] Given the radically opposed ends of commercial republicanism and Marxist oligarchy — the latter having been established for the express purpose of overthrowing the former — world government even in a world threatened by nuclear weapons was obviously an example of what diplomats call a 'nonstarter.' This may be seen by the utter implausibility of the various concrete proposals advanced to bring the nations toward world government. Bertrand Russell, for example, called for a pullout of all "alien" (i.e., American and Soviet) troops from Western and Eastern Europe, then lamely if honestly admitted that this would result in Communist governments in Eastern Europe.[92] The rulers of the Soviet Union never showed the slightest interest in trading the minimal threat of nuclear war for the serious political threat of commercial republics on their country's border.   Only when the political principles of the Soviet rulers had markedly eroded were the Eastern European countries allowed to revolutionize. This had nothing to do with the threat of nuclear war; it had everything to do with the desuetude of Marxism-Leninism among many Soviet oligarchs.[93]   That is, the adoption of commercial republican principles and institutions by the most powerful nations would make world government possible but unnecessary.[94]   (The worldwide adoption of Marxist tyranny or oligarchy would make world government necessary but impossible to bear). Although powerful nuclear weapons are not sufficiently powerful to produce the regime changes needed for a world government. As Aron soon observed, "The present reality is the old game" of political ambition "under different forms" — and not so much forms as moods, moods of increased caution and indirection, even deviousness.[95]

Citizens of commercial republics, like the Soviet rulers, judged the political threat to be more formidable than the death threat.[96] They may have recognized, with Locke and Montesquieu, that the political threat of tyranny is *also* a death threat, that "structural violence has taken many more lives than direct violence."[97] Even as in nature predators kill the weakest of the herd, so human predators, criminals and tyrants, most often destroy the defenseless. Tyrannies and the worst oligarchies therefore see much greater percentages of their populations devoted to military tasks than do commercial republics.[98] Tyrannical regimes fear friendship more than hostility, at home and abroad.[99] Having built a regime with force and fraud, not reasonable consent, such rulers cannot be expected to react favorably to reasoned argument, generosity, or any other decent motive. Fortunately, rulers can at times contradict the spirit of their own regime, but, unfortunately, not as a dependable rule. This gives the citizens of commercial republics a *moral* incentive to match force with force, even as they do everything possible to increase the influence of reason on the rulers and subjects of unjust regimes.[100] Knowing that tyrants will use force, including nuclear force, with few if any moral qualms, commercial republicans have the moral incentive to speak a language clearly understood by their enemies.[101] The extremism of tyranny hesitates only at the countervailing 'extreme' of military power.

In opposition to this it may be argued that the historical determinism of modern tyranny, 'left' or 'right,' commits tyrants to believing in the inevitability of their victory, a victory that will not need military action. "If the socialist forces have a jot of faith in themselves and in the future of socialism, they must also have faith in the force of the influence which by reason of its peaceable and active international policy socialism will have on the total development of present-day mankind," writes the Yugoslav Marxist Edvard Kardelj.[102] In reply, one should note that strong military deterrence of the Marxist regimes does greatly (if not immediately) encourage the redirection of their efforts into such commendably peaceful channels. Inasmuch as Marxism offers no prohibition of military force, the "peaceful coexistence" strategy must be seen as instrumental only, rather as Lenin's New Economic Policy was designed as a temporary, tactical compromise with 'capitalism.'[103] When the Marxist publicist John Somerville urges that "the entire curriculum" of public schools in commercial republics be reorganized around "paxology," that is, "around the theme of the need and value of peace in the age of nuclear weapons," and, as a part of that curriculum, communism as "an ideology" should enjoy "equal rights" with "our ideology," it is hard to resist wondering what he might say on behalf of the ideology of fascism. When Somerville then goes on to argue that Marxism has had more philosophic influence on the "peace movement" than any other secular doctrine, and concludes by claiming that "the amount of social progress" made in the Soviet Union "has indeed no precedent in the past human history," it is hard to avoid suspecting that we are gazing upon an especially rickety and unconvincing Trojan Horse.[104]

It is rather the inferiority of Marxism, the historical failure of this version of historicism, that makes nuclear war increasingly unattractive for commercial republicans and quasi-Marxists alike. For commercial republicans the semi-communism of Hungary and Poland of the mid-1980s began to seem less repellant than the real tyrannies of previous decades, raising the question of whether nuclear war was worth risking anymore. Better dead than Red was one thing, better dead than pink quite another.[105] Simultaneously, the increasingly pale Redness of the communist regimes made them progressively less likely to risk nuclear war for the sake of either conquest or self-defense. The question had to arise: Why defend ourselves against commercial republicanism? Is it not as good or better than Marxist oligarchy?

Far from overwhelming all political considerations or making them obsolete, weapons of mass destruction have highlighted the importance of political regimes. It is not so much that the Japanese, the only nation that suffered nuclear attack, now enjoy political liberty and economic prosperity whereas East Europeans, who never suffered any such attack, waited some forty years for freedom,[106] the nuclear weapons exploded in Japan were small, doing no damage to political and social infrastructure in the nation as a whole. It is rather that, absent a major nuclear war, the regime questions that beset political life before the invention of nuclear weapons have continued to be asked and answered. Even the onset of a terminal illness cannot wipe out the question, 'How shall I live?' Rather, it raises that question with increased urgency.[107]

Those who dispute this argument have claimed that commercial republican foreign policy has no moral content at all, that it is driven merely by the ambition for power. One writer claimed (in 1984 that "all ideological content was long ago squeezed out of the cold conflict with Russia," that Americans "are not engaged in the defense of liberty" as such but only in "*our* liberties," and "at whatever cost in suffering to the weaker peoples of the world."[108] The conflict between the United States and the Soviet Union, another claimed at about the same time, was only "the age-old competition between two powerful nations, each seeking supremacy and nationalistic world hegemony."[109] Both countries exemplify, in the words of still another writer, "the nuclear national security state" — regimes without "democratic control over foreign policy." He adds, "Under present circumstances, without a revitalization of the present forms of representative government, there is little hope that any other approach to the reform of public policy can successfully challenge, except in a minor way, the current role of nuclear weaponry and related militarist dispositions in national security policy."[110] In response, it is sufficient to notice that all of these writers advanced this thesis before regime changes in the Marxist countries were to prove such contentions absurd. Only the dimmest critics of commercial republicanism still assign threats to world peace to some sinister American ambition.

A more plausible variation of this argument does not decry the persistence of meaningful regime differences in the 'nuclear age' but contends that the significance of these differences fades in the blinding light of a prospective nuclear apocalypse. This argument depends upon the claim advanced by Bertrand Russell that a nation is 'Better Red than dead.' It is better to be Red than dead because Redness can change whereas death cannot. No tyranny lasts forever; death does. "The most elementary freedom" is "the freedom to choose survival," without which no other freedom can be possible.[111] Death in nuclear war would not promote any form of freedom. To believe otherwise is "fanaticism." "I will not yield to Patrick Henry, or anyone else, in love of freedom," Russell avers, "but if there is to be as much freedom in the world as possible, it is necessary that there should be restrictions preventing violent assaults upon the freedom of others," including and especially their freedom to survive.[112] To willingly sacrifice one's own life to prevent tyranny can make moral and political sense; to willingly sacrifice all lives in order to prevent tyranny, including the lives of innocents among the tyrant's population, is morally and politically evil. "To the extent to which we forfeit our respect for life and law we forfeit our claim to have any moral superiority to defend against the Communist threat"; commercial republican institutions "would deserve no more respect or loyalty than those of Hitler's Germany" if the last action of their partisans were a nuclear counterattack on tyrants whose innocent subjects would therein perish.[113]

The question of whether secular morality can prohibit absolutely the destruction of innocents is a difficult one that requires careful analysis. At this juncture I shall address only the issue of political justice. The slogan 'Better Red than dead' is true so long as Redness is an ameliorable condition. If technologies of mind control, genetic engineering to produce semi-human living 'robots,' and other inventions thus far happily restricted to the fantasies of science-fiction writers were developed and deployed, the slogan might well give some pause. Death might then be preferable to a universal and permanent tyranny. Absent such inventions, however, Russell's slogan is entirely sensible, although his application of it might be considered somewhat narrow. All-out war between the United States and the Soviet Union might well destroy the human populations of the northern hemisphere; this, however, is not 'everyone." To prevent Soviet tyranny over the southern hemisphere, a nuclear counterattack by the United States might well contribute to the defense of political justice among the remainder of the world's populations. Finally, however, the possibilities for the eventual self-liberation of tyrannized nations might well outweigh these considerations. While this liberation would have been long delayed had the commercial republics disappeared not flourished, it is difficult to claim that the certainty of mass murder in a nuclear counterattack would serve justice better than would refusal to counterattack on the grounds of a hoped-for, uncertain, eventual triumph of political liberty.[114] These imponderables notwithstanding, however, nuclear deterrence need not rest on the conviction that it is always better to be dead than Red. One need only argue that it is better to risk death than to submit to tyranny. (As a corollary, this requires arguing that the various techniques of nonviolent resistance will likely result in failure against a determined conqueror.) Deterrence involves not the military use of nuclear weapons but their political use by commercial republics who are resisting the weapons' "political manipulation" by tyrants.[115] Oliver O'Donovan is therefore not quite correct to argue that "nuclear war creates its own set of values" that "can claim no continuity" with commercial republican principles – principles that treat "all political orders as *relative* values," 'values' not worth the destruction of an entire civil society. To risk nuclear war is not to prefer the destruction of "Western civilization" to its "subjection...to alien political conditions."[116] It is to resist the subjection of commercial republicanism to unjust political conditions. Resistance to injustice in defense of institutions that secure the unalienable rights of life, liberty, and the pursuit of happiness has always required a citizenry willing to risk their own lives and liberty. The risk is more general, now, but it is the same kind of risk. O'Donovan claims that "when someone thinks that it would be better for there to be *no* conditions for individual fulfillment than for the present satisfactory ones to be replaced with others less satisfactory, then he has left the liberal tradition behind him, embracing a form of political totalitarianism" that "matches [one] totalitarian claim" – the Marxist claim to rule all aspects of human life – "with [another] totalitarian claim" – namely, that it is better to be dead than Red. However, to call Marxist tyranny merely "less satisfactory" than commercial republicanism is a laughable euphemism. To claim that the risk of sacrifice run by some commercial republics by their maintenance of a nuclear deterrent (instead of surrender or nonviolent resistance to tyranny) reflects some "totalitarian claim" is again to view the issue narrowly with respect to the populations of those commercial republics at risk, not as part of a worldwide struggle for political liberty. To judge nuclear deterrence as more likely to preserve commercial republicanism than any other policy involves no 'totalitarian' pretensions, only prudential reasoning that may or may not turn out to be mistaken.[117]

It is prudential reasoning that Sidney Hook deploys against Russell's 'Better Red than dead.' Public enunciation of this principle will lead to surrender if the Marxists take commercial republicans at their word and threaten them with nuclear war. Proponents of deterrence seek "to confine the fanaticism of Bolshevism by taming it with the fear of failure." The poorly disguised surrender policy of Russell is "unmitigated political foolishness" that will deter neither the tyrant's war against conquered subjects nor international wars among remaining tyrants.[118]

4.   *The Morality of Nuclear Deterrence*

"Imagination stands appalled" at the effects of nuclear war, Churchill said, but the prospect yields a "curious paradox": "The worse things get, the better." The more appalling the arsenals become, the less likely they will be used. "Then it may well be that we shall by a process of sublime irony have reached a stage in this story where safety will be the sturdy child of terror, and survival the twin brother of annihilation."[119] Deterrence appeals to the low but solid Hobbesian ground, "prevent[ing] an enemy from doing something by making him fear the consequences that will follow."[120] Deterrence rests on trust in the most modest sense, trusting your enemy to perceive and follow his plain self-interest.[121]

     Those who dispute the effectiveness of deterrence ignore or dismiss Churchill's paradox. Because the threat of nuclear weapons has been countered by no very practical physical defense, critics charge that they provide no "security."[122] But this is precisely the point: a would-be attacker's lack of physical security against retaliation yields security for his prospective victim. Although critics claim that retaliation after one's country was devastated by a nuclear attack would be an act of "willful irrationality," retaliation for "vengeance's sake,"[123] it is again precisely the fear that the victim *will* act vengefully that is most likely to impress vicious souls who plot mass murder. Despite protestations that the nuclear deterrent's effectiveness "must be a matter of complete speculation,"[124] that it rests on shaky "credibility" because the weapons are "utterly unusable,"[125] the burden of proof remains on the critics, given the familiarity of deterrence in our everyday lives in everything from law enforcement to child-rearing. The rational "use" of nuclear weapons as a deterrence includes such purposes as "saving lives and preventing conquest" in a set of circumstances that have proven more stable than those provided by 'conventional' weapons alone.[126] Recurrent warnings from some writers notwithstanding − some of the statements are now decades old[127] − the cooperation between enemies that the common possession of nuclear weapons enforces has been seen repeatedly, particularly since the mid-1960s when the United States and the Soviet Union had achieved the capacity substantially to destroy one another.[128] Whereas from 1938 to the present 'conventional' deterrence has failed many times, nuclear deterrence has never failed; in Europe and elsewhere this must be considered a substantial achievement.[129]

Critics understandably prefer to point to the future. New and more dangerous weapons will be invented; nuclear weapons will spread to many more countries; short-range nuclear weapons will erase the borderline between 'conventional' and 'nuclear.'[130] But the mere increase of numbers, power, and accuracy of nuclear weapons will not weaken deterrence so long as the commercial republics maintain their retaliatory capacity.[131] It is not even clear that 'nuclear proliferation' or the acquisition of the weapons by more countries will substantially increase the risk to human life. There is, however, an underlying argument behind all these disputes over credibility and security. Critics dislike nuclear deterrence because it offers no certainty. The effects of nuclear weapons appall the *moral* imagination not only because they 'work' by threatening the destruction of millions of innocent lives but because they cannot be *guaranteed* to work. Only the moral certainty that they will work could possibly justify such a horrible risk.[132] This argument misapplies the theological criteria of faith and absolute certainty to human history or the course of events. Absent prophetic knowledge, it is of course impossible to know if nuclear deterrence will work always and everywhere. This means that it would be better, given the risks, if nuclear weapons did not exist. It does not amount to a sound moral argument against nuclear deterrence in a world in which nuclear weapons do exist.[133] To sustain that argument, the secular moralist has to argue − probabilistically − for a safer and less potentially destructive practicable alternative to nuclear deterrence. No such argument has won the allegiance of anything like a workable majority in a representative government of any major country; in nations that admire pragmatism, no argument for national defense that eschews the nuclear deterrent has been judged to be pragmatic.

And if deterrence fails, what then? If nuclear deterrence of 'conventional' attack fails, then obviously the initial response would be 'conventional' counterattack coupled perhaps with the use of 'tactical' or short-range nuclear weapons.[134] Nuclear attack on the territory of the commercial republics would result, according to their publicly stated policy, in a counter-strike followed by negotiations intended to end the war as quickly as possible.[135] Although some writers assert that "not enough people will survive to make any sustained social cohesiveness a reality,"[136] this depends upon the size of the enemy attack and the governments' ability to end the war. These are "degrees of awfulness," and the Soviet Union itself, along with several other countries in our depraved century, demonstrated a capacity to recover from self-inflicted deaths numbering in the tens of millions.[137] This fact cannot be adduced to prove that tyrannical regimes will or will not be more likely to risk nuclear war − that they will because they believe they can recover, or that they won't because they never want to endure such horrors again[138] − but it does mean that military and civilian planners in the commercial republics had better think about what they will do in case of enemy attack, that such plans will not necessarily be useless and could make a significant difference. A country committed to a policy of nuclear deterrence is morally obligated to plan for the possible failure of that policy, miniscule though that possibility may be. Such planning will have the added advantage of making deterrence more credible. Brodie writes

> For the sake of deterrence before hostilities, the enemy must expect us to be vindictive and irrational if he attacks us. We must give him every reason to feel that that portion of our retaliatory force which survives his attack will surely be targeted against his major centers of population.[139]

Planning will tend to convince an enemy of exactly the opposite: to expect us to be just and rational if he attacks, to expect us to punish him and so far as possible to sustain ourselves.[140] Rather than a mindset of "useless revenge" which "poisons all wholesome thought and feeling in those who allow themselves to be dominated by it,"[141] careful thought about 'what to do if deterrence fails' can limit casualties and make war less likely. The question remains: Can this be done effectively *and* morally? Can a retaliatory strike be designed to be sufficiently frightening to deter enemies and sufficiently limited to be rationally justifiable? The dilemma posed by nuclear weapons is clear. If you are attacked with them, justice requires the punishment of those who caused the attack − presumably, the rulers of the hostile country and their obedient military hatchetmen. Yet the characteristics of nuclear weapons make them ill-fitted for this act of justice. The criminals probably will be hidden in safe shelters underground, preparing to emerge only after they are assured of their own safety. It is rather the innocent, largely unprotected subjects of these criminals who will be most vulnerable to nuclear retaliation. Nuclear deterrence by commercial republics has for most of its history amounted to the statement: If you attack us, we know we will not be able to punish you directly. But we can punish you indirectly. We can destroy many of the instruments of your tyranny: your military facilities, your government offices, your prisons, your propaganda machinery. Above all we can destroy your subjects. We can deprive you of victims to tyrannize. We cannot end your lives but we can end their lives, and therewith your tyranny. We can destroy your reason for living, *qua* tyrants, by preventing you from having subjects to tyrannize. We cannot end your lives but we can make your lives pointless by your own standards, such as they are. In annihilating your slaves we expose your nihilism. We suspect that you prefer not to look your own nihilism too steadily in the face. We suspect you will not attack us so long as we can strike at the instruments and the victims of your will to power.

In making this threat, do commercial republicans expose their own nihilism as well? 'Realists' and 'idealists' alike say so − 'realists' somewhat proudly, 'idealists' indignantly or in shame for their fellow citizens. The 'realists' insist that retribution, the threat to return evil for evil, is "the constituent principle of statecraft." "In principle there has never been a way in which the state's necessities can be acknowledged yet the measures by which these necessities may be preserved always limited."[142] But the State is no god, 'idealists' reply, whose 'necessities' deserve the sacrifice of our moral principles. If the State requires a threat to the innocent in order to survive, let it perish; "few politicians, during peacetime planning at least, are willing to present revenge in and for itself as a respectable goal of policy."[143] But many are quite willing so to present deterrence, of which the credible threat to retaliate forms an indispensable part. A rational policy is not always one that requires a 'rational' action at every stage; a rational policy maximizes the possibility of a good result − in this case the peaceful survival of commercial republics threatened by tyranny.[144] This is not nihilism, though it is surely repugnant.

Given the repugnant character of attacks on innocents, and also given the longtime impotence of effective *defensive* measures against nuclear weapons,[145] can nuclear retaliation be limited to military and governmental targets – to so-called 'counterforce' strikes? 'Counterforce' is "less morally objectionable" than 'countervalue' attacks on innocents; it is also more dangerous to the deterrer, who may only encourage his enemy to use first-strike weapons in a crisis before losing them to a 'counterforce' attack. Will the enemy not misinterpret your intention to *retaliate* with a 'counterforce' strike as an intention (which he may prefer to reserve for himself) to launch a *first* strike?[146] Still, this may be a risk worth taking, given the apparent moral superiority of 'counterforce' to 'countervalue' retaliation. The more serious moral objection to 'counterforce' is that it will cause millions of deaths to innocents, anyway; 'indirect' killing of innocents by the heat and radiation of nuclear explosions at military targets in or near cities is still killing.[147]

What then of bluff? "An enemy has only to believe that we *might* be willing to destroy cities; he has not to know that we will not."[148] Most writers treat bluff so to speak with a pair of tongs, violating as it does the requirements of honesty commended both by Christianity and secular Enlightenment doctrine. Anthony Kenny puts matters in sane perspective by admit-ting, "I wish that the deterrent policy were one of bluff," because "the wrongness of lying is very much less than the wrongness of the intention to commit mass murder." He concludes nonetheless that bluff is both practically impossible – the secret "could never be kept" – and morally impermissible – it would require "the good serviceman" who is too far down in the chain of command to know the policy "to be willing, in the appropriate circumstances, to commit murder on a great scale."[149] These objections are ultimately specious. It should not be beyond human ingenuity, even in a commercial republic, to disarm nuclear weapons secretly, and maintain sufficient secrecy to prevent cautious enemies from believing whatever rumors may arise. As for "requiring" servicemen and women to form an intention to commit mass murder, no one can require a volunteer to do anything, particularly as there could be no sanctions, indeed, no opportunity to disobey any command. It is true that volunteers in missile launching sites around the countries would still intend to kill innocents; it is not clear that harmless custodianship over disarmed yet effective weapons is the worst occupation for such persons. Perfectionists will of course prefer to reform them, to find them a better occupation, and would be free to try. Although one moral perfectionist contends that "the history of ethical speculation has virtually no other instance of the defense of immoral acts under the extenuating circumstances of prudential risk,"[150] both bluffing and punishing obviously exemplify just that. Moralities of enlightenment, religious and secular, typically incline against bluffing and punishment. It is however noteworthy that proponents of these moralities have had recourse to both in certain circumstances.

How morally corrupting can it be to preserve ourselves? Nietzsche agrees with Socrates in arguing that evil is never voluntary; evil is an attempt, a mistaken attempt, to preserve or enhance one's own existence. Moreover (and in anticipation of the command structure governing nuclear weapons), Nietzsche argues, "Much that is horrific and inhuman in history in which one can hardly bear to believe is ameliorated" − a well considered word, that − "when we consider that he who ordered it and he who carried it out are different people: the former does not see it and his imagination therefore receives no impression of it, the latter obeys one set above him and does not feel responsible."[151] Yet this amelioration is precisely what writers who have witnessed twentieth-century history find so horrifying. It is the mindset of Auschwitz and the Katyn Forest, perhaps of Pearl Harbor and Hiroshima.[152] The question facing moralists is, given this mindset in tyrants, the enemies of commercial republics, how may commercial republicans defend themselves without succumbing to it? Again, how morally corrupting can it be to preserve ourselves? Grotius asserts an absolute right of self-preservation of the innocent, even against the innocent:

> ...if otherwise I cannot save my life, I may use any degree of violence to ward off him who assails it, even if he should happen to be free from wrong....The reason is that this right does not properly arise from another's wrong, but from the right which nature grants me on my own behalf.[153]

Grotius does not satisfactorily explain this "right" from a moral standpoint. If both attacker and attacked are free from wrong, what is the standard by which one can choose between them? (Assuming that one can know nothing of the relative merits of the two lives endangered: if I had met the young Einstein on the battlefield in the First World War, presumably most reasonable persons would root for Einstein to prevail; however, on the battlefield I could have known nothing of Einstein's superiority, and my efforts to kill him would be excused by my invincible ignorance.) Perhaps it is the very absence of a standard that justifies Grotius' assertion. The innocent defender defends not in order to punish but in order to preserve his life. This killing in self-defense, does it ruin his innocence? Only if morality can justify *self*-destruction of innocence, which an innocent's refusal to defend himself adequately, his acquiescence in his own destruction by another, must be said to be. Only a judgment by the innocent that his assailant, innocent or not, deserves to live more than the assailed, can justify this choice on a rational and 'secular' basis. In practice this is not always a judgment that can be made.

If this is so, then how much more can one justify the threat of nuclear weapons against tyrannical enemies and their innocent subjects. The argument of Paul Fussell in defense of the bombings of Hiroshima and Nagasaki is not easy to refute. "The purpose of the bombs was not to punish civilians [who were in the event warned beforehand, although they might have needed to assume the warning to have been a bluff] but to stop the war"; "experience whispers that the pity is not that we used the bomb to end the Japanese war but that it wasn't ready in time to end the German one," thereby saving millions of innocent lives from the Nazi death camps.[154] This is an argument for the greatest good for the greatest number of the 'good,' i.e., the innocent. The counter-argument runs as follows: Soldiers should fight only soldiers, not civilians, because soldiers by definition are not themselves innocents. When I pick up a gun, I make myself "a dangerous man."[155] I am morally obligated to recognize the right of those endangered by me to kill me in self-defense; I am also morally obligated not to use my gun against men and women who are not dangerous — e.g., most civilians and disarmed enemy soldiers. The purpose of the destruction of Hiroshima and Nagasaki was to end the war by killing the innocent in order to save the lives of Allied soldiers, who were not innocents; those soldiers remained available to defeat any further military resistance and then to secure the conquest by military occupation. To this Fussell replies *ad hominem* that those who deplore the nuclear bombings are usually not the soldiers who would have had to invade Japan. "In general, the principle is, the farther from the scene of horror, the easier the talk."[156] This argument attempts to upend the claim that the high-altitude bomber pilot or long-range missile launcher crew is more morally culpable (because physically abstracted from the scene of the crime) than is the conscientious person who deplores the mass killing of innocents. The real human beings who are soldiers want the war ended and their lives saved. If the destruction of innocents is the only way to do this (and this assumes that simply going home, retreating, will finally result in another war, another Pearl Harbor – that victory is indispensable to peace) then so be it. The problem is that the frightened American soldier was also physically abstracted from the scene of the crime, if Hiroshima was the scene of a crime. "The farther from the scene of horror, the easier the talk" applies as much to Fussell (in this instance) as it does to anyone else. With respect to Hiroshima, he might as well have been on the moon. "How did the people of Hiroshima forfeit their rights?" Walzer asks, expecting no coherent answer.[157]

What is the foundation of the claim that the rights of the innocent ought never be violated, or, at least, that the right to life of the innocent must never be violated? In secular terms, there can be no recourse to such concepts as the 'sanctity' of innocent life or any other God-given right. Since the eighteenth century many secular moralists have adopted Kant's categorical imperative, claiming that persons may never be used as means but only treated as ends. Nuclear deterrence violates this rule. It "treat[s] human life as a mere object of policy," "justif[ying] the indiscriminate killing of innocent people under certain circumstances."[158] To argue otherwise is nothing but 'consequentialism.' "No consequence can destroy any truth," Algernon Sidney claims, in arguing that the consequences of admitting the people's right to revolution has no bearing on whether that right exists.[159] It is not merely that "a good end, if it cannot be achieved without wholesale slaughter, cannot be achieved at all."[160] Maybe it can. But we have no right to achieve any end by wrongful means.

Why not? Without a doctrine of always treating persons as ends and never as means, there are no conceptual restraints on how we may treat them, Kantians argue. We will descend on a slippery slope to genocide or, alternatively, we will languish on the plain of paralysis, as in Philip Green's argument that a government intending to deter nuclear war could not choose, in the face of it, between all-out war and surrender because "they are both rejected as goals."[161] This second critique of 'consequentialism' fails; it assumes that 'consequentialism' cannot be hierarchical, cannot rest on a hierarchy of ends. All-out war and surrender are both rejected as goals, but neither absolutely so. A government may want neither and nonetheless choose one as the lesser evil.

Will this choice be arbitrary because the goals are incommensurable?[162] That is, can we really compare and contrast in any precise way the moral consequences of surrender with the moral consequences to nuclear war? In a precise way, no: but this may only mean that we should give up the demand for precision where precision is not possible. In a general or imprecise way, we can indeed calculate moral consequences, and do so all the time in everyday life, as when we try not to waste resources that could save many lives in order to save one life. In considering nuclear war, we can avoid these consequences even less because the choices are so stark. With nuclear deterrence we attempt to save millions of lives with the threat, not the act, of destroying millions. Is this threat, involving no loss of life whatever if heeded, not morally superior to deliberately risking the known dangers of surrender or of war? Would carrying out the threat if it is unheeded be worse than not carrying it out?[163] The answer to both questions is likely to be "yes," although the second "yes" will be weaker, based as it must be on calculation of consequences.

Kantians argue that such calculations lead to a slippery slope of self-justification. It is morally safer to refuse to commit an evil act because we know what evil means more clearly than we can calculate the results of employing the means, and we know the goodness of the ends we desire much less certainly than we do the goodness or evil of means. "We are much more certain of the evil we do than the good we hope for."[164] But this is itself a 'consequentialist' argument for non-'consequentialism.'[165] If 'consequentialism' is incoherent without some stable framework whereby consequences may be judged, so Kantianism or 'deontology' is incoherent without calculation of consequences. The slippery slope of 'consequentialism' is mirrored by the idealist vortex of Kantianism – a cyclone that spins upward toward the stratosphere of impossible-to-achieve ends disguised as inviolable 'laws' or methods. Because it can never reach this stratosphere, this cyclone may compel us finally not to moral restraint or duty but to historicism, the most radical 'consequentialism' of all. The Kantian exaltation of duty over happiness effectively makes the means into an end, absolutizing the means in a way that results either in the idealist vortex of historicist millenarianism or the ineffectual dithering of the secular saint – both equally destructive (absent the God secularists eschew) of reasonable means and ends.[166] Kantianism is *moralist* Cartesianism or methodism, inept in practical life. Kantianism is a secularism that wants to evade the chief consequence of secularism, the disappearance of God, by positing rules to be obeyed as if God existed to frame and enforce them. But if God does not exist, only 'History' or 'Man' can take His place, and these are incompetent substitutes for the enforcement of any absolutism, however minutely regulated.[167]

Rational secularism needs the idea of nature. Machiavellian nature is a chaos, and can be employed to justify nuclear deterrence. Because nuclear war would yield an Hobbesian 'state of nature' or war of all against all in which the civil prohibition against killing innocents would dissolve along with all other civil prohibitions, any retaliation against nuclear attack is permissible. The initial attack would not be permissible because the return to the state of nature is the greatest evil, from the standpoint of civil justice. But the response can be unlimited. However, if possible it should not be, because the aim of human beings in the state of nature is to get (back) into the state of civil society, and civil relations with the enemy would be more likely if we showed maximum mercy to innocents.[168] There might even be circumstances in which surrender might be prudentially superior – particularly on the Hobbesian ground that any civil order, including the tyranny that is only monarchy mis-liked, is better than none. Indeed, it is difficult to see how a nuclear war could occur among Hobbesian rulers except by the worst miscalculation.

The weakness of Hobbes' idea of nature ruins the Hobbesian justification of nuclear deterrence. In fact nature is not chaotic. Nature has chaotic or at least entropic tendencies and these will ultimately prevail, according to the Second Law of Thermodynamics. But nature is not simply entropic. Nature is also orderly, order-producing. The natural order, which can be sustained in very small measure by human art or contrivance, is obviously not the product of human art or contrivance. Although nuclear war would be the product of human art at the service not of order but of so-called chaos (itself orderly, inasmuch as no 'law' of nature would be violated by nuclear explosions, which strictly follow the regularities expressed by physicists' orderly equations), even a species-destroying nuclear war could not destroy the nature that produced human nature, the nature that presumably could produce human nature or some other similar nature again. (Only if nature were itself so near entropic collapse as to be unable to produce another 'humanity' would this be untrue.) To call nuclear war a return to a chaotic 'state of nature' is therefore simply incorrect. Even without the human species, natural order would obtain. And if, as is so much more likely, the human species survived the war, the principles of human nature would obtain as before. Hobbes' radical disjunction of natural disorder and political order is a falsehood.

This returns us to considering the relation of politics to the natural order and specifically to human nature. What political orders or regimes best serve human nature, beginning with the 'right to life' or survival of that nature? Which regime or regimes actually do obtain civil and international peace? There is no use in dogmatizing on this matter, given the extraordinary variety of circumstances in which human beings have found themselves. Monarchies, aristocracies, and republics have all served good purposes; in unusual circumstances, so have oligarchies. But in the circumstances under which nuclear weapons have appeared the commercial republics had already established themselves as the likely candidates for the best feasible regime. Experience since the appearance of nuclear weapons has only confirmed this likelihood. This may be seen in considering an erroneous argument of some critics of nuclear deterrence. These critics claim that nuclear deterrence is wrong because it threatens the innocent subjects of tyrannies with harm. We must never do or threaten wrongful harm, i.e., harm to the innocent. If commercial republics disarmed unilaterally, these innocents would be at less risk.[169] The argument is of course nonsensical, demonstrably so even in history as it unfolded in the second half of the twentieth century. Far from increasing the risk of harm to the subjects of tyranny, the commercial republics' nuclear deterrent acted as a restraint on the actions of the tyrants. Tyrannies founded upon expansionist, 'dialectical' ideology could not continue to expand geographically. Trapped within their own geographical borders, they found themselves forced or inclined to grant more and more liberties to their subjects. The tyrannies themselves finally disintegrated. They may or may not be reconstituted or replaced by different tyrannies, or other unjust regimes. Still, the result is clear enough: the threat of harm to their innocent subjects, without whose continued existence they could not tyrannize so long as they were simultaneously deprived of the means necessary to conquer any other desirable population, evidently deterred the tyrannical would-be 'vanguard' of 'world history' from its oft-stated ambitions. Frustrated, these ambitions softened. Tyranny became an imposing shell, vulnerable to revolution, as Tocqueville sees in his *The Old Regime and the French Revolution*, published more than sixty years before the founding of Soviet 'democratic centralism'. The 'hostages' of the commercial republics' nuclear arsenals, the subjects of tyrannies, were substantially better off as threatened by commercial republics than they would have been if ruled without restraint by Marxist-Leninists. The former subjects will be better off still if they establish and maintain their own commercial republics, an opportunity that would have been much delayed had their former tyrants met no strong foreign opposition. This means that the respect for innocent life is one element of and therefore a principle relative to political justice.[170] Political justice is itself relative to the human good, which very often but not always requires the protection of the innocent lives of good human beings.

5.   *The Justice Nuclear Deterrence*

The question of the morality of nuclear deterrence, often posed by secular writers either in Machiavellian or Kantian terms, cannot avoid the issue of political justice. More than either Machiavelli's or Kant's system, however, the constellation of doctrines forming the just war tradition has resulted from the attempt to combine a political morality of rules with prudent adaptation to circumstances. Can 'just war' thought accommodate nuclear deterrence? Evidently not: the just war doctrines generally prohibit the intentional killing of innocents. Many nuclear wars would involve the intentional killing of innocents; nuclear deterrence often involves the deliberate threat to kill innocents.

The key terms in the formula are 'intentional' and 'innocents.' The intention of nuclear deterrence, to avoid both war and surrender, can scarcely be challenged; the deterrer's mediate intention, to directly or indirectly kill innocents, must be challenged by just war traditionalists.[171] Some writers attempt to flee by asserting that no intention need be formed, that the mere possession of nuclear weapons without any firm intention either to use them or not will suffice to deter the enemy. While admirable in the moral decency that underlies it, this kind of casuistry can satisfy almost no one; sooner or later, one may have to make the choice.[172] The only coherent defense of the intention to kill the innocents ruled by an attacking enemy must be to claim that in your judgment the moral good to be gained by forming that intention — an intention vicious 'in itself' — will outweigh the moral evil caused by forming the intention. It is surely true that "the killing of innocents by an aggressor is no worse *as such* than the killing of innocents by those who would oppose him by waging war," that "human beings have as much right to be spared destruction by good people as well as by bad."[173] But do innocent human beings have as much right to be spared destruction by good people whose intention forms part of an effective policy intended to save their own lives *and* those of the innocent among the enemy?[174] Only one who absolutely prohibits murder in all circumstances can deny this with any real confidence. Thus Anthony Kenny: if you would retaliate massively with nuclear weapons after deterrence fails, he charges, you are "a man with murder in his heart"; if you would surrender or at least refrain from retaliation, "then I know that fundamentally we are morally at one."[175] But can secular morality supply a justification for this union of sentiment? Not by any rigorous argument — only by appeal to sentiments. Because moral and other sentiments differ, secular morality cannot justify the just war traditionalists' absolute prohibition of murder. Many 'secular' arguments that attempt to escape this consequence surreptitiously derive from Christian or other convictions that at least putatively originate in no rational argument or natural perception.

Grotius permits himself to observe that Scripture recognizes as a law of nations that innocents are slaughtered: "In the Psalms it is said that he will be happy who dashes the infants of the Babylonians against a rock." Grotius sees that "in war...what is called retaliation very frequently brings harm to those who are in no way to blame for that on which the issue is joined." He does not cite this fact in order to outlaw war but rather to insist on the obligation of restitution by those "who have brought about the war."[176] Leaving Grotius' use of Scripture to one side, there are of course rational reasons for generally prohibiting injury to the innocent. The innocent cause no harm, threaten no one.[177] They have not consented to the war.[178] But consent alone cannot be a morally decisive criterion, unless by consent one means reasonable consent – a definition that reopens the entire argument from prudence. As for the harmlessness of the innocent, it is true that they intend no harm but not true that they are being used by their rulers in a harmless way. If tyrants can with impunity take their own innocent subjects as hostages against international enemies, tyranny ensures its triumph. A coherent *absolutist* secular counter argument to this is not formulable.[179] Rather, in an effort to engage the emotions of their audience, secular moralists usually prefer to concentrate attention on the horror of any massive nuclear strike;[180] or on the difficulty of prudential calculation ("To know that one or more war crimes are both *necessary and sufficient* to win a war would take a greater ability to predict the future than anyone can claim");[181] or on "the human right to life."[182] None of these arguments withstands rational scrutiny: the first because it absents itself from reason altogether; the second because it demands of reason a certainty reason cannot have, while simultaneously ruling out (if it is a strictly secular argument) all superrational aid. The third argument fails, in the words of the writer who formulates it, because "If the person imposing the risk does so on the basis of some right that is stronger than the right of the victim not to be put at risk, then the infliction of risk is morally justifiable."[183] Your right to life cannot outweigh mine; if I save two lives to your one, your right to life has been outweighed, unless you can show that your right to life is not merely unalienable but absolute. No rational secular argument can do this.

A stronger just-war argument against killing innocents attempts to convict proponents of nuclear deterrence of self-contradiction. Proponents object morally to nuclear attack because it would destroy innocent lives; yet their counter-attack equally would destroy innocent lives. "[T]wo wrongs do not make a right."[184] On its own terms this argument is unassailable. At its moral best nuclear deterrence would be a salutary bluff, at worst a most insidious expression of the will to mass murder. However, the terms of the argument do not adequately convey the moral circumstances in which deterrence obtains. A tyrant threatens your government and its citizens' lives with his nuclear weapons. 'Do x or else I strike,' he says. X being morally unacceptable, you reply, 'Strike, and I shall retaliate,' with the intention of deterring him from attack, in full knowledge that your retaliation would kill innocents. (You wish you could retaliate against the tyrant and his collaborators only, but this is physically impossible.) Opponents argue that you may not threaten your enemy's son if your enemy threatens your life, but may at most only threaten your enemy.[185] But what if threatening his son is in your best judgment the only effective deterrent to his attack? And if your enemy rejects your counter-threat, killing you and your son, may not your dying act of retaliation against his son persuade your enemy to take counter-threats seriously in the future? May this not dissuade him from repeating such threats and actions against other innocents? Will your counterattack, if directed primarily at military and governmental targets, not physically prevent him from repeating such threats credibly for a long time to come?

At this point in the argument secular rationalist opponents can raise objections of moral and prudential calculation. Was act x, required by the tyrant, so very immoral that it outweighed the moral evil involved in the retaliatory threat? And will the evils unleashed by retaliation not outweigh the evils unleashed by surrender? Such weighings and calculations bring on a complex of moral/political considerations,[186] and this is just the point. No absolutist or 'legalist' argument will do. Therefore Wasserstrom is wrong to claim that to justify killing of innocents one must imagine that "the nation-state" is "a unitary entity that is neither morally nor in any other way reducible to the individuals who are its members or who happen to reside within its borders."[187] A respect for just political orders or regimes and the consequent desire to protect them against tyrants' threats rests exactly on the rights of individuals governed by and governing those regimes, individuals whose better interests the regimes serve. When we reflect that on one reckoning the twentieth century has seen less than 40 million deaths in wars – some of innocents, some not – and as many as 120 million deaths at the hands of tyrants, almost all of those being deaths of innocents, moral and political calculation alike justify a strong response to tyrants' threats – particularly in view of evidence that tyrants are in fact restrained by serious threats they find credible.[188]

How strong a response? The just-war doctrines require a 'proportionate' response. The good to be saved must be equal to or greater than the good to be sacrificed; there must be no other means to protect the good to be saved; and its protection here and now will "not undermine it in the long run."[189] Under these criteria reasonable cases for and against nuclear retaliation can be made; a still stronger case can be made for nuclear deterrence on the grounds that to threaten an action that may be disproportionate does not constitute a disproportionate threat if the intention animating that threat – avoidance of nuclear war and tyranny – is just and the expectation that the threat will succeed is reasonable.[190] "Outside of their studies even philosophers are unlikely to proclaim that they will literally stop at nothing to achieve the goals they believe to be desirable."[191] Assuming that the unlikelihood of such proclamations arises from moral convictions rather than self-interested concealment, one may impute this shyness to the thought that reason by its nature sets limits, although not the clear and sometimes absolute limits set by divinely revealed laws. The very concept of proportionality, unlike the rule prohibiting the killing of innocents, suggests the metaphors of weighing and balancing. Writers who reject nuclear war and deterrence as disproportionate typically borrow from legalistic concepts of right and quickly have recourse to the ban against killing innocents, which they absolutize.[192] Gerald Dworkin is right to warn that it is not "enough to show that some important values, [e.g.] freedom or national security, are most efficiently secured" by deterrent intentions, "for that merely shows that there is a moral reason in favor of [deterrent] actions." Morality must go on to "put limits or constraints on what one may do to maximize satisfaction or to achieve important issues."[193] Presumably this means also that rational morality must set limits on any moral good, including the very considerable moral good entailed in the protection of innocents.[194] Here the argument of C.S. Lewis (no secular rationalist) in justification of war must apply to secular rationalism with respect to nuclear war. The irreducible moral desire is to "do men good rather than harm" but the rules that derive from this supreme law may conflict in real life − e.g., "lying is bad, but under certain circumstances not-lying is worse." This is *not* "doing evil that good may come" because "the evil character of the means is itself modified by the very fact that it is the only way to a certain kind of good." Doing good in reality means seeking the maximum good under the circumstances. "Life is, unfortunately, full of forced options where, whatever course we may choose, someone will be harmed."[195] Therefore,

> ...conformity to the fundamental principle of always seeking the maximum human welfare *may* involve us in the taking of human life. We cannot therefore say that violence in itself, or killing in itself, is invariably morally wrong, though it is, of course, always evil....War is an evil, as all admit, but it is right if the evil it avoids is a general evil, and that has to be determined in each particular case....It is surely morally irresponsible to refuse to act because the actual situation is not what we think it ought to be. Moral action is surely the choice of the course likely to lead to the greater human welfare out of all *practicable* possibilities of the moment.[196]

It is of course unlikely that as a Christian Lewis could countenance the mass killing of innocents entailed in a major nuclear war. But it is his Christianity that entitles him absolutely to refuse to countenance such killing, if he does, and not any reasoning founded on natural perception (as distinct from arbitrarily selected sentiments that may or may not be natural).

How 'innocent' are the subjects of tyrants? Some deny that subjects have any responsibility whatsoever for the actions of tyrants. Subjects are powerless to change tyrants' policies; if not, the regime is no tyranny.[197] To argue otherwise is to rely "on a primitive theory of collective responsibility."[198] This argument cannot suffice because peoples do in fact overthrow tyrants;

sometimes peoples even install tyrants.[199] Peoples are to an extent morally responsible for the acts of any ruler, whether elected by them or imposed upon them. At least one writer claims that this responsibility abrogates the subjects' right to be considered innocents or noncombatants immune to attack. Those who tolerate tyrants cannot complain if they are killed in retaliation for an attack committed by 'their' tyrants.[200] This is an unusually stern argument. The lassitude of cowed populations under tyranny may be a crime of sorts, but it is hard to call it a capital crime. Tyrannized populations face far greater and more immediate dangers from tyrants than they do from tyrants' foreign adversaries, even when those adversaries brandish nuclear weapons. To blame subjects so strongly for acceding to these immediate and formidable threats comes close to saying that any executed subject of a tyrant deserved to die for failing to resist more effectively, or for failing to resist at all. It may not always be possible to resist tyranny effectively. The just-war tradition's understanding of 'innocent' as 'noncombatant' − one who neither poses a threat nor directly contributes to the efforts of those who do − remains a more prudent guide.[201]

6.   *The Consequences of Nuclear Weapons Policies*

Intentions aside, neither proponents nor opponents of nuclear deterrence can avoid responsibility for addressing the issue of likely consequences. On this issue opponents have almost nothing plausible to say. An absolute 'no' to nuclear deterrence must entail unilateral abandonment of your country's nuclear arsenal, unless you are so fortunate as thereby to inspire your enemy to imitate you. There is no serious reason to suppose that this would occur.[202] Unilateralists must then argue that your enemy will retain his weapons but refrain from using them against you, or that, if he does, his actions will be rendered ineffective by your (non-nuclear) resistance. Such policies as nonviolent resistance, small-scale military resistance, and even appeals to "world opinion" are invoked at this point.[203] Opponents hope that your enemy will not simply destroy you, but also will not be able to conquer or dominate you without destroying you. Given the many kinds of nuclear weapons, ranging from colossi of intercontinental range to small battlefield weapons, it is hard to imagine that competent enemy military planners could not formulate an attack of sufficient measured ferocity to cripple without killing. Of course, they might err, but this would prove poor comfort to you and yours.

Such considerations reduce unilateral disarmers and their sympathizers to the kind of prudential-moral calculations for which they are so often temperamentally unsuited. One writer argues that because unilateral nuclear disarmament by the United States could lead at worst merely to the destruction of the United States in an enemy attack — an outcome far better than the worst result of bilateral strikes and counterstrikes — American unilateral disarmament would be in the best interests of humanity. "Few people are prepared to argue that American nuclear weapons serve humanity."[204] We happy few may do so nonetheless, inasmuch as the writer overlooks a crucial issue: the relative likelihood of the two worst cases. To invite an unanswerable nuclear attack may well be less prudent than not to do so, despite the severer consequences of any failure of nuclear deterrence.

Another writer generously concedes it "dangerous to pass from our present condition [of mutual deterrence] into a state in which one side felt that it could destroy the other with impunity." But, he notices, there is a ready answer to the blackmail threats to which the commercial republics admittedly would be "vulnerable." It is surrender. It is "imprudent" to claim that "we should prepare to kill millions rather than accept the political arrangements of Finland," where "human rights" are enjoyed despite Soviet predominance.[205] This assumes that the rules of the Finnish sideshow would obtain in more important places. It also assumes that the Finnish settlement was uninfluenced by the continued presence of strong commercial republics in Europe and North America. Replace those regimes by tyrannized oligarchies and the *modus vivendi* of Eastern Europe (vintage 1968-1989 would have been rather different. Why would the Soviet model for the commercial republics have been Finland? Why not Ukraine?[206] Absent surrender, there is simply no reason to suppose, given the United States' bombing of Hiroshima and Nagasaki, that a country with a monopoly on weapons of mass destruction would not use them for blackmail and even in military strikes. The abandonment of nuclear deterrence might very well precipitate war. Further, *if* surrender alone would avert war, the deleterious consequences of that surrender almost undoubtedly would outweigh those of a perpetuated nuclear stalemate, with its next-to-nil chances of a general war.[207] What Anthony Kenny says of the pacifism he rejects may therefore be said equally of the nuclear disarmament he espouses. It is "a moral error no matter how noble the respect for life and the love of peace which inspire it" because it "fail[s] to protect" human liberty and justice.[208] "No one has the right to impose martyrdom on the whole community."[209] The choice of martyrdom does not transfer moral responsibility onto the persecutor.[210] Responsibility persists in the martyr. To argue otherwise is finally to insist on moral and political anarchism, the most comprehensive refusal to accept responsibility for the consequences of urged actions.[211] This was seen by one of the founders of commercial republicanism, Algernon Sidney, whose remarks have remained no less true for the invention of mass-destruction weapons:

> From whence should malice and wickedness gain a privilege of putting new inventions to do mischief every day into practice? and who is it that so far protects them, as to forbid good and innocent men to find new ways also of defending themselves from it? If there be any that do this, they must be such as live in the same principle; who whilst they pretend to exercise justice, provide only for the indemnity of their own crimes, and the advancement of unjust designs. They would have a right of attacking us with all the advantages of the arms now in use, and the arts which by the practice of so many ages have been wonderfully refined, whilst we should be obliged to employ no others in our just defense, than such as were known to our naked ancestors when Caesar invaded them, or to the Indians when they fell under the dominion of the Spaniards. This would be a compendious way of placing uncontrolled iniquity in all the kingdoms of the world, and to overthrow all that deserves the name of good....[212]

Although some opponents of nuclear deterrence imagine that the weapons themselves constitute a "tyranny" over the United States,[213] "there should be no confusion over the enduring fact that the causes of war, and hence the conditions of peace, lie in the political character of states and the nature of political relations among states (and possibly in the nature of humanity itself), and only secondarily in the technical details of weaponry."[214] The worldwide possibilities for peace *and* war engendered by the decline of tyrannical oligarchy in the Soviet Union only confirms what any student of political history should have understood all along, namely, the moral as well as the historical significance of political regimes.

The blindness of so many writers may perhaps be traced to their fear of nuclear weapons combined with a misconceived realism. Such 'realists' do not want to hear about regimes. They want to hear about 'powers' great and small, nuclear and non-nuclear, sovereign 'nation-states,' scorpions in a bottle. With this misconception in hand, 'realists' easily pry nuclear weapons strategy loose from complex political circumstances, often establishing some moralistic dichotomy between nuclear weapons and life, or nuclear weapons and justice.[215] They then discover a "radical disproportion" between the means of nuclear deterrence, which risk the destruction of millions of innocents, and the end of nuclear deterrence, which helps to preserve the lives and liberties of Americans, Britons, Frenchmen, and so on.[216] By ignoring the moral significance of regime differences these 'realist' moralizers commit the most astonishing errors of historical judgment. One writer claims that "by starting with the assumption of unmitigated enmity" between commercial republicanism and Marxist-Leninist regimes, we build weapons that make the hostility real.[217] But of course Lenin and the other founders of the tyranno-oligarchy did not merely 'assume' hostility to 'the bourgeois state'; they embodied it, long before they had any weapons to wield against it. Another writer supposes that

> Nothing in the philosophy of Marxism supports the view that communism will come to ascendancy through national conquest, nor do official statements of the Soviet government indicate that they ever had any such intention. This leaves, then, only the conduct of Soviet foreign policy as an area in which to look for evidence of such an intention, and there the evidence is negligible.[218]

This rather unaccountably overlooks such national conquests as those over Ukraine, Uzbekistan, and the eastern European countries, conquests justified in terms of Marxism-Leninism.

The more serious criticism of any regime-oriented understanding of nuclear weapons warns against the use of a political regime, commercial republicanism, as a false absolute. While acknowledging the moral significance of regimes, critics charge that this significance has been grossly overstated by those who justify nuclear deterrence in such terms. It may not always be possible to resist tyranny effectively and morally at the same time. While "hardly any" proponents of nuclear deterrence "have ever expressed real unease about the nature of nuclear war as something one does to others," they wax "moralistic" in condemning the Marxist-Leninist regimes. "[A]ll other considerations" are "made secondary" to a "completely indiscriminate" anti-communism.[219] Subtracting the rhetorical exaggeration from both the critique of anti-Communism and from anti-Communism itself, the substance of the charge can be sustained only by some proof that a policy of nuclear deterrence causes more moral damage to the deterrer and/or to humanity generally than would some other policy. A theologically-minded writer compares proponents of nuclear deterrence to the Whore of Babylon, who appears in the Book of Revelation riding the Beast who will devour her.[220] Of course, many persons and institutions, including some widely regarded as eminently respectable, have been compared to the Whore of Babylon. It is a colorful image. In this case it may be evaluated on the facts of the case, which show that none of the deterrers of dubious repute has been devoured so far. This of course may not satisfy apocalyptic and prophetic personalities, but these by definition are not to be satisfied by the mundane course of human events.[221]

Secular writers will have to assess the moral damage done by nuclear deterrence in less dramatic terms, starting perhaps with the observation that a whore is none the less a whore whether or not he or she gets devoured. One important moral objection to whoredom addresses the way of life of the whore. Whoredom is not a fit life for any human being. Selling one's body degrades and coarsens the human soul. The ethos of the whorehouse depraves the ethical desire and, by habituation, even the capacity to do human beings good rather than harm. Similarly, one may argue, the policy of nuclear deterrence corrupts the ethos of the nation that adopts it. This is of course the moral argument against tyranny, which, as Constant writes, "invites man to voluptuousness through the dangers with which it surrounds him; he should seize each minute, being uncertain of what the next may bring."[222] Weapons of mass destruction operate as tyrants do, bringing with them the prospect of mass destruction. Life lived under the prospect of mass destruction fosters an ethos of 'instant gratification' that may take any form from facile political apocalypticism to (what is more facile for most people) a life spent in front of a television, vicariously experiencing everything but living and loving nothing. Not only the dangerousness of nuclear weapons but also their hiddenness, their remoteness from everyday life, contributes to this effect. Nuclear weapons are easy to ignore, easy not to think about, violating no rights and injuring no bodies directly. Nuclear deterrence works because it is easy.[223] It is easy, all too easy; it leads to an ethos of insecure easiness. "[T]hreatened by imagery of extinction," human beings do not love deeply, marry, raise children; they lose their "sense of immortality" and with it their moral compass. A "new ephemeralism" rules.[224] While military men inflate their souls into fake godliness,[225] ordinary citizens suffer from "psychic numbing."[226] Erich Fromm warns that "to live for any length of time under the constant threat of destruction creates psychological effects in most human beings — fright, hostility, callousness, a hardening of the heart, and a resulting indifference to the values we cherish." This "will transform us into barbarians"; "freedom will be lost." "The real threat to our existence is not Communist ideology...not even Communist military power," but "hollowness."[227]

One may of course call these concerns exaggerated. The very thoughtlessness of people in the 'nuclear age' only duplicates the thoughtlessness of most people in every age, and without thinking much it is hard to be very corrupt.[228] After some four decades of nuclear deterrence actual "evidence of moral deformation" is rather thin.[229] It is clear that absolute weapons at very least do not corrupt absolutely. It is not even true that "once a nation pledges its safety to an absolute weapon, it becomes emotionally essential to believe in an absolute enemy."[230] The safety of commercial republics is still "pledged" to some extent to 'absolute' weapons, yet as I write these regimes are running out of 'absolute' enemies. It is rather the acknowledgment of the existence of 'absolute' enemies — enemies who intend to destroy commercial republicanism — that gives emotional support to the possession of 'absolute' weapons intended to deter any military acts of destruction. Remove the enemy (perhaps by his becoming a friend) and this emotional support will decline.

Nonetheless, however difficult it may be to measure, and however easy it may be to exaggerate, the ethos to which nuclear weapons have contributed can hardly be good for human beings. It will be better if the military necessity for nuclear weapons and other weapons of mass destruction is removed. That necessity can only be removed by the removal of the political causes that gave rise to it. It is to this task, involving the refounding of commercial republicanism where it is and the encouragement of commercial republicanism in countries where it has seldom been but might be, that the efforts of statesmen will now be dedicated.

CONCLUSION

To insist too much on conclusions may put writer and reader alike into the sour mood of Gentili, who mutters at the beginning of an even longer book than this, "I could wish that I had to deal only with the ignorant and not with the perverse as well."[1] This book aims less at imposing conclusions than at inviting thought. A brief conclusion will then be appropriate *and* a relief. If we have endured one another's company this far, maybe peace is more than a light at the end of a tunnel.

War is a problem because war imposes injuriously. Why do we want to injure? Or even to impose? There is an answer offered by anthropologists and ethnologists. War evolved in order to teach human beings to cooperate. It is easier to cooperate when pressed by some common enemy or inflamed by one. Peaceful gathering of vegetation won't do by itself; we also need to be hunters in order more fully to develop our natural capacity for practical reasoning for social purposes.[2]

Whatever 'evolution' may be or mean, the will to injure exists in the human soul, and is associated with what the Greeks call *thumos*, spiritedness. Spiritedness in its simplest form is anger, often a reaction to fear. Refined, it becomes or contributes to such estimable qualities as self-respect, battlefield and civic courage, honor, even magnanimity. Unmoderated it becomes blind rage, rashness, conceit, overweening pride, arrogance. Belittled or perverted it becomes resentment, envy, bitterness, vindictiveness. It enables reason to rule the appetites, but it too wants to rule. It may not be strictly identical to what we now call willfulness, but it is at least a powerful ally of willfulness. The will wants power to enact its intentions. *Thumos* consorts with power-politics in the Machiavellian sense, whether in the often pedestrian ways of Hobbes or in the grand ways of Nietzsche. *Thumos* underlies or animates much of what men have called noble. It equally animates much of what they have called terrible or tyrannical. The same part of the soul both tempts men and women to tyranny and steels them to resist it. It destroys; it defends against destroyers.

The warrior element in human nature need not rule, and in a way cannot rule because it cannot tell itself what it wants. The Greeks taught that *eros* or love tells us what we want. Whether it is the appetite for food, for sexual pleasure, or for the things of the intellect, *eros* not *thumos* motivates us. Tyranny arises when a soul conflates *eros* and *thumos*. The tyrant wants the most and the finest food, the most beautiful women and/or boys, the biggest, the most elaborate lands and palaces. He determines to get them by force and fraud, by the means of war. His fear that others feel as he does and will do as he does further goads his spiritedness. He declares war against his fellow human beings. He wants them, but only as his slaves. A politics one of man's supreme passion must also become a politics of extreme discipline, even destruction, for everyone else.

Attempts to avoid the tyrannical consequence have varied in success. The response of the old philosophers − that reason must rule the spirit and through it the appetites − may be esteemed as personally sound but politically difficult. It was deemed to be flatly impossible by some of those philosophers, who never dreamed of a nation full of philosopher kings, and scarcely took the notion of some ruling class of philosophers as anything more than a specimen of ironic wit. They well understood that any Nocturnal Council would be very nocturnal indeed.

Newer philosophers argued that the Nocturnal Council could be brought to the light of day. Enlightenment meant the public rule of scientists, philosophers who have ceased to wonder and finally know, whose knowledge would win the appreciative consent of a public liberated to fulfill its desires. This fulfillment would be made possible for the first time by scientific manipulation or conquest of nature. The problems with this solution are now well known. On the simplest level, as the pacifist Aldous Huxley saw between the world wars, the techniques of the conquering science do not only liberate. They can also enslave, empowering propagandists, warriors, spies − all the human instruments of tyranny. "For this reason its is enormously important that the principles of non-violence should be propagated rapidly and over the widest possible area."[3]. The year was 1937, already too late − as it usually is for pacifism. More subtly, the problem comes down to the evident fact that the open rule of reason must itself become a kind of orthodoxy or convention. Not everyone can be a scientist. And is there really a science of ruling? What is more, in order to rule a certain spiritedness must infuse this new philosophy. It seeks to conquer nature if not human nature. (And why should it hold back from the attempt to conquer human nature? And yet in the name of what can it make the attempt?) The good Enlightener Jaspers teaches "That mankind has one root and one goal, that true human beings are linked by something that transcends even mortal conflicts" — that is, by reason, which, if served by the technological unity provided by "communication" instruments can united humanity politically.[4] The difficulty, as Jaspers must see, has been identified by modern philosophers themselves. The very will to conquest built into the Enlightenment project turns many of the most powerful and refined ambitions toward the destruction of Enlightenment orthodoxy. Rousseau ends in Marx, or in Nietzsche and Heidegger.

Politically, the result will run in one of a few directions. The scientist will be replaced by the 'leader,' the Weberian 'charismatic,' whether alone or (more usually) acting in concert with some faction claiming to be a truth-bearing race or social class. Inevitably the 'leader' needs a bureaucracy to give some ballast to his man-o'-war, and inevitably the bureaucracy, animated by its own more pedestrian but no less dogmatic will to power, weighs the ship down and threatens to sink it. This will happen only if the ship has been so fortunate as to have avoided getting wrecked by its first captain/shipbuilder.

A more egalitarian form of communalism equally proposes to eroticize politics and thereby to tame spiritedness. Can we not, it asks, have a politics of love and compassion, of inclusiveness not exclusiveness? Spiritedness targets enemies, but is it not better to love each other in all our diversity? The modest or bourgeois, the unardent form of this politics might be termed sentimental liberalism or the politics of toleration. In its more impassioned form it becomes sexual politics, the conviction that the personal is the political, that the polymorphousness of unlimited desire can overcome the crabbed dualities of us and them, friend and foe. The problem with this project is even more readily visible than those that dog the Enlightenment. To universalize tolerance one must establish and maintain the rule of the tolerant over the intolerant. To universalize erotic love or even compassion, one must establish and maintain the rule of the loving and the compassionate over the unloving and the uncompassionate. The good liberal must finally war against tyranny. The good feminist must war against patriarchs, the good erotic against puritans, and so on. Given the inevitability of human disagreement, owing to the imperfection of our perceptions and the persistence of our ambitions, the all-inclusive and all-loving society never quite arrives. Rather, the same combination of *eros* and *thumos* that issues in the crude tyranny of old tyrants and the sophisticated tyranny of new scientists, issues in a tyranny of new rhetoricians, utopians who imagine that all can be had by the manipulation of words, usually couched in the accents of 'rights' – which in this scheme turn out to be nothing more than strongly willed desires. Utopians tell themselves and others that they want no-rule, but of course they must rule in order to obtain no-rule. The orgy of political eroticism, the 'Enlightenment' of eroticism or passion so to speak, is driven by a love, but more by a spirit, that dares not speak its name. As a result, egalitarian communalists are reduced to the status of the Sunday preacher who stoutly maintains that 'Christianity has not failed because it has never really been tried,' because if only everyone would just *agree* peace if not necessarily goodwill could pervade the world. Hobbes has altogether the same view in a way, but he has the honesty to proclaim that peace will come when the tyrant is no longer misliked, when the king's word is consented to precisely because it is above all indispensable *to consent to someone* in order to realize the peace we enter civil society to obtain. It is notable that personal-is-political utopians mean both that politics can be loving and that even the most intimate relations are equilibrations of power, of Hobbesian physics. But the circle cannot square.

Real Christianity, as distinguished from pharisaical sermonizing, proposes a third term in its attempt to negotiate between *eros* and *thumos*. This term is *agape*, a love that desires not the object but the good of the object. In their own way some of the old philosophers understood this when they said that the true lover desires the good for his beloved. This love need not be pacifistic, though it might be. Jesus teaches, Do unto others as you would have others do unto you. He does not teach, If you do unto others as you would have them do unto you, they will likely do unto you as you would do unto them, doing unto you as you would have them do. That is not Christianity; it is Dale Carnegie. *Agape* has not only Spirit but also a degree of spiritedness in it. The Lamb's war is still a war, and it is a war for the good as revealed by God. Physical war may or may not be permitted as an adjunct to the Lamb's War; the question remains controversial. Christian pacifism at its most honest commends martyrdom in the faith that God is all-powerful and will prevail, the soul immortal and finally content and protected if allied with God. Christian just warriors recognize, with Hocking, that Christian "pugnacity wants...to *make the man over*; it wants to create the conditions for the free self-rejection of the evil" and "free self-acceptance of the good." Christianity "expresses the final satisfaction of the will of the fighter in the midst of every good fight."[5]. But to prepare the conditions of willed good, a physical fight may be needed for moral purposes:

> There is such a thing in the world as persistent and self-assured cynicism; and there is such a thing as determined bad-will. It is chiefly these which make wars necessary. War is not to be understood as necessarily a negation of the principle of Christianity; a just war is an attempt to create the conditions under which the opponent is *disposed to* listen to the language of the still, small voice.[6]

Agape works best when those animated by it recognize its stillness and smallness along with its persistence and power.

Unfortunately, this voice does not always want to remain still and small. The Christian undertaking, pacifist or not, does not entirely escape the dilemmas spiritedness imposes. This may be seen in the practice of millenarianism or large prophecy, which the modern scientific 'New Jerusalem' slyly but too uncritically took over, issuing in the deformed visions of 'German' ideology, secular historicism.[7] The American statesman John Adams well described the religious side of the prognostic passion:

> The Crusades were commenced by the Prophets and every Age since, when ever any great Turmoil happens in the World, has produced fresh Prophets. The continual Refutation of all their Prognostications by Time and Experience has no Effect in extinguishing or damping their Ardor.

> I think these Prophecies are not only unphilosophical and inconsistent with the political Safety of States and Nations; but that the most sincere and sober Christians in the World ought upon their own Principles to hold them impious, for nothing is clearer from their Scriptures than that their Prophecies were not intended to make Us Prophets. [8]

This too is the urge to conquer, to conquer by foreseeing all and then aligning oneself with the strongest force. The confusion of piety and policy suffices no more than the Machiavellian insistence on reducing piety to policy. In the end they can amount to nearly the same thing.[9]

After viewing the failures of so many attempts to understand *thumos* and to address the dilemmas it imposes, one conspicuous political success remains. It is commercial republicanism. Commercial republicanism does one thing its competitors have not done. It has delivered on its promise of civil and international peace. It does not do so invariably, or without some wars, or without posing dilemmas if its own. But it does deliver.

The citizen of the commercial republic is not the contemptible 'bourgeois' pilloried by Rousseau and derided by Nietzsche as the last man. The mere bourgeois or last man (really a socialist egalitarian) is a danger to this citizen. He or she might become one, as many have done. But because other, fewer, but more ambitious souls can be depended upon to see the commercial republican as only another bourgeois, their malevolent spiritedness will arouse the citizen's public spiritedness. Or at least this has happened so far, in the nineteenth and twentieth centuries. Blinded by contempt, the men of malevolent spirit lost their wars, militarily and politically.

Citizens of commercial republics avoid the debasing cynicism of realists who know nothing of the realities. They also avoid the self-righteousness of idealists who know nothing of ideas. Idealists are eager to tell you, and themselves, why their ardent pursuit of self-interest is really in the very best interests of God, country, humanity. Commercial republicans want to tell you why doing the right thing is also entirely advantageous to themselves, and also to you.[10]. I am a decent sort, but I am nobody's fool, they want you to know. This is not an inspired or inspiring ethos. It is not always sufficient, particularly in circumstances requiring the last measure of devotion. But it is a peaceable ethos. It will not satisfy the most ardent souls, who sometimes want all the most exquisite agitations of war combined with the safety of peace. But perhaps the most ardent souls should redirect their ardor from grander, political projects that tend not to satisfy the deepest ardor, anyway. Too much ardor armed with too many of the technological resources provided by the modern scientific project makes for dangers unneeded and unwanted. There is a greater need to reconsider the actual components of sound political life − the family and the community that can nurture it. In so reconsidering there will be a need to reconsider real, not 'pragmatic' ideas, including those ideas suggested by the conviction that God exists. Ideas that grant perspective instead of passion will give commercial republicanism a thoughtfulness it needs without committing it to Enlightenment ambitions it cannot sustain.

The strength of commercial republicanism has been its ability to earn the consent of the vast majority of citizens who live with its institutions. Even those who deny the moral and political foundations of commercial republicanism nonetheless habituate themselves to its ways more often than not. Still, there are dangers. The systematic effacement of the principles of commercial republicanism from the curricula of contemporary schools can do it no good. (In the United States, for example, a recent nominee to the Supreme Court sent politicians and journalists scurrying in confusion when they learned he adhered to a strange doctrine called 'natural law'). The Gramscian *Kulturkampf* against commercial republicanism can lead to bizarre efflorescences. More important are the tensions within commercial republicanism itself. Both commerce and republicanism give people what they want. But if they *merely* gave, commerce and republicanism would soon decline into a city of pigs. The reconception of commercial republicanism into a system of giving or charity would be, paradoxically, fatal to peace because the people again would be prey to tyrants, would-be swineherds. Commerce and republicanism rather provide people the chance to earn what they want. Because people's wants differ, and because there is always a scarcity of goods in relation to desires, commerce and republicanism require conflict. Conflict requires souls that bend but do not easily break. Commerce and republicanism require a measured spiritedness. Commercial republicanism, unlike its rivals, rests on a full acknowledgment of the existence and the problem of spiritedness. Commercial republicanism seeks to govern spiritedness, not exalt it, cover it up, or wipe it out. Commercial republicanism does this in a practical not a 'philosophical' way. As such it may need philosophic friends from time to time, to counteract the machinations of its philosophic or (more usually) sophistical enemies.

Those among the old philosophers who do not despair of politics, who recognize that a certain kind of non-partisan political thinking forms an indispensable part of the philosophic enterprise, would appreciate the merits and dangers of commercial republicanism. They understand that reasonableness can rule in politics through a statesmanship that rules by law. They understand the inevitable thumotic divisions between friend and enemy, us and them, and see these not only as a danger to philosophy but as an opportunity for philosophers better to understand nature as manifested in human nature. In pursuing their inquiries and in sharing the results with their fellow citizens – particularly statesmen and young would-be statesmen – those philosophers practice a kind of politics, and their practice instructs the philosophers, as they think about it. ('Everything is political,' but everything is not political in the same way).

In considering commercial republicanism those philosophers would appreciate the way in which it minimizes despotic measures at home and abroad. They would appreciate the ability of commercial republics to fight and win wars against despots while never quite falling in love with war. They would appreciate the variety of human types by this regime, so suggestive of nature's complexities and conflicts. Commercial republicanism does bear some resemblance to the mixed regimes of antiquity, preferred by the most prudent philosophers as the most natural.

These philosophers would see danger in the unmixed character of commercial republican sovereignty founded on the people. Although strictly limited in its exercise by the rule of laws designed to protect unalienable individual rights, popular sovereignty can lead to a redefinition of rights as desires, appetites with spirit. Commerce may then encourage materialism and the denigration of the ancestral. This will become increasingly true as commerce gradually subordinates agriculture, abetting the attempt to conquer nature instead of attaching citizens to the limits imposed by nature. In reaction to this, spirited souls reject commerce and republicanism altogether and seek communalisms of war or peace, exalting the ancestral in various forms of impassioned nationalism and, sometimes, nature-worship. To avoid this descent into despotic passions philosophers may emphasize the distinct-ion between unalienable rights endowed to human nature and pseudo-rights arbitrarily asserted. Because the rule of law can so effectively frustrate arbitrary assertions, it can serve as an ally of philosophy. The struggle over the rule of law between those who see the foundation of such rule in nature and nature's God and those who deny those foundations will continue to challenge commercial republicanism. The results of that struggle will determine the future of war and peace.